BRITISH NAVAL STRATEGY
EAST OF SUEZ 1900–2000

BRITISH NAVAL STRATEGY EAST OF SUEZ 1900–2000

Influences and actions

Editor:
Greg Kennedy
UK Joint Services Command and Staff College

LONDON AND NEW YORK

First published in 2005 by Frank Cass

Published 2015 by Routledge
2 Park Square, Milton Park, Abingdon, Oxfordshire OX14 4RN
711 Third Avenue, New York, NY 10017

First issued in paperback 2015

Routledge is an imprint of the Taylor and Francis Group,
an informa business

Copyright in Collection © 2005 Taylor & Francis Ltd
Copyright in Chapters © 2005 individual authors

British Library Cataloguing in Publication Data
A catalogue record for this book is available
from the British Library

Library of Congress Cataloging in Publication Data
A catalog record for this book has been requested

All rights reserved. No part of this publication may be reproduced, stored
in or introduced into a retrieval system or transmitted in any form or by any
means, electronic, mechanical, photocopying, recording or otherwise,
without the prior written permission of the publisher of this book.

ISSN 1366-9478

Typeset in Times New Roman by
Integra Software Services Pvt. Ltd, Pondicherry, India

ISBN 13: 978-0-415-64626-0 (pbk)
ISBN 13: 978-0-7146-5539-0 (hbk)

CONTENTS

Notes on contributors	vii
Series editor's preface	ix
Maps	xiii

Introduction   1

1   'Wee-ah-wee'?: Britain at Weihaiwei, 1898–1930   4
     T.G. OTTE

2   The idea of naval imperialism: The China Squadron
     and the Boxer Uprising   35
     HAMISH ION

3   'Unbroken Thread': Japan. Maritime power and
     British Imperial Defence, 1920–32   62
     KEITH NEILSON

4   What worth the Americans? The British strategic
     foreign policy-making elite's view of American
     maritime power in the Far East, 1933–1941   90
     GREG KENNEDY

5   'Looking Skyward from Below the Waves': Admiral
     Tom Phillips and the Loss of the *Prince of Wales*
     and the *Repulse*   118
     DAVID IAN HALL

6   'Light Two Lanterns, the British Are Coming by Sea':
     Royal Navy participation in the Pacific 1944–1945   128
     JON ROBB-WEBB

CONTENTS

7   The Royal Navy in Korea: Replenishment and sustainability   154
PETER NASH

8   The Royal Navy, expeditionary operations and the
End of Empire, 1956–75   178
IAN SPELLER

9   The Royal Navy and Confrontation, 1963–66   199
CHRIS TUCK

10   The British Naval role east of Suez: An Australian
perspective   221
DAVID STEVENS

11   The return to globalism: The Royal Navy east of Suez,
1975–2003   244
GEOFFREY TILL

Select bibliography   269
Index   282

NOTES ON CONTRIBUTORS

David Ian Hall is a Lecturer in the Defence Studies Department, King's College London at the Joint Services Command and Staff College, Watchfield, UK. He is also an Air Warfare Historian on the Higher Command and Staff Course at the College. He has a DPhil. in modern British history from the University of Oxford.

Hamish Ion is a member of the History Department at the Royal Military College of Canada in Kingston, Ontario. He is the author of many scholarly article and chapters on American, British and Canadian missionaries in the Far East during the late nineteenth and early twentieth centuries. He is the author of *The Cross in the Dark Valley: The Canadian Protestant Missionary Movement in the Japanese Empire, 1931–1945* (c1990–c1993). His work also deals with issues regarding those three nations' POWs during the war with Japan.

Greg Kennedy is a Senior Lecturer in the Defence Studies Department of King's College London at the Joint Services Command and Staff College, Watchfield, UK. He is the author of the award-winning book *Anglo-American Strategic Relations and the Far East, 1933–39* (2002), as well as many other edited and co-edited volumes. He has published widely in the areas of British and US strategic foreign policy relations and maritime strategy.

Peter Nash is a PhD research student at the War Studies Department of King's College London looking at the extent to which naval logistics was a force multiplier for Anglo-American maritime commitments during the era of transition between World War II and the Korean War. In 2002 he was awarded the Edward S. Miller Research Fellowship in Naval History at the US Naval War College Rhode Island looking at the development of early post-war US naval logistics policy.

Keith Neilson is a member of the History Department at the Royal Military College of Canada in Kingston, Ontario. He is the author of numerous scholarly articles and chapters on Anglo-Russian, Anglo-Japanese and Anglo-European strategic foreign relations in the late nineteenth and early twentieth centuries. He is the author of *Strategy and Supply* (1984) and *Britain and the Last Tsar: British*

NOTES ON CONTRIBUTORS

Policy and Russia, 1894–1917 (1995), and has produced many edited and co-edited books as well.

Thomas G. Otte is a Senior Lecturer in International History at the University of the West of England. He has published widely on aspects of mainly pre-1914 international history and is co-editor of *Military Intervention: From Gunboat Diplomacy to Humanitarian Intervention* (1995) and editor of *The Makers of British Foreign Policy: From Pitt to Thatcher* (2002).

Jon Robb-Webb is a PhD research student in the War Studies Department, King's College London, and a full-time member of the Defence Studies Department at the Joint Services Command and Staff College, Watchfield, UK. His main area of interest is Anglo-American maritime strategy in the Pacific theatre during the Second World War.

Ian Speller is a Lecturer in the Department of Modern History at the National University of Ireland, Maynooth. He also lectures in defence studies at the Irish Defence Forces' Command and Staff School. His research interests include post-1945 British foreign and defence policy, maritime strategy and expeditionary warfare and he is the author of *The Role of Amphibious Warfare in British Defence Policy, 1945–56* (2001).

David Stevens is Director of Strategic and Historical Studies at the Sea Power Centre Australia. He is the author or editor of several publications on naval historical and maritime strategic subjects, including the naval volume of *The Australian Centenary History of Defence* published by Oxford (2001).

Geoffrey Till is the Dean of Academic Studies at the Joint Services Command and Staff College, Watchfield, UK. He is the author of numerous books, articles and chapters on British maritime topics. His most recent work is *Seapower: A Guide for the Twenty-first Century* (2003). He is the series editor for the Cass Series on Naval Policy and History.

Christopher Tuck is a lecturer in the Defence Studies Department, King's College London at the Joint Services Command and Staff College, Watchfield, UK. His research interests include Britain's Confrontation with Indonesia, 1963–66, amphibious warfare, and the American Civil War. He is co-author of *Amphibious Warfare: The Theory and Practice of Amphibious Operations in the 20th Century* (2001).

SERIES EDITOR'S PREFACE

One of the emerging characteristics of the Naval History and Policy series of which this volume is a part has been the close connections between the maritime geography of an area and the role played in its affairs by navies. Accordingly, several volumes have considered the Baltic as one such area, and others have considered the Mediterranean, but this is the first to review the East of Suez area as a uniform background against which the history of the Royal Navy might be assessed.

In comparison with those more confined geographic settings, however, 'East of Suez' is a much more amorphous concept. It could include the Pacific, or it might not. As far as the Royal Navy of the late twentieth century was concerned, the phrase in effect meant almost anywhere outside the North Atlantic, and was taken as a political and terminological justification for the maintenance of a global set of capacities which would keep Britain in the global business. The Navy was uncomfortable with the alternate label of 'Out of Area' because it seemed to imply a very restrictive concept of what *was* the area – almost as though the words 'Britain's proper' were hovering unspoken between the 'of' and 'area.'

The British of an earlier era had no such sensitivities. For them India, and accordingly the Indian Ocean, was the jewel in the crown of the Empire and Commonwealth, and the maintenance of a global maritime capacity to service imperial strategic interests seemed so obvious an imperative that its justification almost went without saying. The matter only arose when Treasury mandarins and others wondered just how sustainable this commitment would prove to be when other and geographically much nearer threats to British interests appeared in Europe itself. The history of the Royal Navy, and its role East of Suez exactly reflects this much larger debate about whether Britain was and is a global player, or merely an offshore island on the edge of the Eurasian landmass. Which interest should predominate? Which threat needed to be dealt with first? How should money, resources and manpower be allocated? As the various contributions in this book show, these were, for the British, the continuing maritime debates of the twentieth century.

To an outsider, and even today, the quintessential characteristic of the British is their liking for the drinking of tea, a habit going back to the late seventeenth century. The traditional paraphernalia of the British tea-drinking ceremony is still the blue-and-white 'willow pattern' cups, saucers and tea plates. This design of course reflects the early designs of the Chinese-export porcelain that came in the holds of countless merchant ships to Europe and especially to Britain from the early eighteenth century in its literally millions of pieces. There were subtle and constant interactions between British and Chinese porcelain producers and between oriental tea producers and British tea consumers. The result was a global network of maritime interests, both commercial and strategic, which transformed Britain, China and India. These linkages were an important part of what these places became. In just the same way the British attitude to 'East of Suez' helped determine what Britain was. As all the contributions in this valuable collection show, how the British saw the wider world reflected the way in which they saw themselves. What was at stake in the naval debate about Wei-Hai-Wei, Borneo or Kuwait was really the sort of navy the British had and the sort of country they lived in.

Geoffrey Till

CASS SERIES: NAVAL POLICY AND HISTORY
Series Editor: Geoffrey Till
ISSN 1366-9478

This series consists primarily of original manuscripts by research scholars in the general area of naval policy and history, without national or chronological limitations. It will from time to time also include collections of important articles as well as reprints of classic works.

1. AUSTRO-HUNGARIAN NAVAL POLICY, 1904–1914
Milan N. Vego

2. FAR-FLUNG LINES
Studies in imperial defence in honour of Donald Mackenzie Schurman
Edited by Keith Neilson and Greg Kennedy

3. MARITIME STRATEGY AND CONTINENTAL WARS
Rear Admiral Raja Menon

4. THE ROYAL NAVY AND GERMAN NAVAL DISARMAMENT 1942–1947
Chris Madsen

5. NAVAL STRATEGY AND OPERATIONS IN NARROW SEAS
Milan N. Vego

6. THE PEN AND INK SAILOR
Charles Middleton and the King's navy, 1778–1813
John E. Talbott

7. THE ITALIAN NAVY AND FASCIST EXPANSIONISM, 1935–1940
Robert Mallett

8. THE MERCHANT MARINE AND INTERNATIONAL AFFAIRS, 1850–1950
Edited by Greg Kennedy

9. NAVAL STRATEGY IN NORTHEAST ASIA
Geo-strategic goals, policies and prospects
Duk-Ki Kim

10. NAVAL POLICY AND STRATEGY IN THE MEDITERRANEAN SEA
Past, present and future
Edited by John B. Hattendorf

11. STALIN'S OCEAN-GOING FLEET
Soviet naval strategy and shipbuilding programmes, 1935–1953
Jürgen Rohwer and Mikhail S. Monakov

12. IMPERIAL DEFENCE, 1868–1887
Donald Mackenzie Schurman; edited by John Beeler

(Continued)

(*Continued*)

13. TECHNOLOGY AND NAVAL COMBAT IN THE TWENTIETH CENTURY AND BEYOND
Edited by Phillips Payson O'Brien

14. THE ROYAL NAVY AND NUCLEAR WEAPONS
Richard Moore

15. THE ROYAL NAVY AND THE CAPITAL SHIP IN THE INTERWAR PERIOD
An operational perspective
Joseph Moretz

16. CHINESE GRAND STRATEGY AND MARITIME POWER
Thomas M. Kane

17. BRITAIN'S ANTI-SUBMARINE CAPABILITY, 1919–1939
George Franklin

18. BRITAIN, FRANCE AND THE NAVAL ARMS TRADE IN THE BALTIC, 1919–1939
Grand strategy and failure
Donald Stoker

19. NAVAL MUTINIES OF THE TWENTIETH CENTURY
An international perspective
Edited by Christopher Bell and Bruce Elleman

20. THE ROAD TO ORAN
Anglo-French naval relations, September 1939–July 1940
David Brown

21. THE SECRET WAR AGAINST SWEDEN
US and British submarine deception and political control in the 1980s
Ola Tunander

22. SEAPOWER
A guide for the twenty-first century
Geoffrey Till

23. BRITAIN'S ECONOMIC BLOCKADE OF GERMANY, 1914–1919
Eric W. Osborne

24. A LIFE OF ADMIRAL OF THE FLEET ANDREW CUNNINGHAM
A twentieth-century naval leader
Michael Simpson

25. NAVIES IN NORTHERN WATERS, 1721–2000
Edited by Rolf Hobson and Tom Kristiansen

26. GERMAN NAVAL STRATEGY, 1856–1888
Forerunners to Tirpitz
David Olivier

27. BRITISH NAVAL STRATEGY EAST OF SUEZ, 1900–2000
Influences and actions
Edited by Greg Kennedy

28. THE RISE AND FALL OF THE SOVIET NAVY IN THE BALTIC 1921–1940
Gunnar Åselius

29. ROYAL NAVY STRATEGY IN THE FAR EAST 1919–1939
Andrew Field

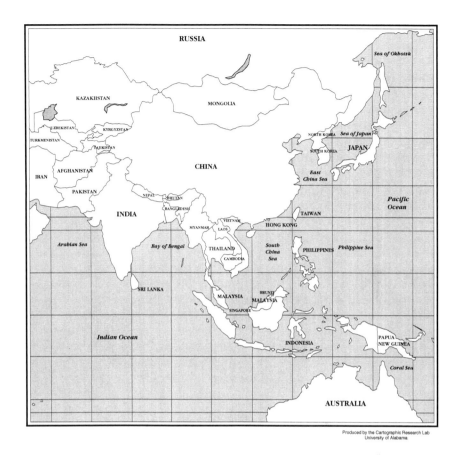

Map 1 East Asia

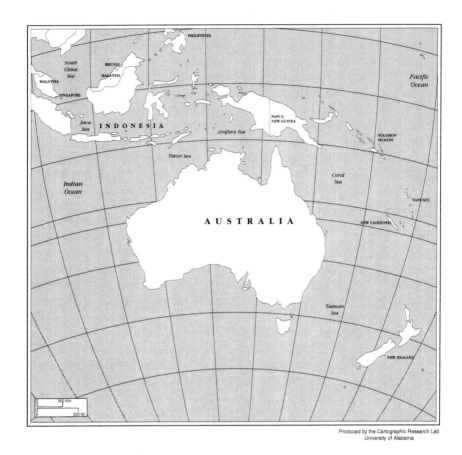

Map 2 South Pacific

INTRODUCTION

The use of the sea as a means of projecting power and influence beyond national borders is one that holds a unique place in the history of Great Britain. Britain's maritime strategic position east of Suez in the twentieth century was a dominant area of interest, whose strategic conditions had an enormous impact in the overall construction of Great Britain's maritime strategic posture.[1] While not the scene of such famous battles as Jutland, Toranto, or the Battle of the Atlantic, which are easily connected in the national mind to Britain's overall effort to maintain its imperial strategic position, the reality of the facts are that Britain's global maritime position was predominantly formed by Far Eastern strategic influences from 1900 to 1945. After that, even in the face of the Cold War and the emphasis on planning for a third European war, strategic influences east of Suez continued to play a major role in the creation of Britain's maritime force structure and in its global strategic foreign policy formulation process.

Directly linked to the concepts of Empire, Great Power status, the global balance of power, alliance and coalition warfare, technological evolutions and revolutions, as well as strategic overstretch, Great Britain's maritime strategy east of Suez, particularly in times of peace, serves as the most useful of historical laboratories for the study of the uses of modern maritime power, in peace and war.[2] This collection of essays, by a panel of international scholars, sheds new light on what some of those strategic influences and considerations were and what strategic actions were taken as a result of Britain's Far Eastern commitments. How much was Britain's ability to play a dominant role in the region a result of economic power, translated into naval power? Was diplomacy and the formulation of a sound strategic foreign-policy the result of Britain's maritime policy in the region, or did the former actually drive the creation of the latter? If so, when and why? Did the Royal Navy always stand alone with regard to protecting imperial interests in this area, or were dominion and imperial ties vital to any success? What were the values of formal and informal maritime strategic relationships? These are just some of the questions and issues that are addressed by the authors whose work is presented in this volume. The idea that the British have gained unique advantages in both war and peace by being a 'maritime power' gained much currency in the nineteenth and twentieth centuries. Leading commentators such as Basil Liddell-Hart suggested that there was a peculiarly maritime 'British Way in Warfare'. In this context, the examination of Britain's maritime strategy in the period indicated by the study is particularly valuable to either support or challenge Liddell-Hart's position. There have been certain undeniable 'truths' associated with that way of warfare, which will be re-examined in this study. It is hoped that the work presented here will form the basis of further studies and explorations, in greater detail, along some of these lines. It is interesting to note that there is as yet no comprehensive, scholarly treatment that evaluates the 'rise and fall' of Great Britain's maritime strategy east of Suez in the twentieth century. Perhaps that time has come.

In an attempt to support Britain's global strategic position overseas, at reduced cost (both political and financial), the Royal Navy was forced to develop and contribute to a maritime strategy based upon the access provided by the sea. Alternative strategies were at times developed and presented, notably by the Royal Air Force, and the fierce debates that resulted demonstrated much about the nature of military and political decision-making at the time. As well, such debates highlight the nature of the decision-making process for the strategic issues dominating the theatre and of the enduring nature of maritime power as the primary protector of Britain's strategic interests. Therefore, as an examination of the influences and actions taken in response to changing conditions, this collection and its theme is of historical interest, but it also retains contemporary relevance.

Today, the oft-repeated idea of a NEW world order and its changed set of circumstances resembles closely, and parallels, the patterns of thought and action in evidence in the period 1920–39 (as well as that in the period from 1945–65) about maritime strategic questions: disarmament, fiscal restraint, the connection between diplomacy and the use of force, use of maritime power vs. land powers, etc. Current policy in both Britain and the United States emphasizes the requirement to be able to project significant military power overseas into the Far East. As military organizations seek to meet this challenge, the utility or otherwise of maritime forces as a means of projecting power is once again a subject that is hotly debated. But still the need for lift, sustainability, power project, defence diplomacy (or assistance to foreign-policy), deterrence, coercion, and combat effectiveness are just some of the myriad missions the modern RN must consider performing today in the area east of Suez. Foremost, however, in most of the chapters presented here, is the nature of the civil – military interactions that created Britain's maritime strategy for the region. The Royal Navy was not the sole, and at times, not the dominant Government body directing the strategic maritime policy for that area. For modern senior naval commanders today, and not only those in the Royal Navy, this is a lesson well worth heeding. This collection will provide a focused theatre case study which contemporary investigations and debates can use as a starting place.

I would like to thank the contributors for their valuable contributions, time and patience in getting this collection to completion. Your efforts will be rewarded in

INTRODUCTION

heaven. I would also like to thank Andrew Humphrys at Frank Cass Publishers for his continued support of the Naval Policy and History Series and my contributions to it. And finally, but by no means least, I would like to thank Frankie Kennedy for her help in preparing the manuscript.

Notes

1. For a similar collective approach which served to inspire this project see John B. Hattendorf (ed.), *Naval Strategy and Policy in the Mediterranean: Past, Present and Future* (London: Frank Cass, 2000).
2. For the uses and creation of maritime history see: Andrew Lambert, Laughton Professor of Naval History, 'Inaugural Lecture' (King's College London, 14 November, 2002); James Goldrick and John B. Hattendorf (eds), *Mahan is Not Enough: The Proceedings of a Conference of the Works of Sir Julian Corbett and Admiral Sir Herbert Richmond* (Newport, RI. 1993); John B. Hattendorf, *Ubi Sumus: The State of Naval and Maritime History* (Newport, RI. 1994); idem, *Doing Naval History: Essays Toward Improvement* (Newport, RI. 1995).

1

'WEE-AH-WEE'?: BRITAIN AT WEIHAIWEI, 1898–1930

T.G. Otte

> Ye Jingoes shout your very best,
>   Ye grumblers cease to cry;
> The East is conquered by the West,
>   We've taken Wei-Hai-Wei.
>
> We none of us know where it is,
>   But that's no reason why
> We should not feel heroic zeal
>   At taking Wei-Hai-Wei.
>
> George Curzon once has seen the spot,
>   And George is pretty spry,
> And George declared that it must be got –
>   We must have Wei-Hai-Wei.
>
> German and Russian fleets, Ah ha!
>   Who cares for you, small fry?
> We laugh at all your warlike feats,
>   We're safe in Wei-Hai-Wei.
>   Sir Wilfrid Lawson, Easter 1898.[1]

The Chinese Empire's defeat in the war with Japan of 1894–95 marked a turning point in China's relations with the outside world. Its rout at the hands of the smaller island power brought before the chancelleries of Europe the full extent of China's internal and external weakness. The Middle Kingdom, it seemed, had joined the ranks of – in the Social Darwinian parlance of the day – 'dying nations'.[2] Its moribund condition raised the prospect of dividing the spoils of the Chinese carcass, and so made it an object of Great Power politics. In the immediate aftermath of the Sino-Japanese War the foreign powers competed for loan agreements, or railway, mining and other commercial concessions. The pace and character of Far Eastern developments, however, changed at the end of 1897, when Germany exploited the murder of two German missionaries to seize Kiaochow Bay in Shantung province, and turned the port of Tsingtao into a naval base. Weakened by the war with Japan, the Peking government was powerless to resist foreign encroachments upon its territory. Indeed, the German move seemed to presage a new, more acute, possibly even the final, phase of the 'China Question'. In retrospect, *The Times* aptly termed the Far Eastern crisis of 1897–98 'a scramble for naval bases'.[3] While Germany and Russia were the principal actors during the crisis, Britain, whose political and trading influence was still dominant in China, was immediately affected by the establishment of fortified German and Russian bases on the Chinese mainland. Already during the final stages of the 1894–95 war France and Russia had significantly augmented their naval squadrons in Chinese waters.[4] At the end of the conflict Germany had joined with these two powers in the so-called Far Eastern *Dreibund* that deprived Japan of her spoils of victory. The coercive cooperation of the three continental Powers, their naval ambitions – albeit in the German case only nascent – combined with China's apparent terminal decline, threatened to undermine Britain's regional position. In consequence, in April 1898 the British government acquired the lease of the port of Weihaiwei on the northernmost tip of the Shantung promontory as a counterpoise to the German and Russian acquisitions of Kiaochow and Port Arthur.

Simultaneously with the northern naval base Britain also acquired the lease of the Hong Kong New Territories. Both leased territories were comparable in size and population; so were the legal and administrative arrangements under the two lease agreements.[5] The fate of the two new leased territories, however, could not have been more dissimilar. While Hong Kong developed into a flourishing, commercially vibrant Crown Colony, and remained under British rule until its retrocession to Peking at the expiry of the lease in 1997, Weihaiwei was a dependent territory, never to be developed as either a naval base or a trading place. It languished in a state of neglect and uncertainty over its future, to be handed over to China in 1930. In the evocative Edwardian grandiloquence of Reginald Johnston, then a district officer and magistrate, and later the territory's last commissioner, Britain's 'robe of empire [was] a very splendid and wonderfully variegated garment'. Pinned to this robe there was 'a little drab-coloured ribbon that is in constant danger of being dragged in the mud or trodden underfoot... This is Weihaiwei.'[6] Indeed, at the time of its acquisition, opposition politicians in London ridiculed the leased territory as 'Wee-hy-Wee', 'Wee-ah-Wee' or 'Why-oh-Why'.[7] Weihaiwei fell into oblivion soon after its unceremonious return to Chinese rule. In scholarly literature, too, it has suffered the same neglect that it suffered at the hands of Whitehall officials during the period of British rule. Insofar as it has attracted the attention of scholars, it has been used as an example of late Ch'ing diplomacy playing a weak hand against encroaching foreign Powers;[8] or a blatant case of the 'irrationality' underpinning late-Victorian British imperialism.[9] It has also been treated as a case study of British colonial administration and the economic and social modernization that it wrought.[10] However, the leased territory's place in British strategy and policy in the Far East in the early part of the twentieth century has not been studied in depth.[11] In fact, Weihaiwei offers an excellent prism through which to study the facets of Britain's regional presence, the constraints placed upon Britain's ability to project its power in East Asia, the metropolitan strategic policy-making process and the wider Great Power context in which British policy in the area operated.

'Cartographic Consolation': The acquisition of Weihaiwei

Part of the reason for Weihaiwei's neglect as a potential naval base lies in the developments that led to its acquisition. At their root was the German seizure of Kiaochow in mid-November 1897, and not Russia's lease of Port Arthur in March 1898. Following the German move the government in London faced pressure on three different fronts. There was, first of all, the danger that a 'policy of grab' by the powers might be unleashed by the German action; and a scramble of this kind was generally anticipated to hasten China's complete disintegration. This concern was hardly allayed by the German ambassador's statement that, if nobody else would, 'the Russians were sure to begin [the scramble] sooner or later'.[12] Then there was the spectre of a revived Far Eastern triplice that haunted senior Foreign Office officials, such as the Assistant Under-secretary Francis Bertie, who supervised Far Eastern affairs. The German action at Kiaochow, he reasoned accurately, had come only after prior consultation with Russia; and Germany's establishment at a northern Chinese port was, in fact, Germany's reward for joining France and Russia in ousting Japan from the Chinese mainland in 1895.[13] St Petersburg's sharp reaction to the German move, and the Russo-German standoff over Kiaochow, which was also coveted by Russia, at the end of November, helped to allay fears about the firmness of Russo-German collusion and its possible poise against Britain.[14] It did not remove, however, fears of a scramble for Chinese territory. Reluctant to commit himself to any definite course to counter the German action at this early stage of the crisis, lest overt British intervention led to a 'scramble for China', the Prime Minister and Foreign Secretary, the Marquis of Salisbury, decided to await further developments.[15] The appearance of a Russian naval squadron in mid-December at Port Arthur at the northern entrance to the Gulf of Pechili, however, increased pressure on Salisbury to formulate a decisive policy. The wintering of the Russian ships in the ice-free port on the Liaotung peninsula was a clear indication of St Petersburg's intention to follow the German move.[16] Sir Nicholas O'Conor, formerly Britain's minister at Peking and now ambassador to Russia, advised that for diplomatic and strategic reasons Britain now required an 'adequate counterpoise to German and Russian actions'.[17] Indeed, Salisbury himself was slowly edging toward the idea of establishing 'a winter station for our fleet near Cheefo [on the southern shore of the Gulf of Pechili] or the constant presence of our vessels there'.[18] On New Year's Eve, he finally instructed the minister at Peking, Sir Claude MacDonald, to demand 'some corresponding concession' in the event of Germany obtaining a permanent base in northern China.[19] During the course of the first week of January 1898 Salisbury and the First Lord of Admiralty 'discuss[ed] various harbours in China'.[20] Thus, the decision to acquire a port in northern China was taken much earlier than is accepted in traditional scholarly assessments. Crucially, it was taken as a necessary countermove to the German seizure of Kiaochow. At this stage in the deliberations, no reference was made to any possible Russian territorial acquisition. In this lies one of the keys to the fate of Weihaiwei after 1898.

However, the government now came under increased pressure on a third front: calls in the press and parliament for forceful British action in China.[21] Demands for 'some sensational action on our part' were echoed by the Colonial Secretary, Joseph Chamberlain, the undoubted strong man of the Unionist administration.[22] Given the importance of keeping the renegade Radical Chamberlain within the Unionist fold, his suggestions could not easily be ignored; nor was Salisbury unreceptive to 'the swing of the pendulum at home'. Whatever his disdain for popular politics, he was resigned 'that "the public" will require...cartographic consolation in China...[A]s a matter of course we shall have to do it'.[23] To fend off mounting public criticism of the government's handling of the Far Eastern situation, leading Cabinet ministers delivered public speeches, declaring the government's resolve to defend British commerce in the region. The Chancellor of the Exchequer, Sir Michael Hicks Beach, even pronounced the government to be 'absolutely determined,...even at the cost of war' to defend British interests.[24] No doubt, the chancellor's bellicose speech was meant as a warning to Russia to respect British rights and interests in China. Such ministerial statements, however, were part of a co-ordinated effort to gain time in order to negotiate a regional understanding with Russia. Such a working agreement would contain the threat of a 'scramble for China'; but would also 'produce some changes in the grouping of the Powers in Europe', as Salisbury noted. For this, he won the backing of the Cabinet.[25] Despite auspicious beginnings, O'Conor's negotiations at St Petersburg eventually ran aground in early March on the twin obstacles of competing attempts to issue another loan to China and Russia's ambitions to secure an expansive sphere of influence in northern China.[26] Indeed, while negotiations for an agreement with Britain continued, Russia extracted from Peking the lease of Port Arthur and Talienwan.[27]

This latest turn of events caused the Salisbury administration considerable embarrassment. On 2 March the government's foreign-affairs spokesman in the House of Commons, Salisbury's Parliamentary Under-secretary George Nathaniel Curzon, had supported a motion, tabled by a Conservative backbencher, pledging London to maintain China's integrity as a vital British interest.[28] Curzon's support for the motion was somewhat precipitate. When the German and Russian occupations were made permanent in mid-March, it highlighted Britain's limited ability to protect her vital interests in the Far East. Throughout March public pressure on the government was mounting to adopt a more decisive attitude. Even in the Conservative-leaning press the government was accused of 'ministerial vacillation, hesitation, and timidity'.[29] Furthermore, in January and February the ruling party lost three parliamentary byelections in supposedly safe seats. On the hustings, Salisbury's 'weak' foreign policy was 'today the theme of every Radical canvasser', as a senior Conservative MP warned.[30] A further, diplomatic factor now entered into Salisbury's equation. At the end of February, the Tsungli Yamên, the Chinese Board of Foreign Affairs, had offered Britain the lease of Weihaiwei. In so doing, Peking hoped to forestall possible British demands for compensation in the rich Yangtze region, but also to play off the foreign Powers against each other.[31] The former headquarters of China's Northern (or Pei-yang) Fleet until the 1894–95 war, Weihaiwei had been under temporary Japanese occupation since then, to be evacuated in May 1898 upon the payment of the last instalment of the war indemnity owed to Japan. Indeed, fearful that the Germans 'had cast their eyes on the place', the Tokyo government signalled that it welcomed a British takeover of Weihaiwei, once the Japanese contingent was withdrawn.[32]

Against this background, the Cabinet assembled to formulate a new China policy. However, the ministers were deeply divided over the Chinese offer of a northern naval base, and it took three Cabinet meetings before the lease was accepted. At the root of the divisions was a fundamental difference of opinion regarding Salisbury's policy of eschewing alliance commitments in peacetime. There was, as the French ambassador observed, a sceptical element in the Cabinet, which was beyond Salisbury's control.[33] The 'anti-Weihaiwei-party' in the Cabinet was largely anti-isolationist. Its members identified Russia as Britain's main adversary in Asia. Its more extreme members, led by Chamberlain, even advocated evicting Russia from Port Arthur by force. This group favoured an Anglo-American-German combination, and was therefore anxious not to antagonize Berlin by occupying a port in the vicinity of Kiaochow.[34] The 'Weihaiwei-party', led by Salisbury with the support of Curzon, who was specially admitted to the Cabinet discussions, was opposed to an alliance with a continental Power. They argued that Russia's establishment at Port Arthur could not be prevented, but that the acquisition of a northern port would act as a check upon both Russia and Germany.[35] Ultimately, Salisbury' supporters prevailed over the sceptics, and on 25 March the Cabinet sanctioned the lease of Weihaiwei.[36]

Two factors provide the key to future decisions regarding Weihaiwei. The first of these were the divisions within the Cabinet. For Salisbury the acquisition of a Shantung port served a dual purpose. It would act as a check on Germany at Kiaochow; and might 'strike a death blow' at her aspirations to turn the province into a German sphere of influence.[37] Furthermore, taking Weihaiwei had a symbolic value, placating anti-Russian sentiments in public and among government supporters in parliament. Indeed, when the government announced the lease in parliament on 5 April, it was presented as a necessary move 'to balance the [Russian] possession of Port Arthur'.[38] To some extent, then, the acquisition of Weihaiwei was a sop to the government's critics at home. However, the continued existence of a strong 'anti-Weihaiwei' group around Chamberlain directly contributed to a key concession to Germany in April. While the ailing Salisbury was absent from London, recuperating in the South of France, the Chamberlain group made an abortive attempt to reverse the decision in favour of Weihaiwei.[39] It was linked to the Colonial Secretary's clandestine alliance talks with the German ambassador, which had commenced on 29 March. Although the attempt to reverse Cabinet policy failed, Chamberlain's alliance overture was not without effect on Weihaiwei's future. Upon being informed of the lease of the port, the German government demanded British recognition of German predominance in Shantung, and an undertaking by London not to build a railway from Weihaiwei into the interior of the province.[40] This pledge was given by Arthur Balfour, the Leader of the Commons, who took charge of the Foreign Office during Salisbury's absence. Balfour tacitly supported Chamberlain's foreign policy alternative, and was anxious to conclude some form of China agreement with Berlin. The prospect of British railway and commercial competition in Shantung, however, was unlikely to induce the German government to conclude such an agreement.[41] At one stroke Balfour's pledge reduced Weihaiwei's value as a tool to keep Germany in check, as was desired by Salisbury and senior British diplomats. It also now prevented the future commercial development of the leased territory since that was dependent upon railway communications.

The second crucial factor was the pressure of time: 'Russia took 30 days, Cabinet give me seven', as the minister at Peking complained.[42] Following consultation with Admiral Sir Alexander Buller, commander-in-chief China Station, the soldier-turned-diplomat MacDonald had already shortly after the German seizure of Kiaochow advocated privately that a coaling station in northern Chinese waters was desirable, provided it was fortified.[43] In early January 1898, before Russia's demands for Port Arthur and Talienwan Bay were made public, Buller favoured either of these two or Thornton Haven in the island of Hayuntao, or preferably the Chusan islands near the mouth of the Yangtze as suitable counterpoises to the German base at Kiaochow.[44] Indeed, as Professor Nish has demonstrated, neither Buller nor Vice-Admiral Sir Edward Seymour, who took over from him in February, were consulted about suitable naval bases to counter Russia at Port Arthur. The 'men-on-the-spot' were exclusively concerned with Germany.[45] Given that the naval squadron on China Station was the main strategic instrument of British power projection in the Far East, this lack of consultation may appear inexplicable. At any rate, it is indicative of the absence of proper policy-co-ordinating mechanisms between various Whitehall departments at the close of the nineteenth century.

It was only when Seymour was instructed on 24 March to assemble and hold in readiness a force at Chefoo that the Admiralty impressed upon him that this force had to be superior to the Russian squadron at Port Arthur.[46] On 26 March, one day after the Cabinet decision in favour of Weihaiwei, he was ordered to collect all available ships to rendezvous in the Gulf of Pechili. The force was to be 'fairly superior to [the] Russian force there'; but the Admiralty also warned Seymour to keep one vessel in southern waters 'to watch the French'. The facility with which Seymour and his second-in-command, Rear Admiral Charles C.P. Fitzgerald, were able to concentrate Britain's naval forces demonstrated the extent to which Britain enjoyed a practical superiority in Chinese waters.[47] There is no evidence to suggest that London expected a warlike response from any of the Powers. The concentration of the squadron was a demonstration of British naval power in support of MacDonald's demand for Weihaiwei.[48] It was the tactical arm of British power in the Far East aiding diplomacy. Indeed, at MacDonald's first interview at the Tsungli Yamên on 28 March, the Chinese ministers prevaricated, raising all manner of difficulties, real and imagined. The Chinese only conceded to MacDonald's demands on 2 April, after two further rounds of talks. They did so under the pressure of Seymour's squadron, now assembled at Chefoo where it maintained a high-visibility presence.[49] MacDonald brought the negotiations to – by Chinese standards – an unusually speedy conclusion, accomplishing the transfer of Weihaiwei to Britain on 24 May, with the formal Anglo-Chinese convention being signed on 1 July.[50] In it Peking ceded to Britain full jurisdiction for the duration of Russia's lease of Port Arthur. The leased territory included the island of Liukung-tao and Jih-tao, which guarded the entrance to Weihaiwei Bay, along with a ten-miles-broad strip of the bay's coastline and all barracks and forts. There was also a British sphere of influence within a radius of some 12 miles of the bay, within which British administration and traditional Chinese forms of government and jurisdiction coexisted. Its frontier-line was 'purely artificial', in some cases slicing Chinese villages into British and Chinese portions. Indeed, the demarcation was not completed until 1900.[51]

Nonetheless, MacDonald had reservations about the suitability of Weihaiwei. Fitzgerald advised him that the harbour was too shallow, and offered only limited anchorage for modern men-of-war. The minister himself warned London that its strategic value would be diminished if Germany proved hostile.[52] It was this warning that encouraged the Chamberlain group in its abortive attempt to reverse the Weihaiwei policy. In yet another illustration of the lack of co-ordination in metropolitan strategic policy-making, Bertie now made enquiries of the Admiralty as to Weihaiwei's strategic potential. The Foreign Office was informed that the bay was open to strong northeasterly gales common in winter and spring; its eastern entrance was also so shallow that warships could only enter it from the West; and the anchorage off the island of Liukung-tao offered berth to only a small number of vessels.[53] Still, it was by now too late: 'The fleet cannot return without good results in its pockets', the First Lord of the Admiralty warned.[54] The Foreign Office and the 'Weihaiwei-party' had advocated the taking of the port without any detailed information on its strategic potential. Indeed, in the House of Commons debate on 29 April Balfour admitted that the leased territory would be 'of the utmost value to us diplomatically at Pekin' during peacetime; and that it was unlikely to be more than 'a secondary naval base'.[55] In one of his more lucid intervals, the German Emperor thought it would 'be a useless expense and indicated a departure from that practical common sense with which Englishmen were usually credited'.[56]

'Strategically too isolated': Britain at Weihaiwei

If the Admiralty was not properly consulted about the lease of Weihaiwei, it played a much larger part in arranging the occupation, and determining the strategic requirements and future role of the leased territory. Indeed, even before the navy took possession of Weihaiwei, its potential as a strategic base formed the subject of public debate. Writing in *The Times* under the appropriately military pseudonym of 'Miles', Colonel G.S. Clarke, then a superintendent at the Royal Arsenal Woolwich, formerly secretary to the Colonial Defence Committee (CDC) and a future secretary to the Committee of Imperial Defence, dismissed the idea that a fortified base at Weihaiwei could neutralize Port Arthur. Fortification involved extensive engineering work; securing the forts properly would require a garrison of 10,000 men. Whereas Russia and Germany could draw on the hinterland of their new bases, Britain enjoyed no such advantage at Weihaiwei. Under such circumstances, Clarke warned, the acquisition of the place as a counterpoise to Port Arthur was 'absolutely futile'. Moreover, events since 1895 had 'inexorably ruled that we cannot exercise a dominating power in Northern China. Wei-hai-wei will be a permanent source of expenditure and weakness to the Empire.'[57] Clarke's doubts were not confined to fellow Engineers, but were shared by the naval officers on China Station. According to the first civilian visitor to the leased territory, the young Francis Dyke Acland, who in later years would become Sir Edward Grey's Parliamentary Undersecretary, the officers had preferred a blockade of Port Arthur to the acquisition of new territory. Still, they conceded that the Japanese had left the place in good condition; and that the mountainous hinterland of the Weihaiwei town offered certain strategic advantages.[58] In Whitehall, by contrast, the Director of Military Intelligence (DMI), Colonel Sir John Ardagh, offered a more positive, albeit preliminary assessment. A fortified naval base at Weihaiwei, he argued, would act as an effective counterpoise to the increased influence of Russia and Germany at the Peking court. Reflecting the contemporary naval consensus, the DMI argued that, for as long as the British squadron operating in the China seas enjoyed a numerical superiority over any potential enemy combination, the fortified port would be secure against a naval attack. Weihaiwei, then, 'would not be exposed to any serious risk of either attack by a fleet or by military expedition over sea, or to a bombardment from the sea, on a large scale'. Although a detailed survey of the new territory had yet to be carried out, and the Colonial Defence Committee had not pronounced on its strategic requirements, Ardagh outlined some key recommendations. Given the nature of the anticipated threat to the base, the two islands, the larger Liukung-tao and the smaller Jih-tao, were the hinges on which the defence of the territory revolved. A small garrison of some 1,500 men, with a nucleus of 500 British troops, should be placed on Liukung; and for the moment only the two islands were to be fortified. However, Ardagh's recommendations were not on a modest scale: 'the works should be of great strength, with enceintes proof against escalade, ample casemated accommodation, very powerful armament, and a liberal employment of steel armour and iron'.[59] The divergent assessments by Clarke and Ardagh reflected the precepts of two different schools of late-Victorian strategic thought, the latter of whom favoured passive defence, based upon 'a policy of "bricklaying"', as opposed to a lighter, more mobile and offensive posture.[60]

On the spot, Seymour was instructed to gather practical information from the departing Japanese, and to conduct a detailed military survey of the new leasehold possession.[61] A first scheme for its defence was developed by Commander A.H. Smith-Dorrien who commanded HMS *Alacrity*. Like Ardagh's preliminary suggestions, Smith-Dorrien's 15-point programme envisaged a defence scheme centred on Liukung-tao, as the mainland would remain a source of weakness. Any landing attempt near Weihaiwei by enemy forces could be scuppered by British cruisers. The island was to be turned into 'an impregnable fortress', secure against 'all attacks'; there ought to be no defensive positions on the mainland; and 'a large basin scooped out' to accommodate six battleships. Such a scheme, the Commander advised, would transform Weihaiwei into 'a useful naval base'. Seymour was sceptical of Smith-Dorrien's plans: ' "Impregnable" is a strong word, and ... inapplicable to the Island of Leu Kung [*sic*].' He contended that an army could be landed on the mainland, but admitted that 'properly defending the mainland is a very large affair', given that the original Chinese forts fell in rapid succession to the Japanese in 1895.[62] Seymour's comment may well have indicated a preference for large-scale fortification. He was favourably impressed by Weihaiwei's strategic potential, and advised the Admiralty that three defence schemes were practicable: an extensive fortification of Liukung-tao and the mainland with substantial naval facilities and a corresponding garrison; a modified version under which only the main island would be fortified and more modest basins and dockyards would be erected; and, finally, a minimum solution, which envisaged merely the repair of existing buildings and facilities with a garrison of no more than 150 men.[63]

Before the Admiralty and the Colonial Defence Committee in Whitehall could decide on the three possible schemes, the 'men-on-the-spot' refined their views on the necessity of fortification. J.F. Lewis, a colonel in the Royal Engineers and member of the surveying party in the territory, concluded in September that the new leasehold possession was 'useless' as a counterpoise to Russia in the event of a war. Any further Russian encroachment upon Chinese territory would come over land, and the British forces at Weihaiwei would be in no position to stop the Russian advance. Indeed, from the Russian perspective, an attack upon the base would be 'a secondary operation'. Under these circumstances, Lewis suggested that the defence scheme be reduced to the defence of the naval establishment. This ought to be concentrated on Liukung-tao; and the island and the floating basin in its lee had to be secured against cruiser attack. This could be achieved by building a breakwater at the entrance to the bay – itself also an effective counter-measure against gunboat and torpedo attacks – equipped with electric sentry and search beams and twelve 12-pounder Quick Fire guns. Half-a-dozen gun batteries on the island and 20 machine-gun emplacements would suffice to make the naval establishment defensible. There should be no fortification of places on the mainland. The total strength of the garrison, comprising one infantry battalion, an artillery company and a section of the Royal Engineers, would be no more than 1,000 men.[64] Seymour's views on the issue had hardened into the conviction that Weihaiwei ought to be made into 'a practical Naval base, capable of resisting the attack of a raiding Squadron'. This was the modified version, which he had highlighted in June. In the Vice-Admiral's assessment Britain had obtained a number of strategic advantages by taking possession of Weihaiwei. With the exception of Port Arthur, it was the only defensible port in northern Chinese waters. It enhanced Britain's presence in the North of the Middle Kingdom at a time when its political and commercial future had become the focus of Great Power rivalries, and it enabled Britain to raid enemy commerce in the Gulf of Pechili and the Yellow Sea. Once equipped with coal bunkers, ammunition and provisions depots, Weihaiwei would increase the operational range and capabilities of the squadron on China Station, as it would be no longer dependent on Hong Kong, some 1,200 miles away. In the event of a war with Russia, Weihaiwei would be key to a naval blockade of Port Arthur and the possible landing of troops on the Liaotung Peninsula in order to 'starve Port Arthur out'. Nevertheless, Seymour insisted that, to have any strategic value in time of war, Weihaiwei 'must be fortified sufficiently to resist for a short period, perhaps very few weeks, the attack of a casual Squadron'. The defences had to be regarded as 'very incomplete' until a breakwater was erected, which alone gave security against torpedo-boat attacks. Given Port Arthur's vicinity, 89 miles off, any Russian attack was most likely to take that form. Seymour's defence scheme was predicated on the assumption of continued British naval dominance. Defence of the base against an enemy with permanent command of the sea and large forces on the mainland – a Crimean War scenario in reverse – 'would be mere folly', involving the expenditure of large sums and the 'locking up of an immense garrison' in peacetime; and if Britain ever lost command over the China seas, 'our holding [Weihaiwei] alone and isolated, were it possible, could scarcely repay us'.[65]

The arguments advanced by Seymour and Lewis were cogent and sensible. They were also echoed in public by a naval officer, R.S. Yorke, who had served on the China Station. The wide entrance to the bay, he observed, exposed the anchorage to strong northeasterly gales, common in the spring. Building the necessary breakwater was, therefore, going to add further to the substantial costs involved in transforming the port into a regular naval base. Port Arthur was impregnable, and given Russia's advantage as an Asiatic landpower, Weihaiwei could never serve as a counterpoise 'to restore the diplomatic equilibrium at Peking'. Russia would attain 'complete mastery' there, and 'we have no means of preventing its accomplishment'. While Weihaiwei could not be retroceded to China, it 'should be "made a Cyprus of", that is to say ignored, and as little expense incurred there as possible'. In its place, Britain ought to acquire the Chusan islands in order to be able better to protect British interests in the Yangtze region in the anticipated event of China's final demise.[66]

Decision-making regarding Weihaiwei's future remained slow. By early 1899 only dredging operations had commenced.[67] Indeed, even though the Admiralty regarded the position of the base as 'similar to that of an advanced post in a hostile country', there still existed no cable communication between Weihaiwei and the Hong Kong naval base.[68] By mid-January the Colonial Defence Committee turned its attention to the new leasehold possession. Since its inception in the late 1880s the committee had developed a tendency to concern itself more with procedural and organizational problems of imperial defence rather than with broader strategic issues. The case of Weihaiwei was no exception. The CDC did not address the fortification issue. Instead, following a suggestion by the commander-in-chief of the army, Field Marshal Lord Wolseley, it examined the strength and composition of the garrison force.[69] The committee recommended that six Chinese infantry companies ought to be recruited in Cantonese-speaking parts of southern China and trained at Weihaiwei, grouped around two companies of British infantry. The total strength of the projected garrison would be just over 900 men. Although this may be taken as an implicit endorsement of Seymour's preferred 'modified version', the CDC did not volunteer any views on the future defence requirements of Weihaiwei.[70] Its recommendations were resisted by the War Office, which throughout the 1890s had striven to bypass the CDC, and which now hoped to reduce the garrison to one Chinese battalion. In the ensuing inter-departmental struggle in Whitehall, the War Office won the support of the Admiralty.[71] A joint committee by the two service departments decided that a naval depot was to be established on Liukung-tao under Admiralty control, while the remainder of the island was placed under the War Office. Nevertheless, the committee fudged the issue of the base's defence, arguing that it was 'impossible to foresee the future requirements at Wei-hai-Wei'.[72]

In this fashion the question of Wei-hai-Wei's future strategic role in the Far East was left unresolved. To an extent this reflected the relative tranquility in Far Eastern affairs in 1899. The Anglo-Russian, so-called Scott–Muravev agreement, on the division of railway spheres of influence, had helped to stabilize the affairs of the Chinese Empire.[73] In so doing it arguably reduced the pressure to define Weihaiwei's role in Britain's regional strategy. Nevertheless, it was something of a wasting asset. As an anonymous commentator observed in mid-1899, there was 'not a fort reconstructed nor a gun mounted'. Weihaiwei was not so much a 'secondary naval base' as 'a miserable, decaying, sixth-rate walled town, at the bottom of a shallow bay'. Examining the potential of the place, he concluded that it could be turned into a first-class naval fortress, albeit at great expense. At a minimum a breakwater ought to be commenced in order to turn the anchorage into a 'splendidly defensible harbour'. Noting the moderate climate and fertile soil of the leased territory, the author concluded that it could 'be turned into a paradise, a sanatorium, and a fortified harbour; but it cannot be held as a secondary naval base in time of war'.[74] Such views were echoed in intelligence circles in Whitehall. In a detailed reassessment of Weihaiwei's position, an anonymous naval intelligence officer argued that the acquisition of the place 'partook more of a political move than one carefully thought-out on a strategic basis'. Weihaiwei was too close to Port Arthur; and given the shallow anchorage and its mountainous surroundings, he opined, it was 'impossible to [sic] adequately defend it as a workable and reasonably safe naval base'. Britain's maritime supremacy and 'due weight with the invertebrate Chinese government' could, therefore, not effectively be secured from Weihaiwei. It was in all respects 'inherently defective as a naval base'.

More suitable secondary bases for the China squadron, he concluded, were Port Hamilton off the Korean coast or the Chusan islands.[75] Ardagh, the DMI, commented that Weihaiwei was not 'an ideal harbour for defence', but defended its acquisition. Moreover, for as long as British naval policy aimed at maintaining naval forces superior to any possible enemy combination in Chinese waters, Weihaiwei was safe against a naval attack or the disembarkation of large enemy land forces in its vicinity.[76] These intelligence discussions did not filter through to political circles. George Curzon was exceptional among senior British politicians in taking some interest in the base. He had been instrumental in the acquisition of Weihaiwei, and therefore took 'a sort of parental interest in that place'. To his mind, London was showing 'inexcusable apathy ... about turning it to some purpose. But then it is part of the Chinese policy of H[er] M[ajesty's] G[overnment] which has always been ... a riddle insoluble by man.'[77] However, by now Curzon was Viceroy of India, and so without any direct influence in the matter.

If Whitehall was unable to determine Weihaiwei's defence requirements, then the territory suffered from delay and neglect in other areas as well. Thus, it was not until March 1900 that a joint Anglo-Chinese boundary commission began the demarcation of the British sphere of influence, though this owed much to procrastination on the part of Shantung governor Yüan Shih-k'ai. When the commission finally commenced its work, the political situation within the territory as well as in northern China had deteriorated. The demarcation was soon marred by violent clashes between British troops and Chinese villagers, apparently led by Chinese soldiers in plain clothes and in collusion with local dignitaries.[78] Against the background of the rising Boxer tide elsewhere in northern China, the government in London decided to remain firm, and not to consider a modification of the boundary. Colonel Arthur Dorward, the commissioner of the territory, eventually completed the demarcation, albeit without Chinese cooperation, after reinforcements arrived.[79] Although there was no evidence of Boxer involvement in the boundary disturbances, the incident highlighted the potential dangers facing British rule. Still, Dorward's firmness paid dividends. With Britain's intention to exert governmental control over the leased territory having been asserted, Weihaiwei remained quiet at the height of the Boxer Uprising. The British contingent of the international China Expeditionary Force made it its principal base for operations in northern China, as well as its chief hospital station.[80] Indeed, it was only under the impression of the Boxer emergency that Weihaiwei was eventually connected to the existing telegraphic cable network.[81]

Further changes were afoot. Locked into an arms race at sea with France and Russia, and in light of the spiralling costs of the South African war and the China campaign, the Admiralty and the War Office were anxious to divest themselves of their shared responsibility for the leasehold. In consequence, the dependency was handed over to civilian administration under the auspices of the Colonial Office on 1 January 1901.[82] However, this still left the issue of its future defence requirements unresolved. As the Secretary of State for War, St John Brodrick admitted, his department had 'no policy; nor have you [viz. Admiralty]; nor have

C[olonial] O[ffice]. No one ever had except George Curzon'.[83] Insofar as the Cabinet had any views on Weihaiwei, it was 'to avoid friction between Admiralty & War Office'.[84] The new army chief, Field Marshal Earl Roberts, suggested that the position at Weihaiwei was so weak militarily that 'we should not establish any extensive form of government there'.[85] He went further: no money should be expended on the territory, and 'a more advantageous harbour' in northwestern China should be secured at the first favourable opportunity.[86] Brodrick concurred. The prohibitive expenditure involved rendered fortification impracticable. As a naval base, however, 'in times of peace or in connection with action in China not involving war with Russia, Wei-hai-Wei has proved most useful'. In the event of a war with the Franco-Russian combination no attempt was to be made to hold the place: 'Nothing, therefore, should be placed there which it would be very costly to abandon'.[87] War Office analysts concluded that the base was 'strategically in too isolated a position for its military occupation in times of war with a naval Power ever to be satisfactory'.[88] Seymour and his successor as commander on China Station, Admiral Sir Cyprian Bridge, by contrast, favoured fortification and the garrisoning of Weihaiwei.[89] Bridge argued that, given its propinquity to the likely theatre of action in any future conflict in China, the creation of a 'considerable garrison [was] absolutely necessary'. Although dismissive of 'secondary bases' as 'new-fangled and un-English predilections' and mere ' "stone frigates" ', he nonetheless urged the Admiralty to consider some fortification so as to create a well-protected anchorage.[90] However, the War Office would entertain no extensive scheme. Brodrick decided that the port should be maintained only as a 'flying naval base . . . for use in a war with China, or a non-naval Power'. In the event of a war with a naval Power, it would be abandoned. The garrison would be reduced to three infantry companies, sufficient to carry out sentry duties at the naval stores and hospital. Moreover, Brodrick also ordered the cessation of all work on the fortification of Weihaiwei.[91] Ultimately, his department prevailed. At an interdepartmental conference of the Colonial Office and the two service departments in January 1902, it was decided that the Admiralty would not retain a large number of stores on Liukung-tao, and that land and buildings there in War Office possession would be handed to the new civil commissioner, James Stewart Lockhart, who resumed his office on 3 May 1902. Under these circumstances the conference also decided that no garrison was now required. Even the Chinese Regiment was eventually disbanded in 1903. The conference marked the end of any plans to convert Weihaiwei into a proper naval base. This decision, however, raised new problems, as Charles Prestwood Lucas, the Assistant Undersecretary of the Colonial Office who was chiefly concerned with Eastern colonies, minuted: 'Our one chance of making the place pay is to get it as much as possible into our own hands. What will be mostly against us will be the impression . . . that England is going to give the place up.'[92]

That impression was not the only problem the Colonial Office needed to address. In a lengthy memorandum George Thompson Hare, a senior official in the Malay civil service, now on special duty in the leased territory as an assistant commissioner, surveyed Weihaiwei's political and commercial potential. The decision by London to stop work on the fortification, and the Admiralty's decision to abandon the port immediately on the outbreak of war, meant that even as a coaling station its value was much reduced. If it was illusory now to think of Weihaiwei as a *place d'armes* against Russia, it was also too far removed from the seat of government in Peking to serve 'as a *point d'appui* for bringing pressure to bear on the Chinese Government...in British interests'. The geographic distance from Peking reduced the effect any joint naval demonstration with Britain's new ally Japan might produce on Russia, if it were to threaten China's integrity. Hare's assessment of Weihaiwei's commercial prospects was equally gloomy. The port and the leased territory had 'absolutely no commercial resources'. Commercial development depended entirely upon the construction of a railway connecting the port with the Shantung hinterland and Tientsin. This, however, London had pledged itself not to undertake. Weihaiwei, then, would remain 'a port of call for the British fleet during the summer, and a health resort for foreign residents in North China during the two or three months of the hot Chinese summer'. Furthermore, without the commercial stimulus of a railway it would remain 'a small burden on the Imperial Treasury'. Hare, therefore, recommended that the place be treated as a navy sanatorium; and that civil expenditure be reduced to a minimum so as to make British administration self-supporting. Indeed, he proposed a more far-reaching programme. Three-quarters of the leased territory were of no use, and should be returned to Chinese rule. In return, Britain should demand Tinghai on the Chusan islands, which was 'capable of being strongly fortified and made into a second Gibraltar and the key to the Yang-tsze Valley'.[93] The metropolitan colonial officials were not inclined to abandon their latest acquisition. C.P. Lucas was convinced that Weihaiwei was capable of sustained, if slow, commercial development: 'It is not fortified places that we want, it is trading, where the Chinese will come'. This still left the problem of Balfour's self-negating railway pledge to Germany. Lucas opined that a Chinese rather than a British-built line to Chefoo, which was not in the Shantung hinterland, and thence to Tientsin would allow circumventing the pledge without breaking it. Lucas' stratagem was more a reflection of Britain's predicament than a realistic policy option; and the idea was not pursued.[94] Hare's bold plan of exchanging most of the leasehold territory for the Chusan islands was received with similar scepticism by the Admiral on China Station.[95]

Lucas' prognosis that Weihaiwei could be transformed into a successful trading place became something of a Colonial Office mantra. The settlement's potential as a health resort would increase public revenue. In general, the department adhered to laissez-faire principles: 'It is not intended to force the development of Weihaiwei in any direction'. However, given its geographic location at the main northern trade route through the Gulf of Pechili as well as its excellent harbour, 'there is no reason for assuming that it must always remain in its present position...and the example of Hong Kong proves that a great port may develop

Table 1.1 Weihaiwei finances, 1901–06.[96]

	Revenue (Silver $)	*Expenditure* (Silver $)	*Grant* (£)
1901–02	22,220	121,877	11,250
1902–03	35,456	102,044	12,000
1903–04	58,586	165,873	9,000
1904–05	90,355	162,282	6,000
1905–06	105,934	146,000	3,000

in spite of the absence of railway communications and customs duties'.[97] This was little more than a pious hope. In reality, the railway problem and London's virtual abandonment of the place as a naval base killed off any commercial interest.[98] Despite his efforts to encourage enterprise, by 1906 the British commissioner was forced to conclude that the dependency did not show 'much sign as yet of permanent commercial activity'.[99] During the first five years of Colonial Office administration expenditure had consistently exceeded the revenue raised in the territory, although the finances improved slightly. A Treasury grant-in-aid had to make up the balance.

'Keeping Its Head above Water': The retention of Weihaiwei

Weihaiwei's commercial backwardness was a permanent concern for the Colonial Office. A further complication was added by the outbreak of the Russo-Japanese War in February 1904. The two, in fact, became entwined. Weihaiwei's 'neglected estate', as revealed in parliamentary reports, provoked press criticism. A strongly worded article by 'Tai Foo', which was given serious consideration at the Colonial Office, argued for energetic efforts to stimulate commercial development. Weihaiwei was in danger of becoming a 'discredited dependency'. German obstruction over the evacuation of Shanghai in 1902–03, a hangover from the Boxer crisis, should be used to revoke the 1898 railway pledge. Once a railway was built, the dependency's commercial future was assured. In addition, the decision to abandon fortification ought to be revised. A protected harbour for ten battleships, complete with a modest garrison, would enhance the commercial prospects and the political utility of Weihaiwei. Such a harbour could also be offered to the Chinese for occasional use by their Northern Fleet. Britain's two Chinese naval bases would then furnish London with 'two levers, working on the common fulcrum of the sea, with which to move the inert mass of China'. If such a programme were carried out, Weihaiwei might still take 'its proper place among the gems in the glittering belt of world-encircling empire'.[100]

However, not only did Whitehall show no inclination to apply diamond-cutters to the rough gem on the Shantung promontory, the linkage in the 1898 lease between Russia's occupation of Port Arthur and Britain's tenure of Weihaiwei now posed a new problem. By May 1904 the fortunes of war had turned against Russia. In view of the possibility of Russia being forced to cede Port Arthur, that vociferous commercial lobby group, the China Association, urged the Foreign Office to readjust the terms of the lease of Weihaiwei, but also to make it the terminus of a railway.[101] The 'necessity to retain Weihaiwei' was also stressed by the new Admiral on China Station, Sir Gerard Noel.[102] The status of Weihaiwei triggered a vigorous policy debate in Whitehall. At the Colonial Office the industrious Lucas championed retention. In its present unfortified state, the base was 'one more vulnerable point in the empire; if fortified it will be a source of anxiety and expense'. Given the harbour's potential and its proximity to the 'main trade route' in northern China, Britain as 'the first naval power in the world' ought not to abandon the place. Liukung-tao was the private property by purchase of the British government. Abandoning the territory would be detrimental to Britain's standing in China, and 'leave Germany in possession of the field in North China'. Even if Weihaiwei was no more than a 'second or third rate watering-place', its healthy climate and sulphur springs made it an ideal sanatorium for Westerners: 'And why should it not pay its way even in pounds, shillings, and pence, if utilised in this manner?' Under no circumstances should the place be given up – 'it would be disastrous in the extreme to do so'. If its commerce was not fully developed, then neither was Hong Kong's in the early years of British rule. Indeed, that thriving trading place was without railway link to the mainland. Lucas suggested that a new 99-year lease, backdated to 1898, should be negotiated with Peking. While he was reluctant to offer the Chinese any quid pro quo, he did not rule out the retrocession of the less valuable parts of the leasehold, as proposed by Hare in 1902, or giving up a site on the island for a dockyard for use by the Chinese fleet.[103] The Permanent Undersecretary, Sir Montagu Ommanney, and the Colonial Secretary Alfred Lyttelton accepted Lucas' argument as to 'the absolute necessity of making our position in the future more assured there'.[104] To strengthen the department's position in the Whitehall battle for retention, the Colonial Office made use of plans by the major China trader Jardine, Matheson and Co. to establish a bean-cake industry in the leasehold. Without some official assurance as to Weihaiwei's future, Lucas warned the Foreign Office, the company would be 'unwilling to sink any capital in the undertaking'. The territory would remain commercially underdeveloped.[105]

Colonial Office representations could not easily be ignored. Nevertheless, the Foreign Office thought any action premature. Lord Lansdowne, the Foreign Secretary, did not admit that Russia's evacuation of Port Arthur would automatically terminate Britain's tenure of Weihaiwei.[106] Given the by no means certain outcome of the war, the diplomatists' preference for inaction was sensible. However, an intervention by the British minister at Peking, Sir Ernest Satow, now complicated the Foreign Office's 'wait-and-see' approach. Under the terms of the original lease, Satow argued, Britain was bound to return the place to Chinese rule if Russia were to cede Port Arthur. Retrocession ought to be accompanied by a general agreement between China and the foreign Powers to guarantee Chinese independence and integrity. Satow regarded such an international guarantee as 'a *sine qua non* to secure us against Germany stepping into our shoes'.[107] What Satow had in mind was a scheme for some form of international protection of China. He feared that the war would lead to a Great Power division of the Chinese Empire '*à la mode de Pologne*'. To his American colleague, William W. Rockhill, he privately suggested an Anglo-American-Japanese combination with the object of 'exercis[ing] together a sort of condominium for the reforms of the administration, justice and finance'.[108] Satow's initiative remained abortive. Lansdowne was in no hurry to terminate the lease, and warned Satow not to encourage the Chinese to raise the matter. Accordingly, the minister stressed London's wish to retain Weihaiwei in his interviews at the *Wai-wu Pu*, the reformed Chinese Board of Foreign Affairs, when officials there touched upon the question of Britain's lease. Satow realized that China's fear of Germany's unchecked predominance in Shantung in the event of a simultaneous Anglo-Russian withdrawal was Britain's strongest card.[109] The German factor in the Weihaiwei equation was more than a reflection of the rising antagonism that began to affect Anglo-German relations in general. German commercial influence in the Shantung province was growing. There was a long-running legal-commercial dispute between the German governor at Tsingtao and a British mining syndicate. The Weihaiwei Gold Mining Company was engaged in mining and prospecting operations in the leased territory, and by late 1902 was anxious to commence work at Lao-ho San (Tiger Hill), an area that was partly outside the British leasehold. Since Britain had recognized in 1898 the predominance of German economic influence and interests in Shantung, the viability of the Tiger Hill enterprise was doubtful.[110] Indeed, a rival German syndicate sprung up, supported by German officials, and imperilled British mining operations. Official neglect had failed to nurse the tender plant of commerce at Weihaiwei; now German competition threatened to trample it underfoot. Once again, the haste with which the lease had been arranged in 1898 was at fault, as A. John Harding of the Colonial Office minuted: 'That convention only contemplated a sort of Eastern Gibraltar & the zone outside the leased territory was to prevent it from being commanded by other powers.' Lucas regarded the 'unfriendly & indefensible proceedings' of the Germans with dismay. '[M]orally we have the strongest case', the Legal Assistant Undersecretary, H. Bertram Cox advised. Still, under the terms of the convention, the Germans were right, 'but their behaviour is as usual unfriendly & disrespectful'.[111] Commissioner Lockhart strongly urged London that German pretensions be 'firmly and emphatically resisted'. Failing that, an impression would be created that British influence in China was in decline. He concluded that '[n]o better illustration...can be found of the selfishness of the policy of Germany in China in general and in Shantung in particular'.[112]

At the Peking Legation Satow, too, had become alarmed at the 'hectoring way of Germany' in China.[113] He instructed his commercial attaché, J.W. Jamieson, to investigate the leased territory's capacity as a commercial centre in relation to the treaty port of Chefoo and the German base at Kiaochow. Jamieson's detailed analysis of trade statistics demonstrated that commerce at Weihaiwei made 'a paltry showing'. Citing the well-known infrastructure problems concerning railway communications and the anchorage, he also highlighted the fact that, as regarded industrial production, all raw materials had to be imported. The Shanghai mercantile community regarded Weihaiwei primarily as a health resort. However, the storage capacity of the bonded warehouses at Shanghai was becoming more limited, leading to increases in storage charges. Jamieson's answer was to suggest turning Weihaiwei into 'a duty free-godown' for certain bulkier articles. Moreover, the place was now a regular port of call for steamers plying their trade between Shanghai and Tientsin. This and Weihaiwei's 'good climate and cheap labour' might also be used to induce the British and American Tobacco Company to relocate there, since the company had been driven out of Japan by the institution of a government tobacco monopoly. Both of these proposals were realistic only if London gave some undertaking of its intention to retain the leasehold. However, Jamieson's trade and finance analysis also revealed that, owing to energetic efforts by Germany, the steady growth of trade at Kiaochow contributed directly to the decline of the other Shantung treaty port Chefoo. If, as Lockhart and the Colonial Office argued, a railway were carried along the coast from Weihaiwei to Tientsin, Chefoo's fate as a commercial centre would be sealed. Chinese agreement to such a railway project could, therefore, not be expected. If, on the other hand, it was planned to connect Weihaiwei with Shantung's interior, the new line could not compete with the already existing German railway. Jamieson's conclusion was pessimistic. Shantung's commercial potential had consistently been over-rated, and the province could not sustain two large ports of entry. Chefoo was about to be overtaken by Kiaochow: 'Will the paling of one star add lustre to that of a new arrival, faintly striving to make itself visible? It is to be feared not, unless Weihaiwei can cover its hill slopes with mulberry trees, attract to itself the beans of Manchuria, or convince merchants in China that it would serve admirably as a duty-free godown.' Jamieson presented London with a dilemma rather than a solution. Commercially, Weihaiwei was unlikely to thrive. On the other hand, he observed that a British role in Shantung 'would tend to counteract German influence'.[114]

The retention of Weihaiwei, then, was a politico-strategic issue. As such it required interdepartmental co-ordination. The newly created mechanism for imperial defence consultation and co-ordination was through the Committee of Imperial Defence. Within Whitehall, the two service departments were anxious to withdraw from the leasehold. Ranged against them was the emerging axis of the Foreign and Colonial Offices, with the latter unsurprisingly acting as the most vociferous advocate of retention.[115] Indeed, there was some dismay at the Colonial Office at the diplomatists' somewhat lackadaisical attitude. The Foreign Office's pretention that while Russia might have ceased physically to occupy Port Arthur, the lease of Weihaiwei was legally not affected was dismissed as so contorted as to be 'an ultra-Chinese argument'. Definite preparations had to be made for the long-term renewal of the lease. Lucas reiterated the idea of obtaining a 99 years lease to place Weihaiwei on a par with Kiaochow and the Kowloon New Territories. Anything less would merely prolong 'the sense of insecurity of which we hear so perpetually as preventing capital from coming to Weihaiwei'. Crucially, he also stressed the fact that retention 'should be backed by Japan'. Lucas' suggestions were adopted by Alfred Lyttelton, who deprecated the Foreign Office's position. The latter, he minuted, bore 'traces of that ingenuity which is generally ascribed to lawyers, but is more often found in lawyers who do not remember that plain sense is at the root of law'.[116] Lyttelton impressed upon the Foreign Office the 'supreme importance ... [of] retain[ing] a foothold in Northern China'. However, Weihaiwei's political value was proportional to its commercial prospects. It should act as a Hong Kong counterpart in the North. However, this could 'never be attained under a hand-to-mouth tenure'. The latter had to be renewed; and as an inducement the Chinese ought to be offered the use by their naval vessels of the waters of the leasehold.[117]

The retentionists' case was strengthened by the need to take into consideration the views of Britain's Japanese ally. During the talks for the renewal and extension of the alliance in the summer of 1905 the Tokyo government urged Britain to remain at Weihaiwei. Continued British occupation was 'indispensable ... as a counterpoise to the German occupation of Kiaochow'.[118] Satow counselled against raising the matter while the US-sponsored peace talks at Portsmouth, New Hampshire, were in progress. If Japan acquired Port Arthur, 'we could come in on her back'. Nevertheless, the minister was doubtful as to Weihaiwei's prospects: 'At best it can keep its head above water, like a half-pay Captain at a small sea-side watering place in Devonshire.'[119] Initially, Satow had hoped to utilize the conclusion of peace to resume his 1904 efforts with the aim of securing a new international treaty, guaranteeing the status quo in China including the rights and concessions obtained by foreign Powers. This idea was motivated by two considerations. A treaty of this kind would stabilize China. But it also had a poise against Germany, for 'it w[ou]ld be necessary for everyone to put his cards on the table, e.g. Germany had been letting us all believe that she had acquired mining rights in 5 areas, whereas it was now certain that agreement had not been signed'.[120] However, he soon realized that such a proposal was impracticable. By mid-October the Foreign Office was petitioned by commercial lobby groups to secure the retention of Weihaiwei. Satow warned that relinquishing the territory would allow Germany to lay claim to the place under article V of the 1898 Sino-German (Kiaochow) convention; Britain's 'political position' in the region would be weakened; and no adequate commercial or territorial compensation could realistically be expected.[121] Satow's telegram and Japanese support for retention strengthened the hands of the Foreign and Colonial Offices in the Whitehall battle. However, as Francis Campbell (chief clerk of the Foreign Office's Far Eastern Department) observed, the two departments were opposed by 'that infernal Committee of Imperial Defence':

> I have no doubt their idea is one point less to have to consider & bother about in the schemes for the defence of the Empire, but I find it difficult to discuss it with patience, & the Col[onial] Off[ice], who are dead set upon making something of the place, are still more angry; but I much fear that the Prime Minister is not sound on the subject.[122]

Campbell's fears about the Prime Minister's soundness were justified. Following comments by Colonel Clarke, by now Secretary to the CID, Arthur Balfour instructed him to examine the case for retention. Balfour suggested somewhat disingenuously that Weihaiwei had originally been acquired at the Admiralty's advice: 'But Boards of Admiralty change, and the circumstances with which they got to deal change, and it may be that the present moment should be taken advantage of for re-considering the situation.'[123] Clarke, once possessed of a viewpoint, was not in the habit of changing it again. His views on Weihaiwei had not changed since his 'Miles' letter in April 1898. He was aware that the Colonial Office 'will not like being deprived of its infant'. The matter was, however, one of imperial defence, and the prospect of commercial development was of no consequence. The longer Britain retained Weihaiwei, he warned, the more difficult would be its eventual abandonment.[124] Clarke echoed Balfour's view that the conditions in the Far East had changed significantly. With only Vladivostok as a naval base, Russia was no longer able to project her naval power in the region. Command of the sea rested firmly with the Anglo-Japanese allies; and given the recent reduction of the squadron on China Station, the conversion of the Weihaiwei harbour into a proper naval base made little sense: 'Strategically, the place has no value, nor does it offer any convenience sufficient to justify retention.' The absence of commercial development or prospects similarly pointed to abandoning the place. Furthermore, the CID Secretary argued that Japan's victory over a European power would encourage China to emulate the smaller Asian nation, and within twenty years a resurgent China would confront the foreign powers. Freeing Britain from 'any territorial entanglements' in northern China would, therefore, be a 'supreme advantage'. If the occupation of Weihaiwei were to continue, Chinese opposition might force Britain into an unwelcome combination with Germany. The Portsmouth Peace Treaty offered an opportunity to relinquish the leasehold 'in the most natural manner', without conveying 'the impression of diminution of our interests or of an abdication of our rights'. All territorial advantages at Weihaiwei should be abandoned, though Clarke conceded that, in view of its 'special climatic merits', the sanatorium there ought to be retained. Indeed, returning the place to Chinese rule, he opined, might encourage France to abandon her southern base at Kwangchow-wan. The only admissible objection to retrocession was Japanese opposition to such a step. The alliance notwithstanding, Clarke insisted that British interests 'must be paramount'. If Tokyo desired a British presence in northern

China on political grounds, Weihaiwei ought to be exchanged for Port Hamilton on a small island off the southernmost tip of Korea.[125] The Prime Minister concurred with Clarke's analysis. The territory had served its strategic purpose; and Colonial Office expectations of some modest future growth were 'no argument ... for keeping Weihaiwei'. Balfour concluded that its tenure ought not to be renewed, provided that China guaranteed not to cede it to another power; that Britain had the right to maintain a hospital or sanatorium there; and that British naval vessels had right of access 'in all contingencies'.[126]

The CID memorandum triggered another round of interdepartmental exchanges. Once again C.P. Lucas emerged as Weihaiwei's strongest champion. Clarke's proposal to abandon it 'would be disastrous in the extreme'.[127] Treasury subsidies had steadily declined, he noted; and, as fortification was no longer envisaged, no military or naval expenditure was asked for. He reiterated his prediction that Weihaiwei would pay its way, provided British tenure of the place was made visibly permanent. No advantages would accrue from abandoning the territory; Japan would be offended; China would not be grateful; British civilians and forces personnel would lose 'an acknowledged health resort' and an inexpensive natural harbour; and Germany would remain as the only European power in northern China. Britain's having 'come and gone' would weaken its position in the China seas. The Colonial Office, Lucas concluded with a flourish, did not demand further funding: 'We ask for a pronouncement that we are going to stay and we will see to the rest.'[128] At the Foreign Office, meanwhile, strong emphasis was laid on the 'wishes of our allies, the Japanese', who hoped that Britain would stay at Weihaiwei so as to keep Germany at Kiaochow in check. Retrocession would produce 'no increase of good-will from the Chinese'. On the contrary, Britain's political position in China would be weakened: 'It would mean loss of "face", and "face" in China is everything.'[129]

The policy rift in Whitehall soured relations between the CID and the Foreign and Colonial Offices, where the retrocessionists were regarded as 'the enemy'. The collapse of Balfour's Unionist administration in December 1905 meant that 'Weihaiwei [was] still trembling in the balance'. The change of government caused further problems; for, while there was no change in the Colonial Office's stance, Sir Edward Grey, the new Foreign Secretary, was 'unsound on the question of W[ei]H[ai]Wei'.[130] Like Balfour, Grey was sceptical of the leasehold's intrinsic strategic value, but accepted that '[t]he conclusive argument for the retention ... [was] the strong feeling of the Japanese'.[131] Decision-making remained slow, however. The government's official line was that the status of Weihaiwei was unaffected by the transfer of the lease of Port Arthur to Japan, and 'no action is at present contemplated with regard to the lease'.[132] Lockhart viewed London's dithering with dismay. Singing '"*Beati Possidentes*"', while declining to renegotiate the status of the leasehold possession, he warned, would perpetuate 'the feeling of uncertainty', and so smother any commercial interest in the place.[133] Together with a Weihaiwei-based group of merchants, the commissioner lobbied the new Colonial Secretary, the Earl of Elgin, for a definite statement regarding the territory's future.[134] Still, it was accepted at the Colonial Office that little 'more than the colourless statements already made' could be expected from the allies at the Foreign Office. C.P. Lucas and his junior clerks remained adamant in their opposition to retrocession. However, to strengthen the department's position within Whitehall, Lucas now advocated the transfer of the administration of Weihaiwei to the governor of Hong Kong. Given the colony's surplus revenue, the small Treasury grant-in-aid to its impoverished northern relative would no longer be required, thereby also removing one of Clarke's arguments in favour of retiring from Weihaiwei.[135] The Colonial Office, however, was impotent in the matter of Weihaiwei's future without Foreign Office support. For his part, Grey favoured retention only in deference to Tokyo's wishes. But he resisted proposals by senior Foreign Office clerks, who echoed Lockhart's demands for some '"declaration" that we shall remain for all time'. He thought any attempt to turn Weihaiwei into a trade centre 'a folly'. Given Britain's 'insecure title', commercial development was possible only under Chinese auspices.[136]

Grey would no doubt have continued to prevaricate on the issue, had it not been formally raised on two occasions by the Chinese minister in London, Wang Tahsieh, in early October 1906.[137] The timing of the Chinese démarche caught Grey by surprise. It added to the mounting complications in Anglo-Chinese relations, which arose over customs, railways and other disputes. In principle, Grey was prepared 'to meet them half-way, but they are too pig-headed to do anything but make difficulties'.[138] At the Colonial Office, Elgin argued that it would be impolitic to yield to Peking in the face of Japanese opposition. On the other hand, since the original lease was to expire in 17 years, there was no real prospect of any revival of Weihaiwei. However, Chinese plans for the modernization of the navy, the Colonial Secretary observed, provided some 'room for a bargain'. As suggested by Lucas in 1904, China ought to be offered the use of dockyard facilities in return for the extension of the lease.[139] As to Tokyo's continued opposition to retrocession there could be no doubt. Similarly, the new minister at Peking, Sir John Jordan, warned that returning Weihaiwei to Chinese rule would strengthen certain elements at Peking who favoured the repudiation of all existing agreements with the foreign powers.[140] Significantly, the Admiral commanding China Station, Sir Arthur Moore, 'consider[ed] retention of [the] greatest importance'. Were Weihaiwei abandoned, the reorganization of the Chinese navy might fall into the hands of the Germans at Kiaochow.[141] The Foreign Office seized upon the Admiral's statement as indicating a volte-face by the Admiralty. Clarke's position of 1905 was now no longer tenable.[142] Indeed, the Foreign Office now dictated the pace and direction of the debate on Weihaiwei. Elgin's suggestion of a dockyard bargain was rejected.[143] The War Office also changed tack. Given the elimination of Russia as a strategic factor in the Far East, and the proximity of the Japanese ally at Port Arthur, Weihaiwei was now judged to be 'secure against maritime attack' or a Chinese onslaught on land. Indeed, the War Office concluded that, in the event of a war with China or of coercive measures against her, 'the possession of Weihaiwei would be an asset of considerable value'.[144]

Grey was desirous to bring matters to a close. A number of factors needed to be weighed, as he limned a possible solution. Recent experience with Chinese recalcitrance in railway negotiations made it inadvisable to make concessions over Weihaiwei. On the other hand, abandoning Weihaiwei was likely to be construed by the Japanese 'as an indication of a ... weakening on our part with regard to possible obligations under the Japanese alliance'. Retrocession was, therefore, inadvisable. Under these circumstances, Grey proposed to inform the Chinese that Britain could not withdraw from Weihaiwei; but that China retained the right to use the waters of the leased territory in peacetime; and that her navy might use facilities there for training purposes. Furthermore, London would welcome the decision by China to establish a branchline to Weihaiwei 'entirely under Chinese auspices'.[145] The Cabinet followed Grey's suggestions on 16 November 1906. Grey accordingly informed Wang that, while Weihaiwei would eventually be restored to China, owing to the still unsettled condition of the Far East, 'it would be exceedingly inconvenient for us to withdraw ... now'.[146] Grey resisted the Chinese minister's attempts to lay down a timetable according to which the issue of retrocession might be raised again; and thus, by early January 1907, the matter was closed.[147]

The Chinese démarche had been half-hearted at best. Nevertheless, the status of Weihaiwei was by no means on a more secure footing. Grey had informed Peking that Britain would not withdraw; and the Chinese had accepted this. The terms and the period of the original lease had not been raised at all. This was also a defeat for the Colonial Office, which had strongly urged the extension of the lease. Indeed, Elgin's Parliamentary Undersecretary, the ambitious and somewhat mischievous Winston Churchill, moved to undermine the department's position on the question. The three naval bases seized by foreign powers in 1898, he observed, 'stand together; & none should be given up without the other'. It would be 'inexpedient' now to raise the question of Weihaiwei's status: 'we should just lie still & say nothing'.[148] The Grey–Churchill combination, thus, put paid to Lucas' hopes of transferring the administration of the leasehold to the Hong Kong governor.[149]

Weihaiwei continued to languish. The reduction of the British squadron in Chinese waters in 1907 depressed business confidence in the harbour's future prospects. Indeed, the deficit in the territory's finances grew, and the Treasury subsidies had to be increased from £3,000 p.a. in 1905 to £10,000 in 1908.[150] The issue of returning Weihaiwei to Chinese rule was raised in Whitehall on two occasions during the First World War, in 1915 after Japan's capture of Kiaochow and further expansion in Shantung province, and in 1918–19 in the context of the Paris Peace Conference.[151] During the preparations for the 1921 Washington naval disarmament conference, naval defence planners accepted as inevitable the loss of Weihaiwei, by now regarded as of no political and strategic value.[152] The head of the delegation at Washington, Britain's elder imperial statesman Arthur Balfour, thought it 'quite useless' and proposed its reversion to China; the 'German and Russian menace' had passed away, and there was no strategic or commercial justification for keeping it.[153] Despite some reservation on the part of Foreign Secretary Lord Curzon, Balfour ultimately prevailed, and the Cabinet agreed to retrocession in order to defuse tensions with China, but also to encourage Tokyo to be more conciliatory over Shantung.[154] On 1 February 1922 Balfour announced the return of Weihaiwei to Chinese rule. As an American delegate noted: 'The gesture was graceful, but all of us knew that England did not want to keep it any longer and had no use for it.'[155] Yet, it still took eight years of protracted negotiations before, on 1 October 1930, the territory was formally handed back to China, while Liukung-tao and its facilities were leased back to Britain. Britain's stay at Weihaiwei finally came to an end on 11 November 1940, when Japanese marines forced the four remaining British sailors to evacuate.[156]

During 42 years of British administration the Weihaiwei dependency remained a 'neglected estate', neither turned into a fortified naval base nor developed into a trading centre. Was such neglect indicative of 'atavistic need' for expansion or 'prestige-driven' and 'unfocused' late-Victorian imperialism?[157] While superficially persuasive, a closer examination of the evidence would suggest a more complex picture. The acquisition of Weihaiwei illustrates the interaction between local crises and Great Power diplomacy as a mechanism of imperial expansion. It also illustrates the weaknesses of the British 'bridgehead' in China. The combination of Chinese obstruction, Great Power rivalries, and insufficient support from London made it difficult to utilize British treaty rights.[158] The lack of a proper policy-coordinating mechanism in Whitehall aggravated the situation. Most importantly, the story of Weihaiwei highlighted Britain's inability, despite her global reach, simultaneously to deal with the systemic Russian threat and emerging powers such Germany and Japan. The object lesson of Weihaiwei, therefore, is not in the irrationality of imperialism; it is in the strategic and systemic limitations of British power in the Far East.

Notes

[*] The Wade-Giles system of romanization has been retained for Chinese place names and terms so as to ensure conformity with the contemporary sources upon which this study is based.

1. Sir W. Lawson and F.C. Gould, *Cartoons in Rhyme and Line* (London: T. Fisher Unwin, 1905), 62.
2. The phrase coined by Prime Minister Lord Salisbury in his speech at the Albert Hall on 4 May 1898, cf. *The Times* (5 May 1898).
3. *The History of The Times* (London: The Times, 1947), Vol. 3, 204. For the crisis cf. T.G. Otte, 'Great Britain, Germany, and the Far Eastern Crisis, 1897–8', *English Historical Review*, 110 (1995), 1157–79.
4. CAB 37/37/42, memo, Spencer, 'British, French and Russian battle-ships and modern cruisers', 1 Dec. 1894; cf. also the figures given in I.H. Nish, 'The Royal Navy and the Taking of Weihaiwei, 1898–1905', *Mariner's Mirror*, 54 (1968), 39.
5. P. Wesley-Smith, *Unequal Treaty, 1898–1997: China, Great Britain and Hong Kong's New Territories* (Hong Kong: Oxford University Press, 1980), 39–44; N.J. Miner, 'Tale

of Two Walled Cities: Kowloon and Weihaiwei', *Hong Kong Law Journal*, 12 (1982), 179–202.

6. R.F. Johnston, *Lion and Dragon in Northern China* (London: John Murray, 1910), 2. Johnston is largely remembered today as the tutor to the last Manchu emperor P'ü-i, cf. idem, *Twilight in the Forbidden City* (London: Gollancz, 1934).

7. Alice Blanche Balfour diary, 30 Apr. 1898, Whittinghame Muniment Mss, National Archives of Scotland, GD 433/2/224; cf. 'Toby, MP' [pseud. H.W. Lucy], 'Essence of Parliament', *Punch Magazine* (28 May and 2 July 1898), 251 and 305.

8. E.Z. Sun, 'The Lease of Wei-hai-Wei', *Pacific Historical Review*, 19 (1950), 277–83.

9. C.B. Davis and R.J. Gowen, 'The British at Weihaiwei: A Case Study in the Irrationality of Empire', *The Historian*, 113 (2000), 87–104. The argument developed in this piece is, in this author's judgement, overdrawn and based on the selective study of the extant archival material.

10. Cf. Pamela Attwell's exemplary study *British Mandarins and Chinese Reformers: The British Administration of Weihaiwei (1898–1930) and the Territory's Return to Chinese Rule* (Hong Kong: Oxford University Press, 1985).

11. A notable exception is Nish, 'Royal Navy and the Taking of Weihaiwei, 1898–1905', *Mariner's Mirror*, 54 (1968), 39–54.

12. FO 800/2, note Sanderson to Salisbury, 19 Nov. 1897, Sanderson Mss.

13. FO 17/1330, memo Bertie, 13 Nov. 1897.

14. Osten-Sacken to Muravev, 10/22 Nov. 1897, in anon., 'Zakhrat Germanie Kiao-chao v 1897 g.', *Krasni Arkhiv*, no. 87 (1928), 49–50; FO 65/1534, Goschen to Salisbury (no. 272), 1 Dec. 1897.

15. FO 17/1330, minute Salisbury, n.d. [*c*. 24 Nov. 1897].

16. FO 65/1534, Goschen to Salisbury (no. 293), 21 Dec. 1897.

17. FO 17/1330, memo Sanderson (on conversation with O'Conor), 23 Dec. 1897; and 3M/A/129/39, O'Conor to Sanderson (private), 24 Mar. 1898, Salisbury Mss, Hatfield House. The crisis underscores John Darwin's argument that British policy in China pursued 'narrowly diplomatic priorities', in his 'Imperialism and the Victorians: The Dynamics of Territorial Expansion', *English Historical Review*, 112 (1997), 632.

18. FO 800/2, memo Sanderson (on conversation with Salisbury), 23 Dec. 1897, Sanderson Mss; also memo Salisbury, n.d. [but before 30 Dec. 1897], Cross Mss, British Library, Add. Mss. 51264.

19. FO 17/1314, tels. Salisbury to MacDonald (nos 76 and 77), 28 and 31 Dec. 1897.

20. Goschen to Salisbury (private), 2 Jan. 1898, Salisbury Mss, 3M/E/Goschen (1897–8).

21. Cf. e.g. H.S. Hallett, 'The Partition of China', *The Nineteenth Century*, 43 (Jan. 1898), 154–64. For a fuller discussion of this cf. T.G. Otte, ' "Avenge England's Dishonour": Parliament, Byelections, and Foreign Policy in 1898', forthcoming.

22. Chamberlain to Salisbury (private), 29 Dec. 1897, Salisbury Mss, 3M/E/Chamberlain (1896–7); P.T. Marsh, *Joseph Chamberlain: Entrepreneur in Politics* (New Haven CT: Yale University Press, 1994), 366–9.

23. Salisbury to Curzon (private), 23 Dec. 1897, Curzon Mss, British Library, India Office and Oriental Collection, Mss. Eur. F.112/1B; and to Chamberlain (private), 30 Dec. 1897, Chamberlain Mss, Birmingham University Library, JC 5/67/88.

24. *The Times* (18 Jan. 1898), also (11 and 27 Jan. 1898) for speeches by Balfour and Curzon; OCON 6/1/15, Sanderson to O'Conor (private), 19 Jan. 1898, O'Conor Mss, Churchill College Archive Centre.

25. GD 433/2/349, Salisbury to Balfour, 6 Jan. 1898, Whittinghame Muniment Mss; CAB 41/24/25B, Salisbury to Queen Victoria, 23 Jan. 1898. For a full account of the debates cf. T.G. Otte, *Global Transformation: Britain, the Great Powers and the China Question, 1894–1905* (forthcoming), Ch. 2.

26. Telegram O'Conor to Salisbury (no. 71, secret), 3 Mar. 1898, in G.P. Gooch and H.W.V. Temperley (eds), *British Documents on the Origins of the War, 1898–1914* (11 Vols, London, 1926–38), 1(22) [hereafter *BD*]. For a comprehensive account of the talks, cf. K. Neilson, *Britain and the Last Tsar: British Policy towards Russia, 1894–1917* (Oxford: Clarendon, 1995), 189–91.
27. FO 65/1553, O'Conor to Salisbury (no. 128), 29 Mar. 1898; and OCON 6/1/14, tel. (private), 23 Mar. 1898, O'Conor Mss.
28. *The Times* (3 Mar. 1898).
29. H.W. Wilson, 'Front-Bench Invertebrates', *National Review*, 31 (Apr. 1898), 300–1.
30. Sir Howard Vincent letter to *The Times* (31 Mar. 1898); for a full discussion, cf. Otte, ' "Avenge England's Dishonour" ', forthcoming.
31. Telegram MacDonald to Salisbury (separate and secret), 25 Feb. 1898, *BD* 1(25); cf. Sun, 'Lease of Wei-hai-Wei', 277–9. It was a classic case of what Ronald Robinson has called 'the imperial take-over', idem, 'Non-European Foundations of European Imperialism: Sketch for a Theory of Collaboration', in R. Owen and B. Sutcliffe (eds), *Studies in the Theory of Imperialism* (London, 1972), 130–2.
32. FO 46/496, Satow to Salisbury (no. 38), 23 Mar. 1898.
33. Memo Courcel, 11 Mar. 1898, in Ministère des Affaires Étrangères (ed.), *Documents diplomatiques français, 1871–1914*, 1st ser. (16 Vols, Paris, 1930–46), 14(80).
34. 3M/E1/11, Curzon to Salisbury (private), 11 Apr. 1898, Salisbury Mss. For an analysis of the ideological divisions cf. T.G. Otte, 'A Question of Leadership: Lord Salisbury, the Unionist Cabinet and Foreign Policy Making, 1895–1900', *Contemporary British History*, 14 (2000), 10–13.
35. F112/63, memo Curzon, 'Memorandum on the Advantages of a British Lease of Wei-hai-Wei', 14 Mar. 1898, Curzon Mss, Mss. Eur.; Curzon to Brodrick, 5 July 1899, Midleton Mss, Add. Mss. 50073; cf. Otte, 'Far Eastern Crisis', 1172–4.
36. CAB 41/24/34, telegram Balfour to Queen Victoria, 26 Mar. 1898.
37. FO 17/1340, telegram MacDonald to Salisbury (no. 71), 10 Mar. 1898; memo Bertie, 14 Mar. 1898, *BD* 2(24).
38. *Parliamentary Debates*, 4th ser., Vol. 56 (1898), cols 225–39; OCON 6/1/15, Sanderson to O'Conor (private), 13 Apr. 1898, O'Conor Mss.
39. Devonshire to Balfour, 30 Mar. 1898, and Chaplin to Balfour, 1 Apr. 1898, Balfour Mss, Add. Mss. 49769 and 49772.
40. FO 64/1437, Lascelles to Salisbury (no. 105), 7 Apr. 1898.
41. Balfour to Sanderson, 9 Apr. 1898, Balfour Mss, Add. Mss. 49738; tel. Bülow to Wilhelm II, 21 Apr. 1898, in J. Lepsius *et al.* (eds), *Die grosse Politik der europäischen Kabinette, 1871–1914* (40 Vols, Berlin: Deutsche Verlagsanstalt, 1922–7), Vol. 14/1, no. 3770.
42. 3M/A/106/9, telegram MacDonald to Barrington (private), 1 Apr. 1898, Salisbury Mss.
43. FO 17/1313, telegram MacDonald to Salisbury (private), 23 Nov. 1897; FO 228/1244, telegrams MacDonald to Buller, 21 Nov. 1897, and vice versa, 22 Nov. 1897.
44. PRO 30/33/6/10, Buller to Satow (private), 4 Jan. 1898, Satow Ms, PRO.
45. Nish, 'Royal Navy and the Taking of Weihaiwei, 1898–1905', 46–7.
46. ADM 125/88, telegram Admiralty to Seymour (no. 47), 24 Mar. 1898.
47. Ibid., telegram Admiralty to Seymour (no. 49), 26 Mar. 1898. For Fitzgerald's movements with HMS *Iphigenia*, *Rainbow* and *Redpole*, cf. ADM 50/379, journal Fitzgerald, entries for Mar. 1898.
48. FO 228/1277, telegrams MacDonald to Fitzgerald, 28 Mar. and 1 Apr. 1898; Goschen to Balfour (private), 27 Mar. 1898, Balfour Mss, Add. Mss. 49706; Nish, 'Royal Navy and the Taking of Weihaiwei, 1898–1905', 46.
49. ADM 125/88, telegram Admiralty to Seymour (no. 54), 6 Apr. 1898; FO 17/1334, MacDonald to Salisbury (no. 73), 10 Apr. 1898. For the minutes of MacDonald's

interviews with the Tsungli Yamên cf. FO 233/44, Chinese Secretary's record books, entries 28, 31 Mar., 2 and 11 Apr. 1898.

50. FO 228/1277, telelgram MacDonald to Seymour, 1 July 1898; King-Hall diary, 24 May 1898, in L. King-Hall (ed.), *Sea Saga: Being the Naval Diaries of Four Generations of the King-Hall Family* (London: Victor Gollancz, 1935), 303–4.

51. CAB 37/47/37, memo Admiralty, 'Transfer of territory at Wei-hai-Wei by China to Great Britain', 2 June 1898. For the text of the convention, cf. J.V.A. MacMurray (ed.), *Treaties and Agreements with and Concerning China, 1894–1919* (2 Vols, New York: Oxford University Press, 1921), 151–2. For a description of the territory and the administrative arrangements, cf. Johnston, *Lion and Dragon*, 77–101; also, Attwell, *British Mandarins*, 11–31.

52. FO 17/1340, telegram MacDonald to Salisbury (no. 108), 29 Mar. 1898.

53. 3M/A/93/30, Admiralty memo, 'Port Arthur – Talienwan – Wei-hai-Wei', 4 Apr. 1898, Salisbury Mss; FO 17/1358, Greene to Bertie, 2 Apr. 1898; cf. O.J.R. Howarth, 'Weihaiwei', in *id.* and A.J. Herbertson (eds), *The Oxford Survey of the British Empire*, Vol. II, *Asia* (Oxford: Clarendon, 1914), 448–53.

54. Goschen to Balfour (private), n.d. [31 Mar. or 1 Apr. 1898], Balfour Mss, Add. Mss. 49706.

55. *Parliamentary Debates*, 4th ser., Vol. 56 (1898), col. 1592.

56. FO 64/1438, Lascelles to Salisbury (no. 168), 26 May 1898.

57. 'Miles' to the Editor of *The Times* (5 Apr. 1898). For Clarke's authorship and his seven letters on the subject, cf. Lord Sydenham of Combe, *My Working Life* (London: John Murray, 1927), 154–5; on his links with Chirol of *The Times*, cf. N. d'Ombrain, *War Machinery and High Policy: Defence Administration in Peacetime Policy, 1902–1914* (Oxford: Oxford University Press, 1973), 165–6.

58. 1148M/add, Acland to father, 6 May (*recte* June) and 15 June 1898, Acland Mss, Devon Record Office.

59. PRO 30/40/14, memo Ardagh, 'Wei-hai-Wei' (confidential), 12 Apr. 1898, Ardagh Mss, PRO.

60. For an instructive discussion, cf. anon., 'British Coast Fortifications: What places ought we to fortify, and to what extent', in T.A. Brassey (ed.), *The Naval Annual 1899* (Portsmouth: Griffin, 1899), 188–97.

61. ADM 125/88, telegram Admiralty to Seymour (no. 82), 17 May 1898; CAB 37/47/34, memo Lansdowne, 13 May 1898.

62. ADM 116/552, memo Smith-Dorrien, 'How to defend Wei-hai-wei at the minimum cost to the country, the least number of troops, and the greatest efficiency for making it into a useful naval base', 25 May 1898, and min. Seymour, n.d.

63. CAB 1/2/35, Seymour to Admiralty (no. 270), 16 June 1898; PRO 30/33/5/10, Seymour to Satow (private), 20 June 1898, Satow Mss. The dependency was eventually to be placed under Colonial Office administration, cf. ADM 125/88, memo Hopkins, 'Civil Administration of the Territory of Wei-hai-Wei', 11 June 1898; CO 521/1/14495, Ardagh to Colonial Office, 29 June 1898.

64. CAB 11/59, memo Lewis, 'Report on the Proposed Defence of the Naval Establishment at Wei-hai-Wei', 11 Sept. 1898; cf. the interview with Lewis in *The Times* (29 Nov. 1898).

65. ADM 125/88, Seymour to Admiralty (no. 481), 17 Sept. 1898; CO 521/1, MacGregor to Colonial Office (no. 17), 23 Dec. 1898.

66. R.S. Yorke, 'Wei Hai Wei, Our Latest Leasehold Possession', *Fortnightly Review*, 64 (1898), 36–43.

67. CAB 37/49/7, memo Goschen, 'Navy Estimates', 31 Jan. 1899; cf. also 'Statement of the First Lord of the Admiralty explanatory of the Navy Estimates for 1899–1900', in Brassey (ed.), *Naval Annual 1899*, 430.

68. CAB 11/59, Greene to Foreign Office, 27 Jan. 1899, and Knox to Admiralty, 2 Mar. 1899.
69. CAB 37/48/88, memo Wolseley, 'Fortification of Wei-hai-Wei', 1 Dec. 1898; cf. Capt. A.A.S. Barnes, *On Active Service with the Chinese Regiment* (London: Little, Brown, 1902).
70. CAB 8/2, memo Colonial Defence Committee, no. 170M, 'Wei-hai-Wei: Strength and Constitution of Garrison', 17 Jan. 1899, also no. 173M, 'Colonial Garrisons: Utilization of Native Troops', 6 Mar. 1899. On the CDC cf. J. Ehrman, *Cabinet Government and War, 1890–1940* (Cambridge: Cambridge University Press, 1958), 9–11.
71. ADM 116/552, Knox to Admiralty (no. 266/41), 11 Feb. 1899, and Greene to War Office (no. M/2085), 21 Feb. 1899. On the War Office's suspicions of the CDC, cf. J. Gooch, *The Plans of War: The General Staff and British Military Strategy* (London: Routledge & Kegan Paul, 1974), 17.
72. Report of Joint Committee, Apr. 1899, ibid.; CAB 37/50/34, memo Lansdowne, 'Armament at Wei-hai-Wei', 10 May 1899.
73. The best analysis of the agreement is K. Neilson, *Britain and the Last Tsar*, 199–203.
74. Anon., 'Wei-hai-wei: Its Value as a Naval Station', *Blackwood's Magazine*, 165 (June 1899), 1069–77; also Lord C. Beresford, *The Break-Up of China* (London: Harper & Bros, 1899), 79–80.
75. PRO 30/40/22/1, anon. memo 'Is Wei-Hai-Wei worth keeping?', n.d. [*c*. 1899–1900], Ardagh Mss.
76. Ibid., memo Ardagh, 'Weihaiwei', n.d. [*c*. 1899–1900].
77. Curzon to Brodrick, 18 June 1900, Midleton Mss, Add.Mss. 50074.
78. FO 288/1353, telegram Dorward to MacDonald (no. 7), 8 May 1900; Attwell, *British Mandarins*, 33–8.
79. FO 17/1418, memo Sanderson, 9 May 1900, and minute Campbell, n.d.; FO 17/1413, MacDonald to Salisbury (no. 104), 28 May 1900.
80. L/MIL/7/16740, Gaselee to Hamilton (no. 474), 17 Aug. 1900, IOR; WO 106/72, War Office memo 'Troops at Wei-hai-Wei', 1 June 1900.
81. CAB 11/59, Knox to Treasury (no. 266/92), 22 June 1900; also CAB 37/53/58, memo Goschen, 'Telegraphic communication between Wei-hai-Wei and Taku', 11 July 1900.
82. ADM 125/110, Lucas to War Office, 9 Oct. 1900; FO 881/7471X, Wei-hai-Wei Order-in-Council, 24 July 1901; Attwell, *British Mandarins*, 38.
83. Brodrick to Selborne, 11 Jan. 1901, Selborne Mss 26.
84. Ibid., Hicks Beach to Selborne, 13 Jan. 1901.
85. WO 32/8244, minute Roberts, 13 Mar. 1901.
86. Minute Roberts, 13 Mar. 1901, Selborne Mss 26.
87. PRO 30/60/36, memo Brodrick, 'Wei-hai-Wei', 19 Mar. 1901, G.W. Balfour Mss, PRO. Although marked for circulation to the Cabinet, there is no copy of this memorandum among the Cabinet Papers.
88. CAB 11/59, Ward to Admiralty (no. 266/WHW/107), 7 June 1901.
89. Seymour to Selborne, 28 Apr. and 28 May 1901, Selborne Mss, Bodleian Library, Selborne 19.
90. Ibid., Bridge to Selborne, 3 July and 19 Sept. 1901.
91. CO 521/2, Ward to Colonial Office (no. 266/WHW/110), 3 Aug. 1901. Dredging continued until early 1905, ADM 125/126, Yorke to Noel (no. 8), 25 Jan. 1905, and minute Noel, 27 Mar. 1905.
92. CO 521/3/2949, minutes of Interdepartmental Conference on Prospects at Weihaiwei, 20 Jan. 1902, and minute Lucas, 23 Jan. 1902; also CO 521/4/20823, Lockhart, 'Report on the Dependency for 1902', 13 Apr. 1903. For Lucas cf. R.V. Kubicek, *The Administration of Imperialism: Joseph Chamberlain at the Colonial Office* (Durham, NC: Duke University Press, 1969), 16.
93. CO 882/6/75, memo Hare, 'The Political and Commercial Importance of Wei-hai-Wei', 31 Mar. 1902; ADM 125/90, Cowan to Bridge (no. 1), 11 Apr. 1902.

94. CO 521/3/25277, minute Lucas, 28 June 1902, on Lockhart to Chamberlain (no. 23), 15 May 1902.
95. ADM 125/90, Bridge to Admiralty, 5 May 1902, and to Lockhart, 5 May 1902.
96. CO 521/6/8538, figures collated from Lockhart to Lyttelton (no. 27), 18 Apr. 1904 (no. 20), CO 521/8/17464, 15 Apr. 1905, and CO 521/9/20401, to Elgin (no. 28), 28 Apr. 1906. For a contemporary survey of commerce, cf. 'F.J.W.', 'Weihaiwei', in A. Wright (ed.), *Twentieth Century Impressions of Hongkong, Shanghai, and other Treaty Ports of China* (London: Lloyd's Greater Britain Publishing, 1908), 773–7.
97. Colonial Office memo, 'Weihaiwei', 1902, Monk Bretton Mss, Bodl., dep. Monk Bretton 98.
98. CO 521/4/20823, Lockhart to Chamberlain (no. 25), 13 Apr. 1902; FO 405/135/163, Lucas to Foreign Office, 11 Sept. 1903; S. Airlie, *Thistle and Bamboo: The Life and Times of Sir James Stewart-Lockhart* (Hong Kong: Oxford University Press, 1989), 124–46; A. Offer, 'The British Empire, 1870–1914: A Waste of Money?', *Economic History Review*, 46 (1993), 243–6.
99. CO 521/9/20401, Lockhart to Elgin (no. 28), 28 Apr. 1906; cf. CO 873/45, Lockhart to Waltz, 16 July 1903. The pessimistic assessment was omitted from the printed version in the Parliamentary Papers. See also H.J. Lethbridge, 'Sir James Haldane Stewart Lockhart: Colonial Servant and Scholar', *Journal of the Hong Kong Branch of the Royal Asiatic Society*, 12 (1972), 68–9.
100. Tai Foo, 'The Neglected Estate of Wei-hai-Wei', *Fortnightly Review*, 75 (Mar. 1904), 406–14. For the Colonial Office reaction, cf. CO 882/6/86, memo Lucas, 'Weihaiwei' (confidential), 7 June 1904.
101. FO 405/143/26 and 34, Welch to Foreign Office, 20 May 1904, and Campbell to China Association, 2 June 1904; cf. N.A. Pelkovits, *Old China Hands and the Foreign Office* (New York: Macmillan, 1948).
102. Noel to Selborne, 28 May and 21 June 1904, Selborne Mss 20; FO 405/143/71, MacGregor to Foreign Office, 27 June 1904.
103. CO 882/6/86, memo Lucas, 'Weihaiwei' (confidential), 7 June 1904.
104. CO 521/7/19814, minutes Ommanney, 13 June 1904, and Lyttelton, 17 June 1904; cf. E. Lyttelton, *Alfred Lyttelton: An Account of His Life* (London: Longmans, 1917), 312–13.
105. FO 405/143/64, Lucas to Foreign Office, 21 June 1904, and correspondence with Jardine, Matheson & Co.
106. FO 405/144/6, Campbell to Colonial Office, 2 July 1904.
107. FO 800/121, Satow to Lansdowne (private), 28 July 1904, Lansdowne Mss; cf. T.G. Otte, ' "Not Proficient in Table-Thumping": Sir Ernest Satow at Peking, 1900–1906', *Diplomacy & Statecraft*, 13 (2002), 185.
108. 46M/386/2377, Satow to Rockhill, 7 July 1904, Rockhill Mss, Houghton Library, Harvard, b*.
109. PRO 30/33/7/3, Lansdowne to Satow (private), 14 Sept. 1904, Satow Mss; FO 800/121, vice versa (private), 20 Oct. 1904, Lansdowne Mss.
110. CO 873/44, Dawson (Weihaiwei Syndicate) to Lockhart, 12 Dec. 1902; FO 405/135/159, Lockhart to Townley (confidential), 5 June 1903.
111. CO 521/7/13985, Campbell to Colonial Office, 19 Apr. 1904, and minutes Harding, 25 Apr., Lucas and Cox, 28 Apr. 1904; cf. FO 64/1593, Lascelles to Lansdowne (no. 95), 6 Apr. 1904.
112. CO 521/8/11731, Lockhart to Lyttelton (confidential), 28 Feb. 1905; Airlie, *Thistle and Bamboo*, 121.
113. PRO 30/33/16/9, Satow diary, 16 Dec. 1905, Satow Mss.
114. FO 881/8284, Jamieson to Lansdowne (no. 15), 12 Sept. 1904. The above from ibid., memo Jamieson, 'Memorandum regarding the Future Prospects of the Leased Territory of Wei-hai-Wei . . .' (confidential), 9 Sept. 1904.
115. CO 323/505/7569, Campbell to Colonial Office, 8 Mar. 1905; and FO 405/155/81, 2 June 1905.

116. CO 521/8/19367, minutes. Harding and Lucas, both 6 June, and Lyttelton, 15 June 1905, on Campbell to Colonial Office, 2 June 1905.
117. CO 521/8/19267, Ommanney to Foreign Office (confidential), 27 June 1905.
118. FO 17/1677, Lansdowne to Satow (no. 151), 13 July 1905; FO 46/594, telegram MacDonald to Lansdowne (no. 247), 13 Oct. 1905.
119. FO 800/121, Satow to Lansdowne (private), 24 Aug. 1905, Lansdowne Mss. The Portsmouth talks commenced on 23 Aug., cf. R.A. Esthus, *Double Eagle and Rising Sun: The Russians and Japanese at Portsmouth in 1905* (Durham, NC: Duke University Press, 1988), 144–5.
120. PRO 30/33/16/8, Satow diary, 1 Sept. 1905, Satow Mss. The Portsmouth talks were concluded on 30 Aug., cf. Esthus, *Double Eagle*, 160–3.
121. Telegram Satow to Lansdowne (no. 185), 16 Oct. 1905, FO 17/1678; cf. FO 405/157/7 and 23, Welch (China Association) to Lansdowne, 6 Oct. 1905, and Bartley (Liverpool Chamber of Commerce) to Lansdowne, 18 Oct. 1905.
122. Campbell to Satow (private), 2 Nov. 1905, Satow Mss, PRO 30/33/7/4; cf. CO 521/8/19367, minute Harding, 24 Oct. 1905.
123. CAB 117/65, Balfour to Clarke, 19 Sept. 1905; and vice versa, 17 Sept. 1905, Balfour Mss, Add.Mss. 49702.
124. Clarke to Balfour, 7 Oct. 1905, Balfour Mss, Add.Mss. 49702. On the rigidity of Clarke's views, See d'Ombrain, *War Machinery*, 130; for his links with Balfour, see J. Gooch, *The Prospect of War: Studies in British Defence Policy, 1847–1942* (London: Frank Cass, 1981), 75.
125. CAB 11/59, memo Clarke, 'Wei-hai-Wei', 7 Oct. 1905. A similar proposal was developed publicly at the same time, cf. D.C. Boulger, 'Wei-hai-Wei and Chusan', *Fortnightly Review*, 78 (Oct. 1905), 656–64.
126. Balfour to Clarke (private), 11 Oct. 1905, Balfour Mss, Add.Mss. 49702.
127. CO 521/8/43877, minute Lucas, on Campbell to Colonial Office, 11 Dec. 1905.
128. CO 882/8/100, memo Lucas, 'Weihaiwei', 8 Nov. 1905.
129. CAB 16/65, Foreign Office memo 'Memorandum respecting Weihaiwei', 2 Nov. 1905 (circulated to Cabinet on 9 Nov., cf. CAB 37/80/167).
130. PRO 30/33/7/4, Campbell to Satow (private), 1 and 15 Dec. 1905, Satow Mss. For Grey's occasionally ambivalent attitude toward overseas possessions, cf. K. Robbins, 'Sir Edward Grey and the Empire', *Journal of Imperial and Commonwealth History*, 1 (1973), 218–19.
131. Minute Grey, 1 Jan. 1906, on MacDonald to Lansdowne (no. 266, confidential), 6 Nov. 1905, *BD* iv, no. 107; CAB 41/30/29, Ripon to King Edward VII, 28 Feb. 1906.
132. *Parliamentary Debates*, 4th ser., Vol. 152 (22 Feb. 1906), col. 505; cf. FO 371/84/675, Campbell to Glasgow Chamber of Commerce, 5 Jan. 1906.
133. CO 521/9/12985, Lockhart to Lucas (private), 6 Mar. 1906, and minute Lucas, 20 Apr.
134. CO 521/9/20401, Lockhart to Elgin (nos. 22 and 28), 28 Mar. and 28 Apr. 1906; CO 873/220, memo Clarke, 'Weihaiwei Trade Report for the Year 1905', 11 Apr. 1906; 'F.J.W.', 'Weihaiwei', 777.
135. CO 521/9/25796, minute Lucas, 19 July 1906, on Lockhart to Elgin (no. 36), 2 June 1906; Airlie, *Thistle and Bamboo*, 145.
136. FO 371/34/29537, minutes Alston, Campbell and Grey, 1 and 3 Sept. 1906, on Lucas to Foreign Office, 31 Aug. 1906; and PRO 30/33/16/9, Satow diary (on conversation with Grey), 19 July 1906, Satow Mss.
137. FO 371/35/33545 and 37533, Grey to Jordan (no. 341), 3 Oct. 1906, and note Campbell to Grey, 31 Oct. 1906.
138. Grey to Campbell-Bannerman, 6 Oct. 1906, Campbell-Bannerman Mss, Add.Mss. 41218.

139. CO 521/9/37201, minutes Harding, 9 Oct. and Elgin, 16 Oct. 1906, on Campbell to Colonial Office, 8 Oct. 1906.
140. FO 371/35/34172, telegrams Jordan to Grey (no. 188), 11 Oct. 1906, and MacDonald to Grey (no. 98), 9 Oct. 1906.
141. ADM 125/127, telegrams Admiralty to Moore (no. 138), 9 Oct. 1906, and vice versa (no. 141), 10 Oct. 1906.
142. FO 371/35/34376, minutes Langley and Campbell, 11 Oct. 1906, on telegram Moore to Admiralty (no. 141), 10 Oct. 1906.
143. FO 371/35/35726, minute Campbell, 23 Oct. 1906, on Cox to Foreign Office (confidential), 22 Oct. 1906.
144. FO 371/35/37307, Brade to Foreign Office (confidential), 3 Nov. 1906.
145. FO 371/35/37533, minute Grey, n.d. [c. 5 Nov. 1906]; and CAB 37/85/82, Foreign Office memo 'Weihaiwei', 6 Nov. 1906.
146. FO 371/35/39381, Grey to Jordan (no. 411), 21 Nov. 1906; CAB 41/30/75, Campbell-Bannerman to King Edward VII, 16 Nov. 1906.
147. FO 371/35/40949 and 42703, Grey to Jordan (no. 425), 3 Dec. 1906, and notes Wang to Grey, 21 Dec. 1906 and vice versa, 4 Jan. 1907.
148. CO 521/9/25796, minute Churchill, 25 Nov. 1906. On the often strained relations between Elgin and Churchill, cf. R. Hyam, *Elgin and Churchill at the Colonial Office, 1905–1908* (London: Macmillan, 1968), 488–506.
149. CO 521/9/43931, Campbell to Lucas, 7 Dec. 1906.
150. CO 521/10/22058, Lockhart to Elgin (no. 14), 14 May 1907; CO 521/11/26023, to Crewe (no. 19), 9 June 1908; also Attwell, *British Mandarins*, 54–8.
151. For a detailed survey, cf. FO 371/6645/F833/10, memo Campbell, 'Memorandum on Weihaiwei', 3 Mar. 1921; cf. D.D. Buck, 'The Siege of Tsingtao', *Orientations*, 8 (1977), 49–53.
152. CAB 4/7/27-B, Naval staff memo, 5 Oct. 1921.
153. Telegrams Balfour to Curzon (nos 28 and 47), 17 and 27 Nov. 1921, in R. Butler *et al.* (ed.), *Documents on British Foreign Policy, 1919–1939*, 1st ser. (London: HMSO, 1966), 14, nos 425 and 453 [hereafter *DBFP*]; cf. D. Armstrong, 'China's Place in the New Pacific Order', in E. Goldstein and J. Maurer (eds), *The Washington Conference, 1921–22: Naval Rivalry, East Asian Stability and the Road to Pearl Harbor* (London: Frank Cass, 1994), 262–4.
154. Telegrams Curzon to Balfour (no. 81), 6 Dec. 1921, and Alston to Curzon (no. 26), 23 Jan. 1922, *DBFP* (1) 14, nos 475 and 561. It is quite ironic that Balfour and Curzon were instrumental in the acquisition and abandonment of Weihaiwei.
155. Roosevelt diary, 1 Feb. 1922, as quoted in H. Sprout and M. Sprout, *Toward a New Order of Sea Power: American Naval Policy and the World Scene, 1918–1922* (New York: Greenwood, repr. 1976), 256, no. 2; telegram Balfour to Curzon (no. 324), 2 Feb. 1922, *DBFP* (1) 14, no. 572.
156. Davis and Gowen, 'Irrationality of Empire', 102–3.
157. The argument developed in ibid., 88 and 103–4.
158. Cf. Darwin, 'Dynamics of Territorial Expansion', 633.

2

THE IDEA OF NAVAL IMPERIALISM: THE CHINA SQUADRON AND THE BOXER UPRISING

Hamish Ion

When a crisis is impending,
When the sky looks like a squall,
When the parleying is over,
And the glass begins to fall;
When diplomacy is ended,
And its failure's been deplored –
Walk up the Little Gunboat,
With a Luff in charge on board[1]

The early summer of 1900 saw the little gunboats and heavy warships of the Royal Navy's China squadron collect off Taku Bar in response to the impending crisis in north China caused by the Boxer Uprising. High adventure, brimming martial spirit and sheer boyish relish for the fight marked the Royal Navy's campaign against the Boxers. As a simple story of naval doggedness and heroism under fire, the Boxer campaign has all the ingredients of naval derring-do which authors of naval fiction from Marryat to Bartimeus, Taffrail and Forrester found in the earlier Napoleonic Wars or the later World Wars.[2] The men of the China squadron brought off what Peter Fleming has described as 'an exploit in the best G.A. Henty tradition'.[3] It is this aspect that makes the story of the Boxer campaign so appealing to the popular historian, as it was obviously also for those who provided copy for contemporary newspapers in 1900. Of interest and practical concern for naval officers was the translation of the high estimation in which the services of the China squadron were held by Queen Victoria's advisers into recommendations that led to promotion or medals, or both, for them.[4] However, there were serious and significant aspects to this campaign and its immediate aftermath both for the Royal Navy and for British foreign policy beyond the valour and courage of individual servicemen. This chapter investigates the role of the China squadron in the Boxer campaign, and in doing so it hopes to illuminate further not only the fighting spirit of the squadron but also, more importantly, the squadron's strategic concerns and their ramifications for the Royal Navy and the future of imperial defence east of Suez.[5] Of particular importance here is the Anglo-Japanese naval relationship during the campaign because of both what it was not – especially close – and what it became barely two years later – a naval alliance. The Boxer Uprising was the first time that the British and Japanese naval forces actively cooperated with each other in wartime.[6] It served to reinforce the notion that both countries had a common agenda in north China and Manchuria, which was to prevent Russia becoming the dominant power in that region. The Anglo-Japanese Alliance of 1902, one result of strategic concerns in the wake of the Boxer Uprising, would not only set the course of British East Asian relations over the next 20 years but also, because it involved Britain acquiring an extra-European ally, alter the balance of power in Europe. While Japanese ships, bluejackets and soldiers participated in the fighting against the Boxers, it was not their military performance that attracted Britain to see Japan as a potential ally but rather their common concern with Russian expansion.[7]

As an important factor in contributing to Britain's turning to a local power, Japan, for help in the defence of British interests in East Asia, the Boxer Uprising can be seen as a transitional watershed. From the point of view of imperial defence, the Boxer Uprising clearly marked a transition from the nineteenth century British use of gunboats and small amphibious assaults to deal with problems in East Asia to the twentieth century, where for reasons of costly new technology and new naval tactics, the British had to adopt new ways to protect their interests. The Anglo-Japanese Alliance of 1902 which, essentially, farmed out local responsibility, in the short term, to a local power was one of the new ways. Another alternative, in the longer term, was to form in the face of a major crisis a larger expeditionary force drawn from flotillas in other regions and to send it to East Asia. Such a stratagem was adopted in the case of the 1927 Shanghai Crisis. In 1900, however, the China squadron was not weak in terms of warships. The problem that confronted the China squadron was that new military technology had allowed the Chinese to become stronger. As the Boxer campaign illustrated, gunboats alone were insufficient to cower the Chinese – a major military effort had to be made. Ultimately, it was diplomacy rather than brute force that restored Britain's political position in China.

While the events of the summer of 1900 in north China took place against a backdrop of rising Chinese nationalism fuelled by anti-Western imperialist feeling, they were also for Britain and Russia an extension of the great game that was being played from the remote hinterlands of West Asia to the furthest marches of East Asia. In China the Anglo-Russian rivalry was exacerbated by the addition of the presence of the other Great Powers also competing to tear off financial, trade and territorial concessions from the moribund carcass of the Manchu empire. In that respect, the actual fighting against the Boxers was only one aspect of the challenge that faced the British. The real struggle was to prevent Russia from taking advantage of the opportunity caused by the chaos created by the Boxers to expand their influence in north China. It was in Britain's interest to try to maintain the status quo as it had existed in 1899, and to save as much as it could of an independent China.[8] The Boxer Uprising, however, revealed that there was a fundamental split in the Cabinet concerning Britain's international position that led to Lord Salisbury's resignation as foreign secretary, although he remained prime minister.[9]

There were strategic restraints on Britain's ability to prevent Russia's occupation of north China and Manchuria because matching the increased strength of the Russian and French fleets in Chinese waters meant transferring assets from the Home and Mediterranean Fleets to the China squadron. This issue was exacerbated by German naval build-up for the South African War, and the Boxer Uprising helped influence the German Reichstag to pass the Second Navy Bill that called for the doubling of the German fleet.[10] The impact of the naval building programme later led to questioning of the wisdom of maintaining large British naval forces against the Russians in East Asia when the Royal Navy in home waters was faced with a growing challenge from Germany. Indeed, as early as September 1901 such were the pressures on the Royal Navy that it was thought that the prospect of reinforcing the China squadron was slight.[11] After 1905, as Nicholas A. Lambert has pointed out, changes in philosophy of naval fighting, coupled with the different strategic climate and lack of perceived threat to British interests in East Asia after the defeat of Russia, as well as budget restraints, led to the removal of British battleships from the China coast.[12] This was attractive as only Britain among the Great Powers had the infrastructure and logistical support east of Suez to allow its transfer of a sizeable fleet to China waters in a time of crisis.[13] In the window of time from the Boxer Uprising to the end of the Russo-Japanese War, however, this view had not full acceptance, with the result that Britain turned to Japan to help offset the naval challenge of Russia in East Asia.

The view that British weakness (and the Boxer Uprising played a part in it) drove Britain into an alliance with Japan is a common one in the Japanese explanation for it. Miyachi Masato, for instance, has noted that Britain, in addition to the need to suppress a strong people's movement like the Boxer Uprising and the need to protect its huge vested rights and interests in China, was also faced with the problem of protecting its interests as Russia looked south. Thus, Britain was driven by circumstances to look for an alliance, as its Army was tied down by the South African War, and to continue its splendid isolation had become impossible.[14] The impact of the Boxer Uprising was also important for both Japan and Russia. Miyachi stresses that Japan was impatient with Russia's strengthening control over Manchuria. The outbreak of the Boxer Uprising during the building of the Eastern China Railway had given Russia the opportunity to invade Manchuria, nominally for the protection of the railway, and at once it occupied the whole of Manchuria. By November 1900 Russia was already engaged in secret negotiations with China in which it requested the railway rights to Peking as well as the monopoly of rights and interests in Manchuria including the garrisoning of Russian troops and compensation for damage to the Eastern China Railway.[15] For its part, Japan had gained confidence in the magnification of its own power as a result of the Boxer Uprising. Japan looked to gain exclusive control of Korea through its railway policies that had the support of the government and General Staff. The Anglo-Japanese Alliance was concluded because Japan thought it was the most efficient way to put pressure on Russia. At the same time, the Japanese calculated that the Alliance would provide Japan with the convenience of obtaining access to British finance.[16] While the Anglo-Japanese Alliance was still two years off, the linkages between the Boxer Uprising and the Alliance should not be overlooked.

Such concerns, however, were not evident to the sailors and marines of the China squadron in the early summer of 1900. At least initially, they were not aware that there was anything different about the Boxers from the unrest that had been witnessed the year before in southern China – that is, the work of one of the secret societies that bitterly resented the encroachment of the Japanese and European powers on China. It was only later that the China squadron came to appreciate that there was something much more formidable facing them.[17] In the absence of readily available ground troops because of the ongoing war in South Africa, the China squadron faced the difficulty of being a naval force that had to confront a military challenge on land. This was by no means an unusual situation for the Victorian Navy, which had never been called upon to defend upon its proper element but had frequently been employed ashore to assist the Army, as indeed it was doing in South Africa. Nevertheless, while the China squadron had been reinforced in the late 1890s in order to allow it to maintain superiority over the Russian fleet, it was hard-pressed to undertake a land campaign. It looked to other navies and other armies for help, and especially to those of Japan.

The campaign against the Boxers, however, clearly did serve as a fillip to Britain in 1900 by showing that the Royal Navy still could be relied upon to be successful or to be hot-headedly gallant in the attempt; thus the importance of its heroic exploits, in contrast to the Army's lacklustre performance in South Africa. The actions of that summer in north China capped the naval successes of the nineteenth century, while those of the Army in South Africa presaged the coming military difficulties of the new century. The Boxer campaign for the Royal Navy was a little war, as inconveniently timed in its beginning but ultimately as one-sided as the two China wars of the middle decades of the nineteenth century. It was a last huzza to the old century.

The Uprising, however, was also a watershed for the rise of Chinese nationalism and a harbinger of new challenges to British interests. The prominence of Manchus among Boxer supporters in both Peking and in the provinces led many to question the dynasty's capacity to lead China. In the ten years following the signing of the Boxer Protocol in 1901, Joseph Esherick has argued, suspicion of the ability of the Manchus to rule gave impetus to the movement for constitutional government and, finally, led to the 1911 Revolution which brought down the dynasty.

Importantly, Esherick has also underlined that the Uprising left the Chinese elite with the greatest fear of the involvement of ordinary people in political affairs, with the result that it was not until Mao Tse-t'ung (Mao Ze-dong)'s instigation of the peasant movement in Hunan in 1927 that anyone dared to rekindle the revolutionary potential of the ordinary people.[18] As for the British, Thomas Otte has suggested, there was a psychological change of attitude after the Boxers, seen in a loss of will to impose things on the Chinese in the same way as before 1900 because the Chinese might fight back. As late as the 1920s the chimera of the Boxers was remembered when a gunboat was requested.[19]

The Uprising did show that the Chinese, so long kept in line by browbeating and the threat of gunboats, could turn vicious and bite back. While the actions of the Navy showed little signs of naval weakness, the strength and the resistance of Boxers, coupled with the immediate serious threat to the diplomatic corps in Peking, required a greater military effort than ever had been contemplated since 1860 and which only an international coalition could provide. In August 1900 *The North China Herald* wrote about the change that had occurred in Chinese military capabilities, pointing out that the battle for 'Tientsin emphasises the lessons of South Africa that modern arms of precision tend to equate soldiers unequal in morale; a Chinaman with a gun at two miles, or a rifle at one, is almost as good a man as a European, and if his weapons are slightly better, he is quite as good a man. The old canons that obtained in fighting between Asiatics and Europeans have to be modified to allow for this new element.'[20] The Chinese were a much more formidable enemy than ever before. In early July 1900 the *Kobe Weekly Chronicle*, pondering the question of why some 15,000 foreign troops then at Tientsin and Taku found it impossible to detach a force strong enough to march less than a hundred miles to Peking to relieve the besieged diplomats, noted that 'for the first time in the century foreign troops are opposed, not by Chinese soldiers alone, but by the Chinese people maddened by superstition and fanaticism and attributing all their troubles to the presence of foreigners in the country'.[21] In early conflicts with the Western Powers, the Chinese population, it was asserted, had not shown much courage. In fact, it was not the Boxers themselves who posed the threat, for they were uncoordinated groups of largely young rural folk with neither the weapons nor the stomach nor the discipline to face trained regular troops of the Great Powers, but rather those elements of the Imperial forces who took up the resistance against the foreign military incursion.

The Boxers, according to one survivor's account of Seymour's relief expedition, were generally armed with knives and only a few of them had rifles of old patterns, and they rushed on to the rifles of the Europeans after the style of the Sudanese and holding the belief that they could not be killed.[22] It was a war in which no quarter was given. *The Japan Weekly Mail* reported in late July 1900 that 'all prisoners taken are shot, the brutalities practised by the enemy on European wounded who fall into their hands justifying such a drastic measure'.[23] The Chinese were not considered a civilized enemy and dum-dum bullets, no longer used in civilized warfare, were used against them.

This was not evident, of course, as the crisis in north China caused by the Boxers began to elicit a naval response.

I

The political and diplomatic aspects of the Boxer Uprising were not immediately apparent to those in Peking or London in early 1900. With Britain's military and financial resources already stretched to the limit by the South African War, Lord Salisbury decided against taking a leading role in Chinese affairs, and held that the Boxers in north China had not affected Britain's main interest in the central area of the Yangtze Valley.[24] Moreover, the early xenophobic activities of the Boxers were directed against foreign missionaries for whose protection Salisbury was not inclined to take vigorous action.[25] In late March Sir Claude MacDonald, the British Minister in Peking, asked for two ships to be sent to Taku for the protection of missionaries and other interests as disturbances had broken out in western Shantung province, and other Western Powers were sending ships there.[26] Lord Walter Kerr, the First Sea Lord, supported this but insisted that Britain should not become involved in any show of force, except to protect British lives and property, without instructions from home.[27] This was in keeping with the view of Salisbury who, L.K. Young has argued, had been shocked earlier in March by the news that MacDonald had suggested to his diplomatic colleagues in Peking that a naval demonstration be used to cajole the Chinese government to take a firm stand against Boxer attacks on missionaries. Salisbury's fear was that one of the demonstrating powers might take the opportunity to demand concessions from China that the British could not effectively protest against because of their commitments in South Africa.[28] In early April the Japanese naval attaché in Peking, Captain Morimura, telegraphed Tokyo to inform them that the alliance of British, American, German and French Ministers in Peking had asked for ships to be sent to Taku in response to the Boxers trespassing between Tientsin and Peking.[29]

The situation, however, continued to deteriorate, with attacks being made on French missionaries. As a result, in late May, MacDonald and his diplomatic colleagues in Peking were once again advocating a naval demonstration by the international powers in order to back an ultimatum demanding that the Chinese government take decisive action against the Boxers.[30] In fact, MacDonald believed that the Chinese authorities were sufficiently alarmed by the Boxers that a naval demonstration would not be needed. Indeed, the Chinese government quickly notified diplomats in Peking that it would take strong measures against the Boxers but did not promise to undertake any of the specific measures demanded in the ultimatum. This led MacDonald to consider the Chinese response as unsatisfactory.[31] Nevertheless, the Ministers in Peking decided to send another letter to the Tsungli Yamên, and failing a satisfactory reply, to apply for more guards for the Legations.[32] By 28 May, MacDonald asked Seymour for Royal Marine reinforcements for the British Legation guard at Peking.[33] While there was difficulty in obtaining permission from the Chinese authorities, an international force of 337, including 75 Royal Marines, were allowed to proceed to Peking.[34] MacDonald also calculated that some 15 foreign warships would soon be off Taku, for the Russian Minister had told him that six Russian warships had been ordered there.[35]

While the China squadron was prepared to respond quickly to the call for marine guards,[36] it is clear that Seymour was not sure about the nature of the threat. In a covering note to a letter containing telegrams from MacDonald since 21 May dealing with the actions of the Boxers, Seymour wrote that they 'include all information in my possession about the movements of the "Boxers", who I believe form a Secret Society, generally unfriendly to foreigners in China, but what their particular object at present is I do not know'.[37] The safe arrival of the Legation guard reinforcements from Tientsin in Peking elicited from MacDonald the opinion that the state of affairs in Peking was now much quieter and the remark that he would be delighted to see Seymour should he decide to visit Peking.[38] Seymour was prepared to land a further 200 reinforcements if needed in Peking.[39] On 2 June, MacDonald wrote that he did not know either how many Legation guards would be needed or how long he would require them because the situation was changing daily, but, at that moment, he felt 75 men in Peking, 50 at Tientsin, with one ship at Tongku and three off Taku would be sufficient. Nevertheless, he still considered the situation to be grave and complicated.[40] By that time, MacDonald believed that no more ships were required off Taku.[41] Already Seymour, however, had collected four ships off Taku with five others, including the battleship HMS *Barfleur*, at Weihaiwei.[42]

The crisis was not restricted to Peking, for Carles, the consul in Tientsin, was also worried that additional guards were needed there because the Viceroy at Tientsin was virtually without any troops to meet an emergency.[43] Again, Seymour was prepared to land more marines and bluejackets if needed.[44] Yet, another issue arose which also required attention. This was caused by the concern expressed to MacDonald by Bishop Scott, the British Anglican missionary bishop of North China, about the safety of a missionary, a Reverend Norman, who it was feared was being held by Boxers at Ningchang, halfway between Tientsin and Peking. Scott implored the Minister to ask Seymour to mount a rescue mission. MacDonald thought that a force of 300–400 Chinese troops stiffened by some marines would be required.[45] Seymour ordered Lt Wright, in charge of the marines in Tientsin, to ask Consul Carles and Bishop Scott if they felt that he had enough men to mount a rescue. Again, Seymour stressed that this would largely be a Chinese rescue attempt.[46] However, MacDonald decided on the advice of Norris, the acting head of the Church of England mission in Peking, to cancel any rescue attempt, for Norris felt that if the Boxers heard of such attempt they would put Norman to death.[47] This was just as well, as Carles subsequently learnt that Norman had been killed as early as 2 June.[48] The Consul also learnt of the death of a second missionary, Reverend Robinson. Carles had stressed to the Viceroy that 'these infatuated Boxers needed a serious blow, and at the present time the death of 300 men might save China from thousands of lives being lost'.[49] As a precaution, Seymour landed a further detachment of marines and ordered them to Tientsin in readiness to depart for Peking, if needed.[50]

By 6 June such a move would have been difficult, for news reached Tientsin that the Boxers had already destroyed a number of stations on the Tientsin–Peking railway line.[51] While it was obviously important that the railway link to Peking should be kept open, the matter of who was going to keep it open became a matter of significant concern. The Hongkong and Shanghai Banking Corporation was afraid that the Russians might seize the property of the Imperial Railways of North China under the pretext of keeping open communications with Peking unless the British forestalled them. Eager to protect their investment, the bankers urged the British government to land troops immediately.[52] The Foreign Office was very much aware of the dangers posed by Russia. Seymour was informed that the situation contained many possible dangers: 'the most serious is that Russia should move to occupy the whole or part of Peking. It would be very difficult to move her out. We must therefore avoid making her wish to occupy Peking, but if she shows signs of intention to do so, we should occupy some important part simultaneously so far as our resources enable us most advantageously do so.'[53] Salisbury indicated that he wanted the China squadron to occupy the Nanking forts or Chusan if other foreign powers began to occupy important points to the detriment of British interests.[54] Clearly, Salisbury was intent on preserving the British position in the Yangtze region. Indeed, as soon as the diplomats were safe in Peking, the attention of the China squadron swiftly turned to the Yangtze valley. Diplomatic negotiations were also undertaken with Germany concerning respective spheres of interest in Shantung and the Yangtze regions and the maintenance of the Open Door.[55] Yet, as the Boxer crisis developed, arrangements with the other Powers elsewhere in China were less important than preventing the Russians from gaining control of Peking. In the light of the gravity of the situation both at Tientsin and in Peking, the British government was prepared to give Seymour wide powers of discretion about what steps he should take.[56] The imperative to stop the Russians from exploiting the situation clearly underpinned Seymour's subsequent actions.

On 5 June at a meeting on board *Centurion* of the senior officers of the warships of the various foreign flotillas off Taku, Seymour stressed that the naval forces were on a peaceful and defensive mission to protect the lives and property of their nationals, and were not at war with China. Nevertheless, he argued that as the Boxers appeared to be stronger than the Chinese government, it was necessary for the international naval forces to assist the government in keeping peace, law and order. He stressed the need for cooperation between the various foreign forces. Most importantly, Seymour argued, if affairs got so serious and urgent that time was not available for them to consult with their superior naval authorities, the various senior officers should consult together.[57] The international forces did not have much to work with; there were 428 foreign troops in Peking, 441 in Tientsin, and a further 961 that could be landed if necessary. At this stage, the Royal Navy had the most men available, with a possible 536 capable of being landed. While the Russians had few troops either in Tientsin or with their flotilla, they had large numbers of men at Port Arthur.

Another meeting of senior officers was held the next day.[58] At it, Seymour stated that he had received a telegram from MacDonald asking for 75 more men,[59] but it was not clear whether the Minister wanted them sent at once to Peking. The British Consul in Tientsin was also urging Seymour to send more reinforcements there and asked that permission be granted to foreign troops 'to take active measures of hostility' against the Boxers for Carles believed that 'our passive position intensifies danger hour by hour'.[60] The US Rear Admiral cautioned against taking the fight to the Boxers, pointing out that the foreign guards at Tientsin were there to protect life and property and to keep communication with Peking. If in doing this, they were attacked by the Chinese, then the Chinese would have to take the consequences.[61]

Seymour had also received an identical telegram from MacDonald which indicated that the situation had become so serious that communications with Peking could be cut at any time and the Legations there besieged, and should that happen that 'immediate instructions be sent to Officers commanding Squadrons Taku to consult together and march to our relief'.[62] Seymour felt that, in light of the gravity of what was apparently happening in Peking, it was advisable for more ships to be brought up to Taku. If the American admiral had earlier been cautious, Seymour could take heart from the attitude of the German senior officer, Gülich of the *Iltis*, who seemed most eager to help.[63]

Yet, while Seymour was satisfied with this meeting to arrange concerted action, he did point out that the French Rear Admiral had suggested that Colonel Wogack, the Russian Agent Militaire in Tientsin, should lead any relief expedition to Peking. Seymour asked for the Admiralty's view of this.[64] The frustration that the China squadron felt at this time was captured by Roger Keyes, the commander of HMS *Fame*, who believed that 'we seem to have been in the hands of the Russians, who no doubt were waiting to exploit the situation to their best advantage, quite indifferent to the fate of their Minister at Peking' and, he added, 'it is obviously impossible for a handful of seamen and Marines from the ships to make war on China, however bad its army may be, whereas the Russians could pour troops in within a few days if they wished, but they seem disinclined to do anything'.[65] Yet it was with a handful of seamen and Marines that Seymour would soon set off to fight a war.

In the light of what was taking place, Seymour had ordered a further two ships to Taku from Weihaiwei,[66] and asked for troops to be sent north from Hong Kong.[67] This latter request was quickly granted, and by 9 June the War Office had instructed the General at Hong Kong to send all available troops to assist Seymour.[68] Events, however, were quickly overtaking the efforts to prepare for such eventualities.

At a meeting of the senior officers held on 9 June, Seymour read a message from MacDonald sent the previous day from Peking which stated that the Boxers were near Yangtson and that Chinese Imperial forces had abandoned the attempt to protect Peking. Added to this was a report from John Jellicoe, Seymour's Flag Captain, that the Boxers were threatening the Tientsin Railway and that a patrol of the Peiho River at Tientsin should be considered.[69] There was also the question of the Ministers in Peking. The Japanese senior officer, Captain Nagamine Mitsuzane of the *Kasagi*, stated that the Japanese Minister in Peking had asked for a further 50 men to be sent there if possible. As if the gathering crisis had almost gone unnoticed, the French Rear Admiral wondered if the time had not come to put pressure on the Chinese government to put down the Boxers, but the German Vice-Admiral felt that such a proposal should originate from the Ministers in Peking.[70]

Late in the afternoon of 9 June Seymour received a telegram from MacDonald, which altered everything. In this, MacDonald stated that the situation in Peking was extremely grave and unless an immediate advance on the capital was made it would be too late for the diplomats there.[71] Late that night, Seymour wrote to Nagamine saying that MacDonald's telegram pressed him to act without delay, and therefore he was 'landing all available men as rapidly as possible to-night and may follow myself before morning. I hope, of course, you may feel able to do the same and act in concert with me.'[72] While the Japanese were willing to do so, they had only some 215 troops in north China under Captain Shimamura at Tientsin, nearly all of them bluejackets from the *Kasagi* and the *Atago*.[73] The Japanese, however, were able to contribute 52 men (the number earlier requested by the Japanese Minister to be sent to Peking), to the Seymour Expedition.[74] A force of some 2,100 marines and bluejackets, to which eight countries contributed men, was swiftly formed.

As senior flag officer afloat, it was Seymour's decision to send a relief force from Tientsin to Peking. Seymour set off from Tientsin on what he thought would be a train journey of about four hours, with two days' provisions and very little spare ammunition.[75] Young has suggested that Seymour's action was gallant but questionable, for the Admiral responded to MacDonald's request for more legation guards by resorting to military force.[76] It was clearly Seymour's concern that the Russians might exploit the turmoil to expand their sphere of interest into north China which lay behind his decision to lead the relief expedition personally in order to prevent a Russian being in command.[77] At the time, it was generally accepted that neither Seymour nor anybody else could have foreseen that his expedition would meet the resistance that it did.[78] Indeed, only a few days before Seymour left for Peking, Komura Jutarō, the Japanese Minister in St Petersburg who had long experience in China, had downplayed the crisis in China in an interview with Charles Scott, the British Ambassador to Russia, and expressed his conviction that 'the Boxers would not be able to offer any serious opposition to even a small European force, as they had no arms of precision and could not use them if they had'.[79]

On 6 June, Seymour had been at pains to stress that the senior officers afloat did not see themselves as being opposed to the Chinese government but 'against a body of rebels, commonly called "Boxers", who seem to overawe the Chinese Government and to be stronger than it is'.[80] As late as 20 June, the senior naval officers made it clear that they intended 'to use armed force only against Boxers and those people who oppose them on the march to Peking to rescue their fellow countrymen'.[81] What the Admirals and senior officers had done by that date was to draw Imperial Chinese forces against them in support of the Boxers. It was these Imperial forces that proved capable of resisting the bluejackets, marines and ultimately soldiers that were landed. It is speculation to suggest that the bloodshed of the summer of 1900 could have been avoided if only Seymour had been more cautious and waited for clarification as to what MacDonald wanted him to do. The Russian Colonel Wogack had objected to the sending of a relief force without artillery.[82] Yet, it was not in the genes of those in the China squadron to be cautious when it came to dealing with the hostile Chinese. It possibly might have been in the interest of the Russians to sacrifice their diplomats in Peking because of the greater compensation that could be exacted from the Chinese government as a result of their deaths. At the same time, for Seymour to act before the Russian military arrived in force in north China and to save the diplomats in Peking would serve to help frustrate Russian desires at any peace settlement. However, the fact that there were nearly a thousand men, women and children in Peking 'caught like rats in a trap, liable to be at any moment the victims of the savagery of the Manchus' was enough to make Seymour attempt their relief.[83]

While Seymour knew full well that railway stations had been burnt on the way to Peking, he was confident that his relief expedition would not be resisted and would reach Peking without inordinate difficulty. Given the telegrams from MacDonald in Peking, and the apparent gravity of the situation in the capital, Seymour was duty bound to attempt some sort of rescue.[84] Indeed, the failure of this attempt (there was little chance of his column suffering the same fate that had befallen those at Isandlhiwana) was due to the fact that his advance to Peking depended upon movement along the railway line, for he did not have the logistic supply train to deploy across country. There was genuine cause for anxiety because of the short supply of ammunition.[85] With the railway line ripped up ahead and behind his clutch of armed trains, Seymour and the relief expedition had little alternative but to slink back to Tientsin, which was reached on 26 June.

II

On 17 June, the deteriorating situation in the area between Taku and Tientsin, and worry for Seymour who had not been heard from since 13 June,[86] resulted in the international fleet issuing an ultimatum for the Chinese authorities at Taku. This called for the surrender of the four forts that guarded the entrance of the Peiho River, which could threaten the movement of troops and supplies landing from the fleet as well as preventing the use of the railway station at Tongku. The fear expressed by Captain Bayley of HMS *Aurora*, the senior Royal Navy officer in Tientsin, was that unless Taku was secured there was a real danger that Tientsin could be cut off and besieged. What Seymour had not foreseen was the possibility that Imperial troops might join the Boxers. Now that this was happening, there was an urgent necessity for reinforcements of men, ammunition and provisions in Tientsin.[87] Clearly, Rear Admiral James Bruce, the second-in-command of the China squadron, and the other senior international officers afloat understood Bayley's concern. They believed that an attack on the Taku Forts, garrisoned as they were by Imperial troops, constituted no unprovoked act of aggression, for they considered Imperial troops were already committed against them.[88] Of the allied ships off the Taku Bar, only the Americans were not prepared to take up arms against the Chinese.

Prior to the attack, allied warships had moved down the Peiho River past the forts to cover the Tongku Wharf and to threaten the Chinese naval dockyard where four Chinese destroyers were tied up. By moving upriver, the allied warships were shielded, being landward, from the full weight of the guns of the forts. While the forts were impregnable from the sea, the allied ships carried landing parties whose orders were to assault the forts from the landside. Prior to this, the four Chinese destroyers were seized by boarding parties from HMS *Fame* and HMS *Whiting* in a manner reminiscent of Cochrane's exploits along the Iberian coast during the Peninsula War. Once this had been done, landing parties were put ashore under cover of darkness. By 7 a.m. the forts had been stormed and taken. Keyes noted that the honour and prestige of the Royal Navy had been worthily upheld by the gallantry and initiative displayed by its officers in attack.[89] In reporting the action on 20 June, the *North China Herald* compared it to the attack on the forts in 1860 and pointed out that 'the capture of these Forts was a very much more serious business forty years ago'.[90] This was true, but in 1900 unlike 1860, the Allies attacked from the rear. Nevertheless, it was an action well carried out with vigour, élan and professionalism.[91]

The attack on the Taku Forts was the first time that Japanese in any number had seen action. Although partially disabled with engine trouble, the Japanese gunboat *Atago* was among the allied ships in the Peiho River. However, it was in its landings that the Japanese contingent, which was second only to the British in size, made their greatest contribution to victory.[92] While the Japanese showed spirit in attack and competed with all in being the first to raise their ensign over captured forts, they also wasted some time, as did the Russians, by bayoneting the wounded Chinese.[93] The Japanese and Russian bloodlust helped to account for the high number of Chinese killed, estimated at 600–800.[94] After the attack, Rear Admiral Bruce found some amusement in the fact that the Japanese put up a flag the size of the dome of St Paul's on the fort they had helped to capture, while the British could only muster a small boat's ensign.[95] While the shadow of atrocities fell over the behaviour of Japanese troops, it was the Russians who were positively loathsome. Bruce described the Russian soldiers as 'very slow, and inhumanly brutal, as they shoot every unoffending Coolie they see at sight'.[96]

This latter practice caused a shortage of coolies, and led to Japanese labourers having to be brought in. However, it was from the Japanese military that Bruce wanted help. In the midst of the growing fighting in Tientsin and before the fate of Seymour was known, Bruce begged that, because 'there are no reinforcements to send suggest pecuniary assistance be negotiated with Japan to send an Army'.[97] At the Admiralty, Lord Walter Kerr certainly hoped that the Japanese would respond favourably to the request for military reinforcements and looked to Foreign Office help in obtaining it.[98]

Close on the heels of the capture of the Taku Forts, the Japanese rapidly increased their forces. This also happened soon after the Japanese government learnt of the murder of Sugiyama of their Legation in Peking.[99] By 13 June Yamagata Aritomo had written detailing the reasons why an Army expeditionary force was being sent to north China. Among these were the desires to ensure the safety of the Legations in Peking, to cooperate with the other powers in the endeavour to secure their safety and to protect the Chinese people in a time of internal confusion.[100] This was certainly in keeping with the diplomatic conversations that the British chargé d'affaires in Tokyo, J.B. Whitehead, had been having with Viscount Aoki, the Japanese Foreign Minister, in which Aoki had stated that 'if the foreign naval detachments which had actually been landed should be surrounded by the Chinese and be in danger of annihilation the Japanese Government would land at once a considerable force to rescue them'.[101] Aoki also noted that a considerable Russian force had been landed at Taku, and expressed the opinion that, if the Russians occupied Peking, 'it would be hazardous to say when they would leave it again'.[102] Yet, until the success or failure of Seymour's attempt to reach Peking was known, it was not clear whether the Japanese troops would, in fact, be needed. The landing of Russian troops, however, was undoubtedly an added incentive for the Japanese to act. Initially, the Japanese planned a two-phased expedition, which would see the Japanese Army begin to land reinforcements on 22 June and gradually built up its strength to 9,000 troops ashore.[103] Events brought changes to the Japanese plans.

On 20 June the *North China Herald* reported that four more warships, including two cruisers, had joined the Japanese flotilla off Taku, bringing its total to ten, and that a regiment had been ordered to leave immediately for north China.[104] Rear Admiral Dewa, the senior Japanese naval officer off Taku, writing on 22 June to Yamamoto Gonnohyōie, the Navy Minister, had urged for even more military forces to be sent immediately.[105] By 28 June the 5th (Hiroshima) Army Division had been mobilized and was preparing to embark for north China in a few days.[106] The need for reinforcements became even more evident when the implications for those besieged in the Legations in Peking of Seymour's failure to relieve them were considered. The British looked to Japan to send more troops, for Salisbury believed that Japan was the only Power that could send significant reinforcements.[107] Even the Russians appeared appreciative of Japanese efforts to help, for the Russian Minister in Tokyo reassured the Japanese that the Russian government 'will not offer hindrance to free action being taken by the Japanese government'.[108] In light of the ominous plight of those besieged in the Legations in Peking after Seymour's failure to relieve them, the need for reinforcements was patently obvious.

Desperate though the situation might have been in the Legations in Peking, serious fighting was also taking place in Tientsin starting on 17 June. This coincided with the naval assault on the Taku Forts which brought the intervention of Imperial troops into the fighting. On 18 June some 5,000 Chinese supported by heavy artillery made a concerted attack on Tientsin Station in the Russian concession which was held by a mixed force of Russians, French, Japanese and British numbering 650.[109] David Beatty of HMS *Barfleur* noted about the sailors under his command that this was the first time any of them apart from himself had been in action and that 'it was a high trial, and they stood it well, steady as a rock. And cool as cucumbers, as if they had been at it all their lives.'[110] Fortunately, the Chinese attack was beaten off, and there was the possibility of capturing a fortified strongpoint across the Peiho River from which the Chinese were shelling the foreign concessions. However, the Russians were too tired to continue and so the opportunity was lost.[111]

Heavy fighting continued over the next few days. Beatty himself was wounded on 19 June. He estimated by 22 June, after some five days of fighting, the Allies had taken nearly 600 casualties.[112] The Russians were apparently all for evacuating Tientsin but, fortunately, on 23 June a strong relief column of nearly a thousand led by Christopher Cradock of HMS *Aurora* arrived. One of those who came up with Cradock was Midshipman Allen who seemed to greatly enjoy the experience of fighting around Tientsin Station. Allen desperately wanted to kill a Boxer with his cutlass but he had to settle for shooting two with his revolver.[113] This testifies to the sense of adventure and excitement with which young midshipmen tackled their first action. With the arrival of Cradock's column, the line of communication with the coast and Taku was re-established. There was also a renewed sense of determination and energy, for Cradock wasted little time in organizing a relief force to extricate Seymour's column, which was known to be besieged at the Hsiku Arsenal some eight miles from the Tientsin foreign concessions.[114]

With Seymour safe, the tenor of the fighting for Tientsin changed, as military reinforcements began to arrive from Taku. On 27 June Brigadier-General R.F. Dorward, the British Commissioner of Weihaiwei, arrived to take command of British troops in Tientsin and brought with him men from the Weihaiwei Regiment, the Hong Kong Regiment and the Welsh Fusiliers. On 28 June the Japanese infantry began to arrive in force. Fighting continued, but the Allied forces were now being steadily strengthened.[115] Even though the military situation was improving, it was reported 'for the first time we have realised the immense strides the Chinese have made in modern warfare since they fought the Japanese, and wonder at their resistance'.[116]

On 10 July Vice-Admiral Seymour left Tientsin for Taku. While some bluejackets including Beatty and his *Barfleur* contingent remained as part of the Tientsin Defence Force, the majority of naval personnel returned to the fleet. Seymour's departure meant that Dorward was the senior British officer in Tientsin. The stage was set for the heavy losses involved in the Allied assault on the walls of the Chinese city of Tientsin, which took place on 13 July.

The plan of attack was directed toward capturing the Chinese batteries on the Lutai Canal and the strong points on the walls. Four thousand Russians together with German bluejackets were to occupy the Canal and the eastern suburbs of the Chinese city, while American, British, French and Japanese troops, starting from the Tientsin Race Course, were to storm the South Gate of the walled city from the south and south-west. The Russians met little resistance, and successfully achieved their objectives. The Japanese found themselves in considerable difficulties. In their attack they were caught in the open within 500 yards of the Chinese city wall and pinned down for some hours by intense fire from the Chinese defenders. Much of the Japanese difficulty was caused when Dorward, in command during this attack, halted the artillery fire, which was covering the Japanese advance.[117] The end result of the attack, however, was only temporarily in doubt. The Japanese were eventually able to rush through a breach in the South Gate, clear the walls and, after much street fighting, the whole of the Chinese city captured by nightfall.

For the Japanese force of 3,500 men under General Fukushima, the battle at Tientsin was the hardest-fought action of the campaign.[118] They took some satisfaction at being the first through the Gate but their losses were higher than the others with some 100 killed and 300 wounded.[119] There was some criticism that the British and Americans took things easy while the French and the Japanese showed vigour in attack.[120] The action of 13 July marked the end of the battle for Tientsin, and the beginning of a lull in fighting as the Allied forces gathered strength before embarking on a second attempt to relieve the Legations in Peking.

The sharp fight at Tientsin and the subsequent lull allowed for the airing of some Japanese views concerning the crisis. In mid-July, the *Kobe Weekly Chronicle* reported that there had been an opinion among foreigners in Shanghai that 'Japan was bound to rescue or attempt the rescue of the refugees in Peking on pain of being regarded as guilty of a crime against humanity'.[121] While the newspaper did not think that the rescue of the diplomats in Peking was more or less incumbent on Japan than on any other Power, it believed that the international jealousy between Russia and Japan had stood in the way of either of those two Powers taking earlier action.[122] There was a feeling in Japan that Germany, and particularly the German Emperor, was overreacting to the crisis in China. In mid-July *The Japan Weekly Mail* reported that the *Mainichi Shimbun*, one of the leading Japanese dailies, in discussing the Kaiser's angry outburst on hearing of the murder of Baron von Ketteler, the German Minister in Peking, had asked, 'why war should be waged against the Chinese Empire because a foreign Minister has been assassinated by rioters in the streets of its capital, and, above all, why a cry of vengeance should be raised against the Chinese Government, because its rebellious subjects have perpetrated a crime. This is not what one expects from the sovereign of a great and highly civilized Christian State.'[123] Later, in August, the Germans offended the Japanese by pressing the Meiji Emperor to have Field Marshal Count von Waldersee as commander of the Second Relief Column.[124] By this time, Lieutenant-General Yamaguchi Motoomi of the Japanese 5th Division had played a significant role in the relief of Peking, but any possibility that he might be named overall commander disappeared with the appearance of the German Field Marshal. By 3 August, a force of 33,000 had been mustered including the 5th Division and 1st Brigade of the 11th Division with a combined strength of 13,000.[125] During the advance to Peking, which lasted from 5 to 14 August, the Chinese opposition was not as spirited as before.

III

A small naval brigade under Captain George A. Callaghan of the *Endymion* took part in the advance to Peking that began in early August but it did not play a major role. The naval brigade brought with it some quick-firing artillery pieces and was able to lay down supporting fire for attacking Russian troops at Peitsang.[126] However, it was mainly occupied in facilitating the transportation of supplies for the advancing troops as they moved toward Peking.[127] The campaign had become a military operation, with Lieutenant General Alfred Gaselee of the Indian Army in command of the British ground forces during the advance. It did not pass unnoticed by the Japanese that out of the 6,000 troops under Gaselee's command, some 4,490 were Indian and 350 were Chinese.[128] This was an imperial affair as far as the British were concerned, for India was the closest place from where to draw large numbers of troops. The China squadron benefited from the Australian Naval Brigade which could be used to help garrison the Taku Forts and so allow British bluejackets to return to duty on board ship.[129]

For the British, the suppression of the Boxers did little to ease their anxiety about Russian ambitions in north China and Manchuria, where the Russians were eager to exploit their position. In particular, British and Russian interests clashed over control of rolling stock and railways in north China and western Manchuria.[130] However, Britain was not the only nation to be worried about the Russians; Japan was also. Indeed, in mid-July the Japanese foreign minister even thought there was a possibility that Japan would find itself confronted by the same coalition of Russia, Germany and France that it had faced in 1895.[131]

Even as the fighting in Tientsin continued in early July, the China squadron had already begun to turn its attention away from Peking to the occupation of Shanhaikuan,[132] the point at which the Great Wall of China touches the sea, and to the protection of the British community in Newchwang. As the *Kobe Weekly Chronicle* indicated in mid-August, the primary concern was Russia, which was seen as the only Power that might not agree to the British policy of the non-partition of China. It was thought that attacks by Chinese troops on Russian territory in the Amur region might lead Russia to demand territorial concessions from China there. The British wanted to ensure that 'another India is not created in Far Eastern waters'.[133] The immediate challenge, however, was to protect the railway lines in north China – in which there was British investment – from being taken over by the Russians. It was in relation to this that Shankaikwan and Newchwang became important. Newchwang had further importance because it was a treaty port through which agricultural products from the Manchurian interior passed. In early September, Seymour pointed out that the railway from Taku to Tientsin and on to Peking was in the hands of the Russians, and that unless the British took measures the Russians would also occupy the railway from Taku to Shanhaikuan. Seymour wrote that 'I attach great importance to our maintaining some hold on this line: the subject is not a Naval one, but I have thought it my duty to acquaint their Lordships and also the General in command in the North with my views'.[134] There was obvious concern that the Russians might also have their eyes on the Newchwang to Shanhaikuan railway line as in early August the Russians had occupied Newchwang after some fighting with Boxers. Although the railway to Shanhaikuan remained in Chinese hands, the Russians retained control of Newchwang, and installed a Russian civilian adminstrator there in place of the Chinese *taotai* (senior official). Seymour could only hope that a return to Chinese rule, which had worked to the benefit of European trade, would come as quickly as possible.[135] Short of sparking a war, the China squadron had only a limited room to manoeuvre because of its lack of reach away from the coast.

Panache and verve did help, however, as was clearly shown in the actions of Lt John Green and the gunboat HMS *Pigmy* at Shanhaikuan. At the end of September the senior naval officers off Taku Bar had decided, at the request of Field Marshal Count von Waldersee, to send a combined naval squadron to occupy Shanhaikuan and Chingwangtao to ensure communications with the Allied ground troops over the winter.[136] *Pigmy* trumped the Russians, who were approaching Shanhaikuan by land as well as by sea, by reaching Shanhaikuan first. *Pigmy* arranged the surrender of the Chinese forces in the fort, and then garrisoned it in order to prevent the Russians, who arrived by land later, from gaining control of it and the town until *Pigmy* received direct orders from Seymour.[137] While serious confrontation between the British and the Russians was avoided at Shanhaikuan, difficulties were clearly seen ahead. In regard to the formal statement by the Russian Admiral that he felt that Shanhaikuan was the left wing of Russian operations in Manchuria and within their sphere, Lord Walter Kerr, the First Sea Lord, noted in early October 1900 that 'The cloven foot shows itself. It is to be hoped that the Powers will insist on international occupation'.[138] Seymour's concerns resonated in some quarters of the Foreign Office but the Cabinet was slow to act.[139]

In the south, British efforts to maintain the status quo met with more immediate success. The Amoy Incident of August 1900 saw the Japanese attempting to use the ploy of a burnt Japanese temple to land bluejackets as the first step to gaining a territorial foothold on mainland China. The importance of Amoy lay in its commercial ties with the Taiwanese tea trade, and its propinquity to Taiwan. (After all, in times past, the Chinese had governed Taiwan from Amoy.)[140] The Japanese landing brought HMS *Isis* to Amoy to assist the British Consul in arranging the withdrawal of Japanese forces.[141] This withdrawal showed that

Japanese leaders still believed that Japan's continental expansion was dependent upon the acquiescence of the major European Powers.[142] However, the refusal of Japan to accept a million pound subsidy from the British government as an incentive to increase Japanese participation in the suppression of the Boxer Uprising[143] also revealed that Japan was no toady of the British.

The Yangtze valley was also a region of concern. In late June the Foreign Office was calling for a warship in every treaty port in the Yangtze.[144] On 24 June Pelham Warren, the Consul-General in Shanghai, warned that the repulse of Seymour's column and the assault on the Taku Forts might lead the sizeable Chinese forces at Woosung, who were armed with modern weapons, to attack Shanghai as had happened at Tientsin. If attacked, Warren warned, Shanghai would fall to the Chinese in a few hours. He also pointed out that there was trouble at Chungking and that the Consul in Ningpo also wanted a gunboat.[145] In early July, in response to information about the number of Europeans in the Yangtze valley, and the suggestion that they should be evacuated to Shanghai, Lord Walter Kerr, the First Sea Lord, minuted that it was impossible, in his opinion, to defend all the treaty ports in the Yangtze from attack by large Chinese forces. Kerr stressed the limitations of the gunboat in such a situation, stating that 'the promise of a ship of War does much and is an excellent deterrent to local risings or desultory attack of small parties, but would be helpless to protect life & property in the event of a general rising'.[146] Lives could be saved, but there was little that the Navy could do to save property. At the best of times, it was difficult (perhaps only just feasible) and certainly time-consuming for gunboats to reach Chungking and other ports in the far navigable reaches of the Yangtze.[147] In early July the *Kobe Weekly Chronicle* reported that the foreign Consuls in Shanghai had issued a proclamation in Chinese calling for calm in the face of rumours that were causing an exodus of Chinese from the city and giving notice that the presence of foreign warships in the river was a measure of precaution for the protection of the European settlement.[148]

In early August, the *Japan Weekly Mail* reported that the British had 11 warships at Woosung and Shanghai and that Seymour himself was in Shanghai, and conjectured that his presence with such a large force had 'some exceptional meaning'.[149] Part of Seymour's role was diplomatic, for he visited the Chinese Viceroy in Nanking in early August. As a result of this, the *Japan Weekly Mail* pointed out, there was a Russian rumour that Britain was taking advantage of the situation to gain an increased hold in the Yangtze valley. For their part, the British thought that the Russians were utilizing the crisis for their own selfish purposes.[150] Certainly Russian suspicions could not have been allayed when in mid-August the British landed some 3,000 troops in Shanghai. By the end of the month, the French, Japanese and Germans had also landed troops there. It was particularly worrying for Salisbury that Germany had troops in Shanghai, for Germany had never recognized that Britain had exclusive rights in the Yangtze basin.[151] However, in October 1900 the Germans were prepared to reach an agreement with Britain over the maintenance of the open-door policy in the Yangtze and Shantung.[152] Given the fact that the China squadron was limited in its capacity to counter a major uprising in the Yangtze valley (and so much depended on the goodwill and cooperation of the Chinese authorities in preventing such an uprising), the diversion of ships and troops to the Yangtze and Shanghai, while the situation in north China remained grave, was unfortunate. This was all the more so as it raised Russian suspicions of British ambitions in the region. Yet Shanghai was not only the centre of British trade in China, but also the centre of rumours and alarms as often-fragmentary reports reached it of events in north China.

Annoying incidents between the China squadron and the Russians, as the latter consolidated their position in Manchuria, still continued. In December 1900 the Russians protested the presence of HMS *Plover* off the Liaotung peninsula on the grounds that Russian lease agreements with the Chinese meant that *Plover* had violated Russian territorial waters.[153] The protection of the British commercial community and its interests in Newchwang came to a head in early January 1902 when Russian military authorities made difficulties about the wintering of HMS *Algerine* at that port.[154] Vice-Admiral Sir Cyrian Bridge, who had replaced Seymour, was adamant that the right of British warships to visit Newchwang and to winter there should be maintained.[155] Given their naval power close at hand and the good political relations that had been enjoyed with Japan since the commercial treaty of 1894, it was not surprising that the Admiralty should look to Japan for help. Likewise, given Japan's concern with Russian ambitions in Manchuria, and its strained relations with Germany, Britain was the only country that could possibly help it against Russia.

In writing in early September 1901 about the possibility of forming an alliance, Lord Walter Kerr noted that while this was a new departure in policy, 'so far as I am able to form an opinion of "high politics" it has been pressing itself upon me for some time past, that with the immense growth of Navies that is now going on and the great strides being made on all sides in creating Naval power, that our hitherto policy of "splendid isolation" may be no longer be possible and that great as the disadvantages in other ways may be, an understanding with other Powers may be forced upon us'.[156] It was, of course, with the Japanese that the British were able to come to an understanding. In early February 1902, Ian Nish points out, Lord Selborne, the First Lord of the Admiralty, stressed to Bridge that the Admiralty hoped to gain two advantages from an alliance with Japan: the ability to reduce the China squadron as part of the fleet redistribution scheme; and the use of Japanese bases for coaling and repairs.[157]

IV

The Boxer campaign is intriguing because of the possibility that it might have had a decisive influence on the course of the Royal Navy over the course of the next two decades. While it was a boy of a midshipman and a young Royal Marine Captain who won the only two Victoria Crosses given out, the naval exploits in this campaign also led to the promotion or high honours for key officers including Bayly, Beatty, Callaghan, Cradock, Jellicoe and Keyes. Fourteen years later at the onset of the Great War, these officers would hold positions of high command and influence. Yet, it is hardly profound to suggest that from the naval experience in the Boxer campaign it can be seen that gallantry and success in action could advance an officer's career. After all, senior officers in every naval age have been men who had distinguished themselves in action when young, and rose in time to encounter problems more intractable than they had experienced as junior officers. It is difficult to demonstrate conclusively that the Boxer campaign was different from so many small wars before and since, and that it had a real influence on the thought and action of Jellicoe, Beatty and Cradock. Further, it is problematic to make an explicit argument, backed with evidence, that Coronel or Jutland might have been fought differently if Cradock and Jellicoe had not been in China in 1900, or that other officers would have been promoted for other qualities but for this episode. The Boxer campaign tantalizes with such suggestions but it does not yield the fruit of evidence to substantiate them.

The China squadron did show admirable courage and valour in fighting the Boxers, but it was the implications of this little war for the strategic situation in China that was important. Seymour was aware of the danger that Russia might take advantage of the Boxers to strengthen its position in north China. This was an important factor in his decision to take personal command of the relief column in mid-June. Throughout the crisis, Seymour was conscious of the need to prevent the Russians from gaining too much advantage. Yet, when it came to stopping the Russians from gaining control of the railways in north China, the China squadron was at a great disadvantage because of its lack of reach beyond the coast. Again, the limitations of naval power were seen in terms of the potential crisis in the Yangtze valley where it was understood that China squadron was not in a position to protect the treaty ports along the river in case of a general uprising. For that matter, no navy could have done so. Happily, no general uprising took place.

The Boxer Uprising also served to stimulate German ambitions in East Asia. The initiative in October 1900 to reach a diplomatic agreement with Germany directed toward the maintenance of the Open Door would appear to be premature and unnecessary, as the gains either in terms of greater security for British interests in the Yangtze or against the spread of Russian influence in north China seem to have been minimal. However, it could also be seen as having been a sop following the failure of more comprehensive negotiations for an Anglo-German alliance. The German naval building programme begun in 1902 stemmed from the German perception that the South African War and the Boxer Uprising had left Britain weak. While the argument that the German fleet was the reason for the redistribution of the British fleet, including the China squadron, has been exploded, the need for economy made possible because of improved communications and faster ships allowed the Royal Navy to be concentrated at key points (Singapore, in the case of East Asia) and then moved where needed.[158] The redistribution led to difficulties for the China squadron fulfilling its traditional role of keeping the Russian fleet in check in northern East Asian waters. In its turn, this contributed to the British seeking out the Japanese as an ally to help them meet the challenge of Russian naval power. The experience of cooperating with the Japanese during the Boxer Uprising, and their willingness to see reason at Amoy, helped to create an atmosphere that would allow the two navies to accept each other as allies. The containment of Russia in East Asia provided the initial common agenda for this alliance.

The China squadron and other foreign flotillas off Taku also looked to Japan and its navy for the repair and recreation facilities in Nagasaki and other ports. Without these rear facilities, it would have been much more difficult to sustain the naval effort in north China. Participation in the naval effort allowed Japanese officers like Vice-Admiral Tōgō Heihachirō, who commanded the Japanese flotilla off Taku Bar, to have the opportunity of seeing foreign naval units at close quarters.[159] As Vice-Admiral Sir Edward Seymour wrote to Captain Shimamura Hayao of the *Suma* in late June 1900, he hoped that Japanese naval participation in his ill-fated relief expedition to Peking would 'help to cement between our respective Nations that mutual good feeling and respect which happily now exists between our Sovereigns, and which, especially in China, is now so desirable in all the best interests of civilisation and advancement'.[160] Whether or not good relations between naval officers were of value in terms of future alliances is a moot point; however, good feeling and respect at the highest level was clearly useful. It was something which the German Emperor had forfeited.

In looking at the China squadron during the Boxer Uprising and its aftermath, little fault can be found with its performance. Seymour, his officers and men acted in a way that was in keeping with the traditions of the China squadron. While the actions of the Navy showed little signs of naval weakness, the strength and the resistance of Boxers coupled with the immediate serious threat to the diplomatic corps in Peking required a greater military effort than ever had been contemplated since 1860, which an international coalition provided. After the fighting was done, it was left to a diplomat, Sir Ernest Satow, the newly appointed Minister in Peking (a person whom Salisbury had passed over earlier in favour of appointing MacDonald),[161] to restore Britain's high position in China over the next few years. This diplomatic restoration turned the suppression of the Boxer Uprising into the first hurray of success of the new century.

If there was British weakness, it lay in the Cabinet division over Britain's international position where the Boxer Uprising served as an excuse to change the course of British foreign policy. The implications of this change for imperial defence in East Asia were far-reaching. After 1900 the China squadron had to content itself with fewer ships. This should not be seen as weakness or as being the fault of the China squadron but merely the result of changes in naval power, which meant smaller numbers of more powerful, faster and expensive ships as well as better communications. While the responsibilities to guard British interests did not diminish, fewer ships meant that the China squadron's resources were stretched. Consequently, the British government had either to look for a local ally to help protect those interests or to make available in times of emergency extra forces that could be sent to East Asia. The Anglo-Japanese Alliance of 1902 provided the assurance of Japan's help in the event of a war with the Franco-Russian alliance. However, in the short term, it did little to resolve Anglo-Russian differences in Manchuria and elsewhere in East Asia (although Russia's defeat in the Russo-Japanese War of 1905 dramatically changed this). The reduction of the China squadron was met with some grumbling and punctured pride. In August 1903, Vice-Admiral Sir Cyprian Bridge, the then CinC of the China Station, lamented that for the first time since the American Revolutionary War 'our fleet on a distant station is outnumbered by that of a single other European nation as far removed as our own from its metropolitan bases and home-waters'.[162] Bridge considered that the state of naval affairs in China was quite without precedent and constituted 'an epoch of immense moment in our Naval history'.[163] In responding to Bridge, Lord Louis of Battenberg at the Admiralty saw matters differently and pointed out that it was the 'Alliance which really governs the present distribution of our ships, and ... the Allied Forces are relatively stronger in the Far East than in Europe'.[164] Further, Battenberg tartly added, 'it would be well to remind the C. in C. that the general distribution of HM Fleet in peace must obviously be affected by other considerations than that of the Russian Fleet alone'.[165] The China squadron had to put up with the naval changes, and depend more heavily on diplomacy. The mixture of diplomacy backed by naval presence served the British well at Amoy in July 1900, for it prevented the Japanese from occupying that Chinese port and showed the Japanese amenable to British persuasion. The future of imperial defence in East Asia would rely on the Alliance for the next two decades. It is a moot question whether the Anglo-Japanese Alliance after 1905 served British interests for the disappearance of a common enemy in Russia after her defeat by Japan, and divergent views on the future of China after 1912 revealed a lack of a common agenda and strained relations between the two allies long before its termination. However, the Boxer Uprising had shown that the Chinese were becoming stronger and that the China squadron needed local allies to help it protect British interests in a major crisis. While the little gunboats with their lieutenants and commanders aboard had proved themselves capable of meeting nineteenth-century challenges, after 1900 the new twentieth century brought new ones driven by the fury of Chinese nationalism that even the most spirited cutlass-wielding midshipman would find beyond his powers to quell. The Boxer Uprising marked the transition into a more complicated era for imperial defence; the age of Henty was past.

Notes

1. Quoted from Joss Chinchinjoss in the *Singapore Free Press* in *The North China Herald and Supreme Court & Consular Gazette* (hereafter cited as *NCH*), 11 July 1900.
2. Taffrail (Henry Taprell Dorling 1883–1963) took part in the relief of Peking. Although he did not write about the Boxers, he published an adventure book dealing with pirates on the China coast in the early 1930s.
3. Peter Fleming, *The Siege at Peking* (London: Hart Davis, 1959), 81, 85.
4. For a list of such recommendations, see ADM 1 7456. S324 1900. W.L. Clowes pointed out that better provisions could have been made for rewarding and honouring the

services and valour of petty officers, seamen and private Marines. See Sir William Laird Clowes, *The Royal Navy: A History From Earliest Times to the Death of Queen Victoria* (London: Chatham, 1997), Vol. 7, 558.

5. Others have looked at the political and diplomatic aspects of this crisis. Most recently are the important works of T.G. Otte, most especially, T.G. Otte, ' "Heaven Knows Where We Shall Finally Drift": Lord Salisbury, the Cabinet, Isolation, and the Boxer Rebellion,' in Gregory C. Kennedy and Keith Neilson (eds), *Incidents and International Relations: People, Power, and Personalities* (Westport CT: Praeger, 2002), 25–45; T.G. Otte, 'A Question of Leadership: Lord Salisbury, the Unionist Cabinet and Foreign Policy Making, 1895–1900', *Contemporary British History*, 14 (Winter 2000), 1–26, and T.G. Otte, 'Great Britain, Germany, and the Far-Eastern Crisis of 1897–8', *English Historical Review*, November 1995, 1157–79. The earlier work of Leonard K. Young, *British Policy in China 1895–1902* (Oxford: Clarendon, 1970) remains invaluable.

6. Ikuta Makoto, *Nihon rikugun shi* (Tokyo: Kyōikusha, 1980), 76. See also Toyama Saburō, *Nihon kaigun shi* (Tokyo: Kyōikusha, 1980), 84.

7. See Ian H. Nish, *The Anglo-Japanese Alliance: The Diplomacy of Two Island Empires 1894–1907* (London: Athlone, 1966), 99–100.

8. T.G. Otte, ' "Not Proficient in Table-Thumping": Sir Ernest Satow at Peking, 1900–1906', *Diplomacy & Statecraft*, 13 (June 2002), 161–200, 162–6.

9. Otte, 'Heaven knows where', 37–8.

10. Holger H. Herwig, *'Luxury' Fleet: The Imperial German Navy 1888–1918* (London: Allen & Unwin, 1980), 42, 47.

11. David Steeds, 'Anglo-Japanese Relations, 1902–1923: A Marriage of Convenience', in Ian Nish and Yoichi Kibata (eds), *The History of Anglo-Japanese Relations: Volume 1: The Political-Diplomatic Dimension, 1600–1930* (Basingstoke: Macmillan, 2000), 197–223, 202.

12. Nicholas A. Lambert, 'The Opportunities of Technology: British and French Naval Strategies in the Pacific, 1905–1909', in N.A.M. Rodger, *Naval Power in the Twentieth Century* (Basingstoke: Macmillan, 1996), 41–57, 48–9.

13. Ibid., 49.

14. Miyachi Masato, *Kokusei seijika no kindai Nihon* (Tokyo: Yamakawa Shuppankai, 1995), 100.

15. Ōkubo Toshiaki *et al.* (eds), *Nihon rekisshi taike 4: kindai 1* (Tokyo: Yamakawa Shuppansha, 1987), 981–2.

16. Miyachi, *Kokusei seijika no kindai Nihon*, 100.

17. Roger Keyes, *Adventures Ashore & Afloat* (London: George Harrap, 1939), 200–1.

18. Joseph W. Esherick, *The Origins of the Boxer Uprising* (Berkeley CA: University of California Press, 1987), 312.

19. Conversation with Thomas Otte, 6 September 2002.

20. *The North China Herald* (hereafter cited as *NCH*), 1 August 1900.

21. The *Kobe Weekly Chronicle* (hereafter cited as *KWC*), 11 July 1900.

22. *The Japan Weekly Mail* (hereafter cites as *JWM*), 21 July 1900. The German officer was Lt Von Krohn.

23. Ibid.

24. T.G. Otte, ' "Floating Downstream"?: Lord Salisbury and British Foreign Policy, 1878–1902', in T.G. Otte (ed.), *The Makers of British Foreign Policy: From Pitt to Thatcher* (Basingstoke: Palgrave, 2002), 98–139, 118.

25. Young, *British Policy in China*, 113–14.

26. ADM 116/116, MacDonald to Salisbury, 23 March 1900.

27. Ibid., Kerr minute.

28. Young, *British Policy in China*, 115.

29. BKTSS. Kaigun: Shinkoku jiken. M33-3, Kaigun Daijin Yamamoto Gonnohyōe to Naikaku Soridaijin Kōshaku Yamagata Aritomo tono, Meiji 33 6 getsu 24 nichi, Hokushin Jihen ni kansuru iken.
30. ADM 125/109, telegram, MacDonald to Seymour, 21 May 1900.
31. Ibid., telegram, MacDonald to Seymour, 25 May 1900.
32. Ibid., telegram, MacDonald to Seymour, 27 May 1900. See also the summation of events in BKTSS. Kaigun: Shinkoku jiken. M33-3, Kaigun Daijin Yamamoto Gonnohyōe to Naikaku Soridaijin Kōshaku Yamagata Aritomo tono, Meiji 33 6 getsu 24 nichi, Hokushin Jihen ni kansuru iken. See also See Kenneth Bourne and D. Cameron Watt (general eds), *British Documents on Foreign Affairs: Reports and Papers from the Foreign Office Confidential Print: Series E: Asia, 1860–1914* [hereafter cited *BDFA*]: Ian Nish (ed.), Vol. 24: *Boxer Disturbances and Siege of Peking, May 1900–August 1900*, Doc. 17, MacDonald to Salisbury, 28 May 1900.
33. ADM 125/109, telegram, MacDonald to Seymour, 28 May 1900.
34. Ibid., see telegrams, MacDonald to Seymour, 30 May 1900; 31 May 1900; Carles to Burke, 1 June 1900, submitted to Seymour as no. 45.
35. Ibid., telegram, MacDonald to Seymour, 30 May 1900.
36. Ibid., Burke to Seymour, Letter of Proceedings, no. 44, off Taku 1 June 1900. J.H.T. Burke was Captain of the first-class cruiser, HMS *Orlando*, which provided the marines.
37. Ibid., Seymour to Admiralty, 31 May 1900.
38. Ibid., telegram, MacDonald to Seymour, 1 June 1900.
39. Ibid., telegram, Seymour to MacDonald, 1 June 1900.
40. ADM 125/109, MacDonald to Seymour, 2 June 1900. This telegram was received after the siege of Peking had been lifted. See also MacDonald to Seymour, 3 June 1900.
41. Ibid., telegram, MacDonald to Seymour, 1 June 1900.
42. ADM 50/380, Enclosure no. 74 in China Letter no. 454 of 30 July 1900: Journal of Sir Edward H. Seymour KCB Commander-in-Chief China, 1 April–30 June 1900. Disposition of Squadron, 1 June 1900.
43. ADM 125/109, Carles to Seymour, 3 June 1900.
44. Ibid., Seymour to Carles, 4 June 1900.
45. Ibid., MacDonald to Seymour, 4 June 1900.
46. Ibid., Seymour to Wright, 4 June 1900.
47. Ibid., MacDonald to Seymour, 4 June 1900.
48. Ibid., Carles to Seymour, 5 June 1900. See also *BDFA*, Vol. 24, Doc. 22, Yu to Carles, 4 June 1900.
49. Ibid., Carles to MacDonald, 5 June 1900. See also *BDFA*, Vol. 24, Doc. 20, Carles to MacDonald, 5 June 1900.
50. Ibid., Seymour to Johnstone, 5 June 1900.
51. Ibid., Carles to Seymour, 6 June 1900. See also *BDFA*, Vol. 24, Doc. 23, Carles to Seymour, 6 June 1900; Doc. 24, memorandum by Mr W. Whittall; Doc. 25, Carles to Seymour, 7 June 1900.
52. ADM 116/116, Bertie to Admiralty, 8 June 1900, enclosure, copy of telegram from Hongkong and Shanghai Banking Corporation, Tientsin, 5 June 1900; enclosure, copy of telegram from Hongkong and Shanghai Banking Corporation, Hongkong, 6 June 1900.
53. ADM 125/109, Admiralty to Seymour, 7 June 1900, no. 80, Secret.
54. ADM 116/116, Villiers to Admiralty, Immediate and Secret, 13 June 1900.
55. Otte, 'Lord Salisbury, the Cabinet, Isolation, and the Boxer Rebellion', 34–7.
56. Ibid., Admiralty to Seymour, 6 June 1900, no. 79.
57. BKTSS, M33-41, Seymour to Nagamine, 5 June 1900; minutes of meeting of senior naval officers in command of Foreign Powers present at Taku, 5 June 1900.

THE CHINA SQUADRON AND THE BOXER UPRISING

58. Ibid., M33-41, minutes of meeting on board *Centurion*, 6 June 1900.
59. ADM 125/109, telegram, MacDonald to Seymour, 6 June 1900.
60. BKTSS, M33-41, minutes of meeting on board *Centurion*, 6 June 1900.
61. Ibid.
62. Ibid. See also ADM 125/109, MacDonald to Seymour, 5 June 1900.
63. BKTSS, M33-41, minutes of meeting on board *Centurion*, 6 June 1900.
64. ADM 125/109, Seymour to Admiralty, 6 June 1900, no. 84.
65. Keyes, *Adventures Ashore & Afloat*, 198.
66. ADM 125/109, Seymour to Admiralty, 6 June 1900, no. 82.
67. Ibid., Seymour to Admiralty, 6 June 1900, no. 83.
68. Ibid., Commodore Hong Kong to Seymour, 9 June 1900.
69. BKTSS., Kaigun: Shinkoku Jihen, M33-41, minutes of meeting on board *Centurion*, 9 June 1900, 89–92.
70. Ibid., 92.
71. ADM 125/109, Seymour to Admiralty, 10 June 1900, no. 88.
72. BKTSS, Kaigun: Shinkoku Jihen, M33-41, Seymour to Nagamine, 9 June 1900, 11.30 p.m., 95.
73. BKTSS, Kaigun: Shinkoku Jihen, M33-41, 148.
74. Ibid., telegram Nomura to Yamamoto, 10 June 1900, 148.
75. Keyes, *Adventures Ashore & Afloat*, 206.
76. Young, *British Policy in China*, 121–2.
77. ADM116/114, telegram no. 84: CinC China to Admiralty 6 June 1900; telegram no. 86: CinC to Admiralty 8 June 1900, see also Lord Walter Kerr's minute on no. 86.
78. *JWM*, 21 July 1900.
79. ADM 116/116, Scott to Salisbury, 9 June 1900.
80. BKTSS, Kaigun: Shinkoku Jihen, M33-41, 72.
81. BKTSS, Kaigun: Shinkoku Jihen, M33-4, Dewa to Navy Minister, 21 June 1900.
82. *NCH*, 4 July 1900.
83. Ibid.
84. BKTSS, Kaigun: Shinkoku Jihen M33-41, 90–7.
85. *NCH*, 18 July 1900.
86. Keyes, *Adventures Ashore & Afloat*, 206.
87. No Imperial troops were sent against Seymour until June 18. See Esherick, *Origins of the Boxer Uprising*, 288.
88. BKTSS, Kaigun : Shinkoku Jiken M33-41, 105–106. This gives details of the Admirals' meetings on 15 and 16 June chaired by the Russian Vice-Admiral Hildebrandt.
89. Keyes, *Adventures Afloat & Ashore*, 226–7.
90. *NCH*, 20 June 1900, 1107.
91. Lieut. Myakishev, 'The Capture of the Taku Forts', *Journal of the Royal United Service Institution*, XLV (January to June 1901), 730-44. See also Vice-Admiral Hildebrant, 'Capture of the Taku Forts by the Allied Forces, 17 June, 1900', 'Ward Room,' trans. *United Service Magazine*, XXVIII (October 1903–March 1904), 11–17.
92. Ibid., M33-3. There are detailed reports of the action as well as translations of newspaper accounts and hand-drawn maps of the fortifications. Of particular interest is the report of Captain Nagamine, 24 June 1900.
93. Keyes, *Adventures Ashore & Afloat*, 225.
94. Myakishev, 'The Capture of the Taku Forts', 738. The total Allied casualties amounted to 9 officers and 129 men wounded or dead. See BKTSS, Kaigun: Shinkoku Jiken: M33-41, Hildebrandt to Dewa, 17 June 1900, 484.
95. ADM116/114, Bruce to Goschen, 25 June 1900.
96. Ibid.
97. ADM125/109, telegram no. 3, Rear Admiral Taku to Admiralty, 20 June 1900.

98. ADM 116/115, telegram no. 17, Kerr minute on Rear Admiral, 9 July 1900.
99. BKTSS, Kaigun: Shinkoku Jiken: M33-41, Nagamine to Yamamoto, 13 June 1900, 298.
100. BKTSS, Kaigun: Shinkoku Jiken: M33-41, Yamagata letter dated 16 June 1900, 393–4. There was considerable correspondence from Katsura Tarō, the Army Minister, to Yamamoto, his naval counterpart, about the reasons for the expedition which needed to be clearly explained to all concerned. See Katsura's orders of 17 June 1900, 392.
101. FO 46/527, Whitehead to Salisbury, 14 June 1900.
102. Ibid.
103. BKTSS, Kaigun: Shinkoku Jiken: M33-41, 404.
104. *NCH*, 20 June 1900. For the changing number of ships off Taku in the first two months of the uprising, see Hirama Yōichi, *Nichi-Ei domei: domei no sentaku to seisui* (Tokyo: PHP Shinsho, 2000), 34.
105. FO 46/527, Whitehead to Salisbury, 24 June 1900, enclosure: Dewa to Yamamoto, 22 June 1900.
106. FO 46/527, Whitehead to Salisbury, 28 June 1900.
107. See FO 46/527, Whitehead to Aoki, 5 July 1900.
108. BKTSS, Kaigun. Shinkoku Jihen, M33-5, report on call made by Minister for Russia upon the Minister for Foreign Affairs, 30 June 1900.
109. *NCH*, 11 July 1900.
110. Rear Admiral W.S. Chalmers, *The Life and Letters of David, Earl Beatty: Admiral of the Fleet, Viscount Borodale of Wexford, Baron Beatty of the North Sea and of Brooksby* (London: Hodder & Stoughton, 1951), 58.
111. Ibid., 59.
112. Ibid., 61.
113. A. Temple Patterson, 'A Midshipman in the Boxer Rebellion', *The Mariner's Mirror*, 63 (1977), 351–8, 356.
114. *NCH*, 4 July 1900. See also ADM 125/109, Seymour to Admiralty, no. 384, 27 June 1900.
115. Ibid., 11 July 1900.
116. Ibid.
117. Beatty was highly critical of Dorward who, he felt, was responsible for many British casualties because he refused to allow troops to move back to cover when the attack was briefly halted by enemy fire. Chalmers, *David, Earl Beatty*, 68.
118. Ikuta, *Nihon rikugun shi*, 76.
119. BKTSS, Kaigun: Shinkoku Jihen, M33-7, Dai roku kai: sentō jōhō Tenshin, shichi getsu jū-yon nichi, 4.
120. Ibid., M33-42, 457.
121. *KWC*, 18 July 1900.
122. Ibid.
123. *JWM*, 21 July 1900.
124. BKTSS, Kaigun: Shinkoku Jihen. M33-4. See, for instance, Kaiser to Emperor, 22 August 1900, 563. See also *JWM*, 25 August 1900, for reaction in the Japanese press on Von Waldersee's appointment.
125. Ikuta, *Nihon rikugun shi*, 76.
126. *The Naval Review 1901*, 187–217, 212.
127. ADM 125/109, Callaghan to Bruce, Letter of Proceedings of Naval Brigade, 1 September 1900.
128. BKTSS, Kaigun: Shinkoku Jihen, M33-42, 541.
129. ADM 116/115, Seymour to Admiralty, 27 August 1900, no. 533.
130. Young, *British Policy in China*, 273–81.
131. FO 46/527, Whitehead to Salisbury, 19 July 1900.
132. Ibid., telegram no. 26, Bruce to Admiralty, 11 July 1900.

133. *KWC*, 15 August 1900.
134. ADM 116/115, Seymour to Admiralty, 10 September 1900, no. 595/3969.
135. Ibid.
136. BKTSS, Kaigun: Shinkoku Jihen, M33-44, 385–97.
137. Clowes, *The Royal Navy*, 559–60.
138. ADM 116/115, telegram no. 210, Kerr minute on Seymour to Admiralty, 1 October 1900.
139. Keith Neilson, *Britain and the Last Tsar: British Policy towards Russia, 1894–1917* (Oxford: Clarendon, 1995), 212.
140. *JWM*, 8 September 1900.
141. ADM 125/109, Henderson to Powell C-20/00 *Isis* at Amoy, 7 September 1900.
142. W.G. Beasley, *Japanese Imperialism* (Oxford: Oxford University Press, 1991), 76.
143. Inoue Kiyoshi, *Nihon teikokushugi no keisei* (Tokyo: Iwanami Shoten 1972), 78.
144. ADM 116/116, from Foreign Office, 21 June 1900, Immediate and Confidential. This asked for approval of sending a warship to each treaty port.
145. Ibid., Cypher Warren, 24 June 1900.
146. Ibid., Kerr minute dated 9 July 1900 on From Foreign Office, 6 July 1900. China: Number of Europeans at Yangtze Ports, telegram. from Act. Con. Genl Warren.
147. See, for instance, ADM 1 1755, S208 1900 [Chungking Expedition: Proceedings of HMS '*Woodcock*' & '*Woodlark*' in River Yangtze].
148. *KWC*, 11 July 1900.
149. *JWM*, 4 August 1900.
150. Ibid., 11 August 1900. For Seymour's movements at the beginning of August see ADM 50/380, enclosure no. 52 in China Letter no. 696 of 16 Oct. 1900: Journal of Vice-Admiral Sir Edward H. Seymour, KCB Commander-in-Chief China, 12 July 1900–30 September 1900. Apart from his visit to Nanking, Seymour was at Woosung or Shanghai from the end of July to the middle of September.
151. Otte, 'Lord Salisbury, the Cabinet, Isolation, and the Boxer Rebellion', 34.
152. Nish, *The Anglo-Japanese Alliance*, 104–6.
153. Young, *British Policy in China*, 273.
154. Telegram CinC to commanding officer, HMS *Algerine*, 31 January 1902; enclosure no. 2 in China Letter no. 89/190, 31 January 1902.
155. ADM 1/ 7590, telegram, CinC to commanding officer, HMS *Algerine*, 31 January 1902; enclosure no. 2 in China Letter no. 89/190, 31 Jan 1902.
156. Selborne Papers, Bodleian Library, Selborne Papers 27, Kerr to Selborne, Secret, 2 September 1901. I must thank Keith Neilson for drawing this quotation to my attention. In late November 1901, Ian Nish points out, Kerr wrote to Vice-Admiral Bridge about the need for diplomacy or alliances to help the Royal Navy out of its predicament caused by the growth of foreign navies; see Nish, *The Anglo-Japanese Alliance*, 184.
157. Ibid., 251.
158. See Ruddock F. Mackay, *Fisher of Kilverstone* (Oxford: Clarendon, 1973), 312–15.
159. R.V.C. Bodley, *Admiral Tōgō: The Authorized Life of Admiral of the Fleet, Marquis Heihachirō Tōgō, O.M.* (London: Jarnolds, 1935), 134.
160. BKTSS, Kaigun: Shinkoku jiken, M33-2, Seymour to Shimamura, 27 June 1900.
161. Otte, ' "Not Proficient in Table-Thumping" ', 162.
162. ADM 1/7652, Confidential Bridge to Admiralty, 14 August 1903.
163. Ibid.
164. ADM1/7652, draft. Battenberg to CinC China, 30 September 1903.
165. Ibid.

3

'UNBROKEN THREAD': JAPAN. MARITIME POWER AND BRITISH IMPERIAL DEFENCE, 1920–32

Keith Neilson

In 1950, Maj.-Gen. F.S.G. Piggott, a former British military attaché in Japan and an ardent Japanophile, published his autobiography.[1] Entitled *Broken Thread*, the book centred on the relationship between Japan and Britain, a relationship sundered, much to Piggott's regret, by the Pacific War. What is less known is that Piggott had attempted to publish the book a decade earlier, in 1941, under the title *Unbroken Thread*, a title chosen to emphasize what he felt was the continuous partnership between the two island kingdoms dating back to the signing of the Anglo-Japanese Alliance in 1902.[2] This latter title is also an appropriate one for an examination of the impact that Japan had on Britain's Imperial defence plans in the period from 1920 to 1932, for considerations of Tokyo run continuously through all such discussions. In particular, Japan was the major focus for the Admiralty. Such issues as naval building, arms control and budgets were intimately linked to Japan, for the latter was deemed to be Britain's most likely naval opponent for the bulk of the inter-war period.[3] And such a linkage also spoke to issues that involved the Treasury and Foreign Office. The former was concerned with keeping Britain's financial house in order and was particularly determined that defence spending should be kept within tight limits. The Foreign Office wanted to ensure that British interests in the Far East were protected. However, it was determined to do so by maintaining both good Anglo-Chinese relations and warm Anglo-Japanese relations, all the while not offending the United States. The goals of the three departments were not always compatible and made for changing alliances within the British foreign policy-making élite. They are also the stuff of British Imperial Defence in the Far East.

The importance of Japan for Imperial Defence did not come into existence only after the First World War. Indeed, the Anglo-Japanese Alliance of 1902 had resulted from Britain's attempts to safeguard its Far Eastern interests against the depredations of Russia by utilizing Japan's burgeoning power in the region.[4] When the threat from Russia rapidly diminished as a result of the Russo-Japanese

War and the subsequent Anglo-Russian Convention of 1907, the value of the Anglo-Japanese Alliance for British Imperial defence waned before 1914.[5] In fact, by 1911, it was evident that the Alliance was of more import as a means of preventing Japan from becoming a threat to the Empire than it was as a check against the European Powers. Indeed, Sir Edward Grey, the British Foreign Secretary, made this point explicitly to the representatives of the Dominions at a special meeting of the Committee of Imperial Defence (CID) in May of 1911.[6]

During the First World War, Japan's implicit threat to Britain's Far Eastern empire became more obvious.[7] While Japan provided useful naval aid during the war, the issuance of the Twenty-One Demands to China in 1915 made it evident that Japan had ambitions in the Far East that were not congruent with British interests. Equally, while there was talk in 1917 and 1918 about using Japanese troops to re-open the Eastern front after the collapse of Russia and to reinforce the British war effort in Mesopotamia, it was clear that employing such forces was opposed by many who felt that Japan could not be trusted.[8] While some argued that it was only natural for the Japanese to wish to exploit Russia's weakness by annexing parts of Siberia and that Japan was a reliable partner, others believed that Japanese participation in the intervention in Russia was for Japan's own interests only.[9]

As the war drew to a close, it was the renewal of the Anglo-Japanese Alliance and how the Alliance might play on the Paris Peace Conference that drew attention. A major consideration involved the United States. As Lord Eustace Percy, who had been posted to Washington in 1917–18 and was now part of the Foreign Office's Political Intelligence Department (PID), wrote in late 1918, 'I think that anyone acquainted with American opinion will agree that the main impulse behind the [American] distrust of the British Navy is the feeling that, after all, the British Empire has certain commitments to Japan and the Far East the full implications of which are uncertain.'[10]

The naval issue was the key item. American unhappiness with respect to the British blockade during the First World War had led Washington to pass a naval building bill in 1916 promising to construct a 'navy second to none'. Throughout the first seven months of 1919, the Cabinet bickered over the Admiralty's budget.[11] Austin Chamberlain, the Chancellor of the Exchequer, made it clear that Britain could not afford a building race with the United States, and argued that, as Japan could not be deterred by a Royal Navy largely concentrated in the Mediterranean, it would not affect Britain's naval position to place more ships in the reserve as a cost-saving measure.[12] While the Admiralty contended that this would put Britain in a position of inferiority as regards the United States, a naval building race with America was deemed to be both expensive and a contest that Britain was unlikely to win. The quarrel between finance and naval power was threshed out in committee and in the Cabinet.[13] Victory went to financial prudence, with the Admiralty being told to make its estimates on the assumption that there would be no war for ten years – the origins of the 'ten-year rule' – and to initiate no new building programmes. This decision had been necessary in order to get the former foreign secretary, Sir Edward Grey, to agree to go to Washington on a special mission with the explicit purpose to inform the Americans that the Royal Navy had never been built against the United States and to assure them 'that is still the policy of His Majesty's Government'.[14]

Thus, by 1920, the issue of the Anglo-Japanese Alliance and Britain's relations with Japan generally were closely tied to Anglo-American relations, naval building policy and Imperial defence. This linkage had been noted as early as November 1918, when the British ambassador to Japan, Sir William Conyngham Greene, had recommended that the Alliance should be allowed to lapse in order that the British might 'resume our liberty of action, whereby we may help to reconcile any divergences of American and Japanese interests in the widening problems of the Far East'.[15] But opinions varied. A year later, the Admiralty warned about the difficulties for Imperial defence should the Anglo-Japanese Alliance not be renewed.[16] In considering the possibility of war with Japan, the Admiralty warned that Britain would 'find ourselves in [a position of] Naval inferiority for a time, the length of this period depending upon the amount of warning of impending trouble which we are given'. This inferiority would be due to two things: 'the days of economy ahead of us and the rapidly increasing strength of Japan'. In these circumstances, Hong Kong as it stood could not be defended. Thus, Their Lordships warned,

> If the Treaty with Japan is not renewed, and if the Port [of Hong Kong] is to be rendered reasonably secure, there appears to be no satisfactory middle course between the two alternatives of (i) keeping a fleet in Eastern Waters capable of dealing with Japan, or (ii) strengthening the defences of Hong Kong sufficiently to sustain a prolonged siege.

> All of this could be dealt with if the Americans were on the side of the British, 'but this cannot be counted upon'.

This analysis set the parameters for all subsequent discussions. The Far East could be defended either by diplomatic means (by means of the renewal of the Anglo-Japanese Alliance, the creation of a suitable successor to it or by an Anglo-American agreement) or by British strength alone. However, the former alternatives were difficult to achieve and possibly incompatible with one another, while the latter solution would be expensive and might affect Britain's diplomatic position adversely.

In late 1919 and throughout 1920, how to reconcile British defence requirements in the Far East with Britain's diplomacy was a constant topic at the Foreign Office. Sir Charles Hardinge, the Permanent Undersecretary (PUS), caught the issue nicely. 'Owing to Japan & the US being apparently irreconcilable', he wrote in December 1919, 'it is very difficult for us to work a policy in the Far East conjointly with them, while it is essential to us, owing to our naval weakness in the Pacific, to have a friendly Japan'.[17] There were also other considerations.

In early 1920, some at the Foreign Office believed that Japan might serve as a useful check to Soviet Russia, just as she had been to Tsarist Russia. This belief was linked to the fear that the new regime in Russia might be dominated by Germany. For Sir John Tilley, the Superintending Assistant Secretary in the Far Eastern Department, the point was clear: 'whether Russia is going to be dangerous on her own account as a Bolshevik Power or dangerous owing to German influence it seems to me that we shall do well to continue the Japanese Alliance – modified to suit the League of Nations'.[18] And, there was another advantage: while Britain's 'relations with Japan in China may be difficult they will probably be less so as she is our ally & much less so than if she is Germany's ally'. However, Tilley concluded, 'it is understood that the alliance must not interfere with our relations with the USA'.

As a result of this discussion, the various British departments were canvassed for their views.[19] The Foreign Office's outline of its own position reflected the points raised above:

> Lord Curzon fully realises the necessity of avoiding any danger of misunderstanding between this country and the United States of America and the difficulty for Great Britain of conducting a policy in the Far East in harmony with both the United States and Japan. In his opinion, however, our naval position in the Pacific renders it desirable to have a friendly Japan, while the existence of some form of agreement with that country would also make it easier for His Majesty's Government to keep a watch upon her movements in China ... [further] it appears to Lord Curzon that this [a powerful Russia] is a factor which it is essential to consider ... There is the further danger that if we abandoned the alliance, Japan might form the alliance with Russia and Germany of which there have already been so many rumours.

The replies made clear the circumstances that played upon the decision for renewal. The Admiralty noted that 'the rehabilitation of China is essential to the preservation of Peace in the Far East', but added that 'without considerable increase in Naval expenditure ... they do not see their way to maintain Forces sufficient to support a strong policy involving a possible coercion of Japan'.[20] As a result, the Admiralty was in favour of the Foreign Office's idea of some sort of modified, 'loose' alliance with Japan.

There is little doubt why the Admiralty found the Foreign Office's proposal attractive. Just a week before the latter had asked for the Admiralty's views, an 'outline of the strategical policy to be adopted in the event of war with Japan' had been sent to the commanders-in-chief of the China and East Indies fleet.[21] In it, the Admiralty had noted that the Anglo-Japanese Alliance 'may not' be renewed and, in that case, 'British interests in the Pacific and Far East generally are likely to be more closely allied to those of the United States than Japan'. While it was thought that Britain and the United States might become allies against Japan, it was noted that any pre-war arrangements with Washington were unlikely. Thus, British naval plans were based on the assumption of hostilities exclusively between London and Tokyo. As '[f]or the present, it is only proposed to maintain in the Pacific and Indian Oceans comparatively small British squadrons which cannot be compared to the Japanese in battle power', the Royal Navy should 'attack by every possible means the Japanese communications, avoiding so far as possible action with superior forces'. The focus of this policy was to maintain a fleet in being and this required forward bases. As defending Hong Kong seemed impossible without a large number of troops being stationed there, the Admiralty contended that it was 'absolutely essential that Singapore should remain in British hands'. With such difficulties in mind, some form of renewal of the Anglo-Japanese alliance was an attractive alternative.

The War Office concurred.[22] That office was particularly concerned with the United States. Since 'the expenditure entailed by adequate preparations to fight her would be so vast as to be out of the question . . . it is therefore imperative that our policy should be so directed as to eliminate any possibility of a rupture between the United States of America and the British Empire'. Given this, while the War Office favoured some sort of continuing relationship with Japan, 'it must be done in such a way as not to embarrass in the smallest degree our relations with America'.

When the views of the two service departments reached the Foreign Office, a comprehensive statement was drawn up to be given to the Colonial Office for transmission to the Dominions.[23] The general tenor of this was that, first, any renewed Anglo-Japanese alliance needed to be brought into line with the Covenant of the newly created League of Nations. Second, for the strategic and diplomatic reasons outlined above, the British should attempt to use 'our friendship with the United States and our alliance with Japan . . . to influence for good the relations between those two countries and to co-operate with both in the rehabilitation of China and the peaceful development of the Far East'. The 'ideal situation' would be 'some sort of tripartite understanding . . . to which France might also adhere', but 'until our ideal can be realised . . . we must content ourselves with the next best arrangement – alliance with Japan; intimate friendship and co-operation with the United States of America and France'.

But these all turned on Japanese and American attitudes. With respect to the former, there were divided opinions. Frank Ashton-Gwatkin, a clerk in the News and Political Intelligence Department of the Foreign Office whose service in the Consular Service in Japan and Singapore gave particular weight to his views about the Far East, argued that Britain should delay negotiations as long as possible.[24] He believed that 'a more democratic regime' would soon establish itself in Japan, leading to a 'decrease' in the 'menace to the British Empire in the Far East', a decline in the probability of 'a rapprochement between Japan and a Russo-German combination' and 'Japan's attitude towards China' improving 'of itself'. To renew the Anglo-Japanese alliance immediately would be to react against these trends: it would 'strengthen the hands of the present oligarchic

Government' and Britain did not 'wish to strengthen the old militarism against the new democratic movement' in Japan.

C.H. Bentinck, H.G. Parlett and E.M. Hobart Hampden, the latter two respectively the incumbent and his immediate predecessor as Japanese Counsellor at the British Embassy in Tokyo, took an opposing tack. Bentinck was 'not so sanguine' as Ashton-Gwatkin about the democratic future of Japan. In any case, he noted that he could not 'see much hope of Japan's attitude towards China improving unless checked by British or American influence, [n]or does it appear probable that the tension between Japan and America will relax'. This, combined with the arguments put forward by the Admiralty and War Office, led Bentinck to contend that a decision concerning renewal needed to be taken no later that the autumn of 1920 due to the need to square it with the Covenant and before Japan found itself 'isolated and free to seek another possible ally'. Parlett agreed. 'Unless we have a very definite promise of American co-operation and support', he argued, 'we cannot afford to leave Japan isolated and thus a potential enemy'. He also felt it 'obvious... that if it is a question of deciding between the United States and Japan our choice must be with the former', leading him to advocate the need to square Washington in advance of whatever decision was reached with respect to Tokyo. Hobart Hampden was not convinced that a 'democratised or labour-ridden Japan' would be better for Britain. Such a state, he suggested, 'would appear to be more exposed that the existing oligarchy to contagion from the red peril and other forces of evil threatening from the direction of Russian Asia'.

As to Washington's attitude, Sir Auckland Geddes, the British ambassador to the United States, opined that, if Britain did not denounce the Alliance on 13 July 1920 (the earliest date possible), this would have two results.[25] The first, partly resulting from the fact that, in July 1920, the 'Democratic Convention will be in full swing in San Francisco, in an atmosphere peculiarly sensitive to alarmist rumours from the East', was that there would be a 'very sensitive prejudice to the already clouded prospects of the League of Nations Covenant in the Presidential campaign'. The second was that it would provide a 'very decided stimulus to the anti-British wave which the campaign is only too certain to evoke'. In these circumstances, it was decided that the prudent course was to inform the Japanese immediately that the Anglo-Japanese Alliance could not be continued in its present form because it was not compatible with the Covenant. By doing so, Cavendish Bentinck argued, Britain had not committed itself or the Dominions to 'anything in advance' and had 'put ourselves right in the eyes of the world and especially of the USA'.

With this done, wider debate began about whether to renew the alliance in any form. From Tokyo Sir Charles Eliot, now the British ambassador to Japan, argued in favour.[26] He believed that the Japanese would be offended if the agreement were abrogated and that, due to Tokyo's 'very real fear of isolation', Japan might turn toward Russia and Germany, despite a strong dislike of Bolshevism. Eliot contended that British interests in the Far East – particularly the security of Hong Kong and Singapore – would be jeopardized by losing the alliance, points that he drove home to Curzon.[27] At the Foreign Office, however, Anglo-American relations were considered much more important. Sir Victor Wellesley, the Superintending Assistant Secretary in the Far Eastern Department, argued, in light of a 'feeler' that the American ambassador to London had made about closer Anglo-American cooperation, that Britain should aim for a tripartite – Anglo-American-Japanese – agreement in the Far East.[28] Wellesley condemned Japan's policy in China, contending that Japan's aggression on the mainland had made the Anglo-Japanese Alliance 'an unnatural and artificial compact based neither on identity of interests nor on sympathy with common aims and ideals'. A tripartite agreement would allow Britain to 'be in a far stronger position to exercise an effective restraint on Japanese ambitions and counteract the insidious ramification of their policy of peaceful penetration' in Asia.

This view was seconded by Beilby Alston upon his return from China via the United States.[29] Alston was convinced that the Pacific was the ideal place to establish a post-war Anglo-American condominium, as it was the 'one quarter of the globe in which Anglo-American interests must be considered identical'. He also pointed out that 'Japan might become a very serious menace to Great Britain or America in the Far East...[as] [n]either Hong Kong, Singapore, nor the Philippines are sufficiently heavily fortified to withstand for long a landing supported by a powerful [Japanese] fleet'. But, 'an adequate Anglo-Saxon fleet in the pacific, based upon say Hawaii and Singapore would...bring the Japanese menace in the Far East to an end'. While Sir Eyre Crowe, soon to be Permanent Undersecretary, was unable to share Alston's 'robust faith in American "cooperation" in China & elsewhere', there was general agreement in the importance of following up the American initiative.

The culmination of these discussions was the establishment, at Curzon's order, of a committee to discuss the whole issue.[30] While this committee was meeting, the entire issue of British naval building policy, with all its implications for imperial defence in the Far East, was considered at the CID on 14 December 1920.[31] The immediate concern was against whom Britain was to build. There were only two possible opponents: the United States and Japan. Prime Minister Lloyd George pointed out that for economic, financial and military reasons, Britain would find it difficult to match the United States, a position given full agreement by Austin Chamberlain, the Chancellor of the Exchequer. In these circumstances, Lloyd George felt that it was incumbent upon the government to explore some sort of 'amicable arrangement' with Washington about naval building.

Winston Churchill, the Secretary of State for War and Air and a former First Lord of the Admiralty, pointed out that any such agreement would involve the possibility of 'counter-building as between the United States and Japan' and this, in turn, 'must bring into review the Anglo-Japanese Treaty'. He argued that the original reasons (defence against Russia) for the Anglo-Japanese Treaty 'had disappeared' and that the Dominions 'had very strong racial objections to the Japanese, and would be disposed to throw in their lot with the United States against Japan in certain contingencies, as they already regarded the United States fleet in the Pacific in light of a safeguard to themselves'. For these reasons, Churchill favoured having 'very frank discussion on the whole question of naval armaments and policy' with the Americans before renewing the Anglo-Japanese treaty. Lloyd George, ever a negotiator, was unwilling to commit himself exclusively to the United States. Instead, he wished also to consider 'the possibility of combining with Japan...for use as an argument if the United States insisted on her attitude' toward building a large fleet. Churchill argued that there could be 'no more fatal policy...than that of basing our naval policy on a possible combination with Japan against the United States'. Lloyd George replied that 'there was one more fatal policy, namely, one whereby we would be at the mercy of the United States'. With no consensus emerging, the meeting adjourned, having decided to ask Auckland Geddes for information about the likely naval attitude of the new American administration.

There the matter rested. In January 1921, the Foreign Office committee on the Anglo-Japanese Alliance reported its findings.[32] These reflected the discussions of the previous months. The 'cardinal feature' of British foreign policy was 'to cultivate the closest relations with the United States and to secure their wholehearted co-operation in the maintenance of peace in every part of the world'. This being so, to renew the Anglo-Japanese Alliance as it stood 'may prove a formidable obstacle to the realisation of that aim'. As the previous reasons for the existence of the Alliance – 'eliminating the power of Russia' and 'checking the ambitions of Germany' – had now vanished, as Japan's policy toward China was inimical to British interests, and as 'present programmes of naval expansion' in Japan and the United States would force Britain to follow suit, the committee recommended that the Alliance should 'be dropped' and replaced by, 'if possible...a Tripartite Entente between the United States, Japan and Great Britain'.

This report languished in the files until 30 May. At that point, the intertwined matters of naval building and the renewal of the Anglo-Japanese Alliance were discussed in the Cabinet.[33] Curzon outlined both options clearly. The fact that the alliance had out-lived its anti-Russian roots irritated the United States, and that it would alienate China from Britain, pointed toward abrogation. The fact that the alliance had been a success, that there might be a recrudescence of the Russian threat (possibly in league with Germany), that it gave Britain a measure of control over Japanese policy and that Britain would find it difficult to exert force in the Far East, pointed toward renewal. Curzon suggested the Foreign Office's preferred alternative: a tripartite pact. After much discussion, it was decided to work toward getting the United States to call a conference on the Far East, while at the same time making it clear to Japan that Britain was not abandoning that country in favour of the United States.[34]

This was an ideal policy, but depended on the attitudes of Japan and the United States. Nor could the British come to a decision until after the Dominions had been consulted, at the Imperial Conference scheduled for June. The result was that, when the defence of the Far East was discussed outside the Cabinet in the spring of 1921, it was considered essentially as a purely military matter. At the beginning of May, the Standing Defence Sub-Committee (which later was treated as having been the CID under a different name), 'strongly emphasised' Singapore's 'vital strategic importance... [as] the gate-way to the Far East and Australasia'.[35] On the eve of the Imperial Conference, on 10 and 13 June, the CID reiterated this view, leaving the final decision for the Cabinet.[36]

This was done on 16 June.[37] Here, Sir Arthur Balfour, Lord President of Council and a veteran of Imperial Defence discussions for twenty years, put emphasis on the need to build a great naval base at Singapore.[38] His argument, which was accepted, was that even the renewal of the Anglo-Japanese Alliance would not eliminate the need for a Singapore base; the latter was needed to provide supplies for the British fleet in the Far East and to assure the Antipodean Dominions of Britain's on-going commitment to their defence (thus heading off any reliance for their part on the United States). The result of the Cabinet's decision was manifest on 17 June, when the CID met again.[39] There it was agreed that, when preparing a paper for the Dominions to consider, emphasis was to be laid on the fact that Singapore was needed whether or not the Anglo-Japanese Alliance was renewed, and it was also deemed 'undesirable' to let the Dominions know that a one-power naval standard had become British policy. As far as they were concerned, 'emphasis should be laid on the necessity of taking such steps as would ensure its being possible to move the main British fleet to the East if the necessity arose'. Although the Dominion premiers had jibbed at some of the British position, by the end of the Conference, they had accepted it and the American and Japanese ambassadors were informed of the British decision.[40] The 'Singapore strategy' had been born, but it was clear that this strategy was not meant to be anything more than a paper promise, a cheque that careful diplomacy must ensure would not need to be cashed.[41]

However, while the Singapore strategy had become policy that did not mean that all British departments of state agreed with it. The Treasury was not convinced by any of the above.[42] Sir George Barstow, the Controller of Supply Services, contended that the one-power standard was unclear: did it 'mean that the British fleet must always be (at least) equal to that of any other Power on the selected area of operations of that Power? If not is it to be equal in our waters, or finally is to be equal on paper?' To pursue the Singapore strategy was 'infinitely more difficult' than defending Britain itself and involved 'enormous preparatory expenditure'. Barstow contended that the Admiralty, 'instead of congratulating themselves on the distance from Japan of these islands propose to seek trouble by preparing to operate in strength in the Pacific'. For him, the issue at stake in the Far East – a possible Japanese descent on Australia – was not of sufficient import to take such action. Besides, to strengthen Singapore at the same moment that the Anglo-Japanese Alliance was being abandoned might 'give Japan some ground of suspicion of our bona fides'. As far as the Treasury was concerned, 'the Cabinet should consider Pacific Ocean policy in the light of all considerations including the financial'. And, finally, the Treasury did not believe in any Japanese threat.

'It seems almost impossible to imagine', Barstow concluded, 'that Japan would in the near future attack the British Empire'.

Despite (or possibly partly because of) the Treasury's arguments, the British decided to see if the problem was amenable to diplomacy. The first venue for this was Washington and the naval conference, for which the Americans had issued a call in August. In the autumn of 1921, the British prepared their position, with warnings from Japan that Tokyo would be 'disappointed' with a tripartite pact and fears that Washington would be unreasonable, due to what Hankey termed the 'imponderabilia of American politics'.[43] The naval position was hammered out at the CID on 14 and 21 October.[44] Here, the views of the Admiralty were generally accepted. The latter put emphasis on the need to develop Singapore, opposed any extension of Japan's naval bases south of Formosa and pointed out that the Royal Navy had been contracted 'since the Armistice... notwithstanding the increased extent of the Empire's commitments throughout the world'. As to restrictions on building, the Admiralty favoured putting a cap on 'capital ships' of a post-Jutland design, since the United States and Japan had extensive building programmes under way in such ships, programmes 'in the present state of national finances' that it would be 'impossible' to match. Churchill made this sleight of hand explicit at the second meeting. The delegates to Washington, he contended, should carry with them a statement of Britain's 'proposed annual building programme, based on the one-Power standard. Such a programme would be a paper one, and we should not be committed to its execution'. Britain could then offer to cut these paper increases in exchange for real cuts by the Americans and the Japanese. Arms control would compensate for financial inability.

During the voyage to the United States in early November, Balfour endeavoured to devise a plan whereby Britain's concerns about Imperial Defence could be met.[45] While Balfour had opposed the original Anglo-Japanese Alliance as costing too much and delivering too little, and believed that the original impetus for it had now disappeared, he now wished to pursue the tripartite alternative without taking action 'calculated to alienate, much less to outrage, Japanese sentiment'. At the same time, he did not want to seem to be 'committing... [the Americans] to military operations', and desired to reassure 'our Australasian Dominions' of Britain's protection.[46] This would be difficult, for the British Delegation found the Anglo-Japanese Alliance 'intensely unpopular' in Washington.[47]

However, by 12 December, Balfour had squared a number of circles. The Four Power Treaty, which was formally signed on 13 December, allowed the Anglo-Japanese Alliance to lapse without alienating the Japanese.[48] The inclusion in it of a clause stating that the Alliance could be renewed if the situation changed had 'convinced the Japanese of our trust in them and that we were not throwing them over'.[49] In fact, Hankey believed that the Four Power Treaty had done a great deal for Britain's strategic foreign policy generally: it 'has not weakened Anglo-Japanese relations; it has relieved us of what was rather an unpleasant liability in certain circumstances; and it has immeasurably strengthened Anglo-American relations'. While Hankey's optimism about Japan's attitude was not shared by Eliot, Balfour had scored a major success.[50]

In the purely naval negotiations that occurred simultaneously, Balfour also was triumphant. Under the terms of the Washington Treaty for the Limitation of Naval Armaments, signed 6 February 1922, ratios were established for the tonnage of capital ships (a ratio of 5:5:3:1.75:1.75 for Britain, the United States, Japan, France and Italy), the issue of cruisers was dropped because the powers could not agree on the topic, and the so-called 'Balfour parallelogram' – which banned new fortifications in the area bounded by the equator and 30 degrees North latitude, and 110 degrees and 180 degrees East longitude (excluding Singapore, Pearl Harbor and New Guinea) – was created. This kept Japan from expanding its naval bases to the south and ensured that British Imperial Defence in the Far East would be secure as long as the Singapore naval base was established to act as its fulcrum. On 6 February, Britain signed the Nine-Power Treaty, by which the signatories guaranteed China's sovereignty and integrity, promised to give China the opportunity to develop an effective government and declared that they would not seek special privileges in that country. In theory, at least, most of the concerns that had been discussed over the preceding four years about Britain's defence of its interests in the Far East had been dealt with successfully.

From 1922 until the early 1930s, Britain's Imperial Defence in the Far East was determined in the context established by the abrogation of the Anglo-Japanese Alliance and the holding of the Washington Naval Conference. As relations with Japan were relatively benign in this period, it appeared as if Balfour's diplomatic patch had solved the issue of the defence of the Far East. However, this did not mean that Japan had ceased to be paramount in British naval planning. This was due to the interlinked matters of naval budgets and naval arms control. Here Japan was an essential part of the debate.[51] With it being agreed that the United States was not to be considered as a likely naval opponent, this meant that British naval planning focused on the possibility of an Anglo-Japanese conflict (although some argued that war with Japan was as unlikely as war with the United States).[52]

In 1923, the Admiralty laid down plans for its defence of the Far East.[53] While Their Lordships accepted the fact that the Four Power Treaty made a Japanese 'bolt from the blue' less likely, they based their plans on the fact that the Washington agreements made 'it possible for Japan to consolidate her political and economic position in that portion of the Globe without active interference on the part of the United States'. In that case, 'Great Britain is now the only Power capable of countering with the requisite Naval Force any aggressive tendencies on the part of Japan in Asiatic Waters and the Western Pacific'. Since Hong Kong could no longer be protected through fortifications, Singapore became 'the only main repair port and anchorage that can be definitely relied on (assuming adequate defences are provided) in a war against Japan'. But Singapore's significance must be seen in the context of British plans for the fleet generally. The Admiralty's remark that '[t]he safety of Hong Kong and Singapore thus depends to a greater extent than ever on the mobility of the British Fleet', reflected the fact that it was proposed that the fleet be concentrated in peace time in the Mediterranean and moved in time of need to where it was required.[54] Only the forces necessary for local defence were to be kept in the Far East.

This policy still did not impress the Treasury. While 'not contest[ing]' the Admiralty's strategic argument about how to defend the Far East, it was not convinced that it needed to be defended at all, particularly as the foreign policy circumstances seemed to make such a large expenditure unnecessary.[55] Barstow again argued that Britain's position was secure. 'Japan appears to be more friendly with Great Britain than [it] is with the USA, and the USA to be more friendly with Great Britain than with Japan', he wrote in February 1923. 'Thus we occupy an intermediate position between those Powers, who are very unlikely to combine against us, while it is probable that in any conflict with either we could have the assistance of the other.' For him, later in 1923, the Japanese earthquake of that year also was an important factor.[56] But, as Barstow made clear, his and the Treasury's arguments against the Singapore base 'are political and not naval'.[57] He derided the possibility that Japan might attack Australia and New Zealand '& passing thence via Singapore attack India' as a 'lunatic's nightmare'. As far as he was concerned, even if Japan were to launch a 'local war in the East against Britain' and 'seize Hong Kong or Singapore & Borneo', this would not be to Japan's advantage.[58] All that would ensue would be a 'perpetual state of war' between Japan and Britain, Japan would have to maintain its forces 'at active strength', not 'trade with the British Empire' and 'the strain on Japanese financial resources would be greater than [it] could bear'.

Despite such arguments, the Treasury was unable to prevent the building of Singapore. In fact, before 1925, the Treasury's voice was not decisive in naval defence matters generally.[59] Politics, however, were able to sidetrack the project. The Labour Government, under J. Ramsay MacDonald, was determined to effect a change in Britain's defence policy, particularly with respect to Japan and France.[60] To this end, on 17 March 1924, the Cabinet decided to stop the construction of Singapore, on the basis that to continue would undermine Britain's position of standing 'for a policy of international cooperation through a strengthened and enlarged League of Nations, the settlement of disputes by conciliation and judicial arbitration, and the creation of conditions which will make a comprehensive agreement of armaments possible'.[61] However, in November the Conservatives returned to power, and reinstated the Singapore project.[62] To underline this change of policy, Hankey consulted with the new Foreign Secretary, Austin Chamberlain, to confirm that the assumption of a possible war with Japan could be used once again in planning.[63]

This did not mean that Chamberlain believed that war with Japan was likely. He made this clear to the CID on 5 January 1925.[64] 'I regard the prospect of war in the Far East as very remote', the Foreign Secretary announced, and 'I cannot conceive of any circumstances in which, singlehanded, we are likely to go to war with Japan.' Unless Japan was to ally itself with Germany or Russia (or possibly both), Chamberlain 'regard[ed] the danger of war between ourselves and Japan as being as remote as the danger of war with any other Great Power'. And, should Japan begin to follow a policy in China 'antagonistic to us or offensive to our sentiments', he believed that such actions would be equally unacceptable to the United States, leading to likely joint Anglo-American actions. Chamberlain was confident that any such change in Japanese policy would be evident to the Foreign Office well in advance and that British policy could be adjusted to meet such eventualities.

He was also in favour of constructing Singapore 'as a necessary link in or line of Imperial communications ... and in itself something of a guarantee for peace, because it is never a guarantee for peace that you should have great territories without defence to possible attack'. However, Chamberlain also 'strongly deprecate[d] anything that can be read here or elsewhere as competitive [naval] building between ourselves and Japan'. This led to substantial debate. Churchill, the Chancellor of the Exchequer, also favoured building Singapore, but suggested that Hong Kong (which he doubted could be defended) should be reduced as the former base was constructed in order to make a 'a gesture which would reassure Japan'. The Admiralty opposed both any cuts to its programmes and the reduction of Hong Kong. The debate between Churchill and Lord Beatty, the First Sea Lord and Chief of Naval Staff, also turned on a discussion about whether Japan (and the United States) constituted a threat to Britain's naval position similar to the threat that Germany had posed before 1914.[65] Churchill, intent on eliminating financial demands from the Admiralty, argued that Japan and the United States were so far geographically separated from Britain (and lacked armies that could threaten British Home defence) that the situation was entirely different. He believed 'it [is] essential that the Committee of Imperial Defence should establish that there is no relation between the pre-war condition *vis-à-vis* Germany and the present position *vis-à-vis* Japan'. Beatty agreed. However, the First Sea Lord contended that the British 'situation to-day *vis-à-vis* Japan is nothing so good as it was *vis-à-vis* Germany in 1914'. He, too, appealed to geography. Before the war, Britain had acted as 'a great breakwater' between Germany and the open sea: 'Nothing could come in and nothing could go out.' Against Japan, things were different: 'We are not in that geographical position which enables us to dominate Japan in naval warfare. Japan ... can deal us a naval blow, a maritime blow, which we are absolutely powerless to prevent' unless Britain held fast in the East. The result of this unresolved debate was the creation of a sub-committee to examine the matter.

This issue was discussed at the Cabinet on 18 March.[66] There, taken in conjunction with previous discussions about naval replacement programmes, the Cabinet decided to ask the CID to consider a number of related matters, including whether the one-Power standard should be retained and whether an attack by Japan was sufficiently likely in the next ten years that the Admiralty should be tasked to prepare for it.[67] When this was done on 30 March, the arguments of the various departments concerned – Foreign Office, Admiralty and Treasury – were paraded.[68] Eyre Crowe, the PUS, stated that the Foreign Office believed that no war with Japan in the course of the next ten years was likely. He also put emphasis on the fact that 'in any conflict in which [Japan] engaged with Great Britain was bound to be affected by the attitude of the United States'. As to the one-Power standard, Beatty was evasive. What he wished to discuss instead was the nature of naval Imperial defence. For the Far East, this meant the ability to 'hold on' at Singapore until the Main Fleet could arrive. Churchill saw immediately that Beatty's discussion of principle, rather than practice, meant that 'the plan outlined by the First Sea Lord added many considerations involving great cost over and above such a one-Power standard', since it made necessary the construction of Singapore with all its accoutrements.[69] The Secretary of State for India, Lord Birkenhead, attempted to clarify matters by contending that Beatty wanted a one-Power standard, but wished to retain the right to keep that fleet 'distributed as necessary'. Beatty and Churchill continued to growl at each other, but the essence of what was to become the 'ten-year rule', that is, that war with Japan within the next ten years was 'not a contingency seriously to be apprehended', had come into existence.[70] Churchill, however, had not ended his dissent nor had Beatty given up on his assumptions. The Chancellor warned the CID that British financial resources were not unlimited, and this had to be remembered, given that 'Fighting departments are always apt to take the standpoint of sons for thinking their fathers' purses inexhaustible', while at meetings of the Chiefs of Staff (COS) held subsequently, Beatty refused to allow that the Fleet could be considered as part of the permanent strength of Singapore.[71] The First Sea Lord also rejected the idea that no war with Japan within the next ten years was possible; those who believed so, he told the COS in July, were 'in reality living in a fool's paradise'.[72]

The interlocked quarrel over Japan, Imperial Defence and finance resurfaced in July 1926 at the CID.[73] Here, Chamberlain made the point that the review of Imperial Defence prepared by the COS put too much emphasis on a danger from Japan.[74] Beatty rebutted that the COS had based their appreciation on the Foreign Office's own list of British commitments and that the latter evaluation had emphasized the need 'to make our strategic position in the Far East defensibly as safe as our resources allow'.[75] Churchill immediately reacted. Noting that he 'had always been in favour of a base at Singapore', the Chancellor stated that 'he had never imagined that that decision would be used as a peg on which to hang far-reaching schemes of alarmist policy and consequent armament'. To make plans on the basis that Britain's possessions in the Far East existed on Japanese 'sufferance', as Beatty contended, was wrong. Britain should not make its plans on the basis of the 'fancied danger' from Japan, but rather focus on a one-power standard based on the United States, a nation that could threaten the entire British Empire, not just that part of it in the Far East. 'By unduly stressing the Japanese danger and expending excessive sums on the defence of Singapore', he concluded, 'the cost of maintaining a Navy, at least equal to the task of defeating the American Navy, was being enhanced'. While the COS's report was approved, clearly there were strong differences of opinion about Japan.

In fact, general concern about threat to the Empire was shifting away from Tokyo and toward Moscow. At the same CID meeting in July, the Secretary of State for India, Lord Birkenhead, had raised the Soviet threat to Afghanistan.[76] Both Churchill and the Marquess of Salisbury, Lord Privy Seal, had noted that the most efficient way of curbing the Soviet threat was in conjunction with Japan, as had been done during the tenure of the Anglo-Japanese alliance. Both men 'regretted' the policy of regarding Japan as an enemy, a contention that clearly also cut across Beatty's bows in the debate about naval expenditures. As Anglo-Soviet relations worsened in the autumn of 1926, the matter of Britain's relations with Japan and Soviet Russia was again discussed at the CID.[77] Here, in an argument that Chamberlain noted, 'coincided entirely with his own convictions', William Tyrrell, PUS at the Foreign Office, put forth the view that 'our policy should be based upon the assumption that Russia is the enemy and not Japan'. Although a return to an Anglo-Japanese alliance was 'so problematical as to be hardly worth the attempting', Tyrrell agreed with Churchill and Salisbury that 'we should maintain our present policy of cultivating the friendliest relations with Japan'.

In these circumstances, the Admiralty began to reconsider its attitude to arms control. With the Treasury's constantly attacking naval estimates and the Foreign Office's asserting that Japan was no danger, the Admiralty began to doubt that it could squeeze out of the government the funds that it required.[78] Thus, arms control, with the possibility that limits could be placed on other countries' building programmes, seemed a possible means to achieve the Admiralty's ends. As it was put in November 1926, '. . . our [Admiralty] material interests coincide with those of an abstract nature [that is, disarmament]'.[79] This new attitude was apparent to all. When, in the spring of 1927, the American government issued a call for a naval arms-control conference – the so-called 'Coolidge Conference' at Geneva – Salisbury noted that the 'atmosphere will be wholly different [from previous attempts at arms control]. The Admiralty wants that [the conference] to succeed'.[80]

It did not. The sticking point at the conference was the issue of cruisers, and this centred on Japan. Throughout the inter-war period, the Admiralty consistently declared that it needed a total of 70 cruisers in order to provide both for the needs of the Fleet and for trade protection, essentially in a war with Japan.[81] But this number was somewhat arbitrary and depended on circumstances. As the First Sea Lord, Sir Charles Madden, noted in 1928, 'the number 70 – 31 with the Fleet, and 39 for trade protection – is based on a war with Japan, and is true only of this special case and assuming Japan has no Allies. This assumption is reasonable, as the Government will not consider U.S.A., and Japan is the next strongest Power, but it is by no means a solid and unchangeable argument'. In fact, '[t]he number of Cruisers we require depends on: (1) What Nations are potential enemies; (2) their strength and accessibility to our trade routes; and the only safe policy is to watch both and act accordingly, so that we should be as free as possible to adjust our requirements'. Churchill was convinced that this was so. He felt that the Admiralty's position for Geneva contained 'three monstrous fallacies'.[82] The first was an 'Anglo-Japanese war scare', the second was the 'American claim to numerical parity' in all classes of ships and the third was the 'Admiralty 70 cruiser guarantee for our food supply'. He blamed the 'fictitious Anglo-Japanese war scare' for pushing the Americans to demand parity and contended that the figure of 70 for cruisers 'was not an absolute standard for the British Empire. If others have none, they are too much. If others have equal, or even half as many, they are too few'. Basing his views on the British experience in the First World War, the Chancellor contended that in time of war cruisers would not suffice to guarantee the sea lanes; that would require convoys composed of 'quite different types of ships than these costly cruisers'.

This differing view of Imperial defence goes far to explain Churchill's position over Geneva. He was quite unwilling to concede naval parity to the Americans, but also unwilling to concede an endless purse to the Admiralty. When the conference bogged down in early July, Churchill argued at the CID that any American building programme was a concern to Britain only inasmuch that it led to a Japanese response.[83] Even here, there was a silver lining, as American building might 'perhaps... bring Japan and Great Britain closer together' – a recrudescence of the Treasury's favoured policy to curb naval expenditure. Chamberlain and the Secretary of State for Dominion Affairs and the Colonies both deprecated such a result, Chamberlain because it would lead either to abandoning the one-power standard or to a naval race; Amery because of the impact that poor Anglo-American relations would have on the Empire, particularly Canada. But, this should not be read as indicating that Churchill was in favour of according parity to the United States. He rejected the idea that Britain should agree to any tonnage ceiling that would limit London's freedom to build what was necessary.[84] What Churchill did propose was a cruiser-building holiday – which would meet the Treasury's concerns about cost – a position that Beatty rejected because it would prevent the Admiralty from carrying out its long-term programme of modernization. The result was that the Cabinet decided in early August to let the conference collapse.[85]

This left the entire issue of Britain's building programme for cruisers unresolved. The debate over this took place at the Naval Programme Committee and in the Cabinet over the period from November 1927 to February 1928.[86] Here, Churchill continued to advocate a cut in the building programmes, arguing that war with Japan was just a bogey used by the Admiralty to justify its budgets. Within the Treasury itself, the Admiralty was castigated for the fact that 'its habits run to unstinted lavishness', a point that spoke directly to the scale of the building at Singapore.[87] A key point was that the Admiralty seemed not, despite its professions to the contrary, to have taken into consideration the fact that the foreign policy situation made war unlikely. With Chamberlain's agreeing that Anglo-Japanese relations remained good, this was not a supportable position.[88] Much also centred on the 'ten year rule'. At the Treasury, the contention by William Bridgeman, the First Lord of the Admiralty, that 'the very fullest weight' had been given to the 'ten-year rule' was termed a 'simple perversion of facts'.[89] Thus, while Churchill was able to block some of the Admiralty's spending, his on-going quarrel with Bridgeman also made him turn aggressively toward a reconsideration of the meaning

77

of the 'ten-year rule'.[90] At the Cabinet on 22 June, Churchill asked that the matter be re-examined.[91] This occurred at the CID on 5 July.[92] Here, Chamberlain again noted (although with some reservations) that Japan 'did not constitute...a menace' at the present moment and that should Japan become so, the United States would be 'a deterrent' to hostile actions by Tokyo. Only Russia, the Foreign Secretary concluded, prevented him from saying 'without any grave doubts that we could reckon on no war of any magnitude occurring during the next 10 years'. With this backing, Churchill was able to get the 'ten-year rule' interpreted as existing on a rolling basis, an interpretation confirmed by the Cabinet a fortnight later.[93]

Matters remained tense between the Admiralty and the Treasury for the remainder of the life of the second Baldwin government. While the Foreign Office attempted to repair Anglo-American relations after the collapse of the Coolidge conference, Churchill continued to snipe at the Admiralty's estimates of cost.[94] When the COS presented their Annual Review of Imperial Defence in 1928, the Treasury saw this as a chance to pare down the defence estimates.[95] That department argued that the Kellogg–Briand Pact provided an instrument that could be used to press for a reduction in spending: 'the political value of such a reduction, as a gesture of faith in the in the importance of Pact and a lead to other nations, is obvious. The opportunity afforded to the Treasury, is thus exceptionally fruitful'. As Sir Warren Fisher, the Permanent Secretary at the Treasury put it in November 1928: 'Our margin in naval strength, the absence of anyone to fight at sea, the Cabinet instruction about no "major" war, the Kellogg Pact, & our financial situation seem to me to provide in the aggregate an overwhelming argument for a drastic cut in naval expenditure.'[96] And, while the Treasury was not convinced that it could delay further expenditure on Singapore, opinion there was that it was 'worth while...to urge further postponement'.[97]

Thus, when Labour came to power in June 1929, Imperial defence in the Far East was uneasily poised between two competing visions. The Admiralty argued for a portable navy capable of defending British interests both in Europe and in the Far East, the key to which was the construction of Singapore and the maintenance of a 70-cruiser fleet. The Treasury's position was that the state of international relations did not justify spending the sums necessary to realize the Admiralty's vision. As the Deputy Controller of Establishments at the Treasury, G.C. Upcott, remarked about the assumptions underpinning the Annual Review of Defence Policy for 1929: 'The most important of these is the ultimate assumption by which Naval policy is governed. This is at present a maritime war in the Far East (but not within the next ten years): & on this assumption depend such immediately practical questions as the Singapore scheme, the building up of the Oil Fuel Reserve, and the size of the British garrisons in China.'[98]

This was a political matter. MacDonald's new government immediately set about dealing with the naval matter at the Fighting Ships Committee, which held its first meeting on 25 June.[99] At this meeting, the First Sea Lord, Admiral Sir Charles Madden, outlined the Admiralty's position with regard to Imperial Defence and found himself opposed by the new Chancellor of the Exchequer,

Philip Snowden, who had been thoroughly briefed in the Treasury's views, including Fisher's opinion that the 'idea of Japan wishing to take on the British Empire is fantastic'.[100] The Treasury remained convinced that the Admiralty's interpretation of the 'one-power standard' was based purely on Japan.

The Admiralty when told to ignore the USA in war plans and to adopt a 'one-power standard' and freed from fear in Europe, interpreted this as authorizing their scheme for equality (meaning of course superiority) against Japan in eastern waters. The cruiser programme, the oil fuel storage programme, the wireless stations programme, the Singapore base, all had the same object of getting the stranglehold on Japan in the Far East.[101] Faced with these divergent views, over the course of the summer of 1929, MacDonald, who was determined both to improve Anglo-American relations and to further arms control, entered into long negotiations with the Admiralty and the Americans over building programmes and the size of cruisers.[102]

The result was that the Admiralty agreed, in exchange for a guaranteed building programme, to reduce the number of cruisers it required to 50, a number confirmed at the London Naval Conference held in the spring of 1930. The new British cruiser fleet was to comprise 15 8-inch-gun ships, 14 new 6-inch-gun ships (to be built on a regular schedule) and 21 older, 6-inch-gun ships. While this reduction has been interpreted by many as the end of Britain's naval superiority and a passing of the torch to the Americans, it marked nothing of the sort.[103] What had occurred was that the had Admiralty decoupled its building programme from the Japanese threat and had obtained agreement as to cruiser size. During the negotiations prior to the conference, the Treasury was alert to the fact that its main interest, the reduction of cost, would not be achieved by this agreement, and suggested instead that an effort be made to freeze the total of naval costs.[104] This, however, was rejected by Snowden as politically 'inexpedient', reflecting the fact that the Treasury had been kept out of the decision-making process when the British position for the London Naval Conference had been established.[105] What reduction did occur was a slowdown in the building of the fortifications at Singapore. However, when the Treasury attempted an assault on the Admiralty's building plans in the immediate aftermath of the Conference, MacDonald quashed the attempt in order to obtain a ready domestic acceptance of the Conference's results by ensuring that the Admiralty remained onside.[106]

In fact, by mid-1931, all seemed for the best with respect to British Imperial defence in the Far East. Britain appeared to be on good terms with all of the leading players in the region, with the exception of Soviet Russia. This was evident in British discussions on general disarmament. In a paper prepared for the Three-Party Disarmament Committee in June 1931, the Foreign Office opined that relations with Japan were generally good and that 'official and public sentiment' in the United States was 'more favourable to Great Britain than has been the case at any time since the war'.[107] However, there were disquieting trends. As Britain prepared for a final push at Geneva toward disarmament, the Foreign Office noted that the 'ten-year rule' rested on shaky grounds due to the 'impetus of Nazism, Fascism, and Bolshevism'.[108] To meet such threats, Hankey was pushing MacDonald to reconsider the 'ten-year rule'.[109]

Everything was turned upside down in the autumn of 1931. Domestically, the Labour government collapsed, and was replaced by a National government of a very different political composition. Abroad, Japan's actions in China led to a deterioration in Anglo-Japanese relations, with the corollary that there were concerns that the naval limitations agreed to at London might prove insufficient for the Admiralty to be able to defend Britain's interests in the Far East. Further, Anglo-American cooperation to check Japan was not forthcoming, as Sir John Simon, the Foreign Secretary in the National government and Henry Stimson, the American Secretary of State, could not find common ground to do so at Geneva.[110] With the coming to power of Hitler in early 1933 and the collapse of the disarmament talks at Geneva, thoughts turned toward rearmament.[111] A new phase in British Imperial defence in the Far East had begun.

What, then, can we conclude about British Imperial defence in the Far East from 1918 to 1932? The first point that needs to be made is the centrality of Japan. With a tight focus on Tokyo, much becomes clear. This is particularly so when considering the positions with respect to Imperial Defence taken by the Foreign Office, the Admiralty and the Treasury. For the Foreign Office, the British position in the Far East after the First World War centred on whether to renew the Anglo-Japanese Alliance. Given that the original reason for the Alliance – preventing Russia from encroaching on British interests in China – had evaporated, and given that a renewal threatened to inflame Anglo-American relations and trigger off an expensive and unwinnable naval race with Washington, the Foreign Office decided not to renew the Alliance. However, it was also unwilling either to offend Japan or to rely on the benign conditions of the post-war to last permanently. Instead, Balfour negotiated a replacement – in the form of the Four Power Treaty, the Washington Naval Treaty and the Nine Power Treaty – for the Anglo-Japanese Alliance.

All of this was to function in the context of the League of Nations and to guarantee that Britain's position in the Far East would remain secure and that any change in the status quo would be achieved through negotiation. This solution lasted from 1922 to 1931 – a period of benign Anglo-Japanese relations. Then, Japanese aggression and the lack of will of the League demonstrated the impotence of the agreements signed at Washington. In such circumstances, the Foreign Office was forced to rely upon diplomacy to ensure Britain's interests. For the rest of the period up to the outbreak of the Pacific War, the Foreign Office attempted to convince the Japanese that they faced a shadowy coalition of Britain, Soviet Russia and, pre-eminently, the United States.[112] This 'no-bloc' policy was the result of Britain's lack of military, particularly naval, might in the Far East.

For the Royal Navy, Japan provided the naval threat – the United States having been ruled out as an enemy by political fiat – necessary to justify its building programmes. While the issue of capital ships had been dealt with at Washington, Imperial Defence in the Far East gave the Admiralty a useful tool both to promote its wish for an extensive cruiser fleet and to insist on the construction of a major naval base at Singapore. However, the Japanese threat proved to be an unreliable lever. By 1926, continued good Anglo-Japanese relations pushed the Admiralty to the realization that it must use naval arms limitation as a means to control both Japanese and American naval construction until a new menace emerged that would provide the public impetus for increased naval building programmes. This effort at arms control occurred at the London Naval Conference, when the Admiralty traded its 70-cruiser requirement (but remained adamant that this was only a temporary measure) for a guaranteed building programme to replace its ageing and obsolescent existing cruisers. Ironically, this happened just as Anglo-Japanese relations deteriorated and Japan re-emerged as a serious naval threat in the Far East. For the rest of the 1930s, the Admiralty pursued two policies. It attempted to ensure that naval arms limitation (both qualitative and quantitative) agreements continued, all the while using the Japanese (and, later, the German and Italian) threat to attempt to pry sufficient money out of the Treasury to build its preferred guarantee – a two-ocean fleet – for British maritime security.[113] Japan was an essential aspect of both policies, particularly given that the building programmes of all the Powers were interlocked.[114]

On the vital issue of cost, Japan was also central to British planning. The Treasury saw good Anglo-Japanese relations as the principal reason to cut back on naval building and hence on costs. They consistently rejected the Admiralty's contention that it was necessary to prepare for possible Anglo-Japanese hostilities either by means of building programmes or the construction of Singapore (at least at the rate the Admiralty preferred). In fact, the Treasury believed that the maintenance of Anglo-Japanese relations should be at the core of British foreign policy. This was particularly evident in the 1930s. At the Defence Requirements Sub-Committee and throughout the remainder of the decade, the Treasury, particularly while Neville Chamberlain was Chancellor, attempted to promote, if not a renewed Anglo-Japanese Alliance then close Anglo-Japanese relations in order both to safeguard Britain's interests in the Far East and to control spiralling naval costs.[115] Due to Chamberlain and the Treasury's profound anti-Americanism, that department preferred a policy of cooperation with Japan in opposition to the Foreign Office's more far-sighted desire to rely on cooperation, however tenuous, with Washington in the Far East.[116] For the Treasury, Tokyo trumped Washington.

These conflicting interests made for shifting alliances among the Foreign Office, the Admiralty and the Treasury. Essentially, in the unusual circumstances of 1921–22, all three departments agreed (albeit for different reasons and with different expectations) with the Washington settlement. However, for the rest of the decade, the Foreign Office and the Treasury tended to make common ground against the Admiralty. This was not due to any animus on the part of the Foreign Office toward the Admiralty (there *was* animus at the Treasury toward the Admiralty), but simply due to the fact that the Foreign Office's reading of the situation in the Far East could be used by the Treasury to suggest that the Admiralty's Japanese-based building plans could be cut back. However, the Foreign Office and the Admiralty were of one mind with regard to the need for Britain to have sufficient force to back up its diplomacy in the Far East, and both supported the construction of Singapore. And, for the Foreign Office, as well as for the Admiralty, the maintenance of good Anglo-American relations was paramount. Any differences between the two departments over this issue (as at Geneva) were more apparent than real. The Admiralty did not wish to have its hands tied by the Americans over the issue of cruisers, but certainly did not wish to risk bad Anglo-American relations. The Foreign Office was adamant about the need for good Anglo-American relations and less so about the need for 70 cruisers (of whatever size). However, there was a basic continuity of interests, as demonstrated at the London Naval Conference when the Admiralty's willingness to submerge its cruisers programme dovetailed nicely with the Foreign Office's desire to improve Anglo-American relations. Once rearmament began, the Foreign Office, in contrast to the Treasury, became a warm supporter of the Admiralty's desire for a two-ocean fleet, a fleet that would provide 'a little straw to make our [diplomatic] bricks' in the Far East.[117]

An examination of British imperial defence in the Far East from 1918 to 1932 also throws some light on other issues, such as the Singapore strategy and the 'decline' of inter-war Britain. With regard to the Singapore strategy, the narrow navalist examinations of the topic obscure the fact that safeguarding Britain's interests in the Far East was a much wider issue, involving Britain's financial and foreign policies as much as its naval policy. The Foreign Office attempted to pursue this issue by means of creating a diplomatic substitute for the Anglo-Japanese Alliance, while the Treasury attempted to ensure Britain's financial stability by means of advocating continuing good Anglo-Japanese relations so that the large costs of deterring Japan by naval power were unnecessary. For the Admiralty and the Foreign Office (and, occasionally, even the Treasury) Singapore had two roles: to deter Japan and, at the same time, to make it possible to pursue a foreign policy ensuring that a contest of arms did not occur in the Far East.

These points also are germane to the debate over whether Britain was a Power in decline after the First World War and that its Far Eastern empire was a classic case of 'Imperial overstretch'.[118] With its focus on economics and finance, such debate has tended to overlook a structural issue: the fact that Japan was an extra-European Power. If the 'Pax Britannica' ever existed, it did so in the context of the European state system of the nineteenth century. In this system, Britain was able to maintain its predominant position – as both a European and an Imperial Power – because it was always able to find allies to maintain the Continental balance of power. However, when Britain's position was threatened by a non-European Power, this option was no longer available (as the Boer War had indicated earlier). In the inter-war, Britain not so much had 'declined' as was faced with a changed international system. This was particularly true when considering the Far East. There, Japan could be checked only by British power alone or by Britain in concert with the United States or the Soviet Union. British power could not be brought to bear in the Far East without compromising Britain's position in Europe. Neither of the latter Powers (both standing largely outside the European system) could be counted on to support London. Japan posed an insoluble problem for imperial defence. By revealing this, it can be suggested that, in fact, Japan brought an end to the British Empire, even before the events of 1941.

Notes

1. F.S.G. Piggott, *Broken Thread: An Autobiography* (Aldershot: Gale & Polden, 1950).
2. See Major G.W. Lambert (WO) to FO, 31 January 1941, FO 371/27965/F546/546/23, UK Public Record Office, Kew (henceforth PRO) and the ensuing correspondence in this file.
3. The standard account of British naval policy in the period is Stephen Roskill, *Naval Policy between the Wars* (London: Collins, 1968–76); Christopher Bell, *The Royal Navy, Seapower and Strategy between the Wars* (Basingstoke: Macmillan, 2000) introduces the later literature in addition to being a valuable account in itself.
4. Keith Neilson, 'The Anglo-Japanese Alliance and British Strategic Foreign Policy, 1902–1914', in P.P. O'Brien (ed.), *The Anglo-Japanese Alliance* (London and New York: Routledge Curzon, 2004) focuses on the subject; for a wider perspective, see Neilson, *Britain and the Last Tsar: British Policy and Russia 1894–1917* (Oxford: Clarendon, 1995), 117–36.
5. What would have transpired for Anglo-Japanese relations had the Anglo-Russian Convention broken down over Central Asia, as seemed likely in 1914, is impossible to guess. For the difficulties in Anglo-Russian relations, see Jennifer Siegel, *Endgame: Britain, Russia and the Final Struggle for Central Asia* (London: I.B. Tauris, 2002).
6. CAB 2/2, PRO, minutes, 111th meeting of the CID, 26 May 1911.
7. See I.H. Nish, 'Japan and China, 1914–1916', in F.H. Hinsley (ed.), *British Foreign Policy under Sir Edward Grey* (Cambridge: Cambridge University Press, 1977), 452–65; Nish, *Alliance in Decline: A Study in Anglo-Japanese Relations 1908–23* (London: Athlone, 1972), 115–262; Peter Lowe, *Great Britain and Japan 1911–1915: a Study of British Far Eastern Policy* (London: Macmillan, 1969); Lowe, 'The British Empire and the Anglo-Japanese Alliance 1911–1915', *History*, 54 (1969), 212–25.
8. For the context with respect to Imperial Defence, see Keith Neilson, ' "For Diplomatic, Economic, Strategic and Telegraphic Reasons": British Imperial Defence, the Middle East and India, 1914–1918', in Keith Neilson and Greg Kennedy (eds), *Far Flung Lines: Studies in Imperial Defence in Honour of Donald Mackenzie Schurman* (London: Frank Cass, 1997), 103–23. For discussions of this policy, see V.H. Rothwell, *British War Aims and Peace Diplomacy 1914–1918* (Oxford: Clarendon, 1971), 186–9; John Fisher, *Curzon and British Imperialism in the Middle East 1916–19* (London: Frank Cass, 1999), 172–6; MSS Eur F 112/118A, British Library, India Office Library Records (henceforth IOLR), Curzon Papers, Balfour to Curzon, 25 September 1917.
9. FO 800/205, Balfour Papers, Sir Charles Eliot (British High Commissioner, Vladivostok) to Balfour, 29 November 1918; FO 371/4355, 'Russian Siberia and Japan', Peace Conference Papers, 80, J.Y. Simpson (Political Intelligence Department, FO); FO 608/188, minutes on FO to British Delegation (Paris), 4 February 1919. There was also a suspicion that Japanese cooperation with Admiral Kolchak's Siberian regime was based on a 'secret agreement' giving Japan concessions in that area, see FO 608/199, minutes on FO to BD, dispatch 3345, 26 May 1919.
10. FO 371/4353, 'Anglo-Japanese Alliance and League of Nations', PC 129, Percy.
11. What follows is informed by J. Kenneth McDonald, 'Lloyd George and the Search for a Postwar Naval Policy, 1919', in A.J.P. Taylor (ed.), *Lloyd George: Twelve Essays* (London: Hamish Hamilton, 1971), 191–222.

12. CAB 24/83, 'Navy Votes. Memorandum by the Chancellor of the Exchequer', GT-7646, 8 July 1919.
13. CAB 23/15, A Minutes, War Cabinet 616A, 15 August 1919.
14. MSS Eur F112/211, Curzon Papers, Curzon to Grey, 9 September 1919. Grey had demanded that the government take up such a position as a condition for his agreeing to go to America; see the correspondence cited by McDonald, 'Lloyd George and the Search', 203–14.
15. FO 371/3234/206006, Conyngham Green to Lord Robert Cecil, 2 November 1918.
16. CAB 24/92, PRO, Naval Situation in the Far East, Cabinet Paper 54, secret, Admiralty, 31 October 1919.
17. FO 371/3816/50925, Hardinge's undated (but *c.* 8 December 1919) minute on B. Alston (Minister Plenipotentiary, Tokyo) to J. Tilley (FO), private and secret, 7 October 1919.
18. FO 371/3816/166706, Tilley's minute (5 January 1920) on B. Alston to Curzon, dispatch 497, 25 November 1919.
19. Ibid., FO to India Office and similar letters to the Admiralty, Colonial Office and War Office, 21 January 1920.
20. FO 371/3816/178570, Admiralty to FO, 18 February 1920.
21. ADM 116/3124, PRO, War Memorandum, secret, Admiralty, M00340, 12 January 1920, final copy dated 20 January 1920.
22. FO 371/3816/178925, B.B. Cubbitt (War Office) to FO, secret, 14 February 1920.
23. FO 371/5358/F199/199/23, 'Memorandum by Mr. C.H. Bentinck on the Effect of the Anglo-Japanese Alliance upon Foreign Relationship', Bentinck (clerk, Far Eastern Department), 28 February 1920; ibid., an untitled memorandum on how any Anglo-Japanese agreement would be affected by the League of Nations, H.W. Malkin (Assistant Legal Adviser, FO), 16 February 1920 and Curzon's minute, 8 March.
24. FO 371/5358/F304/199/23, minute by Mr. Gwatkin on the Anglo-Japanese Alliance and Constitutional Changes in Japan, Ashton-Gwatkin, 23 March 1920 and the minutes on this by Bentinck (26 March), H.G. Parlett (27 March) and E.M. Hobart Hampden (28 March).
25. FO 371/5359/F829/199/23, Geddes to FO, dispatch 599, very confidential, 30 April 1920; the minutes by Bentinck (15 May), Hardinge (nd), and Balfour and Curzon to Sir C. Eliot (now ambassador to Tokyo), telegram 185, 3 June 1920, all attached.
26. FO 371/5360/F1559/199/23, Eliot to FO, dispatch 296, 17 June 1920, and the minutes.
27. MSS Eur F112/216, Curzon Papers, Eliot to Curzon, private, 9 July 1920 and 5 August 1920.
28. FO 371/5360/F2159/199/23, untitled minute, Wellesley, 1 June 1920, and 'Anglo-American Cooperation in the Far East', Wellesley, undated.
29. FO 371/5360F1742/199/23, memorandum by Sir B. Alston respecting Suggestions for an Anglo-Saxon Policy for the Far East, 1 August 1920, and the minutes by Bentinck (9 August) and Eyre Crowe (9 August).
30. FO 371/5361/F2200/199/23, minute by Hardinge (nd, but *c.* 24 September 1920). The Committee's work is discussed in Nish, *Alliance in Decline*, 310–13.
31. CAB 2/3, minutes, 134th meeting of the CID, 14 December 1920.
32. FO 371/6672/F1169/63/23, Report of Anglo-Japanese Alliance Committee, secret, 14 January 1921.
33. CAB 23/25, minutes, CAB 43(21), 30 May 1921; discussed were 'Anglo-Japanese Alliance', CP-2957, Lord Lee (First Lord of the Admiralty), 21 May 1921, CAB 24/123 and a number of Colonial Defence papers, including 'Anglo-Japanese Alliance...', CID C-127, Foreign Office, 27 April 1920, CAB 5/3.
34. Eliot had warned Curzon of the possibility that Japan might look to Germany if the Alliance were abandoned; see MSS Eur F112/219B, Curzon Papers, Eliot to Curzon, 5 May 1921.

JAPAN. MARITIME POWER AND BRITISH IMPERIAL DEFENCE

35. CAB 2/3, minutes, 136th and 137th meetings of the CID, 2 May 1921; CAB 5/3, Naval Situation in the Far East, CID C-119, Admiralty, 31 October 1919, and Defence of Hong Kong, CID C-120, Churchill, 3 February 1920.

36. CAB 2/3, minutes, 140th and 141st meetings of the CID, 10 and 13 June 1921.

37. CAB 23/26, minutes, CAB 50(21), 16 June 1921; CAB 24/125, 'Singapore. Development as a Naval Base', CP-3029, Hankey, 13 June 1921; CAB 5/4, 'Singapore. Development as a Naval Base', CID C-143, Oversea Sub-Committee, CID.

38. For Balfour's position at the time, see Jason Tomes, *Balfour and Foreign Policy: The International Thought of a Conservative Statesman* (Cambridge: Cambridge University Press, 1997), 238–52.

39. CAB 2/3, minutes, 142nd meeting of the CID, 17 June 1921.

40. See the summary found in CAB 23/26, minutes, CAB 56(21), 30 June 1921; FO 371/6675/F2461/63/23, Curzon to Geddes, telegram 416, 9 July 1921 and repeated Tokyo.

41. There is an enormous literature on the Singapore strategy. Two good reviews of it are Malcolm H. Murfett, 'Living in the Past: A Critical Re-examination of the Singapore Naval Strategy, 1918–1941', *War and Society*, 11(1993), 73–103 and Murfett, 'Reflections on an Enduring Theme: The "Singapore Strategy" at Sixty', in Brian Farrell and Sandy Hunter (eds), *Sixty Years On: The Fall of Singapore Revisited* (Singapore: Eastern Universities Press, 2002), 3–28. In addition, there are some articles that throw light on the topic: Galen Roger Perras, ' "Our Position in the Far East would be Stronger without this Unsatisfactory Commitment": Britain and the Reinforcement of Hong Kong, 1941', *Canadian Journal of History*, 30 (1995), 231–59; Ian Cowman, 'Defence of the Malay Barrier? The Place of the Philippines in Admiralty Naval War Planning, 1925–1941', *War in History*, 4 (1996), 398–417; Cowman, 'Main Fleet to Singapore? Churchill, the Admiralty, and Force Z', *Journal of Strategic Studies*, 18, 1 (1995), 79–93; Christopher Bell, ' "Our Most Exposed Outpost": Hong Kong and British Far Eastern Strategy, 1921–1941', *Journal of Military History*, 60 (1996), 61–88; and, most recently, Bell, 'The "Singapore Strategy" and the Deterrence of Japan: Winston Churchill, the Admiralty and the Dispatch of Force Z', *English Historical Review*, 116 (2001), 604–34. There is a useful recapitulation in Malcolm H. Murfett, John N. Miksic, Brian P. Farrell, Chiang Ming Shun (eds), *Between Two Oceans: A Military History of Singapore from First Settlement to Final British Withdrawal* (Oxford: Oxford University Press, 1999), 145–74. In addition, Bell's book, *The Royal Navy, Seapower and Strategy between the Wars* (London: Frank Cass, 2000) and Ong Chit Chung, *Operation Matador: Britain's War Plans against the Japanese 1918–1941* (Singapore: Times Academic Press, 1997) are essential to a wider understanding of the topic.

42. What follows is based on Treasury Office (hereafter T) 161/800S189171/1, 'Naval Policy and Expenditure', Barstow, 15 June 1921.

43. MSS Eur F 112/219B, Curzon Papers, Eliot to Curzon, personal, 25 August 1921; MSS Eur F 112/220A, Curzon Papers, Hankey to Curzon, 18 October 1921. Geddes had written scathingly about the articles in the American press, which he claimed gave him 'occasional feelings of nausea'; see Geddes to Curzon, 16 September 1931, ibid.

44. CAB 2/3, minutes, 145th and 146th meeting of the CID, 14 and 21 October 1921; CAB 4/7, 'Washington Conference on Limitation of Armament', CID B-277, Lee, 5 October 1921.

45. MSS Eur F 112/220A, Curzon Papers, Balfour to Lloyd George, 11 November 1921; for context, Tomes, *Balfour and Foreign Policy*, 253–7.

46. For Balfour's earlier objections to the Anglo-Japanese Alliance, see ADD MSS 49727, BL, Balfour Papers, Balfour to Lansdowne (British Foreign Secretary), 12 December 1901.

47. MSS Eur F112/220A, Curzon Papers, Hankey to Lloyd George, 11 November 1921; see also, Phillips Payson O'Brien, *British and American Naval Power: Politics and Policy, 1900–1936* (Westport CT: Praeger, 1998), 159–60.

48. For the negotiations and the treaty itself, see Nish, *Alliance in Decline*, 368–82.
49. MSS Eur F 112/220B, Curzon Papers, Hankey to Lloyd George, private and personal, 12 December 1921.
50. MSS Eur F112/224A, Curzon Papers, Eliot to Curzon, 17 March 1922. Eliot was prescient. There was substantial unhappiness, particularly in the Imperial Japanese Navy, with the settlement; see Sadao Asada, 'The Revolt against the Washington Treaty: The Imperial Japanese Navy and Naval Limitation, 1921–1927', *Naval War College Review*, 46 (1993), 82–97; Asada, 'From Washington to London: The Imperial Japanese Navy and the Politics of Naval Limitation', *Diplomacy and Statecraft*, 4 (1993), 147–91.
51. For the whole topic, see Bell, *Royal Navy*, 1–47; Joseph Moretz, *The Royal Navy and the Capital Ship in the Interwar Period: An Operational Perspective* (London: Frank Cass, 2002), 65–102; naval expenditures can be found in Jon T. Sumida, 'British Naval Procurement and Technological Change, 1919–39', in Phillips Payson O'Brien (ed.), *Technology and Naval Combat in the Twentieth Century and Beyond* (London: Frank Cass, 2001), 129.
52. ADM 116/3124, C-in-C China Station to Admiralty, secret, 24 April 1924. Such thinking was despite the fact that the British made contingency plans for a war with the United States; see Christopher M. Bell, 'Thinking the Unthinkable: British and American Naval Strategies for an Anglo-American War, 1918–1931', *International History Review*, 19 (1997), 789–808.
53. ADM 116/3124, 'Most Secret. Strategical Policy' M.00351, Admiralty, February 1923, from which the following quotations come. A good examination of plans for naval war with Japan is Christopher Bell, ' "How are we going to make war?": Admiral Sir Herbert Richmond and British Far Eastern War Plans', *Journal of Strategic Studies*, 20 (1997), 123–41.
54. Ibid.; ADM 1/8616/218, 'Proposed Re-Distribution of the Fleet on Strategic Principles', P.D. 01632/21, Plans Division, Admiralty, April 1921.
55. T 161/800/S18917/1, 'Singapore', Barstow, 20 February 1923.
56. T 161/800/S18917/2, his minute, 1 October 1923, on S. Rowntree (Society of Friends) to Baldwin, 26 September 1923. For the impact of the earthquake, see also CAB 2/4, minutes, 178th meeting CID, 19 December 1923.
57. T 161/800/S18917/1, untitled memorandum, Barstow, 26 February 1924.
58. Ibid., 'Singapore', Barstow, 1 March 1924.
59. John Ferris, 'Treasury Control, the Ten Year Rule and British Service Policies, 1919–1924', *Historical Journal*, 30 (1987), 859–83; for a wider context, see George Peden, *The Treasury and British Public Policy 1906–1959* (Oxford: Oxford University Press, 2000), 170–4; 212–16.
60. For this, see John Robert Ferris, *Men, Money and Diplomacy: The Evolution of British Strategic Foreign Policy, 1919–1926* (Ithaca NY: Cornell University Press, 1989), 142–7.
61. CAB 23/47, minutes, CAB 21(24), 17 March 1924; the quotation is from 'Statement of Policy in Regard to Singapore', J. Ramsay MacDonald; see also CAB 2/4, minutes, 183rd meeting CID, 3 April 1924.
62. CAB 23/49, minutes, CAB 63(24), 24 November 1924; CAB 2/4, minutes, 191st meeting of the CID, 11 December 1924.
63. CAB 2/4, 'Note for Office File', Hankey, 20 November 1924, appended to minutes, 187th meeting of the CID, 28 July 1924.
64. What follows, except where otherwise noted, is based on CAB 2/4, minutes, 193rd meeting of the CID, 5 January 1925.
65. For two looks at Churchill's general views toward Japan in this era, see David MacGregor, 'Former Naval Cheapskate: Chancellor of the Exchequer Winston

Churchill and the Royal Navy, 1924–1929', *Armed Forces and Society*, 19 (1993), 319–34 and Ian Hamil, 'Winston Churchill and the Singapore Naval Base, 1924–1929', *Journal of Southeast Asian Studies*, 11 (1980), 277–86.

66. CAB 23/49, minutes, Cab 16(25), 18 March 1925.
67. The naval issues had been raised in February; see CAB 23/49, minutes, Cab 8(25), 12 February 1925; CAB 24/171, 'Naval Estimates', CP 67(25), Bridgeman, 5 February 1925.
68. CAB 2/4, minutes, 198th meeting of the CID, 30 March 1925; CAB 4/12, 'Development of Imperial Defence Policy in the Far East', CID 244-C, Hankey, Cab 5/5; 'The Economic Power of Japan', CID 553-B, Churchill, 29 December 1924; CAB 24/172, 'Political Outlook in the Far East', CP 139(25), Bridgeman, 5 March 1925; CAB 4/12, 'War and Financial Power', CID 599-B, Churchill, 26 March 1925. An expansion of the Admiralty's arguments can be found in CAB 53/1, minutes, 16th meeting of the Chiefs of Staff (COS) Sub-Committee, 24 February 1925.
69. The Treasury had been suspicious of these additional costs earlier; see T 172/1440, untitled memorandum prepared for Barstow, 31 December 1924,.
70. See the bickering over just how the ten-year rule was to be interpreted and how the one-power standard was to be defined in CAB 2/4, minutes, 199th meeting of the CID, 2 April 1925.
71. CAB 4/12, 'War and Financial Power', CID 599-B, Churchill, 26 March 1925; CAB 53/1, minutes, 18th and 19th meetings of the COS, 5 and 19 May 1925.
72. CAB 53/1, minutes, 21st meeting of the COS, 3 July 1925.
73. CAB 2/4, minutes, 215th meeting of the CID, 22 July 1926.
74. CAB 4/15, 'Imperial Defence Policy. A Review of Imperial Defence, 1926, by the Chiefs of Staff Sub-Committee', CID 701-B, COS, 22 June 1926.
75. CAB 4/14, the Foreign Office's contribution to 'Imperial Defence Policy', CID 700-B, various departments, 15 June 1926.
76. The best study of the Soviet threat is Orest Babij, 'The Making of Imperial Defence Policy in Britain, 1926–1934', Unpublished DPhil thesis, Oxford, 2003, Ch 2. I am obliged to Dr Babij for letting me consult an early draft of his thesis. See also Keith Neilson, ' "Pursued by a Bear": British Estimates of Soviet Military Strength and Anglo-Soviet Relations, 1922–1939', *Canadian Journal of History*, 28 (1993), 190–207.
77. CAB 2/4, minutes, 218th meeting of the CID, 25 November 1926; CAB 4/15, 'Foreign Policy in Relation to Russia and Japan', CID 710-B, W. Tyrrell (PUS, FO), 26 July 1926.
78. What follows, except where otherwise noted, is informed by Tadashi Kuramatsu, 'The Geneva Naval Conference of 1927: The British Preparation for the Conference, December 1926 to June 1927', *Journal of Strategic Studies*, 19 (1996), 104–21; Kuramatsu, 'Viscount Cecil, Winston Churchill and the Geneva Naval Conference of 1927: *Si vis pacem para pacem vs si vis pacem para bellum*', in T.G. Otte and Constantine A. Pagedas (eds), *Personalities, War and Diplomacy: Essays in International History* (London: Frank Cass, 1997), 105–26.
79. 'The Limitation of Armaments and the British Programme of New Construction', Plans Division, Admiralty, 15 November 1926, as cited in Babij, 'Imperial Defence Policy', 72.
80. ADD MSS 51086, BL, Cecil Papers, Salisbury to Cecil, 16 April 1927.
81. The following is based on ADM 116/2607, 'The Total Number and Type of Cruisers Required by the British Empire', secret, 13 April 1928, Roger Bellairs (Director of Plans) and the minutes.
82. T 161/295/S3442/1, 'Three Fallacies', Churchill, 25 June 1927.
83. CAB 2/5, minutes, 228th meeting of the CID, 7 July 1927.
84. CAB 2/5, minutes, 229th meeting of the CID, 14 July 1927.

85. CAB 23/55, minutes, CAB 48(27), 4 August 1927.
86. Unless otherwise noted, this is based on Babij, 'Imperial Defence Policy', 85–91.
87. T 161/285/S.33101/3, minutes (29 December 1927) by W.R. Fraser (Treasury) and (6 January 1928) by Waterfield on Bridgeman (First Lord of the Admiralty) to Churchill, 21 December 1927.
88. For Chamberlain's views, see B.J.C. McKercher, 'A Sane and Sensible Diplomacy: Austin Chamberlain, Japan and the Naval Balance of Power in the Pacific Ocean, 1924–1929', *Canadian Journal of History*, 21 (1986), 187–213.
89. T 161/285/S.33101/3, Bridgeman to Churchill, 21 January 1928 and Waterfield's minute (27 January).
90. T161/285/S.3301/4, for the quarrel, see Bridgeman to Churchill, 23 March 1928 and reply, 25 March.
91. CAB 23/58, minutes, Cab 34(28), 22 June 1928.
92. CAB 2/5, minutes, 236th meeting of the CID, 5 July 1928.
93. CAB 23/58, minutes, Cab 39(28), 18 July 1928.
94. B.J.C. McKercher, 'From Enmity to Cooperation: The Second Baldwin Government and the Improvement of Anglo-American Relations, November 1928–June 1929', *Albion*, 24 (1992), 65–88.
95. CAB 4/17, 'Imperial Defence Policy', CID 900-B, COS, 25 July 1928; T 175/35, an untitled memorandum and the Treasury's minutes on this paper, 15 September 1928, Hopkins Papers; CAB 2/5, Churchill's remarks, 238th meeting of the CID, 8 November 1928.
96. T 161/292S34216, Fisher's minute (21 November) on 'Estimates for Fighting Services 1928', Upcott, 19 November 1928.
97. T 161/800/S18917/6, A.P. Waterfield (head of the Treasury's department dealing with defence) to G.C. Upcott (Deputy Controller of Establishments, Treasury), 10 December 1928.
98. CAB 4/18, 'Imperial Defence Policy: Annual Review', CID B-948, COS, 21 June 1929; T 175/35, Upcott's minute (26 June) on Waterfield's discussion (25 June) of this paper, Hopkins Papers. For the issue of how oil factored into the British defence equation with regard to Japan, see Orest Babij, 'The Royal Navy and Inter-war Plans for War Against Japan: The Problem of Oil Supply', in Greg Kennedy (ed.), *The Merchant Marine in International Affairs, 1850–1950* (London: Frank Cass, 2000), 84–106.
99. CAB 27/407, minutes, 1st meeting FS (29), 25 June 1929.
100. T 161/297/S34610, 'Defence Estimates', Fisher to Snowden, 14 June 1929.
101. T 161/299/S.35171, Fraser's minute (2 July 1929) on Madden's remarks at the 1st meeting of the Fighting Ships Committee.
102. This, and what follows, is based on Orest M. Babij, 'The Second Labour Government and British Maritime Security, 1929–1931', *Diplomacy and Statecraft*, 6 (1995), 645–71.
103. For a recent assertion, see Claire M. Scammel, 'The Royal Navy and the Strategic Origins of the Anglo-German Naval Agreement of 1935', *Journal of Strategic Studies*, 20 (1997), 92–118; for a rebuttal, see Gregory C. Kennedy, 'The 1930 London Naval Conference and Anglo-American Maritime Strength, 1927–1930', in B.J.C. McKercher (ed.), *Arms Limitation and Disarmament: Restraints on War, 1899–1939* (Westport CT: Praeger, 1992), 149–72.
104. See Upcott to Fergusson, 20 January 1930; P.J. Grigg (Chancellor's private secretary) to Upcott, 23 January 1930, both T 172/1693.
105. Babij, 'Second Labour Government', pp. 657–8.
106. Babij, 'Imperial Defence Policy', pp. 117–19. The Treasury had been kept in the dark about Macdonald's agreement with the Admirals; see Waterfield's minute to

Upcott, 5 January 1931 and Upcott to Hopkins, 12 January 1931, where Upcott refers to the Admiralty's building programme and notes that 'they claim [that it] was accepted by the PM', both T 161/492/S.36130, for a similar sentiment, see Waterfield's untitled memorandum, 1 January 1931, T 161/486/S.34610/31.

107. CAB 16/102, 'The Foreign Policy of His Majesty's Government in the United Kingdom', DC(P) 35, Foreign Office, 2 June 1931.

108. CAB 16/102, 'Imperial Defence Preparations – The Basis for Service Estimates', DC(P) 46, secret, Foreign Office, 25 June 1931.

109. CAB 21/2093, 'The Basis of Service Estimates', Hankey, secret, 9 January 1931.

110. Christopher Thorne, *The Limits of Foreign Policy: The West, the League and the Far Eastern Crisis of 1931–33* (New York: Putnam, 1973), 202–73.

111. For a development of this, see Keith Neilson, 'The Defence Requirements Sub-Committee, British Strategic Foreign Policy, Neville Chamberlain and the Path to Appeasement', *English Historical Review*, 158 (June 2003), 651–84.

112. On this, see Greg Kennedy, '1935: A Snapshot of British Imperial Defence in the Far East', in Neilson and Kennedy (eds), *Far Flung Lines*, 190–216; Kennedy, 'Symbol of Imperial Defence: The Role of Singapore in British and American Far Eastern Strategic Relations, 1933–1941', in Farrell and Hunter (eds), *Sixty Years On*, 42–67; Kennedy, *Anglo-American Strategic Relations and the Far East 1933–1939* (London: Frank Cass, 2002) and Keith Neilson, 'Defence and Diplomacy: The British Foreign Office and Singapore, 1939–40', *Twentieth Century British History*, 14, 2 (2003), 138–64.

113. For this, see Neilson, 'Defence Requirements Committee'; Bell, *The Royal Navy*, 26–47; Joseph A. Maiolo, *The Royal Navy and Nazi Germany, 1933–39: A Study in Appeasement and the Origins of the Second World War* (London: Macmillan, 1998).

114. For a clear demonstration of this, see Greg Kennedy, 'Becoming Dependent on the Kindness of Strangers: British Strategic Foreign Policy, Naval Arms Limitation and the Soviet Factor: 1935–1937', *War in History*, 11, 1 (2004), 79–105. I would like to thank Dr Kennedy for letting me read this in manuscript form.

115. Neilson, 'Defence Requirements Sub-Committee'; Gill Bennett, 'British Policy in the Far East 1933–1936: Treasury and Foreign Office', *Modern Asian Studies*, 26 (1992), 545–68; V.H. Rothwell, 'The Mission of Sir Frederick Leith-Ross to the Far East, 1935–1936', *Historical Journal*, 18 (1975), 147–69; Kennedy, *Anglo-American Strategic Relations*, passim.

116. For anti-Americanism, see Greg Kennedy, ' "Rat in Power": Neville Chamberlain and the Creation of British Foreign Policy, 1931–1939', in T.G. Otte (ed.), *The Makers of British Foreign Policy: From Pitt to Thatcher* (Basingstoke: Palgrave, 2002), 173–95; Kennedy, 'Neville Chamberlain and Strategic Relations with the US during his Chancellorship', *Diplomacy and Statecraft*, 13 (2002), 95–120.

117. FO 371/23544/F471/471/61, Craigie (British ambassador, Tokyo) to R.G. Howe (Head, Far Eastern Department, FO), private and secret, 15 December 1938.

118. For the issue of decline, see Paul Kennedy, *The Rise and Fall of British Naval Mastery* (pprbk edn; London: Macmillan, 1983), 267–98; Kennedy, *The Rise and Fall of the Great Powers: Economic Change and Military Conflict from 1500 to 2000* (New York: Random House, 1987), 275–346; John R. Ferris, ' "The Greatest Power on Earth": Great Britain in the 1920s' and B.J.C. McKercher, ' "Our Most Dangerous Enemy": Great Britain Pre-eminent in the 1930s', both *International History Review*, 13 (1991), 726–50; 751–83.

4

WHAT WORTH THE AMERICANS? THE BRITISH STRATEGIC FOREIGN POLICY-MAKING ELITE'S VIEW OF AMERICAN MARITIME POWER IN THE FAR EAST, 1933–1941

Greg Kennedy

The mental map possessed by one nation's strategic foreign policy-making elite of another nation's willingness and ability to wage war is a mosaic within which many questions are asked.[1] What is the state of the nation's economic strength, national will, security interests, public opinion, industrial capacity, military capability, and what do the members of its strategic policy-making elite believe? The perceptions held about these various categories by one nation's strategic policy-making elite concerning another are at the root of the conduct of what is known as international relations. They are the key elements with which each nation constructs its own strategic foreign policy.[2] That strategic foreign policy is a reflection of both a nation's own strategic position, interacting with both domestic and external pressures being created by foreign Powers, and internal political conditions. Within this context, in the eight years leading up to the outbreak of a general war in the Far East on 7 December 1941, the British strategic foreign policy-making elite continuously assessed the real and potential worth of the United States as a maritime power in that region.[3] The questions being asked by the British were those of what the North American giant's role in the Pacific was and how that role was linked to Britain's strategic position there. Was America a solid maritime ally, a fair-weather friend, competitor or neutral, and, if any of these, to what degree?

That British elite was made up of many shifting, interconnected, competing and complementary parts. The most important of the governmental agencies involved in the on-going strategic assessment process were the Foreign Office, the Admiralty and the Treasury.[4] The most important aspect of the British mental-mapping process of the American place in the Far Eastern balance-of-power relationship, and the most difficult for British observers to evaluate with great confidence or accuracy, was the question of American will and resolve. Would the United States use its large naval and enormous industrial/economic power to deter Japan? If deterrence failed, would the US bring that vast potential power into a Far Eastern conflict? Would the American objectives in such an act be parallel, if not equal, to British imperial defence interests? Was the opportunity of the possibility of an Anglo-American understanding concerning a combined maritime strategy for the Far East a candle worth pursuing?[5]

Even if answers are thought to be apparent, what of the co-ordination of the various bodies involved in the creation of a strategic foreign policy? In the British case, the Committee of Imperial Defence, as well as the Parliamentary Cabinet system, were co-ordinating bodies that should have provided a coherent fusion of the varied assessments.[6] The reality was, however, that there was no 'amalgamated' solution to the question of worth. The Admiralty, FO, and Treasury all held their opinions, rightly or wrongly, for noble reasons and not, for reasons of personal gain, domestic political leverage, interdepartmental rivalry and ignorance.[7] The reality of the various frictions at work within this process meant that there was no one homogenous British view of the worth of the United States as a possible maritime ally in the Far East.[8] There were three separate views, which in some places, through events and individuals, coincided and allowed policy toward the United States to be made through consensus. In many situations, however, there was consensus, or at least a grudging willingness for cooperation, between two of the three departments against the views of the third. And, more often than not, each group went about its creation of policies concerning the United States in the Far East in an unco-ordinated and separate way, ensuring that nothing approaching a coherent and comprehensive 'American policy' could be produced.[9]

It is important, therefore, to understand when co-ordination and cooperation in the pursuit of an American policy was achieved; when it was not; which departments aligned with another and why; as well as to have an understanding of the importance of individuals in this very human process of assessing the worth of the Americans.[10] It is only by understanding the differences, as well as the commonalities, that an overall picture of what the majority of opinion was in the British strategic foreign policy-making elite. Even then, the majority may not have been powerful enough to carry forward their case, and powerful individuals or groups within the cabinet system could invalidate any judgements made by the majority.[11] Therefore, it is safest to say that, as far as the question of what worth the Americans were in the Far East as a potential maritime ally against Japan, within the British strategic foreign policy-making elite, opinions differed.

The Treasury

In 1933, the Treasury's view of the United States as a potential ally was one of mistrust and, at times, of outright loathing.[12] The reasons for this were threefold. The first was the tense economic relations that existed between the two nations over such issues as monetary policy, silver versus gold standard, the British repayment of War Debts to the United States and a host of other international finance issues.[13] Second, and in some way deriving from the on-going conflicts arising from the first point, there was the influence of key high-level Treasury officials who held rabid anti-American views. As well, Neville Chamberlain, the Chancellor of the Exchequer, was unimpressed with the abilities of the new American President, Franklin D. Roosevelt, and in particular with his radical economic policies.[14] While Chancellors of the Exchequer could come and go, the permanent Treasury officials ensured a continuity of approach to the question of the United States and its strategic relations with Britain. The three most important permanent officials were Sir Warren Fisher, Permanent Secretary to the Treasury and Head of the Civil Service; Sir Frederick Leith Ross, deputy controller of finance; and Sir Richard Hopkins, controller of finance. All held similar views concerning the untrustworthiness of the United States in international affairs, and those views mirrored Neville Chamberlain's.[15] Therefore, among the major personalities involved at the highest level in the Treasury there was a consensus: the United States was no friend of Great Britain's.[16] Last, there was the issue of the Treasury's support for international naval arms limitation and disarmament, an approach that competed with American attempts to build bigger cruisers and perhaps a larger fleet after 1933. For years, the Treasury had been a supporter of the Washington Naval Treaty system. The reason for that support was that the system provided a capital ship building holiday and, therefore, ensured that there were no undue demands on the Treasury for major naval construction. As well, the treaty system set ratios for lesser vessels, thus limiting the demands that the Admiralty could put on the Treasury for future building programmes in the areas of cruisers, destroyers and submarines. The United States was seen as being a possible threat to this system, for if they built ships that either created new classes, or violated the capital ship building holiday, or created a race in cruiser building, the Admiralty would have to follow suit.[17] These fears permeated the Treasury's assessment of the United States as a maritime power. Therefore, when one looks at how the British Treasury viewed the United States as a maritime Power, the term maritime Power is linked not only to the physical ships and their capabilities, but also to questions of economic power and confidence, as well as demonstrations of national will.

Sir Richard Hopkins reflected that combination of frustration and uncertainty that was the British Treasury's attitude toward Roosevelt's United States. On 5 May 1933, Hopkins informed Chamberlain that Britain could not trust the new American administration either to be competent in economic matters or to keep of secrets. In his view, it was '...important to remember that the President is surrounded by a second eleven of amateurs and irregulars where secrecy cannot be relied upon: only Feiss is a regular. Warberg, Bullitt and even Moley must be distrusted on this score'.[18] At the same time, Hopkins and others at the Treasury were attempting to find a way of dealing with the growing demand for increased British defence spending for the Far East. With Japanese aggression in Manchukuo seen as proof of Tokyo's determination to use military force to acquire a greater presence in the region, the Committee of Imperial Defence (CID) witnessed continued requests by the Royal Navy for increased basing facilities at Singapore, as well as considerations for more aircraft, airfields, and both coastal and anti-aircraft gun batteries. The Treasury refused to believe that relations with Japan were as serious as the Chiefs of Staff (COS) were prone to make out.[19] Hopkins and company agreed that the Chiefs of the various military services were all too ready to create an emergency where there was none, in an attempt to stampede the Treasury into giving extra funding for the construction of naval bases, such as Singapore, and the attendant squadrons and garrisons that would have to be a part of the base.[20] This had a basis in foreign policy. Without a maritime alliance in the Pacific, such as the now defunct Anglo-Japanese Alliance of 1902, Britain had no major Pacific maritime power formally allied to assisting in the defence of imperial interests in the region. Therefore, greater spending by Great Britain on its own defensive systems in the theatre was required. While some believed that the United States and its growing maritime strength could help offset Britain's maritime liability in the region, the Treasury was not convinced that this was at all likely. They preferred a change of foreign policy that would once again see a formal ally signed on to the idea of defended British interests in the Far East.

Neville Chamberlain brought the Treasury's longing for a return to the good old days of the Anglo-Japanese Alliance to the attention of the CID in early November, 1933. He informed it that, while British defence preparations, particularly naval preparation, did not and should not take the United States into account as a potential adversary, those same preparations also could not count on that nation being an ally.[21] Sir Maurice Hankey, Secretary of the CID, had explained to Chamberlain the nature of the conditions of the Washington Naval Agreement and the advantages Britain gained navally from the existing condition, but the Chancellor was unconvinced. In fact, Chamberlain was unwilling to alienate Japan as a potential friend in the Far East for the promise of closer relations with the United States. In Chamberlain's view, Japan was not to be accorded as great a priority as a potential enemy as the COS imagined and Britain's contingency planning for a crisis in the Far East could not rely on the United States using its maritime power in support of British interests.[22] Smarting from the international embarrassment and disappointment arising from their encounter with the new Roosevelt administration at the World Economic Conference, Chamberlain and the Treasury were adamant that Britain should not have its strategic foreign policy dictated by American considerations. Thus, in naval disarmament and defence matters, the Treasury allowed Britain's economic interaction with the United States to provide the tone for that department's response to considerations of Anglo-American maritime relations.[23] That anti-American attitude would travel from the CID deliberations to the subcommittee set up by that body to investigate Great Britain's imperial defence position and requirements in the period after 1933: the Defence Requirements Sub-Committee (DRC). The importance of the new subcommittee for understanding the Treasury view of the worth of the United States as a maritime power in the Pacific is due to the fact that the DRC was '...the arena in which British strategic foreign policy was threshed out among competing interests with competing views and, most importantly, the body whose decisions largely determined the path that British strategic defence policy took in the years until 1939'.[24]

The DRC deliberations revealed a number of Treasury views concerning the United States and that department's view of the United States as a potential maritime partner in the Pacific. The two main issues revolved around any future naval disarmament agreements: whether or not the position of the United States was to be considered any more valid than the Japanese calls for naval expansion, and the question of the isolationist attitude of the US. Warren Fisher, the Treasury's representative on the DRC, wasted little time in trying to cast the United States in a negative light. Fisher began his assault on Anglo-American maritime relations by arguing that Britain's acceptance of American naval parity, and the Washington system in general, was a mistake: 'Our policy in the past had been to bow down to America, and Japan doubtless believed that we were now a backboneless nation.'[25] He contended that Britain's security in the Far East lay in a combination economic appeasement and an independent maritime policy that did not give the appearance of following an American lead.[26] Fisher, espousing the Treasury's overall view, believed that Japan was the major maritime power in the Far East, and would be for some time to come. If Japan could once more be brought into an understanding with Great Britain over the balance of power in that region, all would be well. Therefore, if the United States objected to Japan's demand for naval parity with Great Britain and the United States at the upcoming 1935 London Naval Conference, so be it. Britain, Fisher asserted, would be unwise to side with the Americans in disputing the Japanese claim. Instead

> ...it is essential in my view to get clear of our 'entangling' agreement with the USA who should be left to circle the globe with ships if they want, to gratify their vanity by singing 'Rule Columbia, Columbia rules the waves', and to wait and see for how many years the politically all-powerful Middle West will continue to acquiesce in paying a fantastic bill related to not real requirement but primarily to indulge the braggadocio of Yahoodom.[27]

Fisher and the Treasury did not believe that the depression-ravaged United States would respond to any resultant Japanese building programme with a naval construction programme of their own. Indeed, their view was that mid-western

American farmers would take great exception to the idea of having vast sums of federal money spent on naval armaments.[28]

The Treasury's ideal for a solution to the Far Eastern problem was to '... envisage an ultimate policy of accommodation and friendship with Japan and an immediate and provisional policy of "showing a tooth" for the purpose of recovering the standing which we have sacrificed in our post-War period of subservience to the USA'.[29] To do this meant getting back to the conditions of the pre-First World War relationship between Japan and Great Britain. While a return to a formal Anglo-Japanese treaty was a non-starter for a number of reasons, the Treasury believed in the '... necessity of getting back to something like our former relations with Japan; and that, as a stage in this process, we must remove the Japanese opinion that we are (a) materially defenceless and (b) morally spineless sycophants of the U.S.A.'.[30] Moreover, Fisher wished the DRC to admit that the Americans were interested in using the Washington Treaty System only to keep Britain and Japan on awkward terms, and as a means of avoiding having to actually build a major Pacific fleet that would command Japan's respect:

> The American interest in these naval pacts is, in my belief, to keep us on bad terms with the Japanese (and therefore potentially weaker and less able to take an independent line vis-à-vis the USA), and to limit their own expenditure against the bogy which their imaginings make of Japan. As the USA thinks of a first-class war in terms of Japan, she would of course like us involved on her side. (To get us in the meantime to pick the Asiatic chestnuts of the USA out of the fire is a useful preliminary)... If then we emancipate ourselves from thraldom to the USA (who as an institution – and indeed from Colonial days – never has been friendly to us and never will be) and thus free ourselves to establish durable relations with Japan, we can concentrate on the paramount danger at our very threshold.[31]

This was indeed the Treasury policy toward Anglo-American maritime relations throughout the rest of 1934. Although this view was not adopted as the British Government's policy toward the situation in the Far East or as part of the overall recommendations of the DRC's final report, it remained the Treasury's preferred approach, and the Treasury did not relinquish the hope that it could eventually bend the will of the Cabinet and the Service Chiefs to it.

The next opportunity for the Treasury to put forward their case was during the preparations for the Second London Naval Conference, due to commence in the autumn of 1935. In an attempt to wrest control of the preparations for the naval conference from the Admiralty and the Foreign Office, the two departments traditionally charged with overseeing the formulation of Great Britain's policy in such matters, Chamberlain deliberately attempted to increase the Treasury's role in the pre-conference preparations. Stung by continued altercations with the

Americans over the war-debt issue and trade negotiations, Chamberlain hoped to swing opinion in the CID and Cabinet around to the Treasury point of view regarding the unworthiness of the United States as a benevolent neutral in the Far East versus the benefits of a benevolent, activist Japan.[32] In particular, in the light of the DRC's recommendations for defence preparations, and their associated costs, the Treasury hoped that placating Japan and ignoring the United States would alleviate the need for the naval construction and modernization programmes that seemed to be in the offing.[33] Chamberlain argued that better relations with Japan solved a number of Great Britain's imperial defence dilemmas, while any move closer to the American position of limiting Japanese naval power, or appearing to offer to 'pull the American chestnuts out of the fire...', only further jeopardized Britain's strategic position.[34] To the Cabinet he declared the Treasury view on the situation to be that

> ...we should decline to align ourselves with Washington; indicate that we were not prepared to submit ourselves to the limitations of a Treaty, and say we did not mind what America chose to build...At the same time we might go to Japan and say that we had not linked ourselves with America. If this were done Japan would be free from the fear that we might be united with America against her...What we risked by good relations with Japan was (1) trade, (2) deterioration of our relations with America. As to trade, he thought the difficulties were not insurmountable. As to America, what were we going to lose? He doubted if the pursuit of friendly relations with Japan was inconsistent with good relations with the United States.[35]

Some of the Cabinet supported taking this road. But, most importantly, Prime Minister Ramsay MacDonald did not. He was not alone. Pushed by the continued Treasury efforts to gain better relations with Japan at the expense of Anglo-American maritime relations, the Admiralty and FO had come together to try to thwart the Treasury demands for a change in the strategic foreign policy regarding Far Eastern affairs. To the Foreign Office and Admiralty, the British position at the 1935 London Naval Conference was not one of appeasement toward Japan, but rather one of cautious cooperation with the United States on naval disarmament and future Far Eastern maritime strategic questions.[36] They were successful. Defeated by the combined political weight of the Prime Minister, Admiralty and FO, the Treasury would not be able to mount another serious attack on the primacy of Anglo-American maritime relations in imperial defence matters related to the Far East until Neville Chamberlain became Prime Minister in early 1937.[37]

Chamberlain's time in the Treasury, and his attempts to move Britain's strategic foreign policy for the Far East toward the Japanese and away from closer ties with the Americans, had created in the Chancellor a deep animosity toward the FO. That department had been instrumental in thwarting a number of his pro-Japanese plans, and had differed with him in many other foreign policy areas as well, including how to deal with Germany and Italy.[38] In fact, Chamberlain believed that the FO was obstructionist, anti-German, anti-Italian, and certainly anti-Chamberlain, stating that 'I am not too happy about the F.O. who seem to me to have no imagination & no courage'.[39] It was unsurprising, therefore, that upon his becoming Prime Minister in May 1937, the ex-Chancellor of the Exchequer was prepared to make the Foreign Office bow to his will on this matter. However, Prime Minister Chamberlain met with no more success than had Chancellor Chamberlain on the issue. Indeed, his attempts to move closer to the Japanese and further from the Americans cost him a Foreign Secretary, when Anthony Eden (picked by Chamberlain for that office because he believed that Eden was a man who would bend when required) resigned over the Prime Minister's treatment of President Roosevelt and the United States' initiatives aimed at closer strategic cooperation.[40] While the final straw for Eden came in the form of Chamberlain's attitude toward Italy in Abyssinia, the crux for the Foreign Secretary was that the Prime Minister's appeasement of Italy threatened to destroy the closer Anglo-American relations that had been growing over the preceding few years and, in particular, to tear apart the American mental map regarding Britain's strategic foreign policy and its determination to resist aggression in the Far East.[41]

Still, unable to move the FO or the Admiralty toward his view of the worth of the Americans in the Far East, Chamberlain explored other avenues for trying to bring his plans to fruition. One of the Prime Minister's seeds for a possible rapprochement was the planting of Sir Robert Craigie, long-time FO naval disarmament negotiator, to the post of British Ambassador to Japan.[42] Craigie had proven himself a capable and tenacious defender of British naval power in his role as the Foreign Office's, and in large part Britain's, main naval negotiator from 1930 until 1937. More importantly for the Chamberlain/Treasury point of view, Craigie had always been careful to not alienate the Japanese in these various negotiations, and understood the implications of the various naval agreements and Britain's maritime situation in the Far East as well as any other civil servant.[43] Sent by Chamberlain to try to find some middle ground, using naval arms limitation as a possible entrée, with the Japanese and to circumvent the 'obstructionist' and 'anti-Japanese' FO, Craigie became another string in the Chamberlain bow. Unfortunately for the Prime Minister, this new avenue was also thwarted by the FO/Admiralty combination, and continued attempts by Craigie to move Britain's strategic foreign policy away from a pro-US stance to a pro-Japanese stance were unsuccessful.[44]

By September 1939, with continued acts of aggression in the Far East being perpetrated by Japan, with a war in Europe now commanding the British policy-making elites' full attention, and the United States seen as a valued potential ally, or, at worst a benevolent neutral, the Treasury's policy of trying to appease Japan and marginalize the maritime worth of the United States and its vastly improved fleet in the Pacific had come to an end. The need to do so was driven home with great clarity during the Tientsin crisis in June–July 1939. When the British settlement there prevented Japanese military police from arresting four Chinese men suspected of murder, Japan used the incident to pressure Britain into acknowledging that nation's dominance in the region. Walter Runciman, now Lord Privy Seal, advised Chamberlain that, with regard to Britain's ability to project maritime power into the Far East,

> At this morning Cabinet Committee I gathered...that the Chiefs of Staff Report made it most unadvisable for us to risk war with the Japs, in the absence of full support from the USA, partly because of the Japs comparative strength and partly because the Axis powers are looking on with malicious intent. Our naval forces are not large enough to perform successfully in two theatres simultaneously...In the absence of a certain promise of active naval and military help from the USA my view is emphatically against any step calculated to lead to war. For us to adopt a pugnacious attitude in the present position would be most imprudent and might indeed be suicidal...If ultimately we are to be effective in our use of the Fleet it will be wiser of us to look after the European position first of all, and when we are secure in this theatre we can later on deal with the Japanese navy. That I submit is the correct order. With the USA on our side, and provided we played up to neutral opinion, I would go ahead, but to go to war with our present divided forces, without the active cooperation of the USA would in my judgement be disastrous and I could not accept any responsibility for this course.[45]

Clearly, the views of Neville Chamberlain and the Treasury, regarding the worth of the United States as a maritime power in the Far East, had not withstood the tests of time or circumstances between 1933 and 1939. What then were the views and arguments of the Admiralty and Foreign Office regarding the United States' worth that had for over six years held Neville Chamberlain and the Treasury at bay?

The Admiralty

The Admiralty's assessment of the worth of the USN in the Pacific grew after the election of Franklin D. Roosevelt as President of the United States.[46] Under the Roosevelt administration, new money and funds were put into the USN in the form of new ships, new building programmes, new bases, such as Pearl Harbor, which was the catalyst for the mobilization of the American west coast to support greater naval efforts in the Pacific.[47] Admiralty observers in England, the United States, China and Japan provided a steady flow of information regarding the technological, logistical and temperamental state of the USN. This data went to the Cabinet and other strategic policy makers, filtered through the CID, the Chiefs of Staff (COS) and their various subcommittees, the Admiralty's own planning and intelligence departments, and such multi-departmental intelligence organizations as the Industrial Intelligence Committee (IIC) and the Joint

Intelligence Committee (JIC).[48] At all levels, the Admiralty's main concern was to assess the United States Navy's combat capability in the Pacific. It was also concerned with the on-going debate regarding the willingness of the US and the USN to act in concert, formally or informally, with British interests to check Japanese expansionism via maritime policies.

In the highest circles of the Admiralty, a policy of wooing the USN and the new American President were in place by the spring of 1933. No serious commentator within the RN contemplated meeting the USN in any future battle. What concerned the Admiralty during the 1920s and 1930s was whether the USN would choose to become a catalyst for a new naval construction race, or see that the two English-speaking navies would accommodate each other in the post-First World War world. Tellingly, in all legitimate British naval planning for the Pacific, the United States was factored in, either as a benevolent neutral or an ally of some degree.[49] Admiral Sir Reginald Ernle-Earle-Plunket-Drax, Sir Oswyn A.R. Murray (Director of Naval Intelligence, DNI), Rear Admiral G.C. Dickens, Admiral Sir John Kelly (Commander in Chief, CinC, of the China Squadron until February, 1933), and Admiral Sir Frederic C. Dreyer (CinC China Squadron after Kelly) were all openly supportive of any policy that moved the RN and USN closer together in the Far East. As part of a general Admiralty policy they worked, at both the formal and informal levels, to create as cooperative and congenial a relationship between the two navies as possible.[50] However, the key figure in transmitting the Admiralty's assessment of the United States as a maritime power in the Far East to the Cabinet and higher bodies rested in the hands of the First Sea Lord, Admiral Sir A. Ernle M. Chatfield.[51]

While the majority of Admiralty opinion was in favour of closer Anglo-American naval relations, the question of how far those relations would go and what form they would take were crucial strategic questions for Chatfield.[52] In the CID and COS committees, he was constantly aware of the weakness of Britain's maritime position in the Far East. He was also aware, however, that political views were split within the British strategic foreign policy-making elite, and that openly alienating Chamberlain and the Treasury could be a very dangerous manoeuvre, particularly if the RN required increased funding for new building programmes and base improvements, such as those required in Singapore.[53] Chatfield was concerned that, until the Singapore base was completed and either new fleet units procured or a naval arms limitation system that included Japan, Great Britain and the United States was assured, Great Britain could not afford to antagonize Japan needlessly. At the same time, he recognized the strategic reality that, in all likelihood, the only deterrent Japan would respect was the threat of a combined Anglo-American maritime response.[54] Furthermore, he saw the naval rearmament of Great Britain and the United States as the only possible safeguard against Japanese expansion: 'The civilised nations of the world have risen to power over the uncivilised. This is not due to their numerical strength or entirely to their fighting qualities but to their skill in devising and using weapons of war. What the Pacifist says now is "you are not to so use that intelligence but are to do away with the wonderful weapons that your scientific knowledge has produced". If that happens it will mean that the world will no longer be ruled by the most intelligent nations but by the most numerous.'[55] Thus, Chatfield and the Admiralty came to the DRC deliberations with some answers regarding imperial defence issues, but on naval elements regarding the defence of the British interests in the Far East, there were more questions than answers.

The crux of the problem for the Admiralty was the unknown factor represented by the upcoming Second London Naval Conference. If Japan left the Washington system and decided to begin unrestricted naval construction, what then? Did the RN build alone, to create a deterrent to the Japanese, or was the solution to be found in an agreement with the now provoked and alarmed United States, who would view such actions by the Japanese as a direct threat to American security interests in the theatre and thus move closer to the British strategic view of conditions in that region? However, if the USN built capital ships Japan would as well. Such capital-ship escalation would dictate that Great Britain would also have to build such vessels, thus trapping the RN in a 'build or lose parity with the United States' dilemma that was primarily driven by Japanese actions.[56] During the DRC discussions, it was clear that Chatfield was not confident that the United States' maritime power would be used to Great Britain's advantage. He also felt that good relations with Japan were desirable. However, unlike the Treasury, he was not willing to undertake any actions or appeasement that threatened to make Japan a friend at the expense of making America an angry neutral.[57]

Chatfield was mindful of the split in opinion that existed in Cabinet over whether or not Japan should take precedence over America. Not willing to take sides in the swirling waters that surrounded the construction of British imperial defence policy in the spring of 1934, and suspicious of the United States and its navy's motives and willingness to engage Japan in the Pacific, the First Sea Lord worked to stay in step with both the Treasury and the Foreign Office. Writing to Warren Fisher about the DRC deliberations, and in particular the difference of opinion between Fisher and Vansittart over the place of the United States versus Japan in Britain's strategic planning mental map, Chatfield stated that

> We all feel we want to foster really sound relations with Japan and the only difference between you and Van about that is whether it can be done without antagonising the USA and China. The answer to that seems to me to be to move slowly and carefully, but nevertheless to move. We are in a remarkable position of not wanting to quarrel with anybody because we have got most of the world already, or the best parts of it, and we only want to keep what we have got and prevent others from taking it away from us... While, therefore, I am in favour of being as friendly with Japan as possible and letting her know it I do not want that to be looked on as a reason for reducing our Naval world power... I agree with Van to the extent that we do not want to propitiate Japan at the expense of a hostile and jealous United States. At the same time I am

entirely with you that we do not want to tie ourselves as we have done in the past to the United States, because she is unreliable and does not know her own mind and her statesmen do not know the mind of their own country. Nothing that is said by the President or any of their Statesmen can ever be accepted at more than its face value, as we all know ... The one thing which causes all the trouble is the endeavour to make military agreements to limit arms. That is why I should like to see the attempt to make Naval agreements abandoned and substitute for them political understanding, leaving each Nation free to build what she wants. If Japan will not agree to her 5:3 ratio the best thing is to beg to differ and to part on that attempt without quarrelling over it ... There are inherent differences between us and the United States over Naval matters and I do not see how we can get agreement with them unless they are willing to sacrifice their pride.[58]

However, in the aftermath of the DRC recommendations, the actions of Neville Chamberlain and the Treasury in paring down the Royal Navy's funding for the projected programmes caused a serious rift between the Admiralty and the Treasury.[59] Chatfield's view was that, '... if the Chancellor's views are supported we shall have come to the parting of the ways as regards Imperial Defence. A bogus navy inadequate to its responsibilities is not one which any Admiralty could, in my opinion, be responsible for'.[60] The preparations for, and the conduct of, the British naval position regarding the 2nd London Naval Conference would ensure that the gap between the Admiralty and Treasury views concerning Britain's imperial maritime strategy in the Far East widened. In fact, those events would culminate in the creation of an Admiralty/FO vision concerning the worth of the Americans as a maritime power in the Far East that would govern Great Britain's imperial maritime strategy for the Far East until the outbreak of war in 1939.[61]

Chatfield, like the Foreign Office, had little faith in the London Conference's actually reaching any viable conclusion. It was the Admiralty's view that Japan was unwilling to accept anything less than naval parity with the United States and Great Britain, and, as the United States and Great Britain were unwilling to allow such a change to the Washington Treaty, it was most likely that there would be no treaty.[62] However, the First Sea Lord was willing to hedge his bets in late 1934, allowing his negative views of the United States' need for maintaining such a large navy to be used by Warren Fisher and Chamberlain as fodder for the Treasury argument for pursuing Japan.[63] However, it soon became apparent that, despite some similarities between Chatfield's personal views and those of certain members of the Treasury (in particular their common belief in the utility of an maritime appeasement policy toward Japan),[64] official Admiralty policy would not take that route. By 1936, when the naval talks in London were complete, the growing strength of the American navy, continued aggressive acts by Japan in the Far East, and a refusal of the Cabinet to endorse a conference policy that favoured the Japanese position over that of the United States, ensured that the Admiralty was solidly united with the Foreign Office in its pursuit of better Anglo-American Far Eastern relations.[65] In the aftermath of the 2nd London Naval Conference, with the Admiralty now taking a leading position in working for closer Anglo-American naval relations, support for such an initiative was provided by many high-ranking British strategic policy makers.

In February 1937, Hankey prepared a briefing note for Walter Runciman, the President of the Board of Trade, who had recently returned from a visit to the United States where he had held discussions with President Roosevelt regarding Anglo-American trade.[66] Hankey's summary, created at Runciman's request in response to FDR's talks with him about the limitation of naval bases in the Pacific, illustrated the evolving, connected nature of American and British maritime interests in that area. Hankey's note pointed out that Britain and America had a need for such bases if their respective maritime power was to be projected into the Far East. Without effective American and British naval basing systems, Japan would be able to dominate naval operations in the theatre. Hankey advocated Runciman's supporting any lead President Roosevelt made concerning the issue of continuing Article XIX of the Washington Naval Treaty, the article limiting naval base construction, but only if Japan was to be included in the negotiations.[67] Given the open and amicable nature of the talks and the relationship established by Runciman with Roosevelt, there can be little doubt that Anglo-American naval relations in the Far East received a substantial hearing during their discussions.[68] Hankey's response to the Roosevelt probe reflected the cautious and involved nature of trying to move Anglo-American naval relations closer, while at the same time respecting the Treasury/Chamberlain demands that Japan not be unnecessarily excluded from any maritime initiatives. After July 1937, in the aftermath of the Japanese invasion of China, the sinking of the American gunboat *Panay*, and the strafing and wounding of the British Ambassador to China, Sir Hughe M. Knatchbull-Hugesson, there was very little material for those who called for closer ties with Japan to work with.

The Admiralty's appreciation of the worth of the United States as a maritime power in the Pacific increased rapidly and steadily throughout 1938 and 1939. American requests for information regarding the capability of Singapore to support fleet units, Anglo-American plans for joint exercises in the Far East, increased sharing of information on each nation's ability to read Japanese naval and diplomatic codes, as well as an increased flow and exchange of technical naval information, all brought Anglo-American maritime relations closer.[69] The IIC, and the JIC were able to give an accurate appreciation of the maritime power of the United States, and, in particular, that nation's ability to project such power into the Pacific. The speed and scale of the creation of naval support facilities on the American West Coast, as well as the completion of Pearl Harbor as a main fleet base, had added to the belief that the United States was taking Far Eastern matters very seriously, an event that would in all likelihood be beneficial to British interests in that region.[70] In October 1938, Britain and the Royal Navy offered the USN the use of Singapore as a base for operations in the event of any joint actions being required in early 1939.[71] In the spring of 1939, President Roosevelt had agreed to send the American Fleet back to the Pacific early, from exercises in the Atlantic, confirming to the once-sceptical Chatfield, now Minister for the Co-ordination of Defence, that America's maritime presence in the Far East was indeed of great worth to British strategic planning for the Far East. Finally, in June 1939, following earlier exchanges regarding naval planning for the Pacific in 1938, a secret British delegate (T.C. Hampton, Captain RN) travelled to Washington to meet with a small circle of senior American naval officers. During those talks, the USN representatives informed Hampton that if a war in Europe broke out, it was President Roosevelt's intention to send the US Fleet to Pearl Harbor to act as a deterrent, while the RN concentrated in home waters and the Atlantic.[72]

Following the outbreak of the general war in Europe and the resulting British strategic maritime setbacks that followed in 1939–40, particularly the fall of France and the loss of the French Fleet for Britain's naval planning purposes, the USN continued to grow in importance for Britain's Far Eastern imperial defence.[73] That process was only a modification, however, of the strong, informed optimism with which the Admiralty, as a part of the British strategic maritime policy-making elite, had viewed the United States from 1935 onward.[74] The realities and events of the actual war in Europe, and eventually the Far East, only confirmed that that risk, optimism and trust had been well placed. Sir Ronald Lindsay, the British Ambassador in Washington, reported back to the FO and Admiralty that Anglo-American strategic maritime relations were now such that any war in the Far East would be an Anglo-American affair, '... as the present Chief of Naval Operations has stated that he does not consider it likely that the United States would be at war with Japan without the United Kingdom being equally at war with the Japanese, this perhaps explains why the Navy Department do not seem particularly nervous about fortifying Guam'.[75] The Admiralty was not, however, the central department concerned with the maintenance of good Anglo-American maritime relations throughout the period under review. Nor was it the part of the policy-making elite which had led the call for British strategic defence planning for the Far East to take greater account of the worth of the United States as a maritime power.

The Foreign Office

The key department within that policy-making elite was the Foreign Office, which, not always uniformly but consistently, argued from 1933 until the outbreak of the war in the Pacific in 1941 that Britain's interests in the Far East could be pro-tected only by a balance of power.[76] And within that balance of power, as far as maritime strategy was concerned, the United States held the key to British success or failure.[77] Maritime power was the determining factor in any conflict with Japan. British interests in China could be protected by diplomacy, trade, Chinese and Russian influences.[78] However, to protect British interests in Hong

Kong, Malaya, Singapore, Australia and New Zealand meant having superior maritime forces. Throughout the 1930s the Foreign Office, and in particular its Permanent Under Secretary, Sir Robert Vansittart, argued for British naval rearmament.[79] However, the FO also realized that British maritime power alone, given the global nature of imperial defence, would not suffice in any conflict where the Empire faced more than one protagonist at a time.[80] As well, the department understood both the certainty that relations with Japan would be irreparably ruptured if any formal Anglo-American naval bloc were created, and the reality of the lack of desire in both English-speaking nations for such an open alignment due to domestic political constraints.[81] However, and despite this, at the informal level, closer Anglo-American strategic maritime relations were the preferred order of the day between 1934 and 1939, with events from 1939 to 1941 rapidly and assuredly moving the two Powers ever closer together in terms of the acceptance of common mental maps concerning the strategic situation in the Far East and the use of maritime force within that theatre.

Having won the battles within the British strategic foreign policy-making elite for control over the ranking of American maritime power in British strategic planning for the Pacific in the DRC deliberations and during preparations for the 2nd London Naval Conference, the Foreign Office's main task, from 1936 until the outbreak of war in 1939, was to continue to provide evidence that their assessment remained the correct evaluation of the situation.[82] On matters regarding Japanese building programmes, intelligence reports concerning Japanese military and naval intentions, and concerning possible areas of informal cooperation between the USN and RN, the FO acted as a go-between and interpreter. Using the embassies in Japan, China, Washington and London as conduits for providing and obtaining vital information, the FO worked to ensure a synchronization of the British and American mental maps concerning maritime factors in the Far East.[83] Japan's invasion of China, in July 1937, made the need to achieve this more apparent to all, but the rise to power of Neville Chamberlain as Prime Minister dictated that the FO would have to redouble its efforts to prevent the ex-Chancellor of the Exchequer from alienating the thriving Anglo-American maritime relationship.[84] Fortunately, even trusted Chamberlain men such as Sir Walter Runciman, President of the Board of Trade, had to admit that Anglo-American strategic relations were clearly improved. In particular, while on a trip to the United States in January 1937, Runciman reported that 'There is a strong desire here for exchange of information even of a very secret nature between United States Government departments and those of His Majesty's Government'.[85] The Admiralty, guided through these diplomatic channels by the FO, was keen to enhance its standing with Roosevelt by providing the requested information.[86]

While better economic relations between the two nations were a part of that improvement, much of the increased confidence on the part of the US President was a result of strengthened and evolving parallel maritime relations. By the time the Brussels Conference was called in the autumn of 1937 to discuss possible global responses to the Japanese invasion of China that July, both British and

American delegates were certain of each other's position and trusted the other not to try to push them into an uncomfortable leadership role with respect to Japan. As for specific British observations of the willingness of the United States to work with Great Britain in the Far East, the way that the conference evolved consolidated the belief in Anthony Eden's mind that closer Anglo-American relations regarding the Far East and the use of maritime power were a reality.[87] Eden's faith in that relationship was confirmed by the reportage of the new British Ambassador in Tokyo, Sir Robert Craigie, concerning the messages being sent from Tokyo to Washington by Craigie's American counterpart, Joseph Grew.[88] The American Ambassador repeatedly warned the State Department that '...the predominant view in the [Japanese] Foreign Office is that the United States and Great Britain must be considered for all practical purposes in connection with the Far Eastern situation as one unit and that Japan cannot take aggressive measures against the interests of either nation without eventually becoming involved with the other'.[89]

That informal but parallel coincidence of Anglo-American strategic foreign policy was exactly the result the FO had been working toward since 1934 and the DRC debates. Through such an alignment, the maritime power of the United States could be factored into British strategic maritime planning with greater certainty, and with greater prospects of Britain's imperial interests being secured through the deterrent effect of the American fleet in the Pacific weighing heavily now on the Japanese mind.[90] The centre of gravity for the continued progression of this new parallel path was the question of British willingness to stand up to Japan. If Britain was perceived to be willing to appease Japan under Chamberlain's direction, the United States would withdraw and leave Britain's imperial defence to its own devices.[91] In these circumstances, and given the progress made in these areas in the latter months of 1937, it is obvious that, when faced with both Chamberlain's rebuff of President Roosevelt's approaches to work together on world affairs, and the Tory Prime Minister's appeasement of Italy over Abyssinia, Eden had little choice but to resign on 20 February 1938. He did so in order to safeguard the vital Anglo-American relations that protected Britain's interests in the Far East, and, quite possibly in the Foreign Secretary's view, globally.[92]

Although Chamberlain expected Eden's successor, Lord Halifax, to take a more 'favourable' attitude toward the Prime Minister's attempts to manipulate Great Britain's strategic foreign policy, the new Foreign Secretary quickly came to appreciate the centrality of the United States and its maritime power for matters concerning the Far East.[93] By the spring of 1939, conscious of the interdependence of British and American maritime plans for any potential conflict in the Far East, Halifax was anxious to have the Americans understand clearly that His Majesty's Government, if it were involved in any conflict in Europe, '...might not be able at once to reinforce on a large scale their naval forces in the Far East, and that might affect US naval dispositions'.[94] The FO belief in the need for close Anglo-American relations and their linking of that relationship to the provision of Great Britain's security in the Far East remained unchanged until the outbreak of war in Europe in September 1939. At that time, the need for the deterrent effect of Anglo-American strategic maritime relations became vital. However, by that time the FO was confident that 'The President can be relied upon to give the right lead to US public opinion and he is also ready, if need be, to assist in holding the ring in the Far East'.[95] From that point onward, the pace of Anglo-American maritime relations regarding the strategic situation in the Far East quickened. Such was the scope and substance of that evolving relationship that, by November 1940, the United States Navy was in possession of a detailed and extensive amount of information regarding Singapore, its capabilities, capacity and suitability for supporting the US Pacific Fleet.[96]

The year 1940 was a critical one for the Foreign Office and their relations with the American strategic foreign policy-making elite. In the midst of a Presidential election, the Roosevelt administration, still sympathetic to the British security position, was very wary about how far and how fast certain cooperative or parallel actions, especially regarding the disposition of American maritime forces in the Pacific, could go.[97] Unwilling to be tarred as the 'Protector of the British Empire' by his political opponents, Roosevelt was particularly sensitive to any attempt by the British to get the United States to take the 'lead' in deterring Japan. The newly installed British Ambassador to the United States, Lord Lothian, reporting back to members of the British cabinet about the US willingness to assist Great Britain in her time of need, indicated that he believed that

> The present unwritten and unnamed naval alliance with Great Britain is almost as essential to the United States of America if it is to continue to enjoy the kind of existence it has led since 1814 as it is to ourselves. Public opinion is instinctively aware of this, but no politician of importance – even the President, especially in election year – can point openly to these facts for the reason that the logical conclusion is that America must abandon isolation for good and make a permanent naval arrangement with ourselves, with the commitment to war which that implies.[98]

Therefore, until the US election was over and Roosevelt had secured a third term, or until Japanese actions provoked the United States into declaring war, American maritime power remained a deterrent, not a participant, in the Far Eastern balance of power.[99]

Following Roosevelt's re-election in the autumn of 1940, more co-ordinated and wide-ranging, detailed Anglo-American strategic conversations took place. In January 1941, an 'unofficial' team of senior Royal Navy staff officers convened in Washington for talks with their American counterparts. These talks were remarkable not only for the topics that were covered, between a nation at war and a neutral, but also for the maintenance of secrecy that surrounded them.[100] While part of the initial stages of those talks were aimed at possible US naval operations in the Atlantic, the main thrust of the talks throughout the year, until the Japanese attack that December on Pearl Harbor, were directed at Far Eastern matters.[101]

The crucial issue for the British was the continued operation of the US Fleet in the Pacific. The Admiralty admitted that it could not send a capital ship force to the Far East to reinforce the China Squadron, even if the United States and Japan entered such a war simultaneously.[102] Despite earlier discussions between the British and American naval staffs, which had worked on the premise of an American capital-ship force going to and operating from Singapore, by the end of February 1941 Roosevelt and his naval advisers were worried about the Atlantic theatre. The movement of those capital ships to the Pacific was thought by some senior USN officers '...to be inconsistent with fundamental principle of United States policy that the Western Hemisphere must remain secure'.[103] The task for the British representatives now became one of educating the American naval staff and political representatives to the need for the United States to continue to hold the ring in the Far East, and to not weaken the deterrent effect of the US Fleet on the Japanese by moving units to the Atlantic.[104]

On 30 March, Rear Admiral Victor H. Danckwerts travelled to Hawaii to talk with the C-in-C Pacific Fleet, Admiral Kimmel, about how the US and RN fleets would co-ordinate their actions in the event of a war with Japan.[105] In the aftermath of Danckwerts's conversations in Honolulu, a conference of the American naval representatives from the Asiatic Fleet, along with Dutch, Australian and British naval delegates, met in Singapore to discuss a combined naval strategy for the region.[106] Even though differences were arising over the centrality of the Singapore base for combined Anglo-American operations, the variations were of little consequence. The FO, Admiralty, and Prime Minister Winston Churchill were all in agreement: it did not matter the exact order or priority given to certain operational and tactical issues. The First Lord of the Admiralty, A.V. Alexander, was unconcerned about the growing American tendency to downplay both the role of Singapore and the idea of moving Fleet units to the Atlantic to support the British effort in that theatre.[107] In August 1941, prior to Prime Minister Churchill's meeting President Roosevelt to discuss strategic visions, Lord Halifax, now the British Ambassador to the United States, told Churchill that he would '... find the President quite ready to talk freely about Japan, and about the question of joint action with ourselves if the Japs go for ourselves or the Dutch. Opinion has moved so fast during the last few weeks that I don't think you need have any inhibitions about speaking quite freely'.[108] The main point for the British was that, at the highest strategic level, for both the European and Far Eastern theatres now, the United States had to be brought into the war. All parts of the British policy-making elite were convinced that, once the formal participation of the United States in the war began, the war could be won and imperial interests protected.[109] That group now believed that if there were to be a war in the Far East, America would stand alongside Great Britain against Japan. As evidence of that allied attitude British planners could point out that by November of that year, just prior to the sailing of the *Prince of Wales* and *Repulse* for the Far East, Anglo-American preparations for a war with Japan had evolved to a point where arrangements were now in place for British ships to use American bases in the Philippines.[110]

Clearly, the concept of one consolidated, coherent strategic picture being possessed by something as amorphous and de-centralized as a 'policy-making elite' is unsustainable. There were many British mental maps of the American worth as a maritime ally in any possible Far Eastern emergency. Those maps were the product of circumstance, personality, geography, and timing. They were related not only to Far Eastern events, but also to European and Asian happenings as well. Furthermore, trying to ascertain something such as the value of a country to another country's strategic position creates great complications. Issues of will, resources, industry, information or intelligence and infrastructure, as well as training and capabilities, compete for a place of primacy in the final assessment of the question 'what is the worth?' Which of those factors will be the most valued aspect? The element of formal versus informal relationships, particularly when attempting to evaluate the impact of a nation in terms of its deterrent or coercion effect, muddies the waters. Can the actual results of such forces in the deterrence or coercion of Japan be measured incontrovertibly? And, most importantly, how one judges the primacy of the value of the United States is the key point in forming a judgement of the competing views of how Britain should have dealt with the Americans. If the Treasury had dominated the British Cabinet, as Neville Chamberlain often desired, Britain's strategic policy in the Far East would have moved away from believing in the eventual and final worth of the United States and toward the appeasement of Japan. If the Admiralty had not respected the professional and technical ability of the USN, and had not established closer operational and strategic links with the USN in the inter-war period, particularly between 1933 and 1936, confidence in a shared mental map of conditions and possible solutions for the theatre would not have developed.

The Foreign Office was the main creator and defender of Britain's Far Eastern strategic foreign policy during the period under review. It worked tirelessly to ensure that the potential availability of the maritime power possessed by the United States was not jeopardized by events either in Europe or the Far East. Political, economic, military and social issues were all grist to the mill that was the FO's constant attempts to maintain and build as close a relationship as possible with the United States over Far Eastern matters. To that Foreign Office, America's potential maritime power was critical to their considerations not only for the balance of power in that region, but also for the survival of the British empire in that part of the world. Lacking the physical resources to exert sea control in the areas concerned, the British required the deterrent or actual effect of other nations' maritime power to protect their interests. The FO harnessed the Japanese fear of American maritime power being linked with the British and used that threat perception as a shield to protect imperial interests, thus providing protection without the actual Royal Navy units that would have been required if Great Britain had tried to go it alone. Therefore, for the FO and the rest of the British strategic foreign policy-making elite, American maritime power, while not always recognized or appreciated, was vital for the continuance of any significant British presence in the Far East from 1933 to 1942. After the Japanese

WHAT WORTH THE AMERICANS?

attack on Pearl Harbor on 7 December 1941, Britain's imperial position in the Far East became hostage to the reality of American maritime power.

Notes

1. On the idea of mental maps and international relations see: Keith Neilson, *Britain and the Last Tsar: British Policy and Russia, 1894–1917* (Oxford: Clarendon, 1995), xi–xii, 3–50; Zara Steiner, 'Elitism and Foreign Policy: the Foreign Office Before the Great War', in B.J.C. McKercher and David J. Moss (eds), *Shadow and Substance in British Foreign Policy, 1895–1939: Memorial Essays Honouring C.J. Lowe* (Edmonton: University of Alberta Press, 1984), 19–56; A.K. Henrikson, 'The Geographical "Mental Maps" of American Foreign Policy Makers', *IPSR*, 1 (1980), 496–530; Paul M. Kennedy, *The Realities Behind Diplomacy: Background Influences on British External Policy, 1865–1980* (London: Allen & Unwin, 1981).
2. G.T. Waddington's, 'Hassgegner: German Views of Great Britain in the Later 1930s', *Historical Association*, 81 (1996), 22–39; Peter Beck, 'Politicians versus Historians: Lord Avon's "Appeasement Battle" Against "Lamentably, Appeasement-Minded" Historians', *Twentieth Century British History*, 9 (1998), 396–419; Thomas G. Otte, 'Introduction: Personalities and Impersonal Forces in History', in Thomas G. Otte and Constantine A. Pagedas (eds), *Personalities, War and Diplomacy: Essays in International History* (London: Frank Cass, 1997), 1–14.
3. Ann Trotter, *Britain and East Asia, 1933–1939* (Cambridge: Cambridge University Press, 1975); Stephen Endicott, *Diplomacy and Enterprise: Britain's China Policy, 1933–1937* (Manchester: Manchester University Press, 1975); William Roger Louis, *British Strategy in the Far East* (Oxford: Clarendon, 1971); Paul Haggie, *Britannia at Bay: The Defence of Britain's Far Eastern Empire, 1931–1941* (Oxford: Oxford University Press, 1981).
4. John Ferris, *Men, Money, and Diplomacy: The Evolution of British Strategic Policy, 1919–1926* (Ithaca NY: Cornell University Press, 1989); Christopher Bell, *The Royal Navy, Seapower and Strategy between the Wars* (London: Frank Cass, 2000).
5. For these questions see Greg Kennedy, *Anglo-American Strategic Relations and the Far East, 1933–1939* (London: Frank Cass, 2002).
6. For an overview of these various factors see Keith Neilson, ' "Greatly Exaggerated": The Myth of the Decline of Great Britain before 1914', *International History Review*, 13 (1991), 695–725; George C. Peden, 'The Burden of Imperial Defence and the Continental Commitment Reconsidered', *Historical Journal*, 27 (1984), 32–50; B.J.C. McKercher, ' "No Eternal Friends or Enemies": British Defence Policy and the Problem of the United States, 1919–1939', *Canadian Journal of History*, 28 (1993), 257–94; Gordon Martel, 'The Meaning of Power: Rethinking the Decline and Fall of Great Britain', *International History Review*, 13 (1991), 662–94; John Ferris, ' "The Greatest Power on Earth": Great Britain in the 1920s', *International History Review*, 13 (1991), 726–50; David French, ' "Perfidious Albion" Faces the Powers', *Canadian Journal of History*, 28 (1993), 177–88.
7. Erik Goldstein, 'The British Official Mind and the United States, 1919–42', in Thomas G. Otte and Constantine A. Pagedas (eds), *Personalities, War and Diplomacy*, 66–80. See also, G.R. Berridge, Maurice Keens-Soper and T.G. Otte, *Diplomatic Theory From Machiavelli to Kissinger* (Basingstoke: Palgrave, 2001).
8. Although directed at areas not under investigation here, the methodology of the following works is appropriate for understanding the approach taken here. William C. Mills, 'The Chamberlain-Grandi Conversations of July–August 1937 and the Appeasement of Italy', *International History Review*, 19 (1997), 594–619; Roger Fletcher, 'An English Advocate in Germany: Eduard Bernstein's Analysis of Anglo-German Relations, 1900–1914', *Canadian Journal of History*, 13 (1978), 209–35.

9. Other works which illustrate these points of process in other situations are: Sally Marks, 'Ménage à Trois: The Negotiations for an Anglo-French-Belgian Alliance in 1922', *International History Review*, 4 (1982), 524–52; Gerald R. Kleinfeld, 'Nazis and Germans in China 1933–37: The Consulate and the German Community in Tsingtao', *Canadian Journal of History*, 15 (1980), 229–47; Hugh Ragsdale, 'Soviet Military Preparations and Policy in the Munich Crisis: New Evidence', *Jahrbücher für Geschichte Osteuropas*, 47 (1999), 210–26; Trevor Lloyd, 'Ramsay MacDonald: Socialist or Gentleman?', *Canadian Journal of History*, 15 (1980), 307–29.

10. D.C. Watt, 'The Nature of the Foreign Policy-Making Elite in Britain', in D.C. Watt (ed.), *Personalities and Policies: Studies in the Formulation of British Foreign Policy in the Twentieth Century* (Westport CT: Greenwood, 1965), 1–15; D.C. Watt, *What About the People? Abstractions and Reality in History and the Social Sciences* (London: London School of Economics and Political Science, 1983); John McDermott, 'Sir Francis Oppenheimer: "Stranger Within" the Foreign Office', *History*, 66 (1981), 199–207; David F. Trask, 'Woodrow Wilson and International Statecraft: A Modern Assessment', *Naval War College Review*, 36 (1983), 57–68; Michael Jabara Carley, 'Anti-Bolshevism in French Foreign Policy: The Crisis in Poland in 1920', *International History Review*, 2 (1980), 410–31; G. Roberts, 'A Soviet Bid for Coexistence with Nazi Germany, 1935–1937: The Kandelaki Affair', *International History Review*, 16 (1994), 466–90; Donald M. McKale, 'Weltpolitik versus Imperium Britannica: Anglo-German Rivalry in Egypt, 1904–14', *Canadian Journal of History*, 12 (1987), 193–207.

11. W.R. Rock, *British Appeasement in the 1930s* (London: Edward Arnold, 1977); Gaines Post Jr, *Dilemmas of Appeasement: British Deterrence and Defence, 1934–1937* (Ithaca NY: Cornell University Press, 1993); Michael Roi, *Alternative to Appeasement: Sir Robert Vansittart and Alliance Diplomacy, 1934–1937* (Westport CT: Praeger, 1997).

12. The best work on the Treasury and its workings, as well as policies, is George C. Peden, *British Rearmament and the Treasury, 1932–1939* (Edinburgh: Scottish Academic Press, 1979), Peden, *The Treasury and British Public Policy 1906–1959* (Oxford: Oxford University Press, 2000). See also R. Shay, *British Rearmament in the Thirties: Politics and Profits* (Princeton NJ: Princeton University Press, 1977).

13. For some of the literature on the failed World Economic Conference of 1933, see A.P.N Erdmann, 'Mining for the Corporate Synthesis: Gold in American Foreign Economic Policy, 1931–1936', *Diplomatic History*, 17 (1993), 171–200; A. Booth, *British Economic Policy, 1931–49* (London: Harvester Wheatsheaf, 1989), 1–43; D.Kunz, *The Battle for Britain's Gold Standard in 1931* (London: Croom Helm, 1987), 160–3; Kunz, 'When Money Counts and Doesn't: Economic Power and Diplomatic Objectives', *Diplomatic History*, 18 (1994), 451–62; J. Nichols, 'Roosevelt's Monetary Diplomacy in 1933', *American Historical Review*, 56 (1988), 295–317; K.A. Oye, 'The Sterling–Dollar–Franc Triangle: Monetary Diplomacy, 1929–1937', *World Politics*, 38 (1985), 173–99; A.M. Schlesinger, *The Coming of the New Deal* (Boston: Houghton Mifflin, 1939), 200–10; A. Booth, 'Britain in the 1930s: A Managed Economy?', *Economic History Review*, 40 (1987), 499–521; Booth, *British Economic Policy, 1931–1949* (London: Harvester Wheatsheaf, 1989); R. Middleton, *Towards a Managed Economy: Keynes, the Treasury and the Fiscal Debate of the 1930s* (London: Middleton, 1985); Ian Drummond, *The Floating Pound and the Sterling Area, 1931–39* (Cambridge: Cambridge University Press, 1981); P. Williamson, *National Crisis and National Government: British Politics, the Economy and Empire, 1926–1932* (Cambridge: Cambridge University Press, 1992); F.C. Costigliola, 'Anglo-American Financial Rivalry in the 1920s', *Journal of Economic History*, 37 (1977), 911–34; Roberta A. Dayer, 'Anglo-American Monetary Policy and Rivalry in Europe and the Far East, 1919–1931', in B.J.C. McKercher (ed.), *Arms Limitation and Disarmament* (Westport

CT: Praeger, 1992), 158–86. The most useful contextual works on this topic are Patricia Clavin, '"The Fetishes of So-Called International Bankers": Central Bank Co-operation for the World Economic Conference, 1932–3', *Contemporary European History*, 3 (1992), 281–311; Clavin, 'The World Economic Conference 1933: The Failure of British Internationalism', *Journal of European Economic History*, 20 (1991), 489–527; Clavin, *The Failure of Economic Diplomacy: Britain, Germany, France and the United States, 1931–36* (New York: St Martin's, 1996); Kenneth Mouré, 'The Limits to Central Bank Co-operation, 1916–36', *Contemporary European History*, 3 (1992), 259–79; Gyorgy Peter, 'Central Bank Diplomacy: Monagu Norman and Central Europe's Monetary Reconstruction after World War I', *Contemporary European History*, 3 (1992), 233–58.

14. Greg Kennedy, '"Rat in Power": Neville Chamberlain and the Creation of British Foreign Policy, 1931–1939', in T.G. Otte (ed.), *The Makers of British Foreign Policy: From Pitt to Thatcher* (Basingstoke: Palgrave, 2002), 173–189; Sidney Aster, '"Guilty Men": The Case of Neville Chamberlain', in Patrick Finney (ed.), *The Origins of the Second World War* (London: St Martin's, 1997), 62–78; R.A.C. Parker, *Chamberlain and Appeasement: British Policy and the Coming of the Second World War* (New York: St Martin's, 1993); John Charmley, *Chamberlain and the Lost Peace* (London: Hodder & Stoughton, 1989).

15. Treasury, Sir Frederick Leith-Ross, Public Record Office, Kew, London (hereafter T) T188/58, letter from Warren Fisher to Vansittart, 16 December 1932; T188/58, letter from Fisher to Vansittart, 17 December 1932; ibid., secret, note of conversation between Sir R. Lindsay, Sir W. Fisher, Sir R. Vansittart, Sir F. Leith-Ross, Sir R. Hopkins and Sir F. Phillips, 8 February 1933.

16. T175/79, Sir Richard Hopkins MSS, minute by Warren Fisher to Hopkins, 27 March 1933; T175/79, telegram from Leith-Ross to Chamberlain, 2 May 1933; Eunan O'Halpin, *Head of the Civil Service: A Study of Sir Warren Fisher* (London: Routledge, 1989).

17. Roger Dingman, *Power in the Pacific: the Origins of Naval Arms Limitation* (Chicago: University of Chicago Press, 1976); Emily O. Goldman, *Sunken Treaties* (University Park PA: Pennsylvania State University Press, 1994); Malcolm H. Murfett, 'Look Back in Anger: The Western Powers and the Washington Conference of 1921–1922', in B.J.C. McKercher (ed.), *Arms Limitation and Disarmament*, 83–104; Stephen W. Roskill, *Naval Policy Between the Wars*, Vol. 1 (London: Collins, 1968), 70–5; J. Kenneth McDonald, 'The Washington Conference and the Naval Balance of Power, 1921–22', in John B. Hattendorf and Robert S. Jordan (eds), *Maritime Strategy and the Balance of Power* (New York: St Martin's, 1989), 189–213; Erik Goldstein and John Maurer (eds), 'Special Issue on the Washington Conference, 1921–22: Naval Rivalry, East Asian Stability and the Road to Pearl Harbor', *Diplomacy and Statecraft*, 4 (1993); David Carlton, 'Great Britain and the Coolidge Naval Conference of 1927', *Political Science Quarterly*, 83 (1968), 573–98; Richard Fanning, 'The Coolidge Conference of 1927: Disarmament in Disarray', in B.J.C. McKercher (ed.), *Arms Limitation and Disarmament*, 105–28; Greg Kennedy, 'The 1930 London Naval Conference and Anglo-American Maritime Strength, 1927–1930', in McKercher (ed.), *Arms Limitation and Disarmament*, 149–72; Stephen Pelz, *Race to Pearl Harbor: The Failure of the Second London Naval Conference and the Onset of World War II* (Cambridge MA: Harvard University Press, 1974).

18. T172/1815, '1933 World Economic Conference', memorandum from Hopkins to Chancellor, 5 May 1933.

19. For the preliminary Treasury and Admiralty positions in the 1920s and early 1930s see: John Ferris, '"It is our business in the Navy to Command the Seas": The Last Decade of British Maritime Supremacy, 1919–1929', 124–70, and Orest Babij, 'The

Royal Navy and the Defence of the British Empire, 1928–1934', 171–89, both in Keith Neilson and Greg Kennedy (eds), *Far Flung Lines: Studies in Imperial Defence in Honour of Donald Mackenzie Schurman* (London: Frank Cass, 1997).

20. T175/48, Treasury comments on COS Paper 1103-B 'The Far East', undated early 1933; ADM 116/3434, Chamberlain to Sir Bolton M. Eyres Monsell (First Lord of the Admiralty), 10 January 1933.

21. CAB 2/6, minutes of the Meetings of the Committee of Imperial Defence, 261, Meeting, 9 November 1933.

22. Ibid.

23. Greg Kennedy, 'Neville Chamberlain and Strategic Relations with the US during his Chancellorship', *Diplomacy and Statecraft*, 13 (2002), 95–120.

24. The catalyst for the creation of the DRC are found in 'Imperial Defence Policy, Annual review for 1932 by the Chiefs of Staff Sub-Committee', 466–68, and, '"The Far Eastern Situation", memorandum by Chatfield 25 February 1933, prepared for the 107th Meeting, Chiefs of Staff Sub-Committee, CID', 28 February 1933, both in Nicholas Tracy (ed.), *The Collective Naval Defence of the Empire, 1900–1940* (Navy Records Society, 1997). I am grateful to Professor Keith Neilson for allowing me to see an advance copy of his article 'The Defence Requirements Sub-Committee: British Strategic Foreign Policy, Neville Chamberlain and the Path to Appeasement' [now published in the *English Historical Review*, 158 (June 2003)] and from which this quote is taken.

25. CAB 16/109, DRC Minutes, minutes of the 3rd Meeting, 4 December 1933.

26. Ibid.; minutes of 19th Meeting of DRC, 'Note by Sir Warren Fisher', 17 February 1934; CAB 21/434, letter from Fisher to Hankey, Cabinet Registered Files, 17 February 1934.

27. CAB 16/109, minutes of 12th Meeting of DRC, 'Note by Sir Warren Fisher', 30 January 1934.

28. CAB 16/109, minutes of 4th Meeting of DRC, 13 January 1934.

29. CAB 16/109, DRC Paper No. 9, secret, 'Note by Sir Warren Fisher', 12 January 1934.

30. CAB 16/109, DRC Paper No. 12, secret, 'Note by Sir Warren Fisher', 29 January 1934.

31. Ibid. See also CAB 16/109, D.R.C. Paper No. 19, secret, 'Note by Sir Warren Fisher as an addendum to the Defence Requirements Committee Report', 17 February 1934; CAB 16/109, minutes of 10th Meeting, 16 February 1934.

32. CAB 29/148, London Naval Conference, NCM(35), papers, NCM(35)3, 'The Naval Conference: Note by the Chancellor of the Exchequer', 23 April 1934; Chatfield Papers (CHT), National Maritime Museum, Greenwich, 3/2, letter from Warren Fisher to Chatfield and enclosed note from Fisher to Sir John Simon, 1 November 1934.

33. CAB 29/147, London Naval Conference, NCM(35), minutes, 1st Meeting, 16 April 1934; CAB 29/148, NCM(35) 3, 'The Naval Conference, 1935', 19 April 1934. On Treasury attitudes toward rearmament and international issues, see T175/94/2, memorandum from Philips to Hopkins, 31 December 1936.

34. CAB 23/78, Cabinet Minutes, PRO, minutes of meeting 9(34), 14 March 1934.

35. Ibid.

36. Kennedy, *Anglo-American Strategic Relations*, Chapters 4 and 5.

37. In December 1937, even after the Japanese attacks on British and American naval units in China, Warren Fisher still viewed any conflict with Japan in that theatre as a 'Great Britain only' contingency, a contingency he was reluctant to provide funding to prepare for: 'The DRC fleet was based on aggressive power in Europe, and defensive sufficiency in Asia; and while I think some increase in the DRC fleet may be necessary, we neither want nor can we afford the present two-power fleet proposed by the

WHAT WORTH THE AMERICANS?

Admiralty.' Sir N. Warren Fisher MSS (British Library of Economic and Political Science), London (hereafter Fisher MSS) 2.21, memorandum on 'Defence. Sir T. Inskip's New Report', Fisher to Neville Chamberlain, 18 December 1937.

38. Kennedy, ' "Rat in Power" ', pp. 183–5.
39. NC, Neville Chamberlain Papers, Birmingham University Library, 18/1/1020, letter from Chamberlain to sister Hilda, 12 September 1937.
40. The best explanation of Eden's resignation is found in Ritchie Ovendale, *'Appeasement' and the English Speaking World: Britain, the United States, the Dominions, and the Policy of Appeasement, 1937–1939* (Cardiff: University of Wales Press, 1975); Kennedy, *Anglo-American Strategic Relations*, 235–40; V.H. Rothwell, *Anthony Eden: A Political Biography, 1931–1957* (Manchester: Manchester University Press, 1992). A full account of the American question in Eden's decision to resign is found in FO 371/21526/A2127/64/45, department memorandum, 24 March 1938 and FO 371/21547/A14009/1409, dispatch from Lindsay (British Ambassador in Washington) to FO, 22 February 1938 with attached minutes.
41. Anthony Eden MSS (hereafter Eden MSS), PRO, Kew, FO 954/6, memo 'The Far East', Eden to the King, undated November, 1937. Walter Runciman also recognized the danger Chamberlain's actions had created in terms of eroding Anglo-American strategic relations and moved quickly to reassure FDR and his advisers that even though Eden had resigned there were still others in the Cabinet who valued America's help internationally. While Runciman was primarily concerned with ensuring that Roosevelt did not take a more negative view on the forthcoming Anglo-American trade talks, the connections to the issues of appeasement and the Far Eastern situation are clear. Runciman was masterfully practising damage control of the first order. Walter Runciman Papers (hereafter Runciman Papers), Robinson Library, University of Newcastle-on-Tyne, WR 284, 1936–39, letter from Runciman to FDR, 18 February 1938; ibid., letters from Peter Murray to Runciman, 20 and 21 February 1938.
42. On Craigie as Ambassador, see Antony Best, 'Sir Robert Craigie as Ambassador to Japan, 1937–1941', in Ian Nish (ed.), *Britain and Japan: Biographical Portraits* (Folkestone: Japan Library, 1994), 238–51; S. Olu Agbi, 'The Pacific War Controversy in Britain: Sir Robert Craigie Versus the Foreign Office', *Modern Asian Studies*, 17 (1983), 289–517; D.C. Watt, 'Chamberlain's Ambassadors', in Michael Dockrill and Brian McKercher (eds), *Diplomacy and World Power: Studies in British Foreign Policy, 1890–1950* (Cambridge: Cambridge University Press, 1996), 136–70.
43. Kennedy, *Anglo-American Strategic Relations*, 211–61.
44. Ibid.
45. Runciman Papers, WR 284, secret letter from Runciman to Neville Chamberlain, 19 June 1939.
46. Richard J. Aldrich, *The Key to the South: Britain, the United States, and Thailand during the Approach of the Pacific War, 1929–1942* (Oxford: Oxford University Press, 1993); Nicholas Tarling, *Britain, Southeast Asia and the Onset of the Pacific War* (Cambridge: Cambridge University Press, 1996); Antony Best, *British Intelligence and the Japanese Challenge in Asia, 1914–1941* (London: Macmillan, 2002); Kennedy, *Anglo-American Strategic Relations*, 15–41. On the Royal Navy and relations with Japan, the standard is still Arthur J. Marder, *Old Friends, New Enemies: The Royal Navy and the Imperial Japanese Navy* (Oxford: Oxford University Press, 1981).
47. The work on the USN and its various programmes during the period from 1933–1941 is extensive. Some of the better studies for this period are: R.G. Albion (R. Reed ed.), *Makers of Naval Policy, 1798–1947* (Annapolis MD: Naval Institute Press, 1980); G.W. Baer, *One Hundred Years of Sea Power: The United States Navy, 1890–1990* (Stanford CA: Stanford University Press, 1994); Dorothy Borg, *The United States and*

the Far Eastern Crisis of 1933–1938 (Cambridge MA: Harvard University Press, 1964); Robert Dallek, *Franklin D. Roosevelt and American Foreign Policy, 1932–1945* (New York: Oxford University Press, 1979); Kenneth J. Hagan, *This People's Navy* (New York: Collier Macmillan, 1991); J.R. Leutze, *Bargaining for Supremacy: Anglo-American Naval Relations, 1937–1941* (Chapel Hill NC: University of North Carolina Press, 1977). Contemporary observations, from the British Naval Attaché in Washington, Capt. A.R. Dewar, reveal the close watch the RN was keeping on the new American naval programmes; FO 371, PRO, Kew, /16598/A5308/6/45, attaché's report, 18 July 1933.

48. Bell, *The Royal Navy, Seapower and Strategy between the Wars*; Ferris, '"It is Our Business in the Navy to Command the Seas"'; Babij, 'The Royal Navy and the Defence of the British Empire, 1928–1934'; Greg Kennedy, '1935: A Snapshot of Imperial Defence in the Far East', in Neilson and Kennedy (eds), *Far Flung Lines*, 190–216.

49. Ian Cowman, 'Defence of the Malay Barrier? The Place of the Philippines in Admiralty Naval War Planning, 1925–1941', *War in History*, 3 (1996); Louis, *British Strategy in the Far East, 1919–1939*; Bell, *The Royal Navy, Seapower and Strategy between the Wars*; Kennedy, *Anglo-American Strategic Relations*.

50. Drax Papers (DRAX), Churchill College Archive Centre, Cambridge, 2/4, US, letter from Drax to Hankey, 12 November 1933; ibid., letter Drax to Winslow, 29 February 1933; ibid., notes for J.H.R.C, 1 September 1933; ADM 116/2952, China Station Proceedings, Letter No. 1, 1 April 1933; ADM 116/2953, China Station Proceedings. Letter No. 4, 10 July and letter No. 5, 8 August, both 1933; CHT /4/4, Dreyer to Chatfield, 19 August 1933; ibid., Dreyer to Chatfield, 22 October 1934; Admiral Montgomery M. Taylor MSS, Library of Congress, Washington, DC, Container 2, Folder January–February 1933, letter from Taylor to Pratt (Admiral William Veazie), 28 January 1933; FO 371/18168/F57/57/23, Admiralty memorandum, 3 January 1934.

51. Eric J. Grove, 'Admiral Sir (later Baron) Ernle Chatfield (1933–1938)', in Malcolm H. Murfett (ed.), *The First Sea Lords: From Fisher to Mountbatten* (Westport CT: Praeger, 1995), 157–72.

52. Kennedy, 'Snapshot', 204.

53. CAB 53/4, minutes of Meetings of COS, No. 107, 28 February 1933; CAB 4/22, CID Papers Misc. B Series, Paper No. 1103, 'The Situation in the Far East', 31 March 1933; ADM 167/89, 'Naval Defence Requirements, Memorandum by the First Sea Lord', 30 November 1933.

54. CAB 53/4, No. 107, 28 February 1933; CAB 53/4, No. 109, 11 April 1933; CAB 53/ 23, COS Papers, Paper No. 310, 12 October 1933.

55. CHT/3/1, private and personal letter from Chatfield to Hankey, 5 February 1934.

56. CAB 16/109, DRC minutes, 4th Meeting, 18 January 5th Meeting, 19 January and 6th Meeting, 23 January all 1934; CAB 16/109, DRC Paper No. 6, 'Forecast by the Chief of Naval Staff', 20 December 1933; CAB 29/148, NCM(35) 10, Note by First Lord of the Admiralty, 18 May 1934.

57. Neilson, 'New Light on the DRC'.

58. CHT/3/1, secret letter from Chatfield to Fisher, 4 June 1934.

59. CAB 21/388, untitled memorandum by H.J. Batterbee, Assistant Undersecretary, Dominion Office and C.R. Price, Principal Secretary, Dominion Office, 23 June 1934.

60. ADM 116/3434, Chatfield to Eyres-Monsell (First Lord of the Admiralty), 21 June 1934.

61. FO 371/18726/A901/22/45, most secret joint FO/ADM memorandum, 17 December 1935.

62. CHT/3/2, Naval Conference 1935, letter from Chatfield to Madden, 5 October 1934.

63. CHT/3/2, secret draft of note from Fisher to Chamberlain, 12 November 1934.

64. Ibid.

WHAT WORTH THE AMERICANS?

65. Kennedy, *Anglo-American Strategic Relations*, 121–210; FO 371/19809/A2020/4/45, various minutes and memoranda, 10 March 1936.

66. Runciman Papers, WR 284, 1936–39, strictly personal and confidential note, Hankey to Runciman, 'Naval Bases in the Pacific', 22 February 1937.

67. Ibid.

68. Runciman Papers, WR 284, letter from FDR to Peter Murray, 25 February 1937.

69. Kennedy, *Anglo-American Strategic Relations*, 35–37.

70. CAB 56/1, Joint Intelligence Committee Papers, PRO, Kew, most secret No. 28, 'Far Eastern Appreciation', 5 March 1937; FO 371/21490/A1469/1/45, IIC Report, 'US material resources and industry in their bearing upon national war potential', 24 February 1938; FO 371/21546/A9426/1202/45, IIC Report, 'Economic situation in the US in the event of war', 14 December 1938; R[ecord] G[roup] 38, CNO-LNA, Box 1, Folder: British Naval Exercises and Maneuvers, US Naval Attaché's Report, 27 July 1938; CAB 53/45, COS Paper No. 843, 'European Appreciation, 1939–40', 20 February 1939; CAB 16/209, Strategic Appreciation Committee, Minutes, Minutes of 1st Meeting, 1 March 1939.

71. Lawrence Pratt, 'The Anglo-American Naval Conversations in the Far East', *International Affairs*, 47 (1971), 745–63.

72. Kennedy, *Anglo-American Strategic Relations*, 37–41; Reynolds, *The Creation of the Anglo-American Alliance*, 60; James Leutze, *Bargaining for Supremacy*, 15–28; Paul Haggie, *Britannia at Bay*, 115–20; Bradford Lee, *Britain and the Sino-Japanese War*, 131–2; Nicholas Tarling, *Britain, Southeast Asia and the Onset of the Pacific War*, 18; Malcolm Murfett, *Fool-Proof Relations: The Search for Anglo-American Naval Co-operation during the Chamberlain Years, 1937–1940* (Singapore: Singapore University Press, 1984); Richard J. Aldrich, *The Key to the South*, 193; Borg, *The United States and the Far Eastern Crisis of 1933–1938*, 497–9.

73. Reynolds, *The Creation of the Anglo-American Alliance*; Ian Cowman, *Anglo-American Naval Relations in the Pacific, 1937–1941*; H.P. Willmott, *Empires in the Balance: Japanese and Allied Pacific Strategies to April 1942* (Annapolis MD: Naval Institute Press, April 1982); Greg Kennedy, 'Symbol of Imperial Defence: The Role of Singapore in British and American Far Eastern Strategic Relations, 1933–1941', in Brian P. Farrell and Sandy Hunter (eds), *Sixty Years On: The Fall of Singapore Revisited* (Singapore: Eastern Universities Press, 2002).

74. Viscount Templewood, *Nine Troubled Years* (London: Collins, 1954), 400–7.

75. FO 371/22829/2122/1292/45, Lindsay to FO, 3 March 1939.

76. Baron Vansittart Papers [VNST], Roskill Archives, Churchill College, Cambridge, 2/21, untitled memorandum, Lawrence Collier (Head of Northern Dept.), 16 May 1935; VNST 1/19, 'The World Situation and British Rearmament', Vansittart, 31 December 1936; FO 371/20473/W4508/79/98, Cadogan (Sir Alexander, Assistant Permanent Undersecretary) to Eden, with covering note by Vansittart, 15 May 1936; FO 371/20473/W5075/79/98, 'Future Policy of His Majesty's Government in regard to League of Nations' and accompanying minutes, various dates through June, 1936; CAB 24/254, Command Paper (CP) 80, 15 April 1935; FO 371.19359/F1090/483/23, 'Japanese Foreign Policy', 19 February 1935.

77. Kennedy, 'Snapshot'; Kennedy, *Anglo-American Strategic Relations*.

78. I am grateful here for Prof. Keith Neilson's allowing me to read the draft of his forthcoming monograph on Anglo-Russian strategic foreign policy relations, 1933–1941; Greg Kennedy, 'Becoming Dependent on the Kindness of Strangers: Britain's Strategic Foreign Policy, Naval Arms Limitation and the Soviet Factor, 1935–1937', *War in History*, 11, 1 (2004), 79–105.

79. Michael L. Roi, *Alternative to Appeasement: Sir Robert Vansittart and Alliance Diplomacy, 1934–1937* (Westport CT: Praeger, 1997); Neilson, 'The Defence Requirements Sub-Committee'; Bell, *The Royal Navy, Seapower and Strategy between the Wars*, 98–102.

80. CAB 16/109, DRC Paper No. 20, 'Situation in the Far East', 24 February 1934.
81. FO 371/18160/F295/295/61, Wellesley minute, 18 January 1834.
82. For a contrary view see B.J.C. McKercher, *Transition of Power: Britain's Loss of Global Pre-eminence to the United States, 1930–1945* (Cambridge: Cambridge University Press, 1999), 242–77.
83. FO 371/20649/A8110/6/45, letter from Capt. T. Phillips (ADM) to FO and associated minutes, 11 November 1937.
84. Kennedy, ' "Rat in Power" '.
85. FO 371/20651/A665/38/45, secret telegram, Runciman to Prime Minister, 26 January 1937.
86. FO 371/20651/A1155/38/45, letter from Evans to Troutbeck, 12 February 1937.
87. FO 371/20663/A7748/228/45, record of conversation between Eden and Bingham, 28 October 1937; *Papers Relating to the Foreign Relations of the United States (FRUS)*, Vol. III, telegram from Norman David to Cordell Hull, 2 November 1937, 145–7; Nancy H. Hooker (ed.), *Moffat, Jay Pierrepont, 1896–1943* (Cambridge MA: Harvard University Press 1956), 162–5.
88. FO 371/22181/F10611/71/23, all telegrams, memos, and minutes, 12 and 13 October 1938.
89. *FRUS*, Vol. III, telegram from Grew to Hull, 9 September 1938, 282; ibid., letter from Grew to Hull, 1 November 1938.
90. Eden MSS, PRO, Kew, 954/7, letter from Eden to Chamberlain, 31 December 1937; FO 371/20672/A8784/5016/45, draft of memorandum from FO to Colonial Office, Air, Dominions Office, and Admiralty, 4 February 1938.
91. FO 371/21490/A556/1/45, minute by Ashton-Gwatkin, 21 January 1938; Avon Papers, University of Birmingham Library, AP 13/1/45–46, letter from Eden to Lindsay, 25 January 1938.
92. Avon Papers, AP 20/5/27-AP 20/6/23A, Eden to Chamberlain, 9 January and 17 January 1938; AP 20/6/24–29B, minutes of Foreign Policy Committee meetings, Nos 17, 18, 19, 20 on 19, 20, and 21 January 1938.
93. Kennedy, ' "Rat in Power" ', 187.
94. FO 371/23560/F2879/456/23, telegram from FO to Lindsay, 19 March 1939.
95. FO 371/22815/A5899/98/45, Balfour minute, 1 September 1939.
96. Records of the Strategic Plans Division of the Office of the Chief of Naval Operations (hereafter SPD-CNO), Naval Historical Center, Washington Navy Yard, Washington DC, Miscellaneous Subject Files, 1917–1947, Box 71, 'British Empire – Singapore – Naval Base', 23 November 1940.
97. Warren F. Kimball, *Forged in War: Roosevelt, Churchill, and the Second World War* (New York: W. Morrow, 1996), 57; Reynolds, *The Creation of the Anglo-American Alliance*, 65.
98. Letter from Lothian to Sir Samuel Hoare, 1 February 1940, quoted in Templewood, *Nine Troubled Years*, 414–18; FO 371/24722/F4627/4605/61, telegram Lothian to FO, 9 October 1940.
99. FO 371/24674/F4817/57/10, Sir John Brenan minutes, 26 October 1940; FO 371/24716/F2745/2739/61, Ashley-Clarke minute, 18 April 1940; Philip Henry Kerr, 11th Marquess of Lothian (hereafter Lothian Papers), The National Archives of Scotland, Edinburgh, GD 40/17/404, folder 206–413, personal letter from Lothian to Sam Hoare, 8 February 1940.
100. Papers of Edward Frederick Lindley Wood, 1st Earl of Halifax (hereafter Halifax Papers), Borthwick Institute of Historical Research, York University, A7.8.19, 'Most Secret Wartime Diaries, 1941–45', entry for 25 March 1941.
101. J.R.M. Butler, *Grand Strategy*, Vol. II; *September 1939–June 1941* (London: HMSO, 1957), 423–7; Reynolds, *The Creation of the Anglo-American Alliance*, 180–91.

102. FO 371/26219/A1035/384/45, most secret telegram FO to Halifax, 27 February 1941.
103. FO 371/26219/A1134/384/45, most secret telegram Admiral Bellairs (RN) to COS, 23 February 1941.
104. Halifax Papers, A7.8.19, Wartime Diary, entry for 28 February 1941.
105. FO 371/26219/A1760/384/45, most secret telegram Halifax to FO, 13 March 1941; FO 371/26219/A1461/384/45, most secret telegram Halifax to FO, 4 March 1941; FO 371/26219/A1700/384/45, most secret note and COS paper (41) 53(0) attached, from Price (War Office) to Balfour, 9 March 1941.
106. FO 371/26219/A12379/384/45, most secret telegram Halifax to FO, 5 April 1941; FO 371/26219/A2782/384/45, Danckwert's report on conversations in Hawaii, 17 April 1941.
107. FO 371/26219/A1925/384/45, Alexander to Butler, 17 March 1941.
108. Halifax Papers, A4.410.4.11, personal letter from Halifax to Churchill, 6 August 1941.
109. FO 371/26219/A1925/384/45, Alexander to Butler, 17 March 1941.
110. Halifax Papers, A7.8.19, entry for 23 November 1941.

5

'LOOKING SKYWARD FROM BELOW THE WAVES': ADMIRAL TOM PHILLIPS AND THE LOSS OF THE *PRINCE OF WALES* AND THE *REPULSE*

David Ian Hall

On Wednesday 10 December 1941, at two Japanese-held airfields near Saigon, three great parties ran late into the night. Pilots, aircrews and ground attendants of the *Mihoro* and *Kanoya* Air Groups and the *Genzan* Air Group celebrated a momentous victory over the British Royal Navy. Earlier in the day, aircraft from these Japanese Air Groups had found and sunk HMS *Prince of Wales* and HMS *Repulse* on the open sea, 50 miles east of Kuantan, off the coast of Malaya. The battle marked the very first time that aircraft armed with bombs and torpedoes had successfully attacked and destroyed Capital ships at sea where the latter had enjoyed the freedom of manoeuvre. One excited and undoubtedly exhausted reveller was Lieutenant Yoshimi Shirai; he was the pilot who earlier that morning had ordered and led his *Mihoro* squadron in the decisive attack.

For an air historian the tragic saga of the *Prince of Wales* and the *Repulse* tends to reinforce the old stereotype 'air force' view that ships are big targets. In particular, ships that cannot be defended from air attack are indeed big and vulnerable targets. The Japanese action against Force 'Z' proved this point conclusively. But even before 10 December 1941 there had been a number of ominous warnings that aircraft using bombs and torpedoes could sink large ships. In the early 1920s, American Brigadier-General Billy Mitchell ran a series of trials during which aircraft dropping bombs sank two ex-German warships (a battleship and a cruiser) and three old American battleships. Early actions in the Second World War in the North Sea, off the coast of Norway, and in the Mediterranean, also demonstrated the vulnerability of warships to air attack. Yet despite the worrisome nature of the mounting evidence, traditionalist naval officers of all the leading naval powers stubbornly resisted any changes that would entail the eclipse of the battleship fleets.[1] Such views, however, were unsustainable after 10 December 1941, the darkest day in the Royal Navy's long and illustrious history. The era of the omnipotent battleship was over.

The sinking of force 'Z'

Even a cursory look at the orders that were given to the Japanese aircrews sent to sink the British capital ships, their after-action reports and the post-war testimonials, make for disturbing reading, especially for those who count themselves among the romantic supporters of the battleship and battleship-led fleets of the Second World War.[2] The details of this calamitous air/sea battle are well known.[3] Nevertheless, a brief summary with an emphasis on air matters is appropriate.[4]

Shortly after midnight on 8 December, news of the Japanese invasion in northern Malaya and southern Thailand reached British commanders in Singapore. Admiral Tom Phillips reacted quickly and called a meeting of his senior officers where they began their final planning preparations to interdict the Japanese invasion fleets off Kota Bharu (in the north-east corner of Malaya) and Singora (southern Thailand). Phillips thought that his two fast capital ships, aided by the element of surprise and air support, could successfully attack and destroy the Japanese invasion forces. He had little knowledge of Japanese air or naval strength in the area but this did not cause him any real concern. Phillips did not rate the combat capability of the Imperial Japanese Navy very highly, and as the area of his intended operations was more than 300 miles away from the closest enemy airfields he did not fear air attack. On the basis of these assumptions, Phillips sailed with Force 'Z' from Singapore late in the afternoon on 8 December. Force 'Z', which consisted of the *Prince of Wales* and the *Repulse* and the destroyers *Electra*, *Express*, *Vampire* and *Tenedos* – all the effective naval forces at Admiral Phillips's disposal – planned to attack the Japanese invasion fleet at dawn on 10 December. Under Phillips's direction, the entire mission was to be conducted under strictest radio silence.

The question of air support for Force 'Z' had been addressed but not agreed or finalized before Phillips set sail. Phillips had spoken directly with Air Vice-Marshal C.W.H. Pulford three times. Basically, the Admiral wanted pre-arranged reconnaissance and fighter cover to coincide with his movements on 9 and 10 December. This consisted of reconnaissance 100 miles north of his ships from dawn on 9 December, and both fighter cover and reconnaissance off Singora from first light on 10 December. Pulford believed that he could provide the reconnaissance without too much difficulty but he could not guarantee the fighter protection. He would need to use the airfields in northern Malaya to give Phillips his 'fighter umbrella' and the airfields in question were under heavy Japanese air and sea attack. By 9 December, Pulford knew that his worst fears were realized and there would be no fighter cover. This information was passed on to Phillips. But even had the fighter cover been possible, it would only have worked if

Phillips either stuck rigidly to his published plans or notified the Singapore commands of any alterations. In the end, Phillips did neither.

In addition to the more limited air support than Phillips wanted, the surprise that he had so heavily counted on had also been compromised in the early morning hours of 9 December when the destroyer *Vampire* sighted a Japanese reconnaissance plane. Phillips and his fleet were not to know that this aircraft did not spot them but the Admiral was equally unaware that his force had been sighted by a Japanese submarine, *I-65*, at about 13:30 hours. Japanese efforts to attack the British ships in the afternoon and evening of 9 December, however, proved to be a comedy of errors. By the time it all ended, around midnight, the Japanese had nearly bombed one of their own cruisers and lost the location of Force 'Z' altogether.

Phillips's luck was not to last. At 20:15 hours, without breaking his radio silence to inform Singapore of his decision, he abandoned his original plan and set course for Singapore. During the evening, however, he received a series of disturbing reports from Singapore about the progress of the fighting in northern Malaya, including a message at 23:35 hours that said the Japanese were landing in Kuantan. If this last report was accurate, the Japanese would be only 150 miles north of Singapore and in a position to cut off the army's communications with northern Malaya. Phillips therefore changed his plans again, and again he did so without informing Rear Admiral Palliser, his Chief of Staff, who was commanding the naval operations room in Singapore, or Air Vice-Marshal Pulford, who was responsible for the little air support that could be afforded to Force 'Z'.

Before 09:00 hours on 10 December, both a reconnaissance aircraft flown off the *Prince of Wales* and the destroyer *Express* had investigated Kuantan harbour and reported back to Force 'Z' that all was 'complete peace'. The absence of Japanese land and sea forces in Kuantan belied the strenuous air effort that was undertaken by the Japanese throughout the morning to find and destroy the British fleet.

Shortly after 11:00 hours on 10 December 1941, Force 'Z', while operating under strict conditions of radio silence, came under attack some 60 miles east-north-east of Kuantan. Three groups – the *Genzan*, the *Mihoro* and the *Kanoya* – comprising the 22nd Air Flotilla and numbering 88 aircraft (27 bombers and 61 torpedo bomber aircraft) had left their bases near Saigon just after 06:00 hours. They flew a southerly course following a projected route provided by submarine *I-58*, which earlier that morning at around 03:00 hours had sighted and unsuccessfully attacked Force 'Z'. The first wave of enemy aircraft appeared on *Repulse*'s radar at 10:30 hours; ten bombers flying at 10,000 feet attacked just after 11:00 hours. One 500-pound bomb hit the *Repulse* but it did not seriously damage the old battlecruiser. Despite the growing seriousness of the enemy air attack, Force 'Z' still maintained its radio silence. Not only did it forgo the possibility of fighter support, but also its exact whereabouts was still unknown to supporting air and naval commanders in Singapore. Twenty minutes later a second wave of nine torpedo bombers attacked. They were quickly followed by successive waves of nine or ten enemy aircraft that pressed home the attack on the two capital ships over a period of some 90 minutes. Undeterred by the fiercest anti-aircraft fire, the Japanese pilots attacked with skill, daring and resolution.

Both the *Prince of Wales* and the *Repulse* defended themselves gallantly but they stood little chance against the Japanese bomber and torpedo aircraft. In the absence of friendly air cover the two capital ships were reliant on inadequate organic anti-aircraft defences. At 12:33 hours, a little more than one hour after the first Japanese planes began their attack, the *Repulse* rolled over and sank. Some 40 minutes earlier, she had finally broken radio silence and sent an emergency signal – 'enemy aircraft bombing' – to Palliser, in the naval operations room at Singapore. Exactly 90 minutes after receiving *Repulse*'s signal, 11 Brewster Buffalo fighters of No. 453 (Australian) Squadron, from Sembawang airfield in Singapore, arrived to see the Destroyers collecting the survivors from the *Repulse* and the *Prince of Wales*, the latter having sunk at 13:20 hours.[5] It was the darkest of days in the Royal Navy's history and, as RAF official historians Denis Richards and Hilary St George Saunders concluded, 'the end of sea power as Mahan preached and Nelson had practised it'.[6]

Looking skyward from below the waves

Before he set sail on his ill-fated mission, Admiral Tom Phillips had said that he required both air cover and surprise to be successful. In the end he had neither. In a rather one-sided action that lasted just over two hours, the Royal Navy lost two capital ships and 840 officers and ratings. The Japanese lost just three aircraft.[7]

This chapter examines the Royal Navy's first major engagement against the Japanese in the Pacific during the Second World War from the RAF's perspective. What was the Air Staff's view before, during and after the loss of the two capital ships to enemy air attack? Were alternative plans that reflected an air-minded approach offered, and if they were, why were they not implemented? And if such plans did not exist, why did they not? These questions are a reasonable starting point for any enquiry into joint air/sea operations conducted by British forces during the early years of the Second World War. The answers and analysis that follow are pitched at the operational level of war and do not address the higher political and strategic decision-making processes that preceded the dispatch of Force 'Z' to the Pacific. Readers whose interests lie primarily in Britain's Far Eastern strategy during the inter-war period and/or the Admiralty's plans for the reinforcement and deployment of an Eastern Fleet in late 1940 and 1941 are encouraged to consult the rich extant literature on these subjects.[8]

Inter-war rivalries

For many historians, the roots of this disaster are found in the deleterious relations between the Royal Navy and the Royal Air Force during the 1920s and 1930s. Controversies over the respective responsibilities of the Admiralty and the Air

Ministry in the sphere of naval aviation, inadequate equipment, parsimonious defence budgets, and the lack of a common defence policy to guide the two Services in their peacetime strategic direction and training, all conspired against effective air/sea cooperation on almost every level.[9] Air-minded naval officers tended to leave the Royal Navy for careers in the RAF. Those that remained were very much in the minority, both in number and in terms of their status within the RN. The Admiralty also tended to 'navalize' its aviators and put them under great pressure to conform to 'accepted' Admiralty thinking on all naval matters, but particularly doctrine and tactical practice. Such conditions did not facilitate an open and honest debate within the navy on the optimum development of naval aviation. This shortcoming is seen perhaps most acutely in the much-heated controversy between the Admiralty and the Air Staff over the Bomber v. Battleship.[10] Despite being the world leader in the development of aircraft carriers and naval aviation, the Royal Navy placed its faith in the battleship to remain the dominant factor in future naval warfare. The Admiralty concluded that air power was important but that it was very much ancillary. Aircraft, whether they were shore-based or flown off a carrier, had a combat role as air-defence fighters or torpedo bombers but their primary function for the navy was reconnaissance. It was this same intransigence on the growing roles and importance of air power during the last years of the First World War that led to the creation of a independent air force in Britain – the RAF – and the subsequent problems of cooperation between them during the inter-war period. Even the outbreak of war in 1939 did very little to mitigate the differing perspectives of the Royal Navy and the RAF but it did serve as the basis of a truce of sorts. In the spirit of 'getting on with the task at hand', the two Services agreed to disagree. Discussions on aircraft versus ships were avoided in the Joint Planning Committee, and when duty excluded polite avoidance usually a row ensued.[11]

Royal Navy tactical instructions for an enemy air attack at sea

Having failed to understand the potential of carrier air power it is not a surprise that the Royal Navy did not develop modern ideas for the deployment of carrier warfare. Many of the navy's disadvantages, which were exposed during the early years of the war, flowed from faulty designs. The carriers themselves and the aircraft that would fly off them incorporated numerous technical flaws, but equally the Admiralty's Fighting Instructions of 1939 were based on false premises. The Admiralty believed that the main threat to aircraft carriers, just as it was to all other warships, was the gunfire of enemy surface ships. Torpedoes, either fired from a submarine or dropped by a torpedo bomber, were seen as a threat but this was a capability that few foreign navies had developed so it was not considered to be a serious operational problem. Moreover, if the Fleet (or even a single ship) were surprised by an air attack, the main defence was considered to lie in the anti-aircraft guns and the power of manoeuvre of the individual ships. This practice applied equally to carriers. If time allowed, the carrier would recall its aircraft, land them, stow them in their hangers below deck, and defend itself by gunfire. Not all aircraft carrier captains were comfortable with this approach and the unorthodox among them experimented with radar-controlled fighter aircraft defences in the Mediterranean in 1941. This new procedure, however, was not recognized in official Fleet Tactical Instructions at the time of the sortie by Force 'Z' off Malaya in December 1941.[12]

RAF after-action analysis

In terms of a detailed RAF assessment on Force 'Z' and the loss of the *Prince of Wales* and the *Repulse*, there isn't one. There are 13 pages of uncritical narrative in the Air Historical Branch's history of the war in the Far East.[13] What happened, where and when, but very little on why. Many of the published biographies, diaries and memoirs of leading RAF and other British commanders in the Second World War also contain brief mention of the tragedy, but they too ignore the searching questions and concentrate mainly on the unfortunate fate of Admiral Phillips and his force. The most critical comments come, somewhat surprisingly, perhaps, from some of Phillip's colleagues in the navy. In a letter to Admiral Sir Dudley North, dated 11 December 1941, Admiral Sir James Somerville wrote:

> I felt in my bones all the time that [Phillips] would have to pay sooner or later for his lack of practical war experience & his lack of sea sense but I did not imagine it would have to be at such a price... Battleships by themselves are quite useless whilst co-operation with shore based aircraft requires a lot of practice *and* experience. It's all very lamentable and should not have happened.[14]

Ironically, only four months later, while commanding the Eastern Fleet, Somerville himself took far greater risks off Ceylon. Somerville, however, was lucky; Phillips was not. Minus Somerville's blatant self-promotional careerism, Air Marshal Sir Arthur Harris noted in his wartime memoir how he had warned his friend Tom Phillips 'never to get out from under the air umbrella; if you do, you'll be for it'.[15] Others too have commented on the many celebrated battles between Harris and Phillips over bombers versus ships when they were both the Directors of Plans in their respective Services. During one particularly heated argument in June 1940, General Ismay recounts, Harris exploded: 'One day Tom you will be standing on your bridge and your ship will be smashed to pieces by bombers and torpedo aircraft. As she sinks, your last words will be, "That was a...[bloody] great mine!"'[16] And finally, eleven years after the war, Air Marshal Sir John Slessor wrote:

> Tom resolutely and sometimes violently rejected the idea that an aeroplane could be any real threat to a man-of-war. I have never been more

sorry for anyone than on hearing that he had gone down with his flagship, soon after hoisting his flag at sea for the first time, when the *Prince of Wales* and the *Repulse* were sunk by Japanese aircraft in the Gulf of Siam.[17]

Indirectly the airmen had made their point. Ships that went into action without adequate air cover were doomed to suffer under enemy air attack. This was also the one and only 'lesson learnt' to be recorded in the conclusions of the Royal Navy's own battle summary, first published in 1943. The single sentence reads: 'Once again the lesson of Norway and Crete had received tragic confirmation; fighter support for surface forces operating where there is a possibility of strong enemy air attack is a primary necessity.'[18] Having been caught out by the *Luftwaffe* in the Norwegian campaign was a mistake. Making the same mistake a second time in the Mediterranean, in the relief of Crete, was disturbingly disappointing and unfortunate. But out in the Pacific, off Kuantan, it happened again for the third time in less than two years. Three times the same grave error was made; that is a lot.

Who is to blame for Britain's greatest naval disaster in two world wars?

Phillips is not, of course, to blame for the Royal Navy's earlier losses to aircraft off Norway or in the Mediterranean, but he does warrant a great deal of the blame for the loss of the *Prince of Wales* and the *Repulse*. Phillips, like many of his colleagues in the Admiralty, seriously underestimated the threat of air attack on ships. According to Admiral Willis, who had a long talk with Phillips in Freetown when he was on his way to Singapore, 'he was inclined to scoff at the air menace, and advocated facing it with anti-aircraft fire alone'.[19] Phillips also had a low opinion of his Japanese opponents, ranking them well below the British and the Germans and on a par with the regularly disparaged Italians. Moreover, he was a committed centralist. He did not take his staff into his confidence. Accepting the fact that the success of his mission was predicated on surprise, hence his insistence on radio silence, once both of his pre-conditions of air support and surprise were lost, Phillips altered his plans without informing either his shore based naval staff or the RAF.[20]

To blame the entire tragedy on Phillips, however, as some historians have been wont to do, is unsustainable.[21] Faced with similar circumstances, it is almost certain that any other British admiral would have reacted in the same way as Phillips did. Other admirals, as already noted above, went into action without adequate air cover. And as for Phillips's diversion to Kuantan, it is equally inconceivable that another British admiral, hearing of an enemy landing there, would not have made the minor alterations of course to investigate the report. Even the matter of the aircraft carrier *Indomitable*, intended to accompany Force 'Z' to Singapore but delayed in the West Indies for repairs, is a non-issue. Both Churchill and the Admiralty were aware of Phillips's plans and the composition of his fleet, and they did nothing to stop him.[22] Moreover, the Royal Navy's authorized tactical practice for ships under enemy air attack, even if accompanied by an aircraft carrier, emphasized a reliance on the ship's own guns for self-defence and not on organic fighter aircraft protection.[23] Had the *Indomitable*, therefore, been a part of Force 'Z', it too most likely would have been lost.

If the objective then is to find the culprit to blame for this naval disaster then the first place to look is at British military planning and the operational command structure employed at the time.[24] Air Chief Marshal Sir Robert Brooke-Popham was the Commander-in-Chief in Singapore. He was responsible for air and land operations but he had no authority over Phillips or Force 'Z'. Agreeing on a co-ordinated plan was not standard operating procedure in the British armed forces at this point in the war. The cheerless result of the Royal Navy's single-service approach to operations in the waters north of Singapore is, as noted earlier, well documented. It should not come as any surprise that similar problems with equally disastrous results occurred in other theatres of British operations. The lack of effective air and land cooperation between the Army and the RAF in the Battle for France during the summer of 1940 and the early engagements in North Africa against the Deutscher Afrika Korps are but two celebrated examples of a faulty command structure. Except in a few isolated cases, for example the Battle of the River Plate and the Battle of Britain, the Second World War was a war of joint and combined operations. The armed forces that ultimately learned this lesson were the ones that ended the war victorious. British military planning was woefully not joint at the start of the Second World War. All three Services pursued independent strategies and conducted their operations almost in isolation of each other.[25] Costly and hard-earned battle experience eventually led to a more joined-up tri-service approach to operations. Sadly, as the loss of Force 'Z' so clearly illustrates, it was a long and hard lesson for Anglo-American armies, navies and air forces to learn.

Notes

1. See G.A.H. Gordon, 'The British Navy, 1918–1945', in Keith Neilson and Jane Errington (eds), *Navies and Global Defence: Theories and Strategy* (Westport CT: 1995); Jon Sumida, 'The Royal Navy and Technological Change, 1915–1945', in Ronald Haycock and Keith Neilson (eds), *Men, Machines, and War* (Waterloo, Ontario: Wilfrid Laurier University Press, 1988); and John Winton, *Air Power at Sea 1939–45* (London: Sidgwick & Jackson, 1976).
2. Alan Matthews, the War Ships. *The Sinking of the Repulse and the Prince of Wales* (http://www.btinternet.com/~m.a.christie/warship2.htm), 11–12.
3. See S. Woodburn Kirby, *The War Against Japan*. Vol. I, *The Loss of Singapore* (London: HMSO, 1957), 193–200; AHB Narrative, The Campaigns in the Far East. Vol. II: Malaya, Netherlands East Indies and Burma (nd), 35–47; B.R. 1736 (8)/1955 Naval Staff History Second World War, Battle Summary No.14 (revised) 'Loss of H.M. Ships *Prince of Wales* and *Repulse*, 10th December 1941 (London: HMSO, 1955); Henry Probert, *The Forgotten Air Force: The Royal Air Force in the War Against Japan 1941–1945* (London: Brassey's, 1995), 45–8; and Martin Middlebrook and Patrick Mahoney, *Battleship: The Loss of the Prince of Wales and the Repulse* (London: Allen Lane, 1977).

4. The following narrative on the sinking of the *Prince of Wales* and the *Repulse* is based on the accounts provided in official Royal Navy and RAF publications. See B.R. 1736 (8)/1955, Battle Summary No. 14 (revised), 'Loss of H.M. Ships *Prince of Wales* and *Repulse*', 7–18; and Denis Richards and Hilary St George Saunders, *Royal Air Force 1939–1945*, Vol. 2 *The Fight Avails* (London: HMSO, 1953), 24–9.
5. AHB Narrative, The Campaigns in the Far East. Vol. II: Malaya, Netherlands East Indies and Burma, 35–47; B.R. 1736 (8)/1955, Battle Summary No. 14 (revised), 'Loss of H.M. Ships *Prince of Wales* and *Repulse*', 3–18.
6. Richards and Saunders, *Royal Air Force*, 29.
7. Kirby, *War Against Japan*, 198; and AHB Narrative, The Campaigns in the Far East. Vol. II: Malaya, Netherlands East Indies and Burma, 44.
8. A good starting point is Ian Cowman, 'Main Fleet to Singapore? Churchill, the Admiralty, and Force Z', *Journal of Strategic Studies*, 17 (June 1994), 79–93. See also Norman H. Gibbs, *Grand Strategy*, Vol. I (London: HMSO, 1976); Arthur Marder, *Old Friends, New Enemies: the Royal Navy and the Imperial Japanese Navy – Strategic Illusions, 1936–1941* (Oxford: Oxford University Press, 1981); Stephen Roskill, *Churchill and the Admirals* (London: HMSO, 1977); W. David McIntyre, *The Rise and Fall of the Singapore Naval Base, 1919–1942* (London: Macmillan, 1979); and Paul Haggie, *Britannia at Bay: The Defence of Britain's Far Eastern Empire, 1931–1941* (Oxford: Clarendon, 1981).
9. Historical Section, Admiralty. *Naval Staff History of the Second World War*, Vol. I, *The Development of British Naval Aviation 1919–1945* (London: HMSO, 1954); Guy Robbins, *The Aircraft Carrier Story 1908–1945* (London: Cassell & Co., 2001); Geoffrey Till, 'Adopting the Aircraft Carrier: The British, American, and Japanese case studies', in Williamson Murray and Allan R. Millett (eds), *Military Innovation in the Interwar Period* (Cambridge: Cambridge University Press, 1996), 191–226; and Geoffrey Till, *Air Power and the Royal Navy 1914–1945, a Historical Survey* (London: Macdonald and Jane's, 1979).
10. Till, *Air Power and the Royal Navy 1914–1945*, 154–60, 193–4; and David Hamer, *Bombers versus Battleships* (Annapolis MD: Naval Institute Press, 1998).
11. Sir John Slessor, *The Central Blue* (London: Cassell, 1956), 277.
12. PRO ADM 116/4712 Fleet Tactical Instructions Home and Mediterranean Fleets (March 1939); and ADM 239/261 The Fighting Instructions (1939); Historical Section, Admiralty, 'The Development of British Naval Aviation 1919–1945', 4; Hamer, *Bombers versus Battleships*, 28–35; and Till, *Air Power and the Royal Navy*, 149.
13. AHB Narrative, The Campaigns in the Far East. Vol. II: Malaya, Netherlands East Indies and Burma, 35–47.
14. Michael Simpson (ed.), *The Somerville Papers* (Aldershot: Ashgate, 1995), 341.
15. Sir Arthur T. Harris, *Bomber Offensive* (London: Collins, 1947), 275.
16. Sir Arthur Harris as quoted in Lord Ismay, *The Memoirs of General the Lord Ismay* (London:, 1960), 240.
17. Slessor, *The Central Blue*, 277.
18. B.R. 1736 (8)/1955, Battle Summary No. 14 (revised), 'Loss of H.M. Ships *Prince of Wales* and *Repulse*', 19–20.
19. Hamer, *Bombers versus Battleships*, 119.
20. Ibid., 122, 135–6.
21. See Louis Allen, *Singapore 1941–1942* (London: Frank Cass, 1993), 143–6; Marder, *Old Friends*, 365–6; Geoffrey Regan, *Naval Blunders* (London: A. Deutsch, 1993), 68–72; and Norman Dixon, *On the Psychology of Military Incompetence* (London: Cape, 1976), 136.
22. S.W. Roskill, *The War at Sea*, Vol. I (London: HMSO, 1954), 563; Hamer, *Bombers versus Battleships*, 135; and Probert, *Forgotten Air Force*, 46–7.

23. Hamer, *Bombers versus Battleships*, 34, 134.
24. Probert, *Forgotten Air Force*, 47.
25. Sebastian Cox, 'British Military Planning and the Origins of the Second World War', in B.J.C. McKercher and Roch Legault (eds), *Military Planning and the Second World War in Europe* (Westport CT: Praeger, 2001), 103–19.

6

'LIGHT TWO LANTERNS, THE BRITISH ARE COMING BY SEA': ROYAL NAVY PARTICIPATION IN THE PACIFIC 1944–1945

Jon Robb-Webb

When Paul Revere lit two lanterns atop the bell tower of Christ Church in Boston on the night of 4 April 1775 to indicate that the British would come 'by sea' he can scarcely have imagined that 169 years later the Admiral commanding the world's most powerful naval force would be invoking his name and action to describe the imminent arrival of the British Pacific Fleet for participation in the closing stages of World War Two. Admiral Chester Nimitz, Commander in Chief (CinC), Pacific Ocean Area (CINCPAC), wrote to the CinC, United States Fleet and Chief of Naval Operations, Admiral Ernest J. King, in December 1944 telling him that 'I do not need Paul Revere (with his three [*sic*] lanterns) to tell me that the British are coming. The attached paraphrase of six Top Secret dispatches reads like an operation order for an occupation force. Perhaps it is intended to be an occupation force.'[1]

Nimitz's last sentiment was undoubtedly tongue-in-cheek but it does reveal something of the scepticism that presaged the Royal Navy's return to the Pacific. The Royal Navy (RN) was about to make its reappearance in the vastness of the Pacific, a vastness dominated by the United States Navy since 1939. The RN's contribution to the defeat of Japan could not be described as decisive, vital or indeed even necessary. John Winton wrote 'even the most eager British historian could never claim that the British Pacific Fleet (BPF) played anything more than an ancillary part in the war at sea in the Pacific'.[2]

The combat record of the BPF sits uneasily with the fact that the Fleet was probably the most powerful force the Admiralty has ever dispatched.[3] The total operational achievement of the British Pacific Fleet's surface ships amounted to 36 air-strike days, and four bombardments of enemy territory. For a force that comprised four battleships, five fleet, four light fleet and eight escort carriers, 10 cruisers, 40 destroyers and more than 170 minesweepers and support vessels, not counting some 30 submarines, it is not the most illustrious battle roll. In comparison with the fight waged against the U-boat it was a mere drop in the ocean. The Allies lost 12.8 million tons of shipping in the grey Atlantic; the majority of the 73,642 deaths the RN suffered were in European and Atlantic waters.

In spite of the preceding, the British Pacific Fleet was one of the undoubted successes of the RN during the second World War. Not so much because of the damage the Fleet inflicted upon Japan's capacity to continue the war, but rather ironically because of the damage it received. The BPF was a tool of British naval diplomacy. Its limited operational activity was responsible for changing American attitudes toward the RN and the UK, something which was to be of immense importance in the creation of the post-War relationship. Nimitz's attitude went from the undoubted scepticism, illustrated above, through an acceptance 'that "we would make it work regardless of anything"',[4] to a position where he took for granted the BPF's participation and contribution. In order to accomplish this change it was essential that the RN operated 'in company with the US Fleet in their most advanced operations against Japan'.[5] This was not achieved without some considerable difficulty. It was one of the major accomplishments of the Fleet's Commander-in-Chief, Admiral Sir Bruce Fraser, that the BPF were not assigned to the 'many less exacting tasks in the South West Pacific and elsewhere'.[6] Had this occurred, then any political credit that the dispatch of the Fleet had accrued would have been squandered.

The British official history of the Second World War claims that, until the Octagon conference of September 1944, events in the Pacific had 'affected the British only indirectly or by implication'.[7] It was here that the Western Allies then agreed that a British Fleet should be sent as soon as possible to work with the Americans in the main theatre of operations against Japan. The Admiralty had initiated the first scheme to develop fleet bases in Australia as early as 27 December 1941.[8] The loss of Hong Kong two days later followed by the fall of Singapore pushed the RN out of the Pacific. It was to be nearly three years to the day before Admiral Sir Bruce Fraser, CinC British Pacific Fleet, eventually opened offices for a new headquarters in Barrack House, Sydney.[9] Delays in dispatching a fleet were the result of a complex web of politics, economics, resources and strategic priorities. It was following the surrender of the Italian Fleet and the crippling of the *Tirpitz*, during and after September 1943, that a degree of choice entered British calculations with regard to the war against Japan. Until then Britain had been forced simply to respond to Japanese strategy, fighting where it could rather than where it would. After this time, the freeing of naval units in the Mediterranean, and the easing of pressure involved in keeping watch on Germany's last remaining significant surface threat, allowed consideration of how, where and in what form the country could participate in the war in the Far East. At the SEXTANT conference in November 1943, the British high command accepted as a basis for examination the deployment of a fleet to the Pacific, the establishment of its main base in Australia and its advance base in the Solomon and Bismarck islands.

The following spring, however, Churchill presented a paper to the Chiefs of Staff arguing that the British effort should be focused on an amphibious strategy in the Indian Ocean.[10] This was in part prompted by the desire to regain Malaya and Singapore before the Americans completed the defeat of Japan. The PM sought to ensure that when the war ended Britain would be in possession of what, in his view, rightfully belonged to Britain and would not be dependent upon the Americans for the return of lost British colonies.

H.P. Willmott's extensive study of British strategic planning with regard to the Far East theatre argues that much of Churchill's reasoning behind independent action against the Japanese can be attributed to an antagonism toward the adoption of a subsidiary role to the Americans.[11] Correlli Barnett has argued that Churchill's idea for concentrating the British effort in South-East Asia made far better politico-strategic sense. He states that '[i]t would have enabled Britain to win her own, if peripheral, victory against Japan in her own theatre; to play a middle-sized fish in a middle-sized pond.'[12] He continued that operating in the Central Pacific under Nimitz, 'meant playing the sprat in the largest pond in the world [which] could only expose Britain's shrunken relative stature as a power and above all as a naval power'.[13] Willmott's interpretation of Churchill's motives has much to commend it but Barnett's analysis misses much of the purpose of the BPF. British naval power had without a doubt shrunk, but what there was of it performed a vital function that could only be achieved in the Central Pacific.

In contrast to the position taken by the Prime Minister, the Chiefs of Staff saw the United States as a power to be supported rather than guarded against. Their position envisaged the main British and Commonwealth effort intimately bound up with the Americans in the primary operations against Japan. As Admiral Cunningham, the First Sea Lord, recalled,

> For some reason which I never really understood the Prime Minister did not at first agree. He seemed to take the view that the fleet would be better employed in assisting in the recapture of our own possessions, Malaya and Singapore, or it may be he was rather daunted, if daunted he ever was, by the huge demands made upon shipping by the provision of the fleet train.[14]

Churchill was apparently prepared to wait on the defensive until April 1945 if his preferred operation could not be mounted before then, something which the Chiefs of Staff thought would alienate the Americans.

The resources available were indeed strictly limited. It became clear that as the war in Europe dragged on beyond the end of 1944, British manpower could not be stretched to accommodate a significant amphibious commitment in the Indian Ocean or the South West Pacific. Even following the conclusion of European hostilities the demands imposed on manpower resources by the domestic economy and occupation duties threatened to be so heavy that any substantial redeployment of ground forces to the Far East would be impracticable. This was one of the strongest arguments advanced by the Chiefs of Staff in favour of a naval commitment in the Pacific: the dispatch of a far from insignificant fleet was not dependent on the state of the war in Europe. Or so it was argued. This was the case with regard to the availability of the major fighting units – carriers, battleships – which were no longer required in European waters, but the logistical infrastructure for the Fleet Train that permitted them to function was severely handicapped by a lack of shipping. What was available was needed to support the land campaign in north-west Europe, in Italy and supply those parts of the continent that had already been liberated.

Manpower problems were further exacerbated by the desire of the Government to ameliorate some of the hardships inflicted by the war's necessities on the civilian population. This coupled with the need to restore, as far as possible, the nation's capital equipment, particularly homes and industrial machinery, placed severe restrictions on what was available for dispatch to the Pacific. There was also considerable pressure to restore export trade even before the conclusion of hostilities in the Far East. Although the problems faced over manpower were admitted by Cunningham after the war, the truth at the time was that very few involved in planning the Navy's contribution had any realistic idea of what the Pacific under-taking would entail.[15] The distances over which the United States Navy was supporting its Fleet and the scale and rate of its operating were of an order of magnitude greater than anything the RN had previously contemplated.

The restrictions placed on the strategic choices available to the British by the parlous state of the UK economy contrasted starkly with the position that the United States found themselves in. American industrial and military might allowed them to begin offensive operations in the Pacific at the same time as the Allied effort in Europe reached its peak. The British sought to deal with their enemies in turn. In truth they had no option. The Americans possessed such reserves of men and material that were now coming on-stream as to make possible their shift in strategic posture. The British Chiefs of Staff knew that there was no real alternative to a Pacific naval commitment under American command, directed along the shortest route to Japanese surrender. This alone offered the prospect of an early end to a war which Britain could no longer sustain.[16]

It was clear to the Chiefs of Staff that the United Kingdom was so dependent upon American assistance that any failure to make available what fighting strength could be mustered would have serious consequences for the flow of American aid, both in the present and in the future. In addition it was felt that Britain's best hope of securing a voice in the ordering of the post-war world was by fighting alongside, though clearly subordinate to, the Americans in the Pacific rather than by indulging itself in a secondary theatre.[17]

This position was supported by the Foreign Office, which in part derived its stance from an appreciation of possible post-war advantage when seeking to secure loans from the Americans.[18] The Foreign Office's main concern was American attitudes. The North American Desk was of the view that a Pacific commitment was in Britain's best interest in dealing with the question of war debts, the negotiation of future loans, and shipping allocations, and with American public opinion that needed to be assured that Britain had played its full part in the Japanese war.[19]

This analysis echoed the conclusions drawn by British diplomats in the United States. The British Ambassador in Washington, Lord Halifax, suggested that British forces allocated for service in the Pacific should be sent to the Far East via the United States as visual proof of the commitment to continue the war until the defeat of the last Axis partner. Overall, the Foreign Office considered that a failure to participate in the final attack on the Japanese home islands would be a 'very grave handicap to us for years to come in all Anglo-American questions'.[20] In addition, it was understood that the dispatch of a token force would not achieve the desired political objective. It was clear that, in the intensive, efficient and hard-striking type of war that the US Fleet was fighting, nothing but the inclusion of a 'big British force would be noticeable and nothing but the best would be tolerated'.[21]

There is some evidence that similar thoughts for the post-war also occupied some American minds. On 1 September 1944 the US Ambassador in London, John G. Winant, signalled Harry Hopkins, Roosevelt's closest confident and adviser, that '[i]f we allow the British to limit their active participation to recapturing areas that are to their selfish interest alone and not participate in smashing Japan... we will create in the United States a hatred for Great Britain that will make for schism in the post-war years.'[22] Hopkins concurred, replying on 4 September that '[w]e simply must find a way to have Great Britain take her full and proper place in the war against Japan.'[23] Cordell Hull, the US Secretary of State, sent the President a memorandum on 8 September arguing the same points:

> One of the most important objectives of US policy must be to bring the British into the war... in the Far East to the greatest possible extent. The advantages of such a course are obvious... The disadvantages of the failure of the British to participate to the full [are an] immediate and hostile public reaction in the United States.[24]

The effect on Britain's political leadership of American public opinion concerning British participation in the war against Japan had already made itself felt. While visiting Annapolis during the spring of 1943 the Foreign Secretary, Anthony Eden, delivered a speech that attracted 'exceptionally favourable nationwide attention and discussion'.[25] The impact of Eden's speech was made the more important because of a growing uneasiness that had developed in the United States concerning Britain's intentions in the Far East brought about in the main by remarks the Prime Minister had made. Churchill had failed recently to include China on his list of Great Powers, and had commented on a partial demobilization of Commonwealth troops after Germany's surrender. The Foreign Secretary had been at pains to express the United Kingdom and Commonwealth's determination to fight to the end against Japan and his recognition of China was met with, 'universal expressions of relief'.[26] This effort to generate maximum publicity for Britain's declared intention of fighting in the Pacific side by side with the Americans and its subsequent realization was to become a major feature of the BPF's activities.

Criticism in the United States concerning the British failure to participate in the war against Japan had been continuing to grow following the successful invasion of Europe. However, at the end of September 1944 the Embassy in Washington was able, with a degree of satisfaction, to wire that, '... although we do not obtain the full credit we deserve there are signs that the fact that it was we who demanded a greater share in the Far Eastern campaign and the Americans who sought to limit it, has proved a shock to our sincere but misinformed critics'.[27] The efforts of British diplomats to raise the profile of the Commonwealth's participation in the Pacific were beginning to bear modest fruit, as 'it is taken for granted that we will participate as fully as circumstances allow, but it is popularly anticipated that our role will be secondary'.[28]

Despite such optimistic reports from the Washington Embassy, a more realistic assessment of the effect that the British would have was delivered after the BPF strikes on Sumatran oil-production facilities. Described in the RN's *Official History* as the BPF's 'greatest contribution to final victory over Japan'.[29]

> That our war effort in the Pacific is likely to be regarded as purely nominal if known at all to the great majority of Americans is brought out once more by the sparse news coverage given this week to British task forces' attack on oil refineries in the Dutch East Indies. This example once more underlines the lesson that, whatever our actual participation in the Pacific war may be, the general emotional attitude in the United States towards Britain after Germany's downfall will greatly affect the amount of credit we get for our effort.[30]

This assessment placed a premium on the campaign being waged to influence American opinion. The distribution of Government posters and other propaganda material, often bearing the quote from Churchill that 'Britain will pursue the war against Japan to the very end', was not only intended to reorientate the British public toward the Far East as the end in Europe drew nearer, but was also directed at the Allies across the Atlantic.[31] Although the fact of British participation was becoming more widely appreciated there still existed a degree of suspicion with regard to the form and nature of any contribution. In the spring of 1945 General George Marshall, US Army Chief of Staff, and Admirals William Halsey, Commander US Third Fleet, and Chester Nimitz, while in Washington, briefed journalists privately on the broad themes of Allied strategy following the end of the war in Europe.

The broad outlines of Pacific strategy now provided for American forces to tackle Japan direct while other Allied forces would be used for such specialized tasks as removing the Japanese from their conquered overseas territories. The rationale for this division of responsibilities was offered in a succession of inspired broadcasts by Gram Swing,[32] in which he declared

...we are not going to spend American lives and treasure in freeing imperial possessions from the Japanese and then turn them back to their pre-war owners. It is for the British to clear the Japanese out of Malaya and for the Dutch to clear them out of the Netherlands Indies. If the Dutch do not have the strength to do it they must ask the British to help them. We are not going to do it...We see it as our assignment to bear the responsibility of defeating Japan and that we are prepared to do by ourselves.[33]

In this environment British planning deliberations were under way in London. Churchill still favoured the use of amphibious operations descending into Southeast Asia operating independently from the Americans. At the same time, the Americans were urging the British to press their forces forward through Burma with the intention of opening up the route to China, which could eventually be used to support an air campaign against Japanese forces on the continent and ultimately the Home Islands themselves. Designs for these operations, however, were made irrelevant by the quickening pace of American progress in the Pacific theatre. The pressure brought to bear on the UK to carry out these operations reveals that it was not only the British who suffered from confusion in the higher command echelons.

American planning was beset by issues of inter-service rivalry as well as the complications of alliance relations. The balance had to be struck between the competing claims for priority from General Douglas MacArthur's essentially army command, and Nimitz's naval Pacific command, and an independently minded Army Air Force bombing campaign. King and Nimitz agreed that Japan could and should be defeated by blockade, bombing, and submarine warfare.[34] In contrast, the Army held to the view that the Imperial Japanese Army had to be defeated totally, which necessitated a land campaign in China.

Prior to November 1943 the Americans had assumed that as all carrier battles to date had resulted in losses, a worst-case scenario would therefore require some form of British naval commitment. American planners working on the Twelve-month Plan that set a target date of October 1945 for the defeat of Japan came to the conclusion that a British naval presence in the central Pacific was necessary to meet such a timetable.[35] On 2 November 1943 British members of the Joint Staff Mission noted that 'whilst admitting the need for British naval assistance in the Pacific 1944–1945 U.S. still hope against hope that they might be able to bring off decisive fleet action alone'.[36] Although American naval planners were conceding that a role for the RN in the form of 'the greatest contribution by the British naval and amphibious forces to the overall effort...would be to undertake continuing offensive operations in the Southeast Asian areas'.[37] the Chief of Naval Operations, Admiral King, was wholly opposed. In practice this created one of the most unlikely alliances to emerge from the story of Anglo-American grand strategy in the Far East, that of King and Churchill seeking the same policy in opposition to the British Chiefs of Staff and the American State Department.[38]

At the end of June the President approved the US Army's plan for invading Kyushu on 1 November, conveying this and other decisions to the British in a memorandum the following day.[39] This was another demonstration of Britain's junior status. The tentative plans envisaged an invasion of some five million men covered and supported by a Fleet and air force larger than had been used in Overlord. Almost all the forces would be American and of such scale as to absorb almost all of their available strength. It seemed, therefore, to the Joint Chiefs of Staff (JCS) at this stage that their allies could help best by complementary action elsewhere, the British in the South-west Pacific and the Russians, when they entered the war, on the mainland of Asia. Although this looked remarkably akin to what Churchill had been advocating to the British Chiefs of Staff, political and economic factors, as well as a shortage of manpower, cast grave doubts over their practicality.

If the Japanese Home Islands were to be invaded over the next ten months, it was important for political reasons that the British should play a part in the operations. Naval and air support of the invasion, accompanied by 'mopping up' operations far away, were not considered enough. Land forces must participate, on whatever scale, in the invasion itself. Unfortunately, it was unlikely that more than two or three British and Commonwealth divisions could take part, and even then only in the invasion of Honshu (Operation 'Coronet') in the spring of 1946.[40]

British proposals for the use of the BPF and a Very Long Range (VLR) bomber force of ten squadrons (later expanding to twenty) in Coronet (the assault on Tokyo) were acknowledged by the JCS, but the Americans clearly had some reservations concerning the employment of ground troops. Agreeing in principle to the use of a Commonwealth land force in the final phase in the war against Japan, the JCS were worried about a number of key issues. First, the unspecified nature of the commitment made it impossible to draw up detailed plans for the invasion; second, there were perceived difficulties incorporating Indian troops into American operations (language and acclimatization); and third, that the agreement of the other Dominions concerned had not yet been obtained.

In truth, the overstretch brought about by occupation duties in Europe, the falling intake of service personnel and exhausted state of the war economy meant that these plans were exceptionally optimistic to say the least. Japan's surrender saved the embarrassment of being unable to realize them in practice. The only substantial contribution that the British had to offer was a naval one. The question remained whether it would be accepted by the Americans and, if it was, where it would operate.

It was at the Octagon Conference at Quebec, in September 1944, that the major decision concerning British participation was taken. During the meetings, not only was Admiral King forced to accept a British presence, but Churchill also performed an about-face over the substance and form of the contribution. Admiral King recalled after the war that the PM urged that the RAF and the RN be permitted to join the effort against the Japanese as soon as possible.[41] Roosevelt asked King whether 'he needed any help from the Royal Navy', which King declined, arguing that the best occupation for any available British troops, planes, and ships would be the recovery of Singapore. He went on to argue that UK forces should be employed to assist the Dutch in the recovery of the chain of islands from Sumatra through Java to Borneo. Having changed his mind as to where the RN should be employed, such arguments did not please the Prime Minister.

Nimitz also noticed that the Prime Minister was clearly agitated by a Combined Chiefs' proposal that the Royal Navy would not operate north or east of the Philippines.[42] The CINPAC, Nimitz, recognized that the British, with many political and economic interests in the Far East, 'needed a victory in that part of the world to erase from the minds of the Orientals the effect of the crushing defeats of 1941 and 1942'. He believed that Churchill would not be content with the prospect of minor successes in some out-of-the-way corner of the Pacific theatre. The Prime Minister by now wanted British forces clearly and visibly involved in the final defeat of the Japanese homeland. King too was aware of the political motivations behind the British position. In his autobiography King makes it clear that he was suspicious of the offer of British assistance, precisely because he feared that any combined effort would have political strings attached. In particular, he was concerned that it would oblige the USN to reciprocate with help clearing the Japanese out of the Malay States and the Netherlands East Indies, in effect a distraction from the main task. Attempting to deflect the issue, King reported that a paper was being prepared for the Combined Chiefs of Staff on the possible employment of British forces in the Pacific.[43] Churchill raised the question of whether it would not be better to employ the new British ships in place of the 'battle-worn' vessels of the USN. King could only respond by saying the matter was under active consideration, but Churchill continued to press the issue. Roosevelt eventually conceded, saying that '[he] should like to see the British fleet wherever and whenever possible'. This exchange shook Admiral King, his disquiet clearly visible to all the participants. Nimitz recounts that 'Churchill was offended. To him it was inconceivable that an offer of the fleet of Drake and Hawke and St. Vincent and Nelson should not be instantly and gratefully embraced. "The offer of the British Fleet has been made," growled Churchill. "Is it accepted?" "Yes," said Roosevelt.'[44]

This new-found enthusiasm on the part of the Prime Minister for the British Pacific Fleet operating as part of the main campaign against Japan came as something of a welcome surprise to the Chiefs of Staff. Admiral Cunningham declared he was delighted with the Prime Minister's change of thinking and was convinced the Royal Navy needed to be right alongside the United States Navy in the central Pacific, no matter what Admiral King might have liked.[45] Samuel Morrison described the decision on the BPF thus: 'Mr Churchill, as usual, got what he wanted; although Admiral King almost upset the apple cart at the Octagon Conference by letting it be known that he wanted no part of the British Navy in the Central Pacific'.[46] This latter point was something that would come back to haunt the alliance, when it became more widely known and more widely reported while the BPF were actually engaged in operations with the USN.

The day following Roosevelt's acceptance of a RN contribution, 14 September, the UK Chiefs of Staff met their United States counterparts without either the Prime Minister or President and again raised the question of the British Navy in the Pacific. Admiral King, as adamant as ever, hotly refused to have anything to do with it, and argued that the President's acceptance of the offer did not mean what the British interpreted it as meaning. He accepted that it was of course essential to have sufficient forces for the war against Japan but that he was not prepared to accept a British Fleet that he could not employ or support and which might necessitate the removal of some USN elements.[47] The discussion became more heated with King berating not only his supposed allies, but also his fellow members of the Joint Chiefs. Admiral Cunningham recalled how King, having raised his voice to General Marshall, the US Army Chief of Staff, was finally called to order by Admiral Leahy, the President's Chief of Staff, with the remark: 'I don't think we should wash our linen in public.'

> King, with the other American Chiefs of Staff against him, eventually gave way but with very bad grace. The atmosphere was less stormy when we met King next afternoon. He was resigned to the use of our fleet in the Pacific; but made it quite clear that it must expect no assistance from the Americans. From this rather unhelpful attitude he never budged.[48]

Two months later at the end of November, King met with Admiral Nimitz in San Francisco to discuss the situation in the Pacific following the Japanese defeat at the Battle of Leyte. The subject of British participation was again debated. The Americans still had some scepticism concerning whether the BPF would appear at all.[49] King's memoirs claim that these doubts were not the result of any 'lack of good will' on the part of the RN but rather the question was one of actual capability. King's view was that although RN ships had operated throughout the seven seas, they had never in modern times operated for long periods at such distance from any permanent established base, and so had not had the experience of replenishment at sea or of dealing with fleet material and supply so far from home. All kinds of supplies were short, and the whole world lacked sufficient cargo ships. In addition, the RN was not familiar with the administration of carriers in large numbers that had been developed by the United States Navy in the war years.[50] King emphasized that the British CinC would be an administrative, and not operational, designation; that the officer would report to King, who would in turn give him specific directives. King still held to the view that the British should operate as separately from the USN as possible. He intended that the BPF be given certain tasks to carry out independently, rather than for ships of the two navies to be manoeuvred together.

Returning from OCTAGON the Admiralty now believed that they knew what was required: a main fleet of balanced arms whose primary offensive power would be carrier-borne aircraft, supported by a Fleet Train, capable of operating alongside the USN in the most advanced operations against the Japanese. It was, however, a very different matter to make the necessary arrangements to get that policy implemented. In the first instance the feeling remained that neither Admiral King nor the Navy Department in Washington wanted the British Fleet in the Pacific. Second, that because of this, the RN would have to depend entirely upon their own efforts to sustain the commitment. 'We could expect no help from the American organization.'[51]

The agreements of the OCTAGON conference and earlier finally bore fruit on 19 November 1944 when the Far East Fleet was dissolved and replaced by the BPF and the Eastern Fleet. Admiral Fraser established his headquarters in Australia and began attempting to organize his command, which, in reality, only existed on paper. He threw himself wholeheartedly into the task dispatching signals to the Admiralty in London, liaising with the Australian Government to speed along the essential shore work and corresponding at length with Admiral Nimitz concerning the details of the BPF's employment. Fraser eventually arrived with his staff on 16 December at Pearl Harbor where he and Nimitz were able to renew their acquaintance. (They had first met ten years previously when both were captains in the Pacific.) The brief drawn up by Fraser's staff concerning the subjects for discussion at the meeting reveals much of the arguments that were being explored at his headquarters. The fundamental issue remained the details of where and how the BPF would operate. Three proposals were examined. The first was for entirely separate US and British strategic areas. The staff paper advanced two reasons in support of this idea; first, CinC BPF would exercise full operational control, and second, as a consequence of this, it was felt that the BPF would be easier to administer and operate.

Arrayed against these points were three important arguments. First, it was thought that the BPF were unlikely to be allocated anything but an insignificant area. Such a decision would clearly have been in conflict with Fraser's ideas of participating in the most advanced Pacific operations. Second, the practicalities of a separate strategic area gave some concern. The BPF was unlikely to be self-sufficient in either shore facilities or harbour-defence capabilities for a considerable time, which would delay the fleet becoming operational. The final argument against a separate strategic area was the recognition that any such arrangement would be uneconomical in overall naval power. The war in the Far East was highlighting the inability of the British to sustain the war. Their best hope was to bring about as rapid a conclusion to hostilities as possible. Any diversion of military capability into subsidiary activities would be counter-productive.

The alternative proposal under consideration from the British side was combined US and UK strategic areas. The idea was that the BPF would operate as a strategic unit on specific missions as designated by the American High Command. Fraser's staff suggested the example of operating from Manila to cut Japanese North-South supply routes in the South China Sea. This it was felt could be combined with other specific operations – for example, a Highball or XE attack on the Japanese Fleet.[52] When Fraser committed his thoughts on these proposals to paper he wrote,

I favour alternative (2) and it is particularly desired that the British Fleet should operate as near the heart of the enemy as possible. At the same time I want to emphasize that it is unreservedly at the disposal of the American Command for the purpose of bringing the war to a conclusion at the earliest possible moment.[53]

In essence this is what took place during the invasion of Okinawa, Operation ICEBERG. The BPF, operating under Admiral Raymond Spruance, Commander US Fifth Fleet, participated in the main campaign, though they were allocated the task of neutralizing the Japanese air threat to the invasion that could be staged through Sakishima Gunto. This arrangement was not, however, confirmed at the time. Nimitz refused to make any commitments to the British concerning operations. He suggested that they raid the Japanese-held oil installations on Sumatra and implied that, for the time being, the British Pacific Fleet could make its best contribution by attaching itself to Admiral Thomas Kinkaid's Seventh Fleet for operations in the Southwest Pacific Area. This was distinctly not what the British, and in particular Fraser, had in mind. When they objected, Admiral Nimitz said that he might be able to make use of their fleet in connection with the scheduled assault on Okinawa. He then turned them over to Admiral Spruance so that he and his staff could consider that possibility.[54]

It is clear that the British made a very different interpretation of this planning than the Americans. Fraser took this to mean that the BPF would operate either under Spruance and the Fifth Fleet or Halsey, when the Fleet became the Third, in the main operations against Japan, and reported reaching agreement to London. He signalled: 'I intend to operate the British Pacific Fleet to the best possible effect in the most advanced operations in the Pacific and Fleet Admiral Nimitz has agreed that I should do so.'[55] The Americans, however, continued to explore the possibility of a transfer of the British to MacArthur's Southwest Pacific Area command. This reassignment remained a distinct likelihood until August the following year.

The staff talks continued with discussions returning again to the tricky issue of basing requirements. At this stage of the BPF's build-up, the aim was to operate a fully self-supporting balanced fleet from an advanced base as soon as possible and not to call upon the Americans for any support. However, owing to the late arrival of some units, particularly shore-based facilities, the British felt it would probably be necessary to call upon American assistance. Fraser believed that it would be convenient if the BPF's first advanced base was also one used by the USN. Admiral Cunningham in London disagreed with Fraser on this point. He wrote to Fraser, arguing the CinC BPF only had a short-term policy of bringing the greatest force to bear on the enemy as soon as possible. Cunningham believed,

[w]here we differ, as far as I can see, is in our conception of what the course of the war in the Pacific will be... we are strongly of the opinion that we must continue to press for some sort of forward base. The great

difficulty that we are experiencing in getting our demands for the fleet train conceded also makes a forward base with some storage and aircraft facilities essential.[56]

Everything Fraser attempted, however, was constrained by the limited logistics available. He argued with Cunningham's concept of an independent forward base because the BPF simply did not possess the resources to construct or man it.[57] The outcome of this debate left the BPF with rear bases in Eastern Australia and an intermediate base at Manus, a location Fraser described as '...a dismal place'.[58]

The arrangements put in place between the two allies for the command of the BPF reveal something of the complex and tortuous nature of their relationship. Admiral King was reluctant to accept a Commander-in-Chief of Fraser's rank for the RN in the Pacific.[59] King was concerned that Fraser would be senior to the American Commanders afloat if he went to sea. The compromise settled upon by the two navies was that Fraser could be CinC BPF, but exercise that command from shore, with Vice Admiral Sir Bernard Rawlings commanding the Fleet at sea.

Command arrangements between the US and UK became embroiled in not just inter-allied relations but also those between MacArthur (CinC SWPA) and Nimitz. At the end of December 1944 Fraser received a report via the Admiralty in London concerning comments made by General MacArthur to his British liaison officer, Lieutenant-General Sir Herbert Lumsden.[60] Lumsden had written to General Sir Hastings Ismay, Deputy Military Secretary to the War Cabinet, that MacArthur now wished the BPF to operate in the Southwest Pacific Area. This would provide him with a naval capability that was virtually independent of Nimitz. In his somewhat expressive style MacArthur told Lumsden, 'Were the British Fleet here now I could give them ample opportunities of gaining great renown for themselves and great credit to the British Empire.'[61]

The Admiralty advised Fraser in the report that though such arrangements might be 'considered convenient in the future' at the present the fear was that they would exclude the BPF from participating in the major operations planned for the Pacific. Fraser was instructed, 'You should therefore neither discourage it, should it be brought up in discussions in Australia, or with Admiral Nimitz, but refer exact terms of any proposal made to Admiralty.'[62]

Nimitz requested that before coming into the Pacific the BPF's aircraft should attack Palembang, the centre of Japanese petroleum production in the south of Sumatra. Cunningham wondered whether this move by the Americans was designed to delay the arrival of the fleet for political reasons, though he hints that it was possible that it may have been for valid, logistical reasons.[63] Mounting criticisms in the British press were making the political relations between the two fleets more filled with suspicion and creating dangerous frictions.[64]

The storm in the British press was also reflected across the Atlantic in America:

During recent months a great deal has been said and written about the British Fleet in the Pacific. Most of it is erroneous...Concurrent with the arrival of the British Pacific Fleet in Australia, a great deal of unfavourable publicity regarding it was unloosed in the United States. Some said that the British Pacific Fleet was inferior to our own in speed, armament, etc. Others said that it was unwanted in the Pacific – that it should confine its activities to the area around Malaya, the Dutch East Indies, etc.[65]

The row over the employment of the BPF threatened to spill over and become an issue in American domestic politics. The Embassy in Washington reported in May that there had yet to be any specific public speculation as to the exact part that Britain would play in future operations. Members of the legation were very much alive to the difficulties of presenting the British case to the American public, but argued that the best cure for such ills was a vigorous and successful British participation in the closing battles of the Pacific campaign.[66]

To help combat any fears of a British failure to be fully committed to such a campaign, Admiral Fraser made extensive use of his American liaison officer in an effort to publicize and promote the British point of view and counteract any whispering campaign. Capt. Wheeler, USN, wrote a number of contemporary articles that essentially followed the British line, one of which was later reprinted after the war. In it he declared that the British desire to have their fleet participate in the final assault on Japan was linked to their desire for a voice in the post-war settlement of the Far East, 'but before condemning them for this very natural aspiration, let us ask ourselves the question whether we would not do the same thing under similar circumstances. Actually, before the war, British interests in the Far East were far greater than ours'.[67]

By mid-February the BPF had arrived in Sydney following their strikes on Palembang. Fraser wrote to Nimitz about the future employment of his Fleet. The issues of command arrangements had obviously not been settled completely and the BPF found themselves caught again in the middle of a jurisdictional dispute between Nimitz and MacArthur.

I find it now a little difficult to understand what is happening ... directed by you we are trying to plan ICEBERG [the invasion of Okinawa] but (A) we apparently have not been assigned to any command. (B) I am informed that the British Task Force is not available for early stages of ICEBERG. (C) Cominch [King] infers that I should have no communication with Com7th Fleet.

With regard to (C) the only communication I have had are (1) a personal visit on General MacArthur's invitation followed by a proposal to attach liaison officers. (2) A request to CinCSoWesPacArea for the release of some Australian work personnel to assist on airstrip at MANUS. (3) A request to CinC SoWesPacArea to deal direct with commanding General Far Eastern Air Forces over local air matters. (4) Other local questions in AUSTRALIA such as accommodation in SYDNEY.

My only object is to try and bring the BPF into action on the dates you desired, but am beginning to feel a little frustrated. Time is getting short, the Fleet is in SYDNEY, and I have no airstrip allocations at MANUS. Can you help and advise me if we are doing wrong. It hardly seems to me to be practicable to be based in the command of CinCSWPA without having communication on local matters.'[68]

Fraser followed this up with three further signals that outlined his thinking on the employment of the Fleet. He informed Nimitz that his intention was to dispatch the BPF to Manus, MacArthur's command, in the first week of March. From there they would sail for the forward base of Ulithi. The BPF's CinC was proceeding under the impression that even if there were alterations to the planned British involvement in ICEBERG the fleet would be more suitably deployed at Manus, though he would wait for confirmation before moving on. His other concern was that the delay in bringing his Fleet into action was having a negative effect upon its morale. 'In any case you will realise how important it is not to keep the Fleet inactive at SYDNEY for a prolonged period. At MANUS there are few British facilities and you will equally understand how desirable it is that the Fleet should be actively employed within a reasonable time.'[69]

Fraser went on to explain that he regarded Nimitz as his CinC although the complicated state of assignment had still not made their relative positions clear. On the basis of this assumption he proposed that as far as operational assignments were concerned he would not communicate with either the Admiralty or COMINCH. Fraser entreated Nimitz to press King on the matter of assignment hoping that if the BPF were at least assigned to the start of Operation ICEBERG it would be more difficult to redirect them into the Southwest Pacific Area command.

Nimitz took the matter up with Admiral King in Washington. CINCPOA was in a difficult situation. Admiral King retained the right to reallocate the British to MacArthur at seven days notice and had not yet authorized their participation in operations to take the Ryukyus. King's opposition to British involvement in the Pacific War was well known to Nimitz. Without clear authorization and with Fraser pressing the issue it is to Nimitz's credit that he managed very successfully to balance the complex interaction of political and operational matters. In a signal to King, Nimitz stated that 'I am without information as to prospective operations BPF. In order to assist as far as possible in readying them for whatever employment may be required I propose unless otherwise directed to approve [assignment to ICEBERG]. Early clarification of status will be most helpful to both myself and Fraser.'[70] Both Nimitz and Fraser needed to develop their planning and preparations. However, without a clear idea of where and when they might be committed, this was proving to be something of a problem. King replied apparently a little surprised at Nimitz's need for clarification. 'I am at a loss to understand why there should be confusion as to status of British Pacific Fleet. All arrangements for basing British Pacific Fleet are in the hands of Cincpoa including CinCSWPA concurrence where appropriate and always bearing in mind that said Fleet is to be self supporting'[71] King continued by reiterating that it was his authority to commit the BPF to action; 'Allocation of units of British Pacific Fleet for operations remains in my hands.' The COMINCH explained the delay in reaching a decision a consequence of a failure by the JCS to agree on any other future operations. 'I cannot commit units of British Pacific Fleet to ICEBERG (involving 2 to 3 months) or any other operation until Joint Chiefs of Staff decide what operations are due to be carried out other than those already approved. Prospects now are that such decision will be reached by middle of March.[72]

By the time the Fleet left Australia in early March for its intermediate base of Manus, however, a final decision as to where it would operate had still not been taken. This was only partially a result of American reluctance to sanction British participation in the main operations against Japan. It had almost as much to do with inter-American disputes. Difficulties with command arrangements were not limited to the USN and the RN. Those between General MacArthur's Southwest Pacific Area command and Admiral Nimitz's Central Pacific Ocean Area Command also had a bearing on the BPF's fate. The attempts to unite these two independent Area Commanders without appointing a supreme commander were doomed from the start, and it is debatable as to what extent MacArthur would have cooperated with a commander other than himself.[73] Despite the fact that Fraser and Nimitz had reached an understanding at Pearl Harbor, a further complication arose through the fact that King, in Washington, retained for himself the right to reallocate naval forces within the Central and Southwest Pacific Areas.[74] The assignment of the BPF to the Central Pacific Area had only been given on the understanding that it could be moved at seven days notice to the Southwest Pacific Area. Such a change, in fact, very nearly took place shortly after the BPF had become engaged in ICEBERG and it was only the combined representation on the part of both Area Commanders that prevented the Fleet from being switched right in the middle of an operation.

The British were in the unenviable position of operating under Nimitz in the central Pacific, basing in MacArthur's area in Leyte and Manus and under the Australian Government in Australia. Disagreements between Nimitz and MacArthur extended to the complicated issue of base facilities. The problems of basing arrangements, in which operational and political considerations became inextricably linked, were extremely delicate. Despite advocating initially the establishment of their own separate base, Fraser demonstrated a flexibility of mind and eventually came to the conclusion that a joint solution was in the best operational interests of the Fleet.[75] The CinC argued that no operational intermediate base that would make the Fleet any less dependent on Australia could be constructed in under a year.[76] The Admiral had agreed the use of Manus as an advanced base with Nimitz but CINCPAC's fear that control of the island might pass to MacArthur if the BPF were reassigned continued to make operations, if not difficult, then less smooth than they could have been.[77] British basing requests were not welcomed by the USN, who believed that they might result in a permanent post-war occupation – something that Churchill certainly had in mind with his proposals for operations in South East Asia. Admiral Somerville in Washington continued to press Ernie King for a resolution of this issue but did not always receive a sympathetic hearing.[78]

The British Pacific Fleet was eventually utilized in conjunction with the United States Fifth Fleet in its main operation to capture Okinawa, but only after considerable lobbying on the part of Admiral Fraser. When the signal from Admiral King detailing the British to participate in Operation ICEBERG finally arrived at the BPF's headquarters on the evening of 14 March it marked something of a turning point in the RN's history. For the first time a principal, if not the principal, British Fleet passed under direct orders of an Allied Commander-in-Chief. For an organization with the RN's traditions and history it was a momentous development but one that does not appear to have caused any official resentment. As the Fleet's war diary records, '[t]he decision that the Fleet was to be under Fleet Admiral Nimitz and was to take part in Operation ICEBERG gave immense and universal satisfaction not only to ourselves but to every American Naval Officer and man whom we met.'[79] The reality of which nation now wore the mantle of global seapower was apparent for all to see.

The recognition of Britain's changing international position and the part the RN played in it was something that the Pacific experience brought home to all but the most blinkered xenophobe. The importance that this was to have on the post-war world and Fleet became clear. As Rawlings wrote after the end of hostilities, '[s]omething has been forged here between our two fleets...looking back on all that has happened, I begin to see that which matters is not the size of the British contribution, or what we were able to do, but that it is our being a part of that forging which overshadows everything else.'[80]

To a degree Rawlings was right, it was not the size that mattered but the fact that the British were there at all. However, the limited scale in relative terms of the British commitment, which made them susceptible to allegations of shirking, clearly made their voice in the planning of operations a quiet one and made it difficult to counter the 'rumours' that they were unwanted.

The controversy over whether or not the BPF was actually wanted, as opposed to needed, was eventually stifled by Admiral Nimitz who intimated that the active cooperation of the BPF had indeed been welcome. Nimitz visited the British after their participation in ICEBERG telling the assembled officers and men that their most efficiently performed aid in the war against Japan is welcomed by American forces in the Pacific. He denied reports, which he said were circulated in the allied press and verbally, to the effect the United States Pacific Fleet didn't want the British Fleet to come into the Pacific. Speaking extemporaneously to officers and men of the *King George V*, flagship of a British carrier task force, he asserted: 'I assure you that those statements are without foundation.'[81]

The statement received substantial coverage in the American press, much to the relief of the British. Admiral Spruance was also quoted, commending the work of the British ships in supporting the Okinawa invasion, saying the performance 'was typical of the great traditions of the Royal Navy'. Admiral Nimitz declared he wanted to say 'in most emphatic terms' that the work of the British Fleet during the Okinawa operation 'is not only most efficiently performed but of the most valuable service'.[82]

At the end of May 1945 Nimitz again discussed proposals for the future employment of the BPF with Admiral King. Nimitz saw two options. First, the RN would continue to utilize Australia as a main base with an advance base at Manus and operate against Japan with the 3rd Fleet, sharing anchorages (but with no British shore installations) at Ulithi and Eniwetok. Second, they would operate to reopen the Malacca Strait and liberate the enemy-held areas in the British command area. This latter plan had been proposed by the JCS. It was recognized that for this purpose they would need a base in the South China Sea for which Brunei Bay appeared the most appropriate.[83]

Although the British had been arguing for basing facilities in the Philippines, Nimitz disagreed. He saw no need for a base in the Philippines for either category of operations. If the British later operated against Japan he was prepared to countenance Ulithi and Leyte as advanced anchorages. Though mindful of King's strictures regarding the establishment of British base facilities, Nimitz argued that he did 'not regard temporary augmentation of United States carrier aircraft pools et cetera as constituting British shore installations'.[84]

The issue of basing continued to dog cooperation and forward planning. The possibility of reallocation of the BPF, hence Nimitz's caveat regarding continued availability, also complicated matters. Although plans were being prepared regarding the use of Eniwetok in the Marshall Islands as an anchorage from October, until then the Fleet would continue to use Leyte in MacArthur's command as an advanced base. Nimitz informed Fraser directly a few days latter when he signalled that, repairs to damage sustained during ICEBERG permitting, the BPF should anticipate sortieing from Manus in early July for operations with Halsey against the Japanese home islands.[85] By this time it appears that the decision as to whether or not the British would participate in the Third Fleet's operations had been taken almost by default. Although Nimitz was less sure of the timetable of involvement the momentum of a British contribution seems to have carried the day.

The decision having been made that the BPF, designated Task Force 37, would operate in conjunction with the American Third Fleet under Admiral Halsey, Rawlings reported for duty at 06:45 hours on 16th July and took station astern TG38.4. British participation in ICEBERG had avoided many of the issues of how closely the two navies should integrate and how this would effect command arrangements. The BPF had operated as a separate Task Force in support of the American landings on Okinawa. Matters now came to a head, however, when the BPF joined the TF38 for operations off Japan. Rawlings and Vian joined Halsey aboard the USS *Missouri* for a conference on the forthcoming operations. The Americans were fuelling and Halsey used the opportunity to hold a staff conference and become acquainted with both Rawlings and Vian. Halsey describes the meeting as, '... reluctantly I opened the conference. I say "reluctantly" because I dreaded it. When I was informed at Pearl Harbor that the British Pacific

Fleet would report to me, I naturally assumed that I would have full operational control, but when I reread the plan at Leyte, I discovered that tactical control had been reserved.'[86]

Halsey had raised this matter with Nimitz in a signal on 6 June and then again ten days later, 16 June, a few weeks before sortieing from Leyte with the Third Fleet for operations off the Japanese coast. In his first signal Halsey wrote 'I tentatively plan to employ British group as tactical unit of TF38.'[87] He acknowledged that because of a difference in speed and technique the British Service Group would operate separately from their USN counterparts but in the same general vicinity. He concluded that 'British forces can be incorporated into our combat and service operation scheme at any time.' The idea in his mind was to operate TF37 in the same manner as a USN Task Group with the normal inter-group interval. The British in TF37 would conform to the manoeuvres of CTF38. This would permit the RN to make a contribution to and benefit from the USN's defensive umbrella. Halsey argued that this made the most military sense and 'does not infringe on British position guaranteed by Nimitz-Fraser Agreement'.[88] The agreement reached had included the text 'to the maximum practicable extent the British ships will constitute a separate task force with no more direct tactical co-ordination with the US TF's than the situation requires'.[89] Commenting upon this in his dispatches to the Admiralty, Fraser explained that he did not 'mean this to preclude the possibility of a British TG operating in an American Task force, but CinC Pacific appears to have taken it to mean that'.[90]

Nimitz certainly did not concur with Fraser's interpretation. Caught between Halsey's desire for tactical unity and King's insistence upon separation he rejected Commander Third Fleet's proposal and instructed Halsey to '[o]perate TF37 separately from TF38 in fact as well as in name under arrangements which assign to Rawlings tasks to be performed but leave him free to decide upon his own movements and maneuvers [sic]'.[91] This situation was of no little concern to Halsey. The additional fighting power that the BPF represented could easily be negated if co-ordination could not be agreed upon.

Whereas Operation ICEBERG had sidestepped these important issues as to how closely the two navies would integrate because of the detached nature of the BPF's task, matters now came to a head. Rawlings had already expressed what he saw as the key role the BPF would play in forging Anglo-American naval relations when in March he had signalled Fraser: 'My own feeling, for what it is worth, is that the really important side of what we do here is to end up with the White Ensign still looked up to by the Americans. I can not help feeling that in the long run it will do more for us than anything else.'[92] Indeed, mindful of Fraser's oft-repeated intentions that the BPF was to operate in the most advanced operations against Japan, Rawlings reported to Fraser that '[t]he principal points which were settled forthwith were the desire of the British Task Force to work in close tactical co-operation with TF38, conforming to their movements, and that we should take part in Battleship and Cruiser bombardments as well as surface sweeps'.[93] Halsey was content with the close naval relations that this act signalled now existed.[94]

Ultimately Halsey directed all his forces, British and American, into becoming one mutually supporting striking unit. And, although TF37 was weaker than one of the Third Fleet's Task Groups, Fraser was able to report to London that 'Task Force 37, of the BPF, operated in conjunction with the American Task Force 38 under orders of the Commander, United States Third Fleet, with the object of inflicting maximum destruction on Japanese airfields, aircraft and shipping, together with certain other important targets'.[95] The Fleet was formed in four groups in the order from North to South TF37, TG38.1, TG38.4, and TG38.3. This integration within the Third Fleet was something of an occasion and Rawlings noted that '[it] may well be that 4pm on 16 July 1945, will prove a not unimportant milestone on the long road of the world's history'.

The fact that Halsey operated TF37 as a tactical unit of TF38 in the same way as he did TF38's component Task Groups, despite Nimitz's instructions to the contrary, does not appear to have caused him any serious concern. Fraser found such behaviour puzzling, writing that

> It is an interesting sidelight on the American way of thought – in particular on their rigid acceptance of the written word – that CinC Pacific considers it necessary to enforce this small restriction [integration of TF37 into TF38's defensive umbrella]. It is also interesting to note that ComThird Fleet, while accepting the restriction in its normal sense, in fact disregards it completely and continues to operate the British Task Group as a group as part of his own Task Force. Provided he obeys the letter of the law, even if he completely disregards its spirit, every American is quite happy that the right and sensible action has been taken.[96]

This was not the first time that Fraser had noted this aspect of the American character. Back in March, when he had discussed the basing issue with Admiral Cunningham, he had noted that the Americans had been exceptionally generous and helpful with regard to British needs so long as nothing reached an official level. Whereupon 'their hands are rather tied' by King's insistence upon the BPF being self-sufficient.[97]

The final military operations undertaken by the BPF, coastal bombardment and carrier air strikes of the Japanese homeland as part of the American Third Fleet, were again utilized by the British Embassy in support of the Foreign Office policy designed to emphasize Anglo-American solidarity. Publicity for the BPF's participation in the Pacific was vital. The Embassy stressed that 'the part played by British naval forces in the continuing bombardment of Japan receives fair notice in the press and Mountbatten's presence at Potsdam has also served to underline our growing interest and participation in the Pacific war'.[98] The Fleet's activities spoke to several different audiences and press coverage was an important means of reaching many of them, though this was not something that was often welcomed in the Navy. The *Naval Review* was probably speaking for many within the Silent Service when it expressed distaste for dealings with journalists. 'In one of those

Press interviews which now seem to have been accepted as an inevitable horror of total war, Sir Bruce Fraser stated that he would fly his flag in the *Howe* and would have a strong fleet under his command, operating under the control of Admiral Nimitz.'[99]

Fraser may well have not enjoyed the experience, but he certainly recognized the journalist's value in addressing public opinion, informing them of the BPF's existence and emphasizing the relationship with the United States. His intended audiences were not just British domestic opinion but that in the United States and the Dominions as well. When, in November 1945, the Admiral came to compose his report to the Admiralty covering the BPF's activities between November 1944 and July 1945 he included a revised paragraph outlining his public-relations strategy. This clearly indicated that winning the battle for hearts and minds in the United States, Australia and Great Britain was as important as winning any battle taking place against the Japanese.[100]

Such a practice bore some significant results. Admiral Somerville, who was now running the British Admiralty Delegation (BAD) in Washington, wrote to Fraser in April 1945 expressing his pleasure that the American press were carrying stories about British participation in the Pacific.[101] Somerville went on to ask for more publicity photographs and stories that he could use in briefings to the press. He was well aware, however, that caution and a degree of skill was needed when dealing with journalists if the BPF were to be seen in the best possible light. No criticism of the Americans was allowable, nor was any indication that the British Fleet was perhaps not up to the task. The media campaign was all-important now in setting up the post-war Anglo-American relationship in any future governance of the Far East.[102] Although the operational and tactical shortcomings of the BPF were acknowledged by Fraser, his senior officers and, indeed almost all within the Fleet, such issues were for internal consumption only. There were enough stories suspicious of the British in the Pacific without the RN adding to them. In this regard, Fraser would have been most pleased when the *Chicago Daily Tribune* ran an article in June 1945 on Admiral Nimitz's visit to the BPF. While the speech Nimitz gave was delivered to RN personnel its significance was as much for American domestic consumption as for anyone's. Stressing the unity of the Anglo-American war effort, Nimitz paid special attention to the British role in fighting off the dreaded Kamikazi attacks, a tribute which left no doubt as to the BPF's courage and ability.[103] It was just the sort of coverage Fraser and the Foreign Office had hoped for; the Fleet's existence and positive contribution to aiding the USN had come from the mouth of CinCPAC himself.

Professional opinion within the USN was also a target audience and one that would continue to be addressed once the war was over. Articles such as 'We had the British Where We Needed Them' in the *United States Naval Institute Proceedings*, published again at the end of 1946, re-emphasized to the USN officer class the role that the BPF had played in the Pacific.[104] Written by Capt. C.J. Wheeler USN, the article painted a picture of British pluckiness and spirit. The subtext of this glowing piece was undoubtedly that Britain was a trustworthy ally.

The American Administration was under pressure from domestic opinion. It was important for the Executive to avoid any hint that the United States had been involved in propping up Britain's failing Empire in the east. During the first half of 1944 fears grew in the United States that Russia, and in particular Britain, had abandoned the Atlantic Charter and returned to the 'old discredited policies of expediency, national interest and balance of power'.[105] In part the public concern was the result of 'the vagueness of American foreign policy in particular and the Allied war aims in general'.[106] Under such circumstances it was not surprising that the State Department looked unkindly upon ideas such as those proposed by Churchill, which sought to deploy British forces in operations designed to regain imperial possessions. Again in April, the British Government received reports of public and Republican disquiet over the direction of American foreign policy. Antagonism was expressed toward perceived 'secret deals' and concerns over the developing relationship with Russia.[107] The BPF's success had helped avoid any such post-war recriminations between the North Atlantic allies.

The Japanese capitulation provoked a wave of relief and euphoria, nowhere more keenly felt than among the service personnel in the Far East. It also curtailed the more ambitious plans of the BPF to utilize their newly increased forces, which might have continued to make inroads into American public perception. It would be unthinkable to suggest that this was a disappointment – the war was over and many lives had just been reprieved. The defeat of Japan had been accomplished by American resources and forces assisted in small measure by the BPF. Reporting on the celebrations in the United States the Washington Embassy informed London that

> The more sober expressions of victory have been characterized by one central theme – America is now the most powerful nation in the world... Admiral Leahy gave it official sanction in a broadcast in which he said, 'Today we have the biggest and most powerful navy in the world, more powerful than any other two navies in existence... We possess, with our British Allies, the secret of the world's most fearsome weapon.'[108]

The Pacific was always peripheral to overall British grand strategy; Germany was *the* threat, but once that danger was mastered the UK recognized the importance of providing what it could to the Far East. While it is true that the United States Navy's assessment of the British contribution in the Pacific in operational terms is correct – the USN could have done it alone[109] – it ignores the larger significance of the BPF for both Britain and the United States at the grand strategic level.

Navies have long been associated with alliance building and although the degree of importance attached to their political role has waxed and waned over time with the dictates of international relations and developments in naval theory there has been little fundamental disagreement concerning its relevance. From Athenian control of the Delian League, through Papal, Venetian and Spanish opposition to the Ottomans in the fifteenth century, to US attempts at confidence-building measures in the South China Sea, navies have been at the forefront of state foreign policy. Whether or not the attempts by the BPF toward this end have received the academic attention they deserve, it is clear that this aspect of the Fleet's activities was well understood at the time. The British Foreign Office, the Chiefs of Staff and the American State Department all saw British participation as essential, not just as a gesture of allied solidarity directed at Japan, but as crucial for the development of Anglo-American relations in the post-war period.

It is obvious from the foregoing that the RN's experience in the Pacific during the final stages of the Second World War did expose Britain's decline as a naval power when faced with the scale of the USN capabilities. But the central task of the RN's commitment to the Pacific at the Military and Grand Strategic level was political. It welded together the two navies despite the problems of an extremely complex command arrangement. It saw the evolution of new strategic conceptions. The consequences of the British not participating in the final stages of the war against Japan, in the most advanced operations, would have been severe and long-lasting in the minds of those who were to become their most important ally.[110] As the *Chicago Daily Tribune* reported in June of 1945, 'Co-operation in the Pacific between British and American forces is forging a new link toward permanent peace.'[111] Admiral Rawlings, quoted in the article, reflected the British view of participation and the value of naval alliance building. 'At the bottom of everybody's heart is the feeling that if the Americans and us stick together our children and grandchildren will not face another war like this. When you learn to be good fleet mates the stage is set for peace.'[112]

Notes

1. E.B. Potter, *Nimitz* (Annapolis MD: Naval Institute Press, 1976), 347–8.
2. J. Winton, *The Forgotten Fleet* (Warhurst: Douglas-Boyd Books, reprint 1991), 348.
3. Willmott described the BPF as the 'most powerful single strike force assembled by Britain in the course of the Second World War and, relative to its own time, was probably as powerful a force as any raised by the Royal Navy at any stage in its long history'. H.P.Willmott, 'Just Being There', Paper presented to the Institute of Historical Research for the Julian Corbett Prize in Modern Naval History, 1986, 2.
4. Capt. C.J. Wheeler USN [Senior Liaison Officer to Admiral Fraser's Staff], 'We Had the British Where We Needed Them', *United States Naval Institute Proceedings* (hereafter *USNIP*), 72 (December 1946), 1584.
5. ADM 199/118, CinC BPF Despatches, November 1944–July 1945.
6. Ibid.
7. J. Ehrman, *History of the Second World War United Kingdom Military Series Grand Strategy Volume VI October 1944–August 1945* [hereafter *Grand Strategy*] (London: HMSO,1956), 203.
8. ADM 199/2376, Report of Experience of the BPF, January–August 1945, 15 March 1946.
9. Almost immediately Fraser's HQ was transferred to Grenville House, William Street, also in Sydney.
10. CAB 80/79/114, COS (44) 114(0), 'Overall Policy for the Defeat of Japan', 1 February 1944.
11. H.P. Willmott, *Grave of a Dozen Schemes* (Shrewsbury: Air Life Publishing, 1996).

12. C. Barnett, *Engage the Enemy More Closely* (New York: Norton, 2000 [1991]), 877.
13. Ibid.
14. Viscount Cunningham of Hyndhope, Admiral of the Fleet, *A Sailor's Odyssey* (London: Hutchinson, 1951), 598.
15. Ibid., 635.
16. Willmott, *Just Being There*, 8.
17. CAB 80/79/123, COS (44) 123 (0), 'Plan for the Defeat of Japan', 5 February 1944.
18. Willmott, *Just Being There*, 8.
19. Willmott, *Grave of a Dozen Schemes*, 103.
20. FO 954/7/117, Foreign Office internal memorandum, 2 June 1944.
21. ADM 199/118, CinC BPF Despatches, November 1944–July 1945.
22. *Foreign Relations of the United States: Near East, South Asia, Africa and Far East, 1944* (US Government Printing Office, 1965), 254–6.
23. Ibid., 256–7.
24. Ibid., 177–80.
25. Telegram from UK Embassy, 3 April 1943, in H.G. Nicholas (ed.) *Washington Despatches: Weekly Political Reports From the British Embassy* [hereafter *Washington Despatches*] (Chicago IL: University of Chicago Press, 1981), 171.
26. Ibid.
27. Telegram from UK Embassy, 25 September 1944, *Washington Despatches*, 424.
28. Ibid.
29. S.W. Roskill, *History of the Second World War: The War at Sea, 1939–45*, Vol. III pt. II (London: HMSO, 1976).
30. Telegram from UK Embassy, 11 February 1945, *Washington Despatches*, 512–13.
31. See J. Cantwell, *Images of War: British Posters 1939–45* (London: HMSO, 1993); also J. Darracott and B. Loftus, *Second World War Posters* (London: Imperial War Museum, 1972).
32. Raymond Gram Swing (1887–1968), Newspaperman and radio broadcaster, commentator for ABC 1942–48.
33. Telegram from UK Embassy, 17 March 1945, *Washington Despatches*, 527–8.
34. Potter, *Nimitz*, 327.
35. CAB 105/71/342, CAB 122/1075, signal from Strategical Planning Section personnel in Washington to Director of Plans, 7 October 1943.
36. CAB 105/71/392, CAB 122/1075, signal Joint Staff Mission to War Cabinet Office, 2 November 1943.
37. Ibid.
38. Sir Philip Vian, Admiral of the Fleet, *Action This Day* (London: Frederick Muller, 1960) 155.
39. Combined Chiefs of Staff Papers 880/4, British Joint Staff Mission in Washington, Papers and Telegrams, 938.
40. Ehrman, *Grand Strategy*, 264.
41. Adm. E King and W. Whitehall, *Fleet Admiral King: A Naval Record* (London: Eyre & Spottiswoode, 1953), 360.
42. Potter, *Nimitz*, 323–4.
43. King and Whitehall, *Fleet Admiral King: A Naval Record*, 361.
44. Potter, *Nimitz*, 323–4.
45. Cunningham, *A Sailor's Odyssey*, 611.
46. S.E. Morison, *History of the USN in WWII, Vol. XIII: The Liberation of the Philippines* (Oxford: Oxford University Press, 1959), 257.
47. King and Whitehall, *Fleet Admiral King: A Naval Record*, 361.
48. Cunningham, *A Sailor's Odyssey*, 612.

49. King and Whitehall, *Fleet Admiral King: A Naval Record*, 372.
50. Ibid.
51. Cunningham, *A Sailor's Odyssey*, 613–14. In fact, American assistance was more than forthcoming. This was due in no small measure to the efforts and resourcefulness of the BPF's Commander in Chief, Admiral Fraser.
52. Highball – a variant of the 'dambuster' bomb designed for use against shipping. No. 618 Squadron RAF, flying Mosquitos, began trials in April 1943, finally reaching the Far East in January 1945. Highball was never employed and the squadron disbanded in July 1945. XE craft were British Midget submarines built from 1942 onward. Originally employed against the *Tirpitz*, in the Far East they damaged the Japanese cruiser *Takao* and cut submarine telephone cables.
53. Lord Fraser of North Cape Papers National Maritime Museum MS 83/158 File 20 [hereafter Fraser papers].
54. Potter, *Nimitz*, 347, 348–9.
55. Fraser Papers File 20, Operations Section, CinC BPF to Admiralty following N/F1 Pearl Harbor Agreement.
56. Fraser Papers File 23, letter from First Sea Lord to Admiral Fraser, 5 July 1945.
57. Fraser Papers File 23, letter From CinC BPF to First Sea Lord, 17 July 1945.
58. Fraser Papers File 23, letter from CinC BPF to First Sea Lord, 14 March 1945.
59. Fraser Papers File 20, message from COMINCH and C.N.O., 12 November 1944. See also British Admiralty Delegation (BAD) desk diary, 13 November 1944; M. Simpson (ed.), *The Somerville Papers. Selections from the Private and Official Correspondence of Admiral of the Fleet Sir James Somerville,* Publications of the Navy Records Society Vol. 134 (Aldershot: Scholar Press, 1995), 611–12.
60. Fraser Papers File 20.
61. PREM 3/164/4, Lumsden to Ismay, 30 December 1944.
62. Fraser Papers File 20.
63. Cunningham, *A Sailor's Odyssey*, 622.
64. Ibid.
65. Wheeler, 'We Had the British Where We Needed Them', 1584.
66. Telegram from UK Embassy, 13 May 1945, *Washington Despatches*, 559.
67. Wheeler, 'We Had the British Where We Needed Them', 1583.
68. Nimitz Papers Serial 1 Command Summary Book 6, Washington Navy Yard, 12 February 1945, 12037 CINCBPF to CINCPAC [hereafter Nimitz Papers].
69. Nimitz Papers, 190701, 190715 & 190720, CINC BPF to CINCPAC ADV HQ.
70. Nimitz Papers, 192306, CINCPAC ADV HQ to COMINCH, 19 February 1945.
71. Nimitz Papers, 211635, COMINCH to CINCPOA info CINC BPF, CINCSWPA (Nimitz Only).
72. Ibid.
73. Douglas MacArthur's insistence that President Truman should visit him rather than him reporting to Washington perhaps gives some indication of how the General would have responded.
74. Fraser Papers File 21, memorandum of understanding, 'Record of Conference 17–19 December 1944 Employment of BPF', 20 December 1944.
75. ADM 199/118.
76. Fraser Papers File 23, letter from CinC BPF to Admiral Cunningham, 2 June 1945.
77. ADM 199/118.
78. Fraser Papers File 23. The following extract from one of many letters sent to Fraser by Somerville gives something of an indication of the British Admiralty Delegation (BAD)'s difficulties. Somerville 25 April 1945: 'I had a hell of an argument on Saturday with Ernie King touching the matter of a base for the B.P.F. Ernie started off by flying into a rage and saying that the B.P.F. had failed to implement the agreement that it

should be self-supporting. I asked in what respect the Fleet had not been self-supporting, and he barked in reply "Food". I told him I was surprised to hear this in view of the large quantities of food which Australia is supplying to the American Fleet, and I should have thought the B.P.F. would not have had much difficulty in obtaining what they wanted from one of our own dominions. Ernie then became hotter than ever and asked if I wished an itemised list of deficiencies; I said yes, and went on to add that his general demeanour and violence seemed to suggest that he regarded the B.P.F. as a pain in the neck to him, and that possibly he felt quite satisfied he complete the war against Japan quickly and effectively without any assistance from the British. If he thought so he had better say so. Ernie then asked me if I expected him to give an answer to this, and I said "No", he wouldn't have the guts to do it. By this time the temperature having reached boiling point, I told Ernie it was a little odd that we should be fighting like this and suggested we might discuss this matter reasonably and with the heat turned off.'

79. ADM 199/1457, BPF War diary, 3 March 1945.
80. ADM 199/1478, Reports of Naval Operations Against Japan, 17 July–2 September 1945.
81. 'Nimitz Visits British Pacific Fleet' [Chicago *Daily Tribune*, June 1] reprinted in *USNIP*, 71 (July 1945), 864.
82. Ibid., 866.
83. Nimitz Papers, 300526, CINCPAC ADV to COMINCH & CNO, 30 May 1945.
84. Ibid.
85. Nimitz Papers, 050612, CINCPAC ADV to CINC BPF Info COMINCH CINCPAC PEARL COM3RDFLT COMSERON10, 5 June 1945.
86. W.F. Halsey and J. Bryan III, *Admiral Halsey's Story* (New York: Whittlesey House, 1947), 261.
87. Nimitz Papers, 060611, COM3RDFLT to CINCPAC ADV, 6 June 1945.
88. Nimitz Papers, 160007, COM3RDFLT to CINCPAC ADV, 16 June 1945.
89. ADM 199/118, CinC BPF Despatches, November 1944–July 1945, paragraph 94.
90. ADM 199/118, CinC BPF Despatches, November 1944–July 1945, paragraph 95.
91. Nimitz Papers, 170715, CINCPAC ADV to COM3RDFLT, 17 June 1945.
92. Fraser Papers File 23, from V.Adm, 2CinC to CinC BPF, CinC Operational Correspondence with Flag Officers, 28 April 1945.
93. ADM 199/1478, report to CinC BPF from Rawlings, 1 October 1945.
94. Halsey and Bryan, *Admiral Halsey's Story*, 262.
95. ADM 199/118, CinC BPF, 31 October 1945.
96. ADM 199/118, paragraph 96.
97. Fraser Papers File 23, CinC BPF to First Sea Lord, 14 March 1945.
98. Telegram from UK Embassy, 28 July 1945, *Washington Despatches*, 595.
99. 'Notes on the War – The Japanese War', *Naval Review*, 33 (1945), 9.
100. ADM 199/118, CinC BPF Despatches, November 1944–July 1945, paragraph 68.
101. Fraser Papers File 23, letter from Somerville to Fraser, 2 April 1945.
102. Ibid.
103. 'Nimitz Visits British Pacific Fleet', *USNIP*, 866.
104. Wheeler, 'We Had the British Where We Needed Them', *USNIP*, 1583.
105. Telegram from UK Embassy, 11 March 1944, *Washington Despatches*, 327.
106. Ibid., 326.
107. Ibid., 340.
108. Ibid., 602.
109. Morison, *Liberation of the Philippines*, 257.
110. Fraser Papers File 23, undated letter from V.Adm 2CinC BPF in KGV to CinC BPF.
111. 'Nimitz Visits British Pacific Fleet', *USNIP*, 866.
112. Ibid.

7

THE ROYAL NAVY IN KOREA: REPLENISHMENT AND SUSTAINABILITY

Peter Nash

Post-war transition

Introduction

In August 1945, the United States deployed in the Pacific the largest fleet in the world, comprising 4,067 ships, including 2,930 auxiliaries. A less well-known fact was the British had also assembled the largest fleet in its history, with some 247 ships, including 125 acting as logistic support.[1] For warfare at sea had been revolutionized by the ability to deploy large mobile carrier task forces for extended periods from base – thanks to Fleet Trains that were daunting in size and decisive in application. Yet, within five years this embodiment of mobile support was no more. When North Korea invaded the south on 25 June 1950, the total roster of the United States Navy (USN) Service Force Western Pacific had shrunk to a mere handful of auxiliaries.[2] While the British were deploying sizable naval forces in the region at the same time, their mobility too was constrained by a modest Fleet Train that was base-dependent and ill equipped to replenish ships at sea for extended periods.

This chapter will therefore investigate whether the Royal Navy's (RN) approach toward mobility after the Second World War compromised its ability to sustain itself during the Korean War. After reflecting briefly on post-Second World War influences upon naval logistics policy, it will examine the strategic implications of limited ship endurance and how this affected replenishment doctrine. This must be placed into dual context, given the potential for conflict between national 'cold war' global logistic priorities on the one hand and the demands for supporting UN Commonwealth naval forces in a limited war on the other. To date comparatively little has been written on the logistical aspect, partly because it has tended to be taken for granted and partly because for many years the concept of logistics planning was still subordinate rather than integral to strategic or tactical planning and therefore (unlike today) relatively underappreciated in naval officer circles. Since the RN's operational contribution in Korea has already been relatively well studied, description of operations in this chapter will be limited to where this provides appropriate context for the logistic dimension.[3] The practicalities of replenishing at sea, that key enabler for keeping ships at sea for extended periods, is also addressed, particularly in the context of its evolution since 1945 and compared to American experience during this same period.

Logistics planning

Not surprisingly, post-war naval logistics were affected in a number of ways, not least by the sudden but far-reaching transition from a wartime economy (for which logistics was the lifeblood) to a market economy (for which logistics often becomes 'the solution we cannot afford'). The Second World War had cost Britain a quarter of its national wealth and the subsequent necessary economic reconstruction had first priority. Yet Britain's efforts to retain its Great Power status, with '...sea power being an essential component, owing to its strategic mobility worldwide',[4] still required maintaining forces (including overseas garrisons) that by 1948, for example, were costing in percentage of GNP up to twice as much as those of other Western nations.[5] This economic vulnerability was relentlessly forcing the Admiralty both to cut manpower and Fleet size and to moderate its assumptions for carrying out the functions of the Post-War navy. This meant that in addition to performing its immediate peacetime constabulary role throughout Britain's Empire and protecting or promoting British interests, the RN was also expected to be adequately trained and prepared '...with an appropriate backing of ancillary vessels' should war should break out.[6] Such contingency planning, however, generally assumed large-scale global-war scenarios, rather than limited actions – a mindset that affected how both British and American navies prioritized their resources for the Korean crisis when it eventually came.

That such plans had assumed the next war to be global was, to some extent, a reflection of recent history exacerbated by the growing fear of nuclear confrontation. The consequent vulnerability of fixed bases to potential atomic attack would, it was submitted, require the Fleet to be dispersed at sea for long periods. It was this concern and the successful legacy of mobile carrier power that soon coalesced to the point where Fleet Trains in general and replenishment at sea in particular were once again considered essential.[7] Although the model was based on Pacific experience, its application was directed nearer to home, stretching from the Mediterranean to the Arctic and Atlantic. This became increasingly focused, once the Korean War became perceived as a Soviet-inspired diversion to the main threat directed toward Europe.[8] Trying to reconcile the financial and practical consequences for retaining such mobility was nevertheless difficult. For many officers, logistics had represented a relatively static concept concerned only with bases and supply departments, but the Pacific War challenged the navy to become more flexible and mobile. With the challenge in 1945 being met by assembling, with difficulty, a large fleet of auxiliaries, the question now was about the degree to which Britain could afford or need to be so mobile in the future. The debate would come to influence attitudes and priorities over what type of naval logistic support was required before and during the Korean War.

The essence of the British Pacific Fleet (BPF) Train had been to provide mobile bases replete with floating medical, repair and salvage facilities and to transport fuels, aircraft and all forms of supplies via such bases out to the Fleet while it remained on station, often thousands of miles from its main base. The final link in this long supply chain, replenishing the Fleet underway, was the critical enabler for ensuring sustainable mobility. As such, it had to be carried out with the utmost dispatch to minimize interference with the operation in progress or risk damage from enemy action. The level of efficiency, therefore, attached to such an operation had significant strategic and tactical ramifications. If there is one determining factor found in any formula associated with sustainability, it is 'distance'. Combatant endurance, transportation routes, potential enemy targets all demand global logistic expedition. Operation ICEBERG in 1945, often regarded as the benchmark for comparison because it involved both American and British naval task forces, was about 4,700 miles equidistant from their respective bases in Pearl Harbor and Sydney; under-way refuelling through consolidation routinely occurred up to 2,000 miles from fuel-depot bases.

An indicator of the extent to which replenishment at sea had become a key operational task can be gauged by looking at ship endurance capacity. Extensive American wartime experience suggested that built-in endurance capacity at sea could last 30–90 days provided that resupply of fuel and ammunition was assured every three to five days.[9] For the British, escort endurance was particularly acute, given their relatively smaller hull size that made regular replenishment inevitable. With endurance defined as '... [t]he period during which war rates of expenditure, with full war complements, could be sustained without replenishment of victualling, medical and naval stores, including spare gear', the Admiralty's planning guidelines by 1950 set minimum acceptable endurance periods from base as 90 days for aircraft carriers, 70 for battleships and 45 for destroyers and below.[10] Some regarded this as ill conceived, since war-fighting capability would have to be sacrificed to achieve this extreme sufficiency. Still, the fact that fuel was notably excluded from the equation confirmed that regular refuelling at sea had by then become recognized as sine qua non.[11] However, post-war Fleet composition comprised an ever-increasing proportion of small warships which, being less self-reliant, required base support for repair, supply and accommodation.[12] Since these would be increasingly vulnerable to air attack, the question was raised as to whether and how such support should be dispersed overseas.[13] New mobile bases (which today are called Forward Logistics Sites) in a dynamic war risked immobilizing logistic support and could prove uneconomic. The alternative, keeping stores afloat, provided flexibility but risked tying up scarce shipping. So, while the Fleet Train concept had, in Commodore Fisher's earlier words, 'come to stay', its ideal composition was undetermined for years while this economic conundrum remained unresolved.[14]

The post-war theoretical assumption for how long ships might have to remain at sea was, if anything, being constantly extended, particularly when patrolling near 'enemy' territory during periods of strained relations short of war. Since this would invariably demand extending ship endurance beyond normal base-replenishment cycles, so the limitations on endurance became significant. Looking at fuel for example, wartime manoeuvres above 20 knots seriously exacerbated consumption. For US Essex-class carriers, increasing speed from 14 to 30 knots would increase consumption by 520 per cent. For destroyers, usually the least self-sufficient ship, the increase was 975 per cent.[15] With destroyers having as low as eight days' endurance at cruising speed, the problem becomes particularly compelling since this would drop further under sustained high-speed circum-stances, such as responding to submarine or aircraft attack. Not only would constant replenishment be essential, but it would also have to be expedited quickly to minimize both mission distraction and vulnerability to submarine or air attack. This demand for extra speed was nevertheless a problem for auxiliary/ commercial ship design. Every extra knot determines the size of the propulsion plant and consequently fuel-consumption rates, thereby affecting cargo capacity and, ultimately, operating profitability.[16] Replenishment ship design therefore had on the one hand to accommodate extra power to handle winches and pumps that could operate under all conditions, while on the other, in peacetime, matching the overriding commercial requirement for economy. As the Americans had discovered in the Second World War, only the contingencies of actual war justified building a fast tailor-made tanker fully equipped for the fleet. After 1945 the Admiralty tried to finesse the problem by operating, or chartering out when not required, a variety of different 'commercial' tankers while enthusiastically designing fast Fleet tankers and Fleet issue ships '...for a Fleet conducting ocean warfare'. While these plans were more advanced than anything on even American drawing boards, absent war they remained for several years just that...plans.[17] The continuous pressure for faster replenishment could only be partially satisfied by further ad hoc modifications to replenishment gear on what were still under-powered inadequately designed commercial hulls. While this was expedient, at some point the law of diminishing returns would apply. A more radical approach in rig technology and hull design had to be found, therefore, to enable ships to be replenished under way against increasingly severe time and weather constraints.

The next leap in progress was therefore pivotal and the Admiralty was reassured by the most important development achieved by either the British or Americans to date. This emanated from a series of replenishment-at-sea trials undertaken from 1947 onward, using the captured German replenishment ship *Nordmark*, renamed HMS *Bulawayo*, manned by naval personnel. A newly fitted rig, called the Jackstay Fuelling rig, enabled a larger hose to be supported by four troughs slung on travellers that ran along a jackstay, or taut wire stretched across a much wider channel of water between the ships.[18] Despite encouraging results, even at 20 knots compared to the normal 12–14 knots adopted by USN and RFA tankers, the rig unfortunately could not be fitted to other tankers. This was because it required either installing more powerful steam winches that were unavailable or incorporating an efficient means of automatic compensation, such as the tensioning winch, that was still under development by both navies.[19] By 1950, at the end of the trials, the proposal to refit *Bulawayo* for more permanent replenishment duties was rejected on financial and other grounds, so she was placed into reserve. While her legacy was to have provided the vital groundwork, it was the Korean replenishment experience that would provide the catalyst culminating, in 1955, with the first non-commercial tailor-made Tide-class naval replenishment tanker built in the UK – the origins of which were derived from the early planning concepts in 1946.

The practicalities of replenishment at sea

For the RN replenishment at sea, in some form, had been around during most of the twentieth century, although it remained more or less in arrested development until about 1944, mainly for refuelling convoy escorts in the Atlantic. By then, everyone was forced to recognize that open-ocean warfare was becoming, above all else, a routine but complex practical application that demanded a well-honed logistics support system. In 1945, American insistence required that any British contribution to the Pacific campaign must be self-sufficient, so a Fleet Train had to be created virtually from scratch, to provide the necessary afloat logistic support. Its success was not without considerable trial and tribulation, a great deal of improvisation and more American support than had been originally envisaged. But the priorities upon scarce Allied shipping, particularly to sustain Britain and support Europe, ruled out sending modern auxiliaries to the Pacific. Not surprisingly, with none of the auxiliaries designed for the exacting Fleet standards demanded by continuous oceanic replenishment, performance remained well below that of their relatively well equipped and more experienced American cousins.[20] Five years later this difference, particularly in refuelling, had narrowed significantly but experience during the Korean War by both navies brought home the need for revolutionary changes to both ship design and equipment.

There were two basic methods of transfer, either from astern or abeam the supplier. The maximum number of ships that could be grouped around most tankers was one on each beam with two astern. The Astern method, which dominated the early years until 1944/45, required the tanker to deploy a buoyant hose that would be picked up and connected to a warship about 400–600 feet behind.[21] This method was not popular with the USN except in emergency. Although it still retained support from RFA masters, particularly when fuelling light vessels in bad weather, by 1952 it was rarely used.[22] Because of the carriers' starboard bridge structure they only refuelled on the tanker's port beam; cruisers preferred the same, while destroyers generally fuelled from its starboard. Apart from two small port oilers and a freighting tanker in the region, there were two main types of British tanker deployed in Korea. The primary group were eight 14-knot Wave-class, originally built as freighting tankers which, apart from one, were fitted with four hose derricks/rigs, two either side, deploying up to 10 hoses for fuel oil, aviation gas and water. Two smaller Ranger-class were capable of astern fuelling but otherwise equipped with a single fuelling derrick on the port side supporting one water and two fuel hoses. Aviation gas or stores had to be transferred by separate jackstay on the port side although not at the same time, which made for inefficient replenishment.[23]

Initial contact would be established when the receiving warship had approached abreast the tanker gradually edging in to usually no less than 75 feet, to avoid disturbance to ship handling caused by the interaction effects of the two ships running in parallel. The suction could be strong enough to cause a collision if unchecked, particularly if one ship was smaller. A coston gun was then fired from the supply ship to hurl a line across the gap, except for aircraft carriers where, to protect the aircraft, it was the reverse. Attached were lines called messengers, usually one for distance and telephone lines and the other for passing the hose line. The rubber hose was secured in troughs slung outboard from the supplying ship's derrick or crane. The underlying principle was that if any rolling or yawing occurred, enough slack had to exist in the rig to ride through the motion, providing the ships kept station. As each ship reacted differently to the effects of waves and swell, the challenge was in the ability to adjust, through the use of winches, the hose bight lines to avoid either dunking or stretching them to breaking point.[24] The other principle was that the burden of rigging and handling was normally assumed by the supplier ship, thereby enabling warships to respond to any attack with the minimum of delay. Until the introduction of extra winches in 1945, the constant adjustment of the hose bight lines was hand-tended and therefore more precarious.[25] Rigs using booms and saddles, like the American 'Close in' or the British standard 70-foot 'Large Derrick', became the traditional method of transfer by the end of the Second World War. The gap between the ships nevertheless varied, being determined by the type of rig, the sea state and weather conditions. Korean experience indicated best working practices of between 95 and 130 feet but when alongside American tankers, using the Elwood or Span-Wire rig with British hose adaptors, the preference was 80–120 feet for cruisers or carriers and 60–100 feet for destroyers.[26] Even by 1952, however, not all British replenishment ships had gyrocompasses, so station-keeping was down to good seamanship.[27] Heavy swells, particularly on the quarter, would badly affect steering and manoeuvring. Automatic pilots received a mixed reception from RFA masters because with only one source of power supply the ship would not be under immediate control in an emergency.[28]

Often, the tanker set the limitation on speed. Pumping and heating the fuel absorbed on average two knots of power, so typical replenishment speed varied between 8 and 15 knots. Below eight knots made steering ineffective and 12–14 knots became normal. Cruisers, destroyers and carriers typically received two 6-inch hoses from a Wave-class tanker rated to pump up to 780 tons per hour (tph).[29] The speed at which warships could fill their fuel tanks without throttling would usually determine the upper limit and because of their internal pipe and tank design this was still generally poorer than American receiver rates. The record from a British tanker in Korea was 612 tph, using three hoses to a cruiser and destroyer (this incidentally being exactly the same rate as *Bulawayo* pumped to the battleship *Duke of York* in trials, using just one new 7-inch hose in 1947).[30] Those frigates and destroyers capable of only connecting one hose typically received oil at between 127 and 230 tph, the highest recorded being 243 tph. By eventually using two hoses destroyers averaged 300 tph, but this was still some way below 350 tph which American destroyers typically received using one hose. Aviation gas to carriers, using two hoses, was pumped across at 75 tph.[31] All these rates were broadly an improvement on those of 1945 due in part to technique, or by using additional hoses for each evolution.[32] The pressure for introducing night transfers as a regular practice did not really materialize until the Korean War and was mainly confined to the USN, due to the sheer volume of ordnance and jet fuel consumed by their carrier task force every day.

The amount of time it took to conduct an evolution depended on a variety of factors including the volume required, prevailing sea conditions, pumping velocity and manhandling efficiency. Transferring and then connecting the hoses, for example, typically took about seven minutes and their disconnection and retraction a further five.[33] When refuelling from American tankers this more or less doubled, mostly due to unfamiliarity with each other's gear. Regular rivalry among Allied destroyers to reduce these times eventually evolved into quite a competition that was eventually to be won by HMCS *Athabaskan*, in one minute 45 seconds![34]

Broadly speaking, the advantages of refuelling abeam rather than astern were shorter hoses, easier handling, higher pumping rates and higher ship's speeds. Light stores such as mail could also be transferred simultaneously and telephone communication was possible.[35] The biggest advantage however, was that it would allow for eventual improvements in fuel-rig design, using jackstays stretched between the ships to provide more latitude in ship motion while keeping ships further apart.[36] A third method was also introduced, known today as drafting up, whereby a tanker was permanently anchored in an exposed anchorage, such as at Taechong-Do, which enabled Commonwealth destroyers to come alongside using fenders or, if there was too much swell, by fuelling astern.[37]

Whichever method was adopted there was always the real risk of damage or worse, particularly given the appalling winter weather and sea conditions encountered in the Yellow Sea. Doubtless reflecting the skill of the practitioners and the underlying strength of the doctrine, any damage during the Korean War was not in fact caused while under way, but when they were stationed alongside, as ships' overhanging superstructures clashed in exposed anchorages due to the swell.[38]

Transfers of solids, from frozen provisions to ammunition, posed numerous and peculiar problems given the different types of 'customer', the nature and quantity of stores and the constraint that supply ships '... are not loaded to capacity but for mobility'.[39] The limiting factor for provisions was usually volume not weight, and transfer rates were slow, often influenced by how fast the receiver ship could actually accommodate the loads. No British supply ships deployed in Korea were fitted with the heavy jackstays for handling under-way loads up to one ton. However both warships and tankers were fitted with a light jackstay for transferring up to 500 pounds, typically provisions, controlled by a winch. If personnel were being transferred, a common occurrence in Korea, or other rigs were being operated simultaneously, then the receiver ship would detail about twenty men to manhandle the lift. This was because British tankers, unlike their American counterparts, were never designed to accommodate the size of crew necessary for multi-rig operations and simultaneous handling of miscellaneous stores, hoses, etc.[40] Although the methodology and weight limitations for solids transfers were broadly similar in both navies, the USN operated a wider variety of rigs to suit different needs and ships, particularly for ordnance. Despite requests, there were no RFA armament supply ships with under-way capability available for Korea.[41] On occasions, Commonwealth ships therefore resorted to receiving British ammunition from American ammunition ships, to avoid returning to base.

Korean operations

Mobilization

As mentioned earlier, the Admiralty had a number of options for augmenting the fleet over phased periods following the outbreak of war. The most expedient, and the one adopted for Korea, was to mobilize warships from reserve. These had been considerably expanded since 1945 with any surplus either scrapped or sold. On 1 September 1945, for example, total Fleet resources numbered 8,915 vessels, including 1,151 major combatants. Some 30 per cent of the total, 2,685 vessels were in reserve of which 302 were major combatants.[42] By June 1950, the active Fleet and overall personnel levels were the lowest since the Second World War, reflecting the severe reductions in naval estimates over the previous two years.[43] For example, by June 1950 total Fleet resources had been dramatically cut by 85 per cent to 1,381 vessels of which 60 per cent were by now in reserve; of the 495 major combatants, 310 were in reserve.[44]

However, the Korean War would change this. 1951–52 was the first complete year of the rearmament programme providing additional carriers and destroyers, the largest the country could afford without going over to a war economy. Following a moratorium on ship disposal, commercial work in royal dockyards was suspended to refit 100 mostly smaller warships, and the active Fleet was soon increased by about a third. By July 1952, the Reserve Fleet contracted to its lowest post-war level of 232 major combatants, reflecting the need to replenish gaps in the active fleet.[45] While the reserve policy had therefore been vindicated, the combination of stretched manpower and the complexities of mobilization nevertheless left their mark on operational efficiency that would influence their eventual deployment. For the Fleet Train the motive for placing ships into reserve was somewhat different and depended on, *inter alia*, the size and type of ship. It was accepted that retaining in peacetime a permanent large Pacific-style fleet train for a future war was both uneconomical and an unnecessary drain on skilled manpower. Many vintage ships were therefore scrapped, some converted back to civilian service and others sold. Only a small proportion of the remainder, particularly the large depot/repair ships and some small oilers, were reduced to reserve.[46] Others, such as freighting ships that could not be manned, stocked up and brought forward at short notice for Fleet duty, were employed to transport the Admiralty's own stores and fuel worldwide, with any surplus capacity chartered out to earn their keep.[47] Requisition of civilian ships for conversion, a traditionally important strategy for the Admiralty, was confined to two 10,000-ton tankers, being privately built for Polish owners, that in 1951 were outfitted for freighting.[48] Meanwhile, construction since 1945 was limited to four small port oilers, the last of the war-building programme and eight replacement 1,500-ton attendant oilers scheduled from 1952 onward. The only modernization had been to eight of the existing twenty Wave-class tankers, four of which had served with the Fleet Train in 1945, while two freighters were converted to ammunition supply ships. The Fleet Train for Korea (see Table 7.1) was therefore drawn from both naval and civilian services with the vast majority un-modernized. Hospital and head-quarters ships were white ensign; the rest, such as tankers, transports, stores issuing ships for armaments ('ASIS.'), or provisions ('VSIS.') or naval stores ('NSIS.') were operated by the civilian manned Royal Fleet Auxiliary (RFA) under the blue ensign.

When South Korea was invaded on 25 June 1950, the RN was deploying 22 warships in Far Eastern waters on various patrol duties or extending courtesy visits to Japan. Currently enjoying a summer training cruise in Japanese waters were the light carrier *Triumph*, cruisers *Belfast* and *Jamaica*, two destroyers and three frigates under Rear Admiral Andrewes, Flag Officer Second-in-Command Far East Station (FO2FE). In support was a small Fleet Train, comprising the stores ship RFA *Fort Charlotte*, the tanker RFA *Wave Chief* and two station tankers RFA *Green Ranger* and RFA *Brown Ranger*. Admiral Sir Patrick Brind, Commander in Chief of Far East Station Hong Kong swiftly offered this force for UN operations off Korea, under the command of Admiral Joy, Commander in Chief US Naval Forces.[49] With so many tasks to be undertaken with so few available ships, Admiral Joy was 'heartened' by the offer. Within days the British task force joined the carrier, cruiser and eight destroyers of the US 7th Fleet in Okinawa to form Task Force 77, charged with attacking military targets in North Korea.[50] Further reinforcements from Australia and New Zealand were quickly committed to assist in a blocking campaign. The west coast was allocated to the Commonwealth navies, including a carrier in the Yellow Sea, while the USN blockaded the east coast, with the US carrier group TF 77 operating as a strike force from the Sea of Japan.

Table 7.1 Ships of the fleet train employed in the Korean war

Name	Type (gross registered tons)	Comment
Tankers		
RFA *Birchol*	1,440 tons harbour tanker	Stationed in HK for some years
RFA *Oakol*	1,440 tons harbour tanker	Stationed in Singapore
RFA *Brown Ranger*	3,417 tons Fleet Attendant	Limited under-way capability
RFA *Green Ranger*	3,313 tons Fleet Attendant	Limited under-way capability
RFA *Echodale*	8,219 tons	Freighting only
RFA *Wave Chief*	8,097 tons Fleet tanker	Fitted for under way replenishment
RFA *Wave Conqueror*	8,141 tons Fleet tanker	
RFA *Wave Knight*	8,187 tons Fleet tanker	Intermediate modification
RFA *Wave Laird*	8,187 tons Fleet tanker	Intermediate modification
RFA *Wave Premier*	8,175 tons Fleet tanker	Intermediate modification
RFA *Wave Prince*	8,197 tons Fleet tanker	Fitted for under way replenishment
RFA *Wave Regent*	8,184 tons Fleet tanker	Freighting only
RFA *Wave Sovereign*	8,182 tons Fleet tanker	Fitted for under way replenishment
Naval Stores and Victualling Issue Ships (N.S.I.S) & (V.S.I.S.)		
RFA *Fort Charlotte*	7,201 tons N.S.I.S/V.S.I.S.	Sasebo: Stores depot
Armament Supplies Issuing Ships (A.S.I.S.)		
MFA *Choysang*	1,500 tons Temporary A.S.I.S.	Sasebo and freighting from HK
RFA *Fort Rosalie*	7,335 tons	Sasebo Sept. 1950 to June 1952
RFA *Fort Sandusky*	7,300 tons	June 1952 onward
MFA *Fort Langley*	7,285 tons	Transferred to RFA in 1954
White Ensign Naval Manned Ships		
HMHS *Maine*	7,515 tons Hospital	
HMS *Tyne*	HQ Sasebo	April–July 1953
HMS *Ladybird*	Headquarters Ship	Ex-SS *Wusueh*
HMS *Unicorn*	Repair/Maintenance Ferry carrier	July 1950 to July 1953

Sources: B.R. 1736(54) Naval Staff History *British Commonwealth Naval Operations, Korea 1950–1953* Appendix B1.
Captain E.E. Sigwart, *Royal Fleet Auxiliary* (London: Adlard Coles, 1969).
ADM 1/27143 'History of the RFA Service 1919–1958', Public Record Office Kew.

Within months Britain's force level had stabilized and more or less remained the same for the remainder of the war. This was not without difficulty, as the RN was soon stretched by its worldwide commitments, particularly given its ageing Fleet that required increasing maintenance support. Apart from heavy responsibilities for the defence of Europe and Atlantic sea-lanes, deployments extended to Grenada, Persian Gulf, Malaya and China followed later by the Gulf of Akaba, Jamaica and Egypt.[51] Only Korea, however, presented the type of wartime logistic challenges last experienced in 1945, which would once again demand competing for scarce resources against other global imperatives.

Logistic challenge

The RN's temporary base was Sasebo in Japan, some three days' sailing or 1,079 miles from Hong Kong and about 10,580 miles from Britain.[52] From Sasebo to Inchon on Korea's west coast would typically take 21–28 hours at 20 or 15 knots to steam the 420 miles, while the 560 miles to Chinnampo would take 28–37 hours.[53] Deploying warships for considerable periods off either coast would require replenishment at sea to reduce the number of journeys back and forth. Initial arrangements for establishing logistic support for any naval force away from its base, particularly if time and plans are scarce, would typically be haphazard and expedient, relying on whatever was available to hand. Establishing the Fleet Train in 1945 provided ample evidence of just how challenging this could be. Five years later, no naval logistic plans existed, other than for major or global wars, so the only solution for those on the spot was to improvise. As the Director of Plans (Q) was to reflect in 1951, '... Too often in the past logistic planning has been left with the hope that it will sort itself out somehow.'[54] Even the much-vaunted US Fleet Train had been virtually disbanded with only a destroyer tender, a refrigeration ship, an oiler on shuttle duty, fleet tug and an LST to support the Western Pacific. Their only hospital ship and stores-issue ship had been decommissioned. The rest of the 91 auxiliaries of the Pacific Fleet Service Force were mostly located in west-coast ports or at Pearl Harbor, covering east central and south Pacific.[55]

The problem for both navies was the uncertainty about the course and duration of the war. At least for the British, the early days proved less of a logistic problem than expected mainly for two reasons. First, experienced Supply and Engineering officers arrived to plan and co-ordinate logistical arrangements.[56] Second and most fortuitously, arrangements had already been made for supplying the ships for the Summer Cruise, so the majority of provisions and naval stores were available from the RFA *Fort Charlotte*. She had just been topped up but could replenish at Kure, other than for fresh vegetables, which were obtained through local USN sources. With some 5,000 bodies to feed and clothe there were inevitable difficulties, but at least this provided enough breathing space until a routine could be established for keeping Sasebo adequately stocked.[57] This was accomplished by having her return every six weeks to Hong Kong for a month to replenish, but her absence '... created a constant battle of wits to keep the wolf from the door'.[58] While this arrangement proved relatively satisfactory initially, serious shortages in spare gear arose later as ships expended their stores, endurance. The dearth of radio and radar valves, for example, '... endangered the operational capacity of the Fleet'.[59]

Fuel was available from the tanker RFA *Wave Chief*, while the RFA *Green Ranger* and RFA *Brown Ranger* acted as station tankers at Sasebo. Some ammunition supplies were kept at Sasebo in SS *Choysang*, a converted merchant on charter, joined by RFA *Fort Rosalie* three months later, carrying the bulk of the Korean war reserve and replacements for what had been expended already.

Thereafter the future supply into theatre of all fuel, spare gear, ammunition and stores of all kinds was dependent on Singapore and Hong Kong.[60] American depot ships meanwhile willingly provided temporary ship repair.[61] Indeed American generosity was unbounded. Rear Admiral Andrewes reported that Vice-Admiral Joy was keen to offer a depot ship and provision and refrigeration ships from their now highly organized Fleet Train and, despite being pleased to learn that supplies were satisfactory, he '…pressed us to use American repair facilities or anything we wanted to the utmost'.[62] Unfortunately this had, in reality, limited practical value until some level of standardization was achieved, since only some 50 per cent of victualling items were common-user, with naval stores and clothing being completely different.[63] While general maintenance was satisfactorily handled under British supervision by, for example, the Sasebo Shipbuilding Company – the third largest shipyard in Japan – the need for a dedicated British depot repair ship became quite pressing as ships deteriorated with age and wear.

Sasebo itself provided a good but defenceless harbour, with overstretched facilities due to the increasing volume of American and Commonwealth ship activity. Accommodation presented a particular problem, but American assistance helped until the British commissioned the SS *Wuseheh* as HMS *Ladybird* in September, to act as HQ ship until eventually relieved by HMS *Tyne* in April 1953.[64] Lack of amenities meanwhile remained a constant headache, particularly when ships reached full war complement by October 1950. It eventually proved so difficult to arrange any healthy recreation that ships were diverted either to the Commonwealth zone of occupation in Kure managed by the Australians, or to the US base at Yokosuka nearer to Tokyo.[65]

Conduct of the war

In total, 55 ships of the Commonwealth navies served in the Korean war for various periods: 32 from the RN (five light fleet carriers, six cruisers, seven destroyers, fourteen frigates), nine from the Royal Australian Navy including a carrier, eight from the Royal Canadian Navy and six from the Royal New Zealand Navy. In addition, two naval HQ ships, a hospital ship as well as sixteen RFA auxiliaries and two merchant fleet auxiliaries served in the Fleet Train.[66]

The war developed in four phases. The first period until the Inchon landings was a retreat to a defensible perimeter, with all military effort devoted to maintaining a single bridgehead around the port of Pusan. The second phase was the UN counter-assault at Inchon mid-September nearly reaching the Yalu River, when it appeared the war might be over. In early November 1950 the third phase evidenced the Chinese intervention and UN counter-attack in early 1951; this eventually led to the static stalemate that prevailed until the armistice of July 1953. Five Commonwealth operational carriers were engaged, some more than once, with most undertaking between seven and eleven patrols over periods of between five and seven month tours at a stretch. Three tours entailed fewer patrols over shorter periods. *Triumph* was initially part of the US Task Force 77 on the west coast followed by the Inchon landings, being replaced at the end of September by *Theseus*, which covered the mobile war post-Inchon until the long stalemate period.[67] The task of blockading was divided between Commonwealth ships supplemented by others from France and the Netherlands on the west coast and the USN on the longer east coast. The two forces periodically exchanged ships, usually destroyers and frigates for bombardment or escort duties. For a short period a USN light or escort carrier alternated with the Commonwealth carrier on the west coast, both remaining under command of FO2FE.[68]

A routine for refuelling the task groups at sea was developed to optimize the time on-station, which proved relatively straightforward but not without mishap. On-station carrier cycles were 10 days, with refuelling at sea undertaken every fifth day; a similar period, less passage time, was spent at base.[69] Initially RFA tankers were temporarily attached to the US mobile Logistic Service group until *Triumph* was reassigned to the west coast. Some tankers were not well prepared for handling the tasks involved, which caused delays or even postponements to replenishment evolutions that demanded urgent remedial attention.[70] Refuelling at Inchon was also undertaken at anchor but owing to the height of the tanker's superstructure, which in a swell was apt to foul the sponsons of the carrier, this option was subsequently confined to smaller ships.[71]

One of the immediate challenges was how to replace and upkeep *Triumph*'s obsolete aircraft without draining logistics in the forward area. This was resolved by using the carrier *Unicorn* as a ferry carrier, leaving its repair department and workshops in Singapore. The original peacetime concept of acting as a full repair ship, permanently based in port, was abandoned as inefficient for a variety of reasons.[72] In fact her new role was quite multifaceted. Replacement aircraft and stores from the UK for all five operational carriers were ferried on *Unicorn* from Singapore or Hong Kong to Kure. These were then either flown off or transferred by a large 30-ton crane on a floating pontoon, moored between the carriers, in exchange for time-expired or unserviceable aircraft.[73] Initially, this meant a six- to eight-week routine back and forth but when *Theseus* arrived with new aircraft, these could be more efficiently maintained or repaired on board *Unicorn* herself, provided she stayed for longer periods in Japan. Her large hangers also provided suitable space for all types of cargo stores, ammunition, troops, etc. between Singapore, Hong Kong, Japan and the operating area. She also occasionally flew her own spare aircraft or acted as spare deck in the forward area.

During the first six months of 1951 concern grew about possible submarine activity, particularly during replenishment when ships were at their most vulnerable. ASW screening was increased both for the carrier and, equally importantly, for the replenishment ships to and from the operating areas. An unusual, but not unique occurrence was the transfer of contaminated avgas that forced the *Glory* back to Sasebo; there was, however, no truth to the rumours in the press of sabotage.[74]

Meanwhile, in March 1951, the first of a number of Reports was submitted by FO2FE to the Admiralty, which covered, *inter alia*, various concerns about the logistic arrangements and shortfalls. While *Ladybird* proved to be valuable as a communications HQ her capability was limited. A depot/repair ship was requested to provide facilities to manage the various logistic and administrative needs of the Fleet. '...Above all, a depot ship provides mobility.' Undue reliance was meanwhile being placed upon the three American depot/repair ships in Sasebo.[75]

Second, although it was acknowledged that '...[n]othing in the way of a major replenishment has been attempted', concerns were raised about the state and capability of some of the supply ships.[76] These not only lacked adequate speed to permit replenishment under way but lacked adequate seaworthiness, an ability to steer a steady course with insufficient power to cope simultaneously with pumps, etc. Tankers were severely undermanned and only ad hoc arrangements existed to meet the heavy additional demands from the destroyers and the carriers for water. The contention rested on the belief that only by acquiring the right tools to do the job properly could a Fleet be successfully sustained at sea. The wide diversity in replenishment gear and rigging, it was argued, must either be standardized among warships and RFAs or, preferably, replaced by new designs.[77] It was stressed that every major fleet 'should have a properly fitted and manned Fleet oiler attached to it as well as ASIS and VSIS. As an immediate measure it was therefore recommended that *Bulawayo* be re-commissioned as a peripatetic replenishment training ship'.[78]

After due study by the Admiralty's 'Replenishment at Sea committee, some sympathy and assurance was given, with corrections promised as the opportunity offers'. In reality, of course, these problems were to be expected, given the age and design of the ships. The only solution, it was conceded, rested with the new 15,000-ton naval tankers, long on the drawing boards but still to be built. It was hoped these could incorporate all the necessary requirements – particularly for flexible power, speed and the provision of new fuel jackstays – that had already shown such promise in the *Bulawayo* trials.[79] As for bringing *Bulawayo* out to Korea, this was apparently 'not realistic' on financial and other grounds, as her machinery was no longer adequate for prolonged replenishment duties.[80] Meanwhile other ships that would qualify for Korea, it was claimed, were 'already allocated to various fleets'. These, however, were the very ships being criticized in the report as either inadequate (Ranger-class) or still to be modernized (Wave-class). As for sending a repair /depot ship, this was dismissed as simply not possible 'due to the essential duty allocated to the six available in the event of global war'.[81]

In effect, while London sympathized with FO2FE's concerns, there was little or no change in direction because the die was cast. As the Director of Plans (Q) was thereafter prompted to record, 'it is essential if false conclusions are not to be drawn that the logistic aspect of the Korean naval operations must be viewed in correct context, the requirements of a two theatre strategy...Had there been no question of prejudicing European defence it would not have been too difficult to have filled all Korean wants'.[82] Perhaps inevitably, this conflict between the global strategic imperative and coping with a relatively limited local war would be the first of several over the next year or two.

In July 1951, a second report was submitted that dealt in some length with the many 'difficulties and differences of approach between British and US methods' relating to the methods for exercising command.[83] From the logistics perspective it had to be determined whether to have two separate organizations, or 'graft a limb into the American set-up'.[84] Although initially the Americans had wanted to separate British operational and administrative command by attaching the RFAs to their Service Force, this would have divided Admiral Scott Moncrieff's command and split his staff. Fortunately the strong operational links since forged between both naval logistic groups was such that Britain retained control of its own logistic force.[85] As in the previous report the opportunity was taken to request a depot/repair ship as a headquarters ship, for '...[e]very development of this war has shown more and more conclusively how valuable a headquarters/ accommodation ship would be with this type of force and operations... [which]...has to be an essential part of any Fleet in the future.'[86] There then followed a similar list of suggestions for achieving a properly equipped mobile Fleet Train including repair facilities. But once again London's persuasive logic poured cold water on the request, for instance arguing that no repair ship was needed while there existed favourably located Japanese bases and adequate assistance from the USN in need, and while warships were free from the effects of wear and tear caused by any submarine or air attack.[87]

As the war moved into the long final stalemate from mid-1951 onward, blockade and bombardment operations continued unabated, as did escorting duties for the auxiliaries and carrier. With the war entering its third year the front lines remained static, and naval operations on both coasts assumed a form that was to remain unchanged until the end. Much of the ensuing months from April 1952 were devoted to supporting guerrilla operations, but as ammunition expenditure was getting high and with the whole of the RN's needs supplied from only one ammunition ship, the RFA *Fort Sandusky*, commanders were instructed to restrict expenditure to observable targets.[88] The other problem brewing, however, was that since neither Singapore nor Hong Kong was on a wartime tempo and their respective dockyard facilities barely adequate, reliance upon Kure had to be rationed as maintenance backlogs increased.[89] To make matters worse, on 28 April 1952 the Japanese peace treaty was signed with the USA and British Commonwealth, bringing with it legal and diplomatic problems over using Kure. This resulted in the RN losing its cruiser dock, and having to rely on the USN as rent-free tenants in Sasebo, for the rest of the war.[90]

Following the signing of the Armistice on 27 July 1953, the activities of the Commonwealth forces began to wind down except for continued patrols within reach of the coast and assisting in evacuations from the west-coast islands. On 18 November 1953 Rear Admiral Clifford hauled down his flag as FO2FE at which point the involvement of HM naval ships in the Korean War came to an end.

Analysis

Global versus limited war

The Korean War was the first limited war since 1945, involving significant United Nations forces to which the RN was a primary contributor. It occurred while concern was developing about the prospects of a global war against the Soviet bloc, with the centre of gravity as Central/Southern Europe and the Atlantic. Both the British and American navies were consequently obliged to adopt a two-theatre strategy, which required retaining a substantial proportion of their fleets in the European arena, acting either as a deterrent or for mounting a response should war break out.[91] Against this was the subsidiary need to ensure the Commonwealth naval forces in Korea were adequately supported, logistically, to fulfil their mandate. A major handicap in planning the appropriate type and level of support was the open-ended uncertainty about the duration of the war that pervaded all three years. This, combined with significant shortages in trained personnel (if not necessarily the ships) throughout the navy, exacerbated the difficulties in striking the right balance. One way to augment fleet levels relatively quickly, for example, was to mobilize reserves that had been laid up in varying degrees of readiness. Due to manning and equipment shortages, however, delays occurred before they were properly worked up prior to Fleet assignment where gaps had arisen as reliefs were being retained in the Far East Fleet. As for augmenting logistic support, London's dilemma was more acute. Even if circumstances had eventually arisen to justify sending a depot ship to Sasebo, there was no guarantee that one would be found. For this, as the Director of Plans noted, the Admiralty was 'loath to do because it would have involved a disproportionately large increase in the manpower requirement engaged in the Korean War and it would have dissipated resources which might be urgently needed in the west should global war break out'.[92]

Fleet trains: Korean experience versus expectations

It will be recalled that post-Second World War logistic plans incorporated a model based primarily on the experience of the BPF in 1945, designed to quantify fleet train levels in general and to define the rationale for replenishment at sea in particular. It was predicated on several underlying assumptions related to operating distances from base, ships' speed and therefore endurance and how these combined to determine how and what type of fixed or afloat support might be appropriate. As it transpired, Korea did not fit the model. In a logistic sense, this had been a relatively benign war. First, the lack of air or submarine attack, despite the threat, curtailed the need for constant but erratic high speeds, thereby improving fuel consumption and endurance. Wear and tear was consequently less debilitating and enemy damage very minor. Second, plans envisaged that forward base facilities might be relatively remote and/or far from the operating area. In Korea, however, distance was only a factor in terms of freighting fuel or spares from the UK or elsewhere. Hong Kong and Singapore thereafter served their purpose as interim bases while Japan, located so near to the operational zone, contributed invaluable host-nation support. All these factors were more favourable than in 1945 or compared to the earlier post-war paradigm.

Adequacy of logistic support in Korea

Looking at fuel first, RN warships alone steamed a total of 2,100,550 miles and consumed 632,150 tons of fuel, with the RFA steaming a further 300,000 miles in the zone of operations. Of the 70 fleet auxiliaries operated by the Admiralty during this time, approximately one third contributed to the Korean War effort carrying the fuel and stores to the Far East and distributing to the ships in the zone of operations. In the first two years, some 90,000 tons of fuel was transferred at sea.[93] This was exactly half the amount transferred under way from 21 tankers to the BPF's 4-carrier task group in Operation ICEBERG during two four-week periods.[94] While this cannot be a fair comparison in isolation because environmental conditions, fleet composition, and distances were completely different, it places into context the decision to have just two tankers always available in the Korean operational zone as being adequate, given the less extreme circumstances. While in the initial period, progress and improvement would have been quicker if auxiliaries had been better equipped or if the BPF's earlier replenishment experience had been widely available, what is remarkable is that despite the age and wear of both ships and equipment that had seen action in the Second World War, it proved possible with practice to achieve the same or occasionally improved operating performance during replenishments.[95]

If the distances from base had been greater, or enemy counter-attack more intense and the carrier air complement comprised jets, not piston-engine aircraft, this would have had severe logistic ramifications that might have proved irreconcilable. The USN practice of keeping the fast carrier task force on-station for longer cycles, despite the proximity to Japan, created such a constant demand for air ordnance and jet fuel that by the end of the war replenishments took up to nine hours where 'nightly replenishment became the rule'.[96] As a consequence, oiler availability became so marginal that in-port fuelling became dependent on British or Japanese tankers.[97]

The distribution of additional ammunition was inhibited by the absence of an ASIS with the speed and ability to transfer under way. Carrier cycles were consequently constrained to about ten days with the need to restock with air ordnance at Sasebo, while bombardment warships occasionally had to rely for further British ammunition from American supply ships within the theatre.[98] There is no evidence to suggest that air operations were seriously compromised as a result, since the distance to Sasebo for replenishment was only a day's sailing, and there were benefits to efficiency by having more dockside time anyway. Again, the conclusion might be different if the number of planes carried and type of ordnance used had been more in line with American naval air performance, or if the larger Fleet rather than Light carriers had been deployed. As for bombardment ammunition, both navies were eventually forced to invoke a more disciplined approach in the choice of targets to conserve ammunition but generally speaking demand outstripped supply. While a more mobile delivery system would have alleviated this, its absence was not critical to the eventual outcome.

The next major logistics concern was that of having adequate facilities to uphold maintenance levels, since ships remaining on station for longer periods between proper docking periods were depleting their spares, endurance. Cruisers and smaller were planned to deploy on a 36-day cycle, of which 18 were in the operational area, on passage, with minimum on maintenance at Kure every alternate harbour period, leaving days available on hours' notice. That was the theory, but by 1952 maintenance and notice for steam had to be increased to keep many ageing ships on schedule. Still, the average target of 67 per cent at-sea on operations over the long term was actually achieved, but this was mainly due to well-equipped Japanese dockyards 'without which a depot repair ship would have been *sine qua non*'.[99] Whether the Admiralty would ever have been able to provide one was another matter. Finally, there was the question of whether the overall management and administration of fleet logistics had been effective. It will be recalled that FO2FE was concerned that, without a depot/HQ ship to supplement *Ladybird* acting as communications HQ, mobility was being compromised due to the lack of accommodation and facilities to manage the myriad aspects of logistic support. The fact that logistic demands for fuel and provisions (and ammunition to some extent) became relatively predictable over such a long time should theoretically have helped. This must, however, be tempered by the effects of continuous uncertainty over how the war would evolve. As the Naval Staff History would record, '[h]ad [the British Authorities] been aware that it would drag on for years, much more extensive administration provision would have been made from the first'.[100] Since the nature of any logistic challenge varied widely, depending on whether it arose at the beginning or after long continuous use, the level of responsiveness was conditioned by the quantity and quality of the resources available throughout this period. At various times this proved inadequate, but sufficient alternative solutions were found to ensure that, overall, the task was still accomplished.

Multinational command

A significant and oft-repeated lesson of the Second World War was that the commander must have control of his logistic support to ensure proper responsiveness and, conversely, that the logistics support system must be in harmony with the deployment and operation of the fighting force.[101] Putting scale to one side, the comparatively more modest Korean experience at the operational level appeared to corroborate this. While the Anglo-American command relationship was complicated by the different expectations and practices for how command should function, the logistic arrangements between the two navies in fact worked extremely well. Evidence for this working relationship can be seen by the extraordinary progress achieved in reaching new levels of standardization in replenishment doctrine between the two navies. In 1945 British warships would only occasionally refuel from American tankers. Korea, however, witnessed ships of several navies able to replenish from either American or British tankers as a matter of routine, this latter point being the fundamental objective for any successful replenishment doctrine. It happened because both navies realized the mutual benefit to be derived from achieving safe, efficient and fast transfers at sea between each other's ships, which were increasingly expected to be operating together globally.

The RN's replenishment doctrine was derived mainly from the British Pacific Fleet War Orders issued to its Fleet Train in 1945.[102] The first publication to the whole navy was in 1947, entitled 'B.R. 1742 Replenishment at Sea'.[103] Contemporaneously, 'USF-83 Fueling and Replenishment at Sea' was published by the USN, which included inter-operability procedures with the RN. These formed the foundation for a localized version in Korea that was revised in 1951, following further Anglo-American replenishment experience, and subsequently promulgated throughout the Far East Fleet.[104] The combination of this document and the experience of new replenishment techniques in the *Bulawayo* trials was then codified and promulgated throughout the RN in 1952.[105] Two subsequent addenda prescribed how ships of the RN, Royal Canadian Navy and USN should replenish from each other – a vital and necessary step toward convergence that was universally welcomed.[106] Simultaneously, the USN issued its 'NWP-38 Replenishment At Sea', reflecting some of the procedural lessons gained from Korea.[107] Two years later came ATP-16 'Replenishment At Sea', which in many respects was identical to NWP-38 but, most importantly, included procedures and rig descriptions for operating with navies from NATO and France.[108] The American ATP-16 and the British B.R. 1742 thus became mutually compatible and, although modified from time to time since, ATP-16 remains today the governing doctrine for replenishment at sea by the USN and all its NATO partners.

RN/RFA relationship

A significant difference between the RN and USN both in the Second World War and Korea was that American auxiliaries were naval-manned whereas British vessels were civilian-manned and unionized. The relationship between the RN and RFA was complex, reflecting the mutual interdependence on the one hand yet each subject to such different traditions, command and employment practices. Fleet replenishment, it had been felt by naval officers for some years, should be separated from commercial freighting and integrated into the RN to ensure common discipline and harmony of management structures. This debate continued well into the 1950s.[109] Most of the difficulties in Korea stemmed, however, from the poor condition of the Wave-class tankers on arrival in the forward area. Occasionally there was evidence of poor performance by some of them, usually due to lack of preparedness. In general, however, provided that their crews had been well selected, a very good service was provided.[110] Many a compliment from both British and American warships was recorded in the Reports of Proceedings; perhaps no better description of their worth was the appreciation that the tankers 'have spent many weeks on end on the West coast often operating in vile, and recently cold, weather during their periods of duty, with practically no harbour time. In spite of having supposedly "difficult" British crews, every call has been answered with willingness and efficiency.'[111] Perhaps the most important recognition of all was the Admiralty's announcement in August 1951 to appoint a Commodore in the RFA, reflecting not only its important contribution to Korea but also the extent to which reliance would be placed upon it for mobility in the future.

Summary

The RN's post-Second World War concept of logistic mobility for a global war was modelled after the experience of providing afloat support to the BPF in the Pacific. The combination of economic stringency, reduced fleet size and manpower severely restricted the Admiralty's ability to meet both peacetime and potential wartime requirements. Available contingencies included mobilizing reserves, requisitioning civilian ships and modifying freighting or commercial ships to under-way replenishment capability. However, none was designed for the increasingly exacting demands for fleet support but they would have to suffice until new naval replenishment ships were built. To this end, successful trials of new transfer equipment for replenishment at sea were conducted that laid the groundwork, and it was the subsequent experience in Korea that precipitated the arrival of the first tailor-made fast naval replenishment ship in the RFA and RN's history.

The Korean War itself was a limited but protracted and open-ended operation that bore little logistic resemblance to the post-war 'Pacific' model. The comparatively modest distances, virtual absence of enemy attack and excellent host-nation support provided a relatively benign logistic environment. The growing concern that global war might break out required the Admiralty to uphold a two-theatre strategy. With limited available resources, this therefore meant that many requests from Korea for additional afloat support were declined. Despite being stretched and often inadequately equipped as a result, the logistic arrangements were not critically impaired and, with help and improvisation, the Commonwealth forces were sustained throughout. One important legacy was the convergence in under-way replenishment doctrine between the USN and RN that would underscore how coalition mobility could become a key force multiplier in global expedition.

Notes

1. Rear Admiral W.R. Carter, *Beans, Bullets And Black Oil* (Washington DC: Dept of Navy, 1953) 9; ADM 199/1766, 'Fleet Train Records 1944–1946': Reports of Rear Admiral Fleet Train Vol. 2, Appendix A 'Staff Organization', Public Record Office Kew (PRO).
2. James Field, *A History of UN Naval Operations: Korea* (Washington DC: GPO Naval History Center, 1982), 78.
3. See for example Stephen Prince, 'The Contribution of the Royal Navy to the United Nations Forces during the Korean War', *Journal of Strategic Studies*, 17 (1994), 94–120.
4. ADM 167/124, 'The Post War Navy and the Policy Governing its Composition', Paper B424 of 17 July 1945, p. 208.
5. Norman Friedman, *The Post War Naval Revolution* (London: Conway Maritime Press, 1986), 14.
6. CAB 131/1, Cabinet Defence Committee Paper DO (46) 5th meeting; See also ADM 167/124, 'Composition of the Post War Navy', paper B435, 12 September 1945.
7. Capt. P.C.S. Tupper Carey RN, 'Fuelling At Sea', *Journal of the Royal United Services Institute*, 91 (1946).
8. ADM 116/5824, Director of Plans to Fifth Sea Lord, 'Appreciation Report', 8 April 1947; 'Requirement in Replenishment of Carriers and Aircraft Transports in Peace & War'.
9. Rear Admiral Henry E. Eccles, *Logistics In The National Defense* (Harrisburg PA: Stackpole, reprint 1989), 143.
10. ADM 1/19983, Director of Technical and Staff Duties memorandum, 'Fleet Train Requirements 1946–1951', 5 May 1950.
11. ADM 219/304, DNOR Report 19/46 'Report on Fleet Carriers – Maximum Period away from Base or Fleet Train', 18 April 1946, paragraph 23.
12. ADM 167/124, B435; See also ADM 205/83, 'Future Size and Shape of the Navy'.
13. Carey, 'Fuelling At Sea', 384.
14. ADM 1/19248, Commodore BPF Fleet Train memorandum, 'Admiralty Comments concerning Recommendations', 26 April 1946; Enclosure No. 4, 'Logistic Support of a Fleet Engaged in Ocean Warfare'; 'Fleet Train Skeleton Organization for the Future based off BPF Experience'.
15. *Farragut, Gearing* and *Fletcher*-class figures vary. Derived from 'War Service Fuel Consumption of US Naval Surface Vessels' NAVPERS 91085 (1 July 1946 modified 1947 & 1948); BUSANDA Navy Supply Corps School, NJ; RG 143 Records of Bureau of Supply and Accounts, 143010 Supply Management Publications and Documents 1943–1964, Box 50, National Archive And Records Administration, Maryland, USA (NARA II).
16. Thomas Wildenberg, *Gray Steel and Black Oil: Fast Tankers and Replenishment at Sea in the U.S. Navy 1912–1992* (Annapolis MD: Naval Institute Press, 1996), 65.
17. ADM 199/1457, 'Report of Experience of the British Pacific Fleet January to August 1945' Part III 'Recommendations for Fleet Conducting Ocean Warfare', Section II 'Staff Requirements for Ships'; C-in C BPF, 15 March 1946. These plans evolved into the new *Tide* class tankers built in 1955. For an American appreciation of the advances in British replenishment design see Captain Pare, *'Mobile Fleet Support'* (1948), RG-15 'Guest Lectures', Naval War College RI, USA. Captain Pare was the leading authority on under-way replenishment in the USN.
18. B.R. 67(2) 'Admiralty Manual of Seamanship' Vol. II (London, 1951) 468.
19. B.R. 1742(52); B.R. 1742B 'Liquids' (52) and B.R. 1742C 'Solids' (53). See this chapter's notes 105 and 106 below.
20. ADM 116-5813, G. Carter MBE, 'History of Fuelling at Sea', 31 March 1948; 'History of Naval Stores Department 1939–1945', Vol. 3 'Role of Yards and Depots Overseas; Fuelling at Sea'.

21. B.R. 1742(52) 1.
22. ADM 1/23443, 'RFA *Wave Chief*: Report by Master of Experience Gained in Korean Waters', 31 December 1951. See also ADM 116/6231, 'Far East Fleet Memoranda' paragraph 4 (g)(i), 1 February 1952; 'Replenishment at Sea – Fuelling', FEFM 29/51 (Revised).
23. FEFM 29/51.
24. I.McD. Black, RCNC, 'Fuelling at Sea', *North East Coast Institution of Engineers and Shipbuilders*, 68 (1951–2), 138.
25. ADM 116/5813, paragraph 47 and Appendix 1.
26. FEFM 29/51.
27. B.R. 1742(52).
28. ADM 1/23443.
29. FEFM 29/51.
30. Ibid.; ADM 1/21061, 'Report of Replenishment At Sea Trials carried out by HMS *Bulawayo* and Ships of the Home Fleet'.
31. FEFM 29/51; ADM116/6231, FO2FE, 'Third Report – Report of Experience in Korean Operations July 1951–June 1952' part III section vi.
32. ADM 116/5813.
33. ADM 1/23434, 'Oiling at Sea: Reports by HMS *Cossack* and Other Ships 1951–1952'.
34. B.R. 1736(54), Naval Staff History, *'British Commonwealth Naval Operations Korea 1950–1953'* (1967) Naval Historical Branch MOD, 128. This type of refuelling is illustrated in the jacket photograph, where *Athabaskan*'s sister ship HMCS *Nootka* is refuelling from RFA *Wave Sovereign* with HMS *Ocean* also alongside.
35. B.R. 1742(52) 1.
36. Rear Admiral C.C. Hughes Hallett, 'Naval Logistics in a Future War', *Journal of the Royal United Services Institute*, 95 (1950), 238.
37. ADM 116/6229, 'Korean War Reports of Proceedings December 1951–February 1953' No. 47, paragraph 16, 9 January–4 February 1952; 'Report of Proceedings Korean War' December 1951–February 1953.
38. ADM 116/6231; FEFM 29/51, paragraph 9.
39. Each hold must have sufficient space to enable access to different stores that can then be broken out through the hatches to the transfer points.
40. Temporary drafting of ten ratings helped but the lack of available skilled crews meant that the complement of British tankers was generally only 20% to 40% of USN oilers. ADM 1/23431, 'Additional Personnel required when employed on Replenishment at Sea', 1952. See also Rear Admiral Fleet Train, 'Re Oiling At Sea 1945–46, section 2 'Report on US methods re USS *Platte*'; ADM 199/1756 (PRO), 'Fleet Train Records' part 17.
41. ADM 116/6231, Minute Director of Victualling, 27 April 1948.
42. ADM 116/5864, 'Major combatant' defined as Fleet minesweepers and larger. See Appendix to Cabinet Paper 'Sale and Scrapping of Warships September 1945', 'Obsolete Warships: Policy on Refitting or Disposal', 1945–55.
43. Statements of the Naval Estimates 1947–1960 (Net Figures).
44. Pink Lists 20 June 1950; Reserve figures derived from Operational/Supplementary/ Extended categories, 'Z' lists, reserve refits and ships being placed into reserve. Active Fleet includes training ships, active refits or 'non-operational' but excludes foreign-manned or loans to other countries. RFA ships not recorded.
45. Pink Lists 20 June 1951; 1 July 1952.
46. Pink Lists 24 June 1946; 23 June 1947; 30 June 1948; 30 June 1949; 20 June 1950; 26 June 1951; also ADM 1/27413, 'History of the RFA Service', 1919–1958.
47. ADM 1/27413.
48. *Surf Pioneer* and *Surf Patrol*.

49. Malcolm W. Cagle and Frank A. Manson, *The Sea War in Korea* (Annapolis: Naval Institute Press, 1957), 35.
50. Ibid., 32.
51. 'The RN – Incidents since 1946: Notes of HM Ships involved', MOD WP5U13.40.
52. Naval Staff, *Operations*, 19.
53. FO2FE/21175/1 CTG 96.8 Operation order no. 1 to C/Os of all ships, 8 July 1950, 'Korean War Records of Proceedings 1–29', ADM 116/5794, '25/6/50–21/1/51 Activities at Sasebo Fleet Base'.
54. ADM 116/6230, Director of Plans (Q) note of 18 October 1951 re DTSD reference sheet to VCNS, 'Report of Experience in Korean Operations : FO2FE July–December 1950', 6 November 1951.
55. Field, *A History of UN Naval Operations: Korea*, 78.
56. Naval Staff, *Operations*, 72.
57. ADM 116/5794, 'Korean War Report of Proceedings', 14–16 July 1950, paragraph 25.
58. ADM 116/6230, 'Supply at Sea' logistics part iv section 111, Appendix X.
59. Naval Staff, *Operations*, 32.
60. ADM 116/6228, 'Report No. 3, 29 July 1950–10 August 1950', paragraph 60; ADM 116/6230, Part IV Administration, Maintenance and Logistics Section 3 Logistics.
61. ADM 116/6228, 'Report No. 3, 29 July 1950–10 August 1950', paragraph 61.
62. ADM 116/5794.
63. ADM 116/6230.
64. Naval Staff, *Operations*, 20.
65. John Landsdown, *A History of UN Naval Operations: Korea* (Worcester: Square One, 1992), 11, 48.
66. Naval Staff, *Operations*, 298.
67. Thereafter *Glory*, HMAS *Sydney* and *Ocean* operated a number of tours until the end.
68. Naval Staff, *Operations*, 103–12.
69. This compares to American carriers' operating for 21 days, with full replenishment undertaken every third day. See ADM 116/6230, Second Report, Part IV: 'Administrative Lessons'.
70. ADM 116/5794, paragraphs 113–14.
71. Ibid., paragraph 104.
72. Landsdown, 439.
73. ADM 116/6230, Part IV Administrative Lessons: General Administration.
74. Naval Staff, *Operations*, 154.
75. Ibid., 68–9.
76. ADM 116/6230, 'Supply at Sea', Logistics part iv section 111 Logistics.
77. Ibid., Appendix X.
78. Ibid.
79. ADM 116/6230, P.S. Newell memorandum, ref DNE 1218/51 to C in C FES, 7 November 1951.
80. Ibid.
81. ADM 116/6230, Director of Plans (Q) minute, First Report July–December 1950, 5 December 1951.
82. ADM 116/6230, Director of Plans (Q) minute, 'Supply at Sea', 18 October 1951, Logistics part iv Section 111, Appendix X.
83. ADM116/6230, Rear Admiral Scott-Moncrieff letter, 'Second Report: Report of Experience in Korean Operations', 27 July 1951.
84. ADM 116/6230, Second Report, Part II 'Command', paragraph 67.
85. Ibid., paragraph 38.
86. Ibid., Part IV 'Administrative Lessons,' paragraph 80.

87. Military Branch, 'Summary of Collection of Departmental Remarks', re 'Special Report of Experience in Korean Operations: FO2FE January–June 1951', 6 October 1951; ADM 116/6231 (PRO), 'Report of Proceedings Korean War December 1951–February 1953'.
88. Landsdown, *Carriers*, 239, 247.
89. ADM 116/6231, 'Third Report – Report of Experience in Korean Operations July 1951–June 1952', FO2FE, paragraph 43 'operational and maintenance cycle'.
90. Landsdown, *Carriers*, 203.
91. Field, *A History of UN Naval Operations: Korea*, 398.
92. ADM 116/6231, Director of Plans Minute ref M02227/51 Folder C in C FES 916/FES/1190/31/1 13/8/51 Report of Experience in Korean Operations January to June 1951.
93. Naval Staff, *Operations*, 299 and Appendix J.
94. BSR 493, 'Fleet Train History', Appendix D 'Logistic Support Group statistics parts 1& 2', Naval Historical Branch, MOD.
95. Several examples exist but see ADM 116/6230, Part III section 4 'Handling of the Fleet'.
96. Field, *A History of UN Naval Operations: Korea*, 380.
97. Ibid., 378.
98. Naval Staff, *Operations*, 71.
99. Ibid., 72.
100. Ibid., 68.
101. Eccles, *Logistics In The National Defense*, 224.
102. Pacific Fleet War Orders – Part III 'Fleet Train', revised 1 July 1945 promulgated by Rear Admiral Fleet Train (RAFT) FT 2610/438. BSR 493/477 'Fleet Train History'; Naval Historical Branch, MOD.
103. 'B.R. 1742/47'. See ADM 116/6231.
104. FEFM 29(51) See note 22 for full title.
105. ADM 234/393 'B.R.1742/52'. 'Replenishment at Sea'.
106. 'B.R. 1742/52B', 'Transfer of Liquids at Sea' and 'B.R. 1742/52C', 'Transfer of Solids at Sea'. Both documents noted elsewhere as 'B.R. 1742/52B' and 'B.R.1742/52C'. ADM 234/394 and ADM 234/395. See also ADM 116/6231, 'Fourth Report' of 'Report of Experience in Korean Operations 1 July 1952–30 April 1953' by FO2FE, paragraph 11.
107. NWP-38 (1953).
108. ATP-16 'Replenishment at Sea: Corrected Version', Office of CNO, Washington, June 1955 Registered Publications, USN Operational 1918–1970; RG 38 'Records of the Office of Chief of Naval Operations', Box 11, NARA II.
109. For example, see 'Replenisher', 'What is Wrong with the R.F.A.?' *Naval Review* (1957).
110. ADM 116/6231, Fourth Report part IV 'Navigation and Replenishment at Sea'.
111. This, for example, from ADM 116/6229, 'Report of Proceedings Korean War No. 47 9 January–4 Feb 1952', 4 February 1952.

8

THE ROYAL NAVY, EXPEDITIONARY OPERATIONS AND THE END OF EMPIRE, 1956–75[1]

Ian Speller

In the period 1966–75 Britain progressively reduced its military involvement beyond Europe. This process was not inevitable, nor indeed was it anticipated far in advance by the leadership of either main political party.[2] Immediately prior to this, Britain had enhanced significantly its ability to project power beyond the NATO region.[3] A tide of nationalism in Africa and Asia had accelerated the process of decolonization and threatened to rob the British of the system of overseas bases upon which their military posture depended. That land bases might prove of little use in times of crisis was demonstrated in 1956 when Jordan, Libya and Ceylon all refused to allow British bases within their territory to be used for operations against Egypt. In order to reduce the reliance on such bases the British military sought to enhance the strategic mobility of their forces. The Royal Navy responded to the challenge that this presented by developing a concept of mobile amphibious task groups supported by large aircraft carriers. This chapter will focus on the way in which this concept evolved and the degree to which it supported the protection of British interests overseas.

Despite the decisive contribution that amphibious forces made to victory in the Second World War, the British neglected expeditionary capabilities in the post-war decade. The Royal Navy concentrated its limited assets on the tools required to secure sea control in a war against the Soviet Union. During the 1950s a change in strategic assumptions brought a new emphasis on expeditionary forces, and in response to this the Royal Navy reversed previous policy and placed a high priority on power-projection capabilities able to support national policy overseas. The navy developed a concept of mobile amphibious task groups, supported by large aircraft carriers and the necessary escorts and replenishment ships. These forces were to concentrate in the Indian Ocean and Western Pacific, in the region described by the British as 'east of Suez'. Almost inevitably this brought them into conflict with the Royal Air Force (RAF) who had developed their own scheme for the projection of power overseas, based upon the use of land-based aircraft. In the debates that followed, the various strengths and limitations of either case were discussed exhaustively and the value of both was tested in a number of actual operations. The debates are of historical interest because their outcome had a fundamental impact on the shape and size of the British armed forces in the 1970s, 1980s and beyond. They may also be of contemporary value as they highlight issues that remain important today, particularly as the United Kingdom once again seeks to project power overseas in a fashion that is militarily effective, politically acceptable and economically sustainable.

The future role of the Navy

The failure of British arms to secure a satisfactory outcome to the 1956 Suez crisis highlighted the inability of the armed forces to react rapidly and effectively to events outside Europe. The time required to build a response to Colonel Nasser's nationalization of the Suez Canal and the military shortcomings of the force that conducted Operation MUSKETEER demonstrated that British expeditionary capabilities had been allowed to atrophy. As a result, the 1957 Defence Review articulated a shift toward smaller, professional forces and greater strategic mobility to meet the demands of limited conflict beyond Europe. The role of the navy in major war was declared to be 'somewhat uncertain' but this rather alarming statement was offset by a new emphasis on the value of the Royal Navy and Royal Marines as a means of 'bringing power rapidly to bear in peacetime emergencies or limited hostilities'.[4]

The 1957 Defence Review was not as revolutionary as it appeared. The new role that it identified for the Royal Navy was in reality a reflection of existing Admiralty plans that pre-dated the debacle at Suez. As early as 1955 the Service Chiefs of Staff had agreed that major war in Europe was unlikely and that the armed forces should also cater for contingencies overseas in order to 'maintain and improve Britain's position in the cold war'.[5] By June 1956 the Chiefs of Staff agreed that preparation for 'global war' would receive the lowest priority while forces devoted to 'limited war' and 'cold war' contingencies would be built up.[6]

Anticipating a requirement for change the First Sea Lord, Lord Mountbatten, established the Way Ahead Committee to draw up recommendations into the future structure and organization of the navy. The early findings of this committee were reflected in the 1956 Navy Estimates and these intimated a move away from preparations to fight a long drawn-out war in Europe.[7] In response to the changing appreciation of strategic requirements the navy submitted their new concept for the *Future Role of the Navy* to the Chiefs of Staff Committee on 20 July 1956, six days before the nationalization of the Suez Canal.[8] The paper announced that forces devoted to global war would be reduced and resources reallocated to cold war and limited war tasks. At the centre of this new concept was the creation of a task group built around an aircraft carrier and a new 'commando carrier' that would be based at Singapore. Supported by a cruiser and four destroyers, this task group would be capable of launching air attacks against targets ashore and of landing a self-supporting Royal Marine Commando unit. According to the concept paper, 'the Navy's task in the Cold and Limited war is broadly to protect British interests, support the civil power, produce a rapid show of force in an emergency and uphold prestige and influence'. The new concept represented a fundamental shift in naval priorities. Prior to 1956 the main emphasis in naval plans and procurement had been preparation for a major conflict with the Soviet Union. Power-projection capabilities in general and amphibious forces in particular had received a low priority.[9] The change did not occur without some opposition. Some members of the Board of Admiralty were concerned by the plan to curtail expenditure on traditional sea-control assets such as anti-submarine and minesweeping vessels in favour of a more expeditionary focus.[10]

Despite these misgivings, in the years after 1956 the navy embraced their new expeditionary role. In 1957 Mountbatten successfully secured agreement for the conversion of a light fleet carrier into a new commando carrier (or LPH).[11] As a result, in January 1959 work to convert the 20,000-ton carrier HMS *Bulwark* was begun at Portsmouth Dockyard and the ship was commissioned in its new role on 19 January 1960. *Bulwark* was designed to embark a battalion-sized Royal Marine Commando unit. It could provide complete administrative support for one unit for 14 days at intensive rates and for 42 days at reduced rates. In an emergency an extra Commando unit could be embarked.[12] *Bulwark* was equipped with four small landing craft carried on gantries and had an initial air complement of 16 Whirlwind helicopters. These were later replaced by the more capable Wessex. The conversion of *Bulwark* proved to be a success and, in 1962, its sister ship HMS *Albion* underwent a similar conversion in order to provide a second LPH. Capabilities were further enhanced by the replacement of the obsolete Landing Ship Tanks (LSTs) of the Amphibious Warfare Squadron with the new assault ships (LPDs) HMS *Fearless* and HMS *Intrepid*. These capable new vessels entered service in 1965 and 1967 respectively. Follow-on support and logistic lift would be provided by the six Landing Ship Logistic (LSL) launched between 1963 and 1967. Originally operated by the Ministry of Transport, these vessels were transferred to the Royal Fleet Auxiliary in 1970.

Amphibious ships were only one component of this new expeditionary capability. Aircraft carriers were at the centre of the proposed new task force. The Minister of Defence, Duncan Sandys, had begun his defence review with a sceptical attitude toward the value of aircraft carriers. However, Mountbatten had skilfully overcome this opposition by demonstrating their value in support of operations overseas.[13] Unfortunately, gaining and maintaining approval for the replacement of the existing ships would prove more difficult.

In 1960 the Chiefs of Staff undertook a study of 'Military Strategy in Circumstances Short of Global War'. Their conclusions were discussed by the Cabinet Defence Committee and formed the basis for a later paper entitled 'British Strategy in the Sixties'.[14] As part of this review process the Admiralty undertook a study of the shape and size of the navy under the following circumstances: if Britain retained its current bases; if the navy ceased to have an operational role east of Suez; and if the role east of Suez remained but no bases were available except in Australia.

Three alternative fleets were outlined, Fleets A, B and C respectively. Under Fleet A the navy remained as currently projected, with four aircraft carriers (but only three air groups), two LPHs and two LPDs. For this fleet to be viable beyond the 1960s new aircraft carriers would need to be built. The Admiralty accepted that aircraft carriers were not required for Fleet B and that in these circumstances the existing large carriers would not need replacing. This was a surprising admission given later events. The case for Fleet C offered the most demanding challenge to the navy. With no bases east of Suez, the Admiralty proposed to deploy military power from a Joint Services Seaborne Force. The force would be able to put ashore a balanced brigade group, if necessary against armed opposition. In order to maintain the permanent availability of the force, two powerful amphibious groups would be required. Dubbed the 'Double Stance', this approach called for a total of four LPHs and four LPDs supported by six large aircraft carriers operating four air groups. By rotating these ships, a powerful military presence could be maintained off a trouble spot almost indefinitely and without recourse to land bases. The combination of balanced amphibious forces and powerful air groups would give Britain the ability to bring power to bear in most conceivable circumstances.[15]

The First Sea Lord, now Admiral Caspar John, emphasized that the Joint Services Seaborne Force was not an attempt by the navy to 'go it alone'. The Force was a joint concept that would be developed in partnership with the other services. In particular, he stressed that sea- and land-based aircraft were complementary and did not claim that aircraft carriers would eliminate the requirement for land-based aircraft east of Suez. He did not claim that Britain could do without bases east of Suez but rather tried to demonstrate that a seaborne strategy offered the best way of making do with a reduced number.[16]

The utility of the Admiralty's concept of employing amphibious forces and aircraft carriers in support of British interests overseas was demonstrated during the 1961 Kuwait crisis. In response to a perceived threat to Kuwaiti independence from Iraq the British deployed to Kuwait a reinforced infantry brigade group supported by air and maritime assets. Under Plan Vantage, the existing plan to reinforce Kuwait, the majority of troops were to arrive by air and join equipment held in stockpiles in Kuwait and Bahrain. However, in the first days of the crisis both Turkey and Sudan refused to allow overflight of their airspace and this, in conjunction with the 'air barrier' of unfriendly states in the Middle East, seriously undermined the plan. Indeed, 24 hours after the initial Kuwaiti request for help on 30 June the only full unit in Kuwait was No. 42 Commando landed from HMS *Bulwark* and supported by half a squadron of tanks from the LST HMS *Striker*.[17]

Unimpeded by political restrictions and able to poise over the horizon in international waters, ostensibly slow amphibious ships proved quicker and more mobile than the air-transported alternative. In addition, and in contrast to troops arriving in long-range transport aircraft, the troops landed by helicopter from *Bulwark* did not need airport facilities to arrive and could, if necessary, secure theatre entry in a non-benign situation. In the event, the amphibious force was able to adopt a covering position to secure the entry of the follow-on forces arriving by air and no Iraqi attack materialized. It was noteworthy that despite the existence of airfield facilities at Kuwait and Bahrain, the RAF was unable to secure a satisfactory air-defence environment before the arrival of the aircraft carrier HMS *Victorious* on 9 July.[18]

Despite the experience at Kuwait the Double Stance was considered to be too expensive. The Chiefs of Staff study 'British Strategy in the Sixties', completed by the end of 1961, accepted that the Double Stance was the most desirable strategy for the next decade given the uncertain tenure of Britain's overseas bases but ruled it out on the grounds of cost. The paper noted that, in order to compensate for the inevitable reduction in overseas bases, forces east of Suez would have to be mobile and flexible. Reliance would be placed primarily on forces based at Singapore and in the Persian Gulf and these should be capable of mutual reinforcement. For this purpose an Amphibious Group would be maintained in theatre. In order to ensure the constant availability of the necessary shipping and in view of the decision that no specialist amphibious capability was required in the west, the study concluded that both LPHs and both LPDs should be maintained in commission east of Suez.[19]

Prior to the arrival of the new LPDs, the amphibious presence east of Suez rested on either *Bulwark* or *Albion* and occasionally both. The drawback that this posed in such a vast region was obvious. In December 1962 when the Brunei revolt broke out, the only LPH in theatre, HMS *Albion* with No. 40 Commando embarked, was at the other end of the Indian Ocean, off Mombasa. Ordered to Brunei on 8 December the ship arrived six days later. Infantry transported by air from Singapore arrived within hours. Clearly the maritime amphibious capability was better suited to situations where an immediate response was not necessary or where prior warning allowed the force to poise offshore.

The 1962 Defence White Paper reflected the conclusions reached in 'British Strategy in the Sixties' and enunciated the new concept of operations. It stated that '[w]e must insure against the loss of fixed installations overseas by keeping men and heavy equipment afloat, and by increasing the air and sea portability of the strategic reserve.'[20] The paper announced that a fully effective joint-services amphibious force would be permanently maintained east of Suez. By 1964 the Admiralty[21] was planning on the basis that within two years an Amphibious Group consisting of three operational ships (with the fourth ship undergoing refit) would normally be maintained in theatre. In operations the Amphibious Group would normally be supported by an aircraft carrier, the necessary escorts, a replenishment group and the new LSLs.[22] Aircraft-carrier strength was limited to one, and later two such vessels maintained in commission in theatre.[23]

By 1964 all of the ships of the Amphibious Group were in service or being built. The situation regarding aircraft carriers was less satisfactory. The hulls of all of the existing ships had been laid down during the Second World War. HMS *Victorious*, the oldest vessel, was due to reach the end of its useful life by 1970 and the remaining carriers, *Ark Royal*, *Eagle* and *Hermes* were all due to retire in the years that followed. Expensive modernization programmes might extend the lives of some of these ships but it was clear that if the navy was to maintain a fleet of at least three operational carriers into the 1970s new construction would be required. The Admiralty favoured large carriers over smaller, less capable vessels. Despite some concern that large and therefore costly vessels might encounter political opposition, in June 1962 the Admiralty approved a design concept for a ship of 53,000 tons capable of carrying 30 fighter/strike aircraft and costing between £55 and £60 million to construct.[24] This brought them into conflict with the RAF who had their own ideas about the best way to deploy air power overseas. The vicious debate that followed brought out many of the supposed advantages and limitations of maritime forces operating in support of national policy overseas.

The Joint Services Seaborne Force versus The Island Stance

The RAF rejected the case for large aircraft carriers, but was not dogmatic in their opposition. The Air Ministry were willing to contemplate smaller less capable ships. In 1961 the Chief of the Air Staff, Air Marshal Thomas Pike, argued in favour of a multi-purpose vessel that could be used in a variety of different roles according to requirements. Dubbed the *Pike Ship* this vessel could be used to carry troops, operate as a platform for anti-submarine aircraft and defensive fighters, or as an advanced landing ground with limited servicing facilities for land-based close-support and fighter aircraft.[25] A joint Admiralty/Air Ministry study group examined the proposal but was unable to agree on the basic concept for this dual-purpose ship. The Chiefs of Staff referred the issue to a neutral party, Field Marshal Festing,[26] and he concluded that a specialist aircraft carrier capable of providing air defence for an amphibious force and close support for troops ashore was required. In 1963 the Minister of Defence, Peter Thorneycroft, resurrected the idea of small, dual-purpose aircraft carriers, this time dubbed the offshore garage (an indication of their limited support facilities) or the Thorney craft. Once again the Admiralty rejected the ship as entirely inadequate, considering it as a potential supplement to conventional aircraft carriers but certainly not as a replacement. With some justification the Air Ministry complained that the Admiralty were deliberately exaggerating the costs and limitations of this ship in order to strengthen the case for a large aircraft carrier.[27]

The navy scheme for intervention overseas was based on the ability to land a balanced infantry brigade group, including armour and artillery, against a hostile shore supported by a powerful maritime force of surface vessels and a large aircraft carrier.[28] Based at Singapore, this force could operate anywhere within the Indian Ocean littoral without recourse to other land bases. Should Singapore become unavailable due to political developments, the force could operate from a new base on the west coast of Australia. The Admiralty did not claim that it would remove the requirement for land-based aircraft, but rather, the different capabilities of land-based and sea-based forces were seen to complement each other.

The RAF developed a very different case. In what became known as the 'Island Strategy' or 'Island Stance', they claimed that British interests could be supported through the application of long-range air power deployed from a notional series of bases that could be established across the region.[29] The strategy offered a more limited intervention capability based around the use of long-range strike aircraft and air-transported troops. It provided for intervention by a parachute battalion and an infantry brigade group, without armour, up to 1,000 miles from the mounting base. Assault operations would be limited to a battalion, as only the parachute troops would be trained for airborne operations. Follow-on forces would only arrive if a suitable airfield could be captured and held. Similarly, any assault operations would be limited in range to within the operating distance of the short-range transports from which troops could land. The majority of the military force would be left in the United Kingdom and deployed into theatre if required. Small detachments of troops and tactical transport would be maintained at island bases in order to provide a rapid intervention capability. Likewise, long-range strike aircraft would base in the UK and Cyprus and from where they could concentrate in theatre should the requirement arise. Fighter aircraft would have to remain based east of Suez as their limited range would preclude rapid deployment east in any crisis.

The Admiralty correctly interpreted the Island Strategy as an attack on their plans for aircraft carriers and amphibious ships east of Suez. There was no place for either in the RAF plan. They responded with a series of papers criticizing this approach. Notably, in January 1963 the Minister of Defence was sent a report by Vice-Admiral Frewen[30] that explained that the strategy was fatally flawed on three major grounds: those of strategic reality, political feasibility and military practicality.[31] Frewen claimed that the strategy was not realistic because it was inflexible. Being tied to static bases it would be unable to adapt to meet new threats in different areas. Therefore the strategy did not provide the worldwide military options needed to match changing circumstances. He also questioned the political feasibility of maintaining all of the island bases that were required. Facilities at Masirah and Aldabra and in Thailand were all vital to the strategy. The continued use of facilities at Masirah after withdrawal from Aden was at best doubtful and the willingness of the Thai government to allow Britain to develop a stockpile there was questioned. Frewen anticipated that any move to develop facilities in Aldabra would provoke a hostile reaction from Afro-Asian nations and would be interpreted as a threat to the newly independent East African nations. This might result in an increase in Chinese or Soviet influence in the region.

Frewen pointed out that the military feasibility of going into battle at ranges of up to 1,000 miles was untried and was dependent on there being no worthwhile opposition in the air. The vulnerability of transport aircraft dictated that any airborne assault would require undisputed command of the air. This could not be ensured unless the force was protected by fighter and ground-attack aircraft. Fighters were required to stop enemy air attack, and ground-attack aircraft were necessary to subdue anti-aircraft fire. Long-range interdiction was not sufficient on its own. As Frewen explained:

> Even if (which is unlikely) political approval were to be forthcoming for long-range interdiction strikes in advance of a landing, these could not by themselves be expected to establish command of the air in the landing zone. During a period of tension, a potential opponent could withdraw his air squadrons to airfields remote from Island Bases. Alternately, in the future, with VTOL[32] aircraft which can readily be dispersed, the effectiveness of interdiction strikes would be largely nullified; moreover, it should not be overlooked that current intelligence shows that Egypt, Iraq and Indonesia, for example, are all acquiring surface to air guided weapons for point defence of towns and airfields.

He claimed that in the absence of carriers, fighter/ground-attack aircraft could not be flown forward to the landing zone in any state of readiness, nor could a radar environment be established. Even under the most favourable conditions, with four days' warning, it would still take between eight and ten days to undertake the unopposed airlift of a brigade group 1,000 miles forward. There was little difference between this figure and the reaction time for a seaborne lift. The air-transported troops would have the additional disadvantage of arriving unacclimatized. With few land and air forces permanently based in the theatre the strategy would also lack the physical deterrence associated with seaborne forces. Frewen stressed that the Admiralty did not advocate a purely seaborne strategy any more than it could accept a purely airborne one. They considered air and naval power as complementary, each balancing the weakness inherent in the other.

In order to assess the relative merits of the RAF and navy cases, an inter-Service panel was set up under the chair of the Chief Scientific Adviser, Professor Zuckerman. The Panel heard evidence from all three services and completed its report in April 1963.[33] They concluded that the most likely case of intervention would be at the invitation of a threatened regime or for internal security reasons. It was therefore reasonable to expect that an airhead would be available and that initial opposition would be slight. Such intervention did not require carriers, nor did it require the full range of bases projected by the Air Ministry. It did, however, require maintenance of the present planned RAF strength of transport and fighter/ ground-attack aircraft. As the level of opposition rose, it would become more difficult to establish the essential airhead until a point was reached where the carrier/ amphibious solution was the most effective and enduring. The panel recognized that such operations against 'moderate opposition' were the least likely forms of intervention, but considered that, nevertheless, the Government should still be prepared to carry them out. Moderate opposition was defined as 'opposition which would be supported by Russian type equipment though not of the latest patterns'.

The debate was conducted in the context of bitter inter-service rivalry, although both sides in the dispute were willing to accept a degree of compromise. The Admiralty never claimed that seaborne forces alone could suffice. They advocated a partnership with the RAF in order to achieve a credible strategy. Likewise, the Air Ministry were willing to contemplate small, multi-purpose aircraft carriers such as the *Pike Ship* or Thorney craft. However, the Admiralty were unable to compromise on the requirement for large, modern aircraft carriers, and the RAF consistently found this unacceptable. In the short term, the short-comings of the RAF Island Strategy and the superior intervention capability of carrier/amphibious forces against moderate opposition ensured the success of the Admiralty case. On 30 July 1963 the Cabinet agreed that the aircraft-carrier force should be maintained at three ships into the 1970s and that a new ship should be built to replace HMS *Ark Royal*. That afternoon Thorneycroft announced to Parliament the decision to build an aircraft carrier of about 50,000 tons costing around £60 million.[34] Although only one ship had been approved, the Admiralty clearly hoped that more would follow. Indeed, they went so far as to agree a name for the second vessel. Unfortunately, this success was to be short-lived. The new carrier, codenamed CVA-01 and due to adopt the old battleship name, HMS *Queen Elizabeth*, did not progress beyond the drawing board.[35]

The Royal Marines

The Royal Marines prospered under the navy's new role. The Commando Brigade expanded from three to five active Commando units and consideration was given to raising a sixth. The brigade also received additional artillery and logistic support elements provided by the army. These were designed to allow the brigade, or individual commando units, to operate independently in an expeditionary role. The mobility possessed by the combination of amphibious shipping and embarked Commando, and the excellent recruitment figures for the Marines, provided a means of alleviating the problems faced by an overstretched and undermanned army. For this reason, in October 1961 the Minister of Defence, Harold Watkinson, advocated raising a sixth Commando unit.[36] Unfortunately, the army would not accept this. Incensed at what they saw as an expansion of the Marines at their expense, the War Office lobbied the Admiralty against any such move. There were even some suggestions that army regiments with a historical maritime connection could be given an amphibious role. In order to placate the army, and to win War Office support for the aircraft carrier replacement programme, the Admiralty agreed not to form a sixth Commando, and even suggested disbanding the fifth. The opposition of the Commandant General, Royal Marines was ignored.[37]

The Admiralty soon regretted the agreement and in 1964 a new deal was struck. The Army accepted the maintenance of five active Royal Marine Commando units, with three based east of Suez. In return the Navy acknowledged that the Marines were specialist amphibious troops, and that while they were also trained as conventional infantry they were less suited to this role than army infantry battalions. It was agreed that it would be wrong to make infantry battalions redundant by using Commandos in a purely land role, or to make Commandos redundant by excessive employment of infantry at sea.[38] Despite this agreement the army displayed a periodic interest in the amphibious role. This had less to do with a genuine commitment to amphibious operations than to a belief that by replacing one or more Royal Marine Commando units they might be able to avoid cuts to their own infantry regiments. Such attempts became particularly vigorous as the defence review initiated by the new Labour Government in 1964 began to bite.

For example, in the wake of the 1966 Defence Review the army made a serious attempt to gain some responsibility for the provision of amphibious infantry. The Chief of the General Staff argued that the army should provide one of the two battalions required for the amphibious force that was now to be maintained east of Suez. The Admiralty recognized the value of including the army in this role as a means of guaranteeing their hitherto shaky support for the amphibious concept. However, they were not willing to do this at the expense of the existing amphibious specialists, the Royal Marines. As such, the Admiralty rejected army suggestions that they could replace one Commando unit with an infantry battalion, that command of the Commando Brigade could rotate between the two services and that Wessex helicopters allocated to the LPHs could be used primarily for counter-insurgency operations ashore, with amphibious warfare relegated to a secondary role.[39]

In defence of his Commando units the First Sea Lord identified the particular advantages of the Royal Marines when compared to their army counterparts. He noted that it was not militarily sound or practical to have units of different services with different standards, training and conditions of service as the embarked force of the Amphibious Group. For this reason the Marines should continue to provide the two units of the embarked force, with the army providing a third unit in a follow-on role. He also noted that as the Royal Marine Commandos provided the specialist infantry element of the brigade it was logical that they also should command it. This was, after all, the only opportunity for Royal Marine officers to exercise command in the field above battalion level. The fact that the Royal Marines had a wealth of experience in training for, planning and conducting amphibious operations was emphasized. In stark contrast to army officers who possessed very little knowledge of maritime operations, Marine officers spent approximately 66 per cent of their career engaged in amphibious activity. He stressed that it would be very difficult for the army to replicate the depth of experience gained by the Marines over a period of years and in numerous operations.[40]

There was clearly an economic aspect to this debate. It made little sense to replace a fully manned Commando unit with years of experience in amphibious operations with an army battalion that would have to start from scratch. In addition, the Marines' process of trickle drafting between their UK-based and overseas Commandos was more economical than the army alternative for overseas duty. In order to maintain one army unit overseas a total of three units were required for rotational purposes. If the unit was to be unaccompanied by family members then four units were required for rotation. This had clear advantages for the army, as by replacing just one Royal Marine Commando unit they could save three or four infantry battalions from the threat of cuts. It made no sense in terms of the wider national interest.

In September 1966 the Chief of the General Staff finally accepted that the two infantry units of the Amphibious Group should be provided by the Royal Marines. However, he reserved the right to change his mind should further defence cuts be advocated.[41] Thus, as the defence review continued, the army abandoned this position and reopened the assault on the Marines. It is hard to portray this as anything other than cynical single-service politics. As the Admiralty pointed out, it made little sense for the already over-stretched army to take on a new responsibility at the expense of the Royal Marines who were fully manned and turning away prospective recruits. In the event the gathering pace of change made the debate rather academic as the role that was being fought over was abandoned. Nevertheless, the debate over who should provide the infantry element of an amphibious force, and the degree to which specialist skills are required, has proven to be an enduring one that can still invite controversy today.

Protecting British interests overseas

The Royal Navy contributed toward the protection of British interests overseas in a variety of ways during the 1960s. This was particularly true of the east of Suez region. From exercises with allies and port visits by individual vessels, to participation in the ANZUK naval force and provision of the Hong Kong frigate guard ship, the navy was an everyday feature of the military and diplomatic life of the region. Maritime forces took part in operations in Borneo during the 'Confrontation' with Indonesia and provided support for counter-insurgency operations in Aden. Frigates deployed to the Persian Gulf offered support to friendly rulers and provided a visible sign of British commitment while other vessels participated in the thankless Beira Patrol, attempting to enforce economic sanctions against the rogue regime in Rhodesia. The conceptual basis for the navy's policy was founded on the belief that the mobility and access provided by the politically free environment of the sea offered the ideal means of projecting power over a wide area and in response to unforeseen circumstances. They also believed that on many occasions the threat of air strikes by distant (and thus unseen) bombers would be insufficient to deter opposition and that troops arriving at secure airports in long-range transport aircraft would not suffice in all circumstances. They might also have noted that in the 1950s, during the Abadan crisis and in the various plans for intervention in Egypt prior to 1956, the independent use of airborne forces against formed opposition had consistently been ruled out as too dangerous.[42]

In January 1964 the navy once again had the opportunity to demonstrate the political and military utility of its concept for intervention. In response to a mutiny by the Tanganyikan Army the British prepared military options to intervene. The only LPH in theatre was off Borneo and thus, in order to guarantee a rapid response, the aircraft carrier HMS *Centaur*, at the time off Aden, embarked No. 45 Commando, a troop of scout cars and some tactical transport and sailed to the trouble spot immediately. Without a mandate to intervene, the carrier, now joined by the destroyer HMS *Cambrian*, deployed out of sight of land in the Zanzibar Channel. Thus, when President Nyerere asked for British military help on 24 January 1964 they were well placed for immediate action. Within a matter of hours the ships closed the area north of Dar es Salaam and, after a gunfire demonstration by *Cambrian* designed to cow the mutineers, the marines conducted a helicopter landing near the main rebel barracks at Colito at first light on 25 January 1964. HMS *Centaur* later provided air cover with its *Sea Vixen* fighter/ground-attack aircraft. Within 40 minutes of the first landing the rebels had surrendered. The marines then proceeded to occupy Dar es Salaam and the main airfield. In subsequent operations order was restored to the hinterland. In the space of about 24 hours the amphibious force had secured an area the size of the UK, with a population of 6 million, for the cost of only four rebels killed and seven wounded.[43]

Operations in Tanganyika demonstrated how a maritime force could poise over the horizon, available for immediate operations should the need arise. The combination of the embarked landing force, organic helicopter transport, fighter and ground-attack aircraft and naval fire support from the destroyer gave this improvised force a potent range of capabilities. It was very flexible. Although capable of causing heavy casualties through a combination of naval gunfire and carrier air attack, it was also able to adopt the politically more acceptable approach of minimum use of force. The speed of response was impressive, striking at the heart of the rebel opposition and disarming them quickly and effectively and virtually bloodlessly before opposition had time to crystallize. After restoring order in Tanganyika No. 45 Commando embarked in the LPH HMS *Albion* to stand by in order to intervene in neighbouring Zanzibar should the need arise. The amphibious force remained poised offshore for three weeks although in the event no intervention was required.[44]

The End of Empire

The new Labour government elected in 1964 was initially as committed to the world role as had been its Conservative predecessor. Unfortunately, the Wilson Government inherited a balance-of-payments deficit of £800 million and faced an urgent requirement to cut government expenditure. One of the results of this was a stipulation that defence spending would be held at £2,000 million at 1964 prices, an effective cut of £400 million on Conservative long-term spending plans. The result was a defence review by the Minister of Defence, Denis Healey, which would have far-reaching consequences.[45]

In this context the new carrier was particularly vulnerable as it represented a large, discrete amount of expenditure on a project that had not progressed beyond the design stage. It would thus be relatively easy to cut. The project was also vulnerable politically. The Admiralty had already admitted that carriers were not required west of Suez and independent studies had concluded that they were only needed east of Suez for operations against moderate opposition. Such a capability was desirable but not absolutely vital for national defence. Should the government decide to reduce the capacity for independent action in this region, the navy's concept of capable but expensive carrier/amphibious task forces might become redundant. The navy's position was further undermined by the report of a joint services study group that concluded that aircraft carriers were not required in order to fulfil any purely maritime task east of Suez.[46] The implication of this was that the only role for which carriers were a necessity was that of support for military intervention against moderate opposition beyond the effective operating range of land-based aircraft. The First Sea Lord, Admiral David Luce, had serious reservations about the conclusions of the study group but, ominously, Denis Healey described the report as 'a useful – indeed, essential' step in the defence review.[47]

The 1966 Defence Review announced the decision to cancel CVA-01. In future, aircraft operating from land bases would take over the strike, reconnaissance and air-defence activities previously conducted by carrier aviation. The decision was based upon new limitations on the use of military force beyond Europe. The review announced that although the UK would maintain a 'major military capability outside Europe' three constraints would apply:

1. Britain would not undertake military operations of war except in cooperation with allies.
2. Britain would not accept an obligation to provide another country with military assistance unless that country provided the facilities to make such assistance effective in time.
3. There would be no attempt to maintain defence facilities in an independent country against its wishes.

In order to improve the ratio of home to overseas service it was announced that in future a higher proportion of troops would be based in the UK, relying on quick reinforcement by air when necessary.[48]

Much has been written about the decision to cancel CVA-01. A significant proportion of this literature has attempted to portray the decision as a bad one and points to an alleged 'dirty tricks' campaign conducted by the RAF in collaboration with the Treasury.[49] It is certainly true that the RAF vigorously opposed plans for the new carrier and actively promoted their alternative of land-based air power. The Royal Navy was equally vigorous in defence of their own concept for the projection of military power overseas. However, their argument was fatally undermined by the question of cost. Unlike the RAF, the navy did not claim that they alone could provide intervention capabilities east of Suez. As such, expenditure on the carrier would have to be in addition to the proposed RAF aircraft and bases. There was simply no way that this could be accommodated within the new ceiling on expenditure without unwarranted cuts in other areas. The RAF may have been culpable in claiming too much for their alternative strategy. However, by 1966 the government was willing to accept a much reduced intervention capability based around providing support to allies and explicitly excluding the possibility of conducting amphibious operations against moderate opposition beyond the range of land-based aircraft. Aircraft carriers would continue to play a useful role into the 1970s in the transitional period when British interests were reduced; they would have no role thereafter.[50]

As a result of the decision to cancel CVA-01 both Admiral Luce and the Navy Minister, Christopher Mayhew, resigned. Prior to this, in a meeting of the Admiralty Board on 7 February 1966, Luce had pleaded with Healey not to cancel the carrier, arguing that the vessel was required to ensure 'a proper and orderly changeover from the carrier system to something else'. He emphasized the difficulty of maintaining the current carrier force through the transitional period in the 1970s without new construction.[51] This may have been a tactical ploy to try to save CVA-01, but it demonstrates that Luce realized that although carriers could be defended in terms of protecting current British interests overseas, in the more restricted vision now supported by Healey they had less long-term relevance. Unfortunately for Luce, by the time CVA-01 was due to enter service in 1973 the transitional period would be more or less over.[52] It is also worth noting that Mayhew did not resign because the carrier was cancelled. Indeed, he was far from a convinced advocate of this ship. He resigned because he did not believe that commitments had been cut to match the planned reduction in military capabilities.[53] Clearly he did not feel that Healey's proclaimed limits on British military assistance east of Suez would actually translate into political reality.

The loss of the carriers did not cause the navy to lose interest in the expeditionary role east of Suez, now increasingly being described as the Indo-Pacific region. The Future Fleet Working Party, established by the First Sea Lord in April 1966 to produce an overall plan for the future navy, maintained that an expeditionary capability was still a key role for the fleet.[54] The Admiralty believed that, if anything, the planned reduction in the British presence overseas made such a force more valuable than before, and continued to espouse the virtues of a sea-based intervention capability. In April 1967 the First Sea Lord, now Admiral Varyl Begg, explained to Healey that military effectiveness away from the UK would be measured increasingly in terms of freedom of political manoeuvre and flexibility of response. Against this background, '[T]he politically free medium of the sea assumes increasing importance, and the role of naval forces, largely self-supporting and with modest overseas currency requirements, becomes correspondingly more significant.'[55]

The utility of such forces had been demonstrated at Kuwait in 1961 and again during intervention at Tanganyika in 1964. Maritime forces contributed to British military efforts during Confrontation and generally provided a useful military tool for sending political signals. For example, in May 1967 HMS *Bulwark* was sent to Hong Kong as a graphic demonstration of British resolve and capability to meet the challenge caused by communist-inspired instability in that colony.[56] On the other hand, maritime forces could also offer unobtrusive presence, providing military options without political commitment. In the summer of 1960 contingency planning had taken place to cover the reinforcement of Nyasaland and Northern Rhodesia in case of possible violence linked to the Nyasaland Constitutional Conference in July. Provision of troops from the UK would have required the cancellation of leave and this was prohibited by the government on the grounds of the publicity that this would receive. Political inhibitions about staging troops through Nigeria and a prohibition of using troops stationed in Aden due to the risk of coincident trouble there led to the decision to use HMS *Bulwark* and its embarked Commando as a floating reserve in case of trouble. This unit would be supported by a brigade headquarters, two units from the Theatre Reserve in Kenya and a battalion based in the UK. *Bulwark*, with No. 42 Commando embarked, was able to sail from Singapore to Mombasa without any fanfare, unobtrusively boosting in-theatre capabilities until the state of tension relaxed in September 1960.[57]

The question of what to do with the amphibious fleet was examined by the Ministry of Defence in the course of a major study into future operations by the Intervention and Amphibious Capability Working Party (IAWP) in 1967. The working party was set up after a request by Healey for an investigation into the balance required between the planned amphibious capability and the forces required in future intervention operations where 'red carpet' facilities were provided for the entry of air and military forces. The IAWP conducted a detailed study looking at potential intervention operations in the Seychelles, Muscat, Kenya and Fiji covering 21 variants ranging in intensity from assistance to the civil power through to counter-insurgency operations, and in scale from a single battalion to a brigade group. Critically, the analysis was limited to calculating the times that would be taken, using alternative methods of delivery, to bring the forces to the scene of the operations. No attempt was made to assess the effectiveness of the forces specified. The result was a superficially impressive set of dates and figures that reflected the pseudo-scientific approach to defence matters popular in the 1960s.[58]

Unsurprisingly the report concluded that when intervention took place on a small scale and without any prior warning or preparatory action the quickest response could be provided by airlifted troops. However, for larger operations, where a force of brigade strength was called for, the use of amphibious shipping in addition to air transport brought a quicker response. The advantage was particularly marked where points of entry were not secure. According to the IAWP the particular advantages of amphibious forces were that they were not limited to a specific point of entry and unlike air-transported troops they provided a mobile, self-contained force capable of landing in a fully tactical posture. Maritime forces had the additional advantage that, given sufficient warning, they could sail early and poise in international waters ready for the call to intervene. In such a way a nominal deployment time of seven days for an intervention in Kenya could be cut to only a few hours. The reaction time of air-transported troops could also be reduced given prior warning, notably by concentrating the landing force at the appropriate mounting base. The main constraints in air transport were distance from the mounting base, overflight limitations, pilot fatigue and the handling capacity of the various airfields employed. These could not be significantly reduced with warning and aircraft did not have the poise capability of their maritime counterparts.[59]

In November 1967 the Admiralty had the perfect opportunity to demonstrate the utility of their carrier/amphibious task group concept during the final British withdrawal from Aden. In order to extract British forces from what promised to be a volatile situation ashore, all four key amphibious ships were deployed in addition to a destroyer, two frigates and eight auxiliary ships. Air cover was provided by the aircraft carrier HMS *Eagle*. The last troops ashore were the Royal Marines of No. 42 Commando who covered the withdrawal before being evacuated by helicopter to the commando carrier HMS *Albion* waiting offshore. The withdrawal was a prime example of precisely the kind of operation that could only be conducted by sea. It was also an example of the kind of operation that the British did not expect to have to conduct in the 1970s. Despite this, in 1968 *Albion* and her embarked Commando were off Aden again, poised in case instability ashore required the evacuation of British civilians.[60]

In July 1967 the government announced further cuts to the military presence east of Suez. British forces in Malaysia and Singapore were to be halved by 1970/1 and withdrawn in the mid-1970s. This was to be offset by the maintenance of a special Military Capability for use in the area. The Royal Navy would continue to contribute toward this capability.[61] Unfortunately, Britain's economic woes continued and this, allied to an increasing lobby in favour of reducing overseas commitments, led to the announcement in February 1968 that all British forces in the Middle East and East Asia would be withdrawn by 1971. In addition no 'special capability' for intervention would be retained; only a 'general capability' was promised.[62] The 1975 Mason Defence Review carried the logic of 1968 to its ultimate conclusion, withdrawing almost all of the small forces that remained east of Suez and concentrating British assets in central and northern Europe.[63]

This had obvious implications for the armed forces. The Royal Navy's concept of mobile intervention forces had been specifically designed to support a national strategy that would soon no longer exist. The RAF suffered similarly. With no requirement to project airpower east of Suez the planned purchase of 50 US-built F-111 strike aircraft was cancelled. The navy fared slightly better. The amphibious ships already existed and represented a significant investment of capital. Maintaining the existing amphibious forces cost the nation only £14 million per annum, compared to the £115 million price tag associated with strategic and tactical air transport.[64] The ships and marines found a new role in support of NATO's northern and southern flanks and this was announced in a July 1968 Supplementary Statement on Defence.[65] The command cruiser identified by the navy as a vital element of the post-carrier fleet survived, and this eventually metamorphosed into the Invincible-class through-deck cruiser.[66] Nevertheless, without the east-of-Suez role expeditionary capabilities were unlikely to prosper. By the time of the 1981 Nott Defence Review the Commando Brigade was back to its pre-Suez strength of three Commando units, the commando carriers *Bulwark* and *Albion* had been decommissioned and the navy's last conventional fixed-wing-aircraft carrier, HMS *Ark Royal*, had gone to the breaker's yard. The LPDs survived, although only one was to remain active at any one time. Planned replacements for these ships were removed from the Long Term Costings in 1975.[67]

Conclusion

In the decade between 1956 and 1966 British maritime expeditionary capabilities underwent something of a renaissance. Old, obsolescent war-built amphibious ships and craft were replaced by a modern mix of helicopter-equipped commando carriers, dock landing ships and logistic landing ships. For the first time since 1945 the Royal Navy accepted amphibious warfare as a high-priority task and the Royal Marines prospered. The utility of large aircraft carriers was reaffirmed and, for a period, the superiority of the carrier/amphibious combination to the alternative of land-based airpower brought government approval for CVA-01. Despite the strength of the maritime approach the Admiralty did not claim that they alone could meet the need of British foreign and defence policy overseas. They consistently portrayed their concept for a maritime strategy overseas as being inherently joint. Army units would provide support and follow-on elements for the amphibious group while RAF land-based aircraft were acknowledged as a vital supplement to carrier-based aviation. Inevitably, however, the concept of a Joint Services Seaborne Force was liable to attract funds to the navy budget and at the expense of the other services. The 'Double Stance' was ideally suited to British needs east of Suez but a navy that included six large aircraft carriers and eight major amphibious ships could only be afforded if radical cuts were made in other areas of the defence budget. This was never likely to happen. The Single Stance approach adopted in the 1960s placed a much smaller burden on the budget but this reduced capability made it inevitable that scarce ships would sometimes be in the wrong place at the wrong time.

When reception facilities could be guaranteed, air-transported troops promised faster arrival times than the maritime alternative. Likewise land-based fighter and strike aircraft could provide a cheaper alternative to carrier aviation when crises occurred within range of their bases. Neither situation could be relied upon. In situations where 'red-carpet' reception facilities were not available, or where larger forces requiring heavy equipment were needed, a mixture of maritime and air-transported assets could build up a balanced military force faster than by air alone. Experience at Kuwait and Tanganyika showed that when a warning period allowed ships to poise offshore, maritime assets could offer an extremely rapid intervention capability. Strike aircraft operating from island bases lacked the mobility, flexibility and physical deterrence associated with a forward-deployed maritime force. There was also a serious question about the long-term viability of the bases from which they operated.

The concept of a task force comprising an amphibious group, a large aircraft carrier and appropriate escorts and supported by joint assets was extremely well suited to British needs. The attributes of mobility and flexibility, both military and political, were demonstrated in numerous operations. Able to travel freely across international waters without reliance on forward bases, host-nation support or overflight rights, maritime forces could offer influence without provocation in a way that could not be matched by land-based alternatives. Unfortunately, the operations that they were designed to support were essentially those of choice rather than necessity. When the government chose to concentrate resources on more immediate tasks, the maritime approach was doomed. For a period the government sought to use airpower as a means of maintaining a very limited intervention capability. This did not occur because air power could do the same job better, or more cheaply. Rather, it was a reflection of the fact that the task had changed. Britain no longer aspired to maintain the robust, multifaceted intervention capability that the maritime force provided. Despite residual commitments around the globe, British defence priorities would in future concentrate on Europe.[68] In future, with the exception of a small number of patrol craft at Hong Kong, the UK maritime presence east of Suez was to be limited to periodic visits and exercises conducted by ships devoted to NATO contingencies.

The military and political value of the Joint Services Seaborne Force concept was belatedly demonstrated during the 1982 Falklands conflict. The task force that recaptured the Falkland Islands was in essence a smaller version of the force envisaged by the Admiralty twenty years earlier. Unfortunately, it lacked the scale and range of capabilities envisaged in the 1960s, and for this the sailors, marines, soldiers and airmen were to pay a heavy price. However, the ability of a balanced maritime force to respond rapidly and effectively to unforeseen circumstances was demonstrated once again. The task force that sailed from Britain in April 1982 provided a visible sign of British determination and offered the politicians a variety of political options including, ultimately, the reconquest of the disputed islands. This could not have been achieved by any other means. British land-based aircraft made only a minor contribution to the conflict. Army units operated ashore alongside their Royal Marine counterparts; however, the amphibious experience of the latter was vital for the successful planning and conduct of operations. The arguments deployed by the Navy in the 1960s were vindicated once again.

Notes

1. This chapter is based on a short presentation that was to have been given at the cancelled 15th Naval History Symposium at Annapolis on 12 September 2001. The presentation was subsequently published in outline form, along with other presentations from the symposium, in the April 2002 edition of the *International Journal for Naval History*.
2. For a detailed examination of the decisions leading to withdrawal see S. Dockrill, *Britain's Retreat from East of Suez: The Choice between Europe and the World?* (Basingstoke: Palgrave, 2002).
3. North Atlantic Treaty Organization.
4. *Defence: Outline of Future Policy 1957*, Cmnd. 124 (London, 1957).
5. COS (55) 176, 25 July 1955: UK Public Records Office, Kew (henceforth PRO): DEFE 5/59.
6. At this time the term 'global war' war was usually used to describe a major global conflict with the Soviet Union. 'Limited war' and 'cold war' operations were small-scale conflicts ranging from civil unrest to outright war fighting that would not include open conflict with the Soviet Union, although it might involve groups or states supported by them. Most frequently it was used to describe operations of low intensity and limited duration.
7. Notably the Reserve Fleet, static and thus vulnerable to nuclear attack, was cut back ruthlessly. *Explanatory Statement on the Navy Estimates 1956–1957*, Cmnd. 9697 (London, 1956).
8. *The Future Role of the Navy*, COS (56) 280, 20 July 1956: PRO: DEFE 5/70.
9. For a detailed examination of this see Ian Speller, *The Role of Amphibious Warfare in British Defence Policy, 1945–1956* (Basingstoke: Palgrave, 2001).
10. ADM 167/146, Board Minute 5016 and Board Minute 5021, PRO.
11. Landing Platform, Helicopter.
12. DEFE 5/85, COS (58) 219, 18 September 1958, PRO.
13. E. Grove, *Vanguard to Trident: British Naval Policy Since World War II* (London: Bodley Head, 1987), 199–209.
14. DEFE 5/123, COS (62) 1, 'British Strategy in the Sixties', PRO; DEFE 7/2231, PRO; DEFE 7/2234, PRO and DEFE 7/2235, PRO. For 'Military Strategy for Circumstances Short of Global War' see PREM 11/2946, PRO.
15. ADM 205/192, 'Presentation of Alternative Long Term Naval Programme', 17 May 1961, PRO.
16. Ibid.
17. DEFE 5/118, COS (61) 378, 18 October 1961, PRO.
18. Ibid.
19. DEFE 7/2235, PRO; CAB 131/27, D (61), 1 meeting, 12 January 1962, PRO.
20. *Statement on Defence 1962: The Next Five Years*, Cmnd. 1639 (London, 1962).
21. During the 1964 reorganization of the Ministry of Defence the Board of Admiralty was replaced by a renamed Admiralty Board of the Defence Council. For ease of reference the term 'Admiralty' will continue to be used throughout this chapter.
22. DEFE 5/150, COS 109/64, 2 April 1964, PRO; DEFE 4/167, COS 26 mtg/64, 2 April 1964, PRO.
23. CAB 131/25, D (61) 28, 16 May 1961, PRO; ADM 1/29638, PRO.
24. ADM 167/160, Board memo B.1421 and Board Minute 5535, PRO.
25. AIR 8/2328, PRO.
26. Field Marshal Festing was Chief of the Imperial General Staff between 1958 and 1961.
27. AIR 8/2328, PRO; E. Grove, 'Partnership Spurned: the Royal Navy's Search for a Joint Maritime-Air Strategy East of Suez, 1961–63', in N.A.M. Rodger, *Naval Power in the Twentieth Century* (Basingstoke: Macmillan, 1996), 227–41.

28. The Chiefs of Staff agreed that operations against 'heavy opposition' requiring a full-scale assault would not be attempted without the help of allies but that British forces might have to conduct operations where 'the points of entry would be in hostile hands, requiring us to face opposition to establish ourselves'. DEFE 7/2235, COS (61) 499, 20 December 1961, PRO.
29. AIR 8/2354, PRO.
30. The Vice Chief of the Naval Staff.
31. AIR 20/11423, PRO.
32. Vertical Take Off and Landing.
33. AIR 8/2354, 'Report of Enquiry into Carrier Task Forces', 22 April 1963, PRO; AIR 20/1124.
34. CAB 128/37, CC (63) 50th Conclusions, cabinet meeting on 30 July 1963, PRO; *Parliamentary Debate (Hansard)*, Vol. 682, column 237–8 and 992–4.
35. The second ship was to have been called HMS *Duke of Edinburgh* in the tradition of naming major warships after the reigning monarch and his or her consort. ADM 1/29044, PRO.
36. DEFE 7/1681, PRO.
37. ADM 205/185, PRO; ADM 205/191, PRO.
38. DEFE 5/150, 'The Royal Marines and the Requirement for Royal Marine Commandos', COS 133/64, 15 April 1964, PRO.
39. ADM 201/135, 'Post Confrontation. Composition of the Amphibious Force', PRO.
40. Ibid.
41. Ibid.
42. Speller, *The Role of Amphibious Warfare*, Ch. 4.
43. ADM 1/29063, 'Operations in East Africa', PRO; Lt-Col T. Stephens, 'A Joint Operation in Tanganyika', *RUSI Journal*, 637 (February 1965).
44. ADM 201/135, PRO.
45. For further details see Dockrill, *Britain's Retreat, passim*.
46. DEFE 13/746, PRO.
47. DEFE 13/746, Denis Healey to the Chief of the Defence Staff, 22 April 1965, PRO.
48. *Statement on the Defence Estimates 1966. Part 1. The Defence Review*, Cmnd. 2901 (London, 1966).
49. For example see Grove, *Vanguard to Trident*, 269–76; P. Beaver, *The British Aircraft Carrier* (Cambridge: Patrick Stephens, 1982), 191–2; D. Wettern, *The Decline of British Seapower* (London: Jane's, 1982), Ch. 20; N. Polmar, *Aircraft Carrier: A Graphic History of Carrier Aviation and its Influence on World Events* (London: Macdonald, 1969), 688–90; T. Benbow, 'British Naval Aviation: Limited Global Power Projection', in G. Till (ed.), *Seapower at the Millennium* (Stroud: Sutton, 2001), 60–1.
50. *Statement on the Defence Estimates 1966. Part 1. The Defence Review*, p. 10.
51. ADM 167/166, minutes of Admiralty Board Meeting, 7 February 1966, PRO.
52. Dockrill, *Britain's Retreat*, 138–44.
53. C. Mayhew, *Britain's Role Tomorrow* (London: Hutchinson, 1967), Ch. 12.
54. See DEFE 13/540, PRO and DEFE 24/128, PRO.
55. ADM 201/135, Chief of the Naval Staff to Denis Healey, 18 April 1967, PRO.
56. Wettern, *The Decline of British Seapower*, 291.
57. ADM 167/166, PRO.
58. DEFE 13/479, 'Report of the Working Party on Intervention Operations and Amphibious Capability 1967', PRO.
59. Ibid.
60. Grove, *Vanguard to Trident*, 298–300; J. Thompson, *The Royal Marines: From Sea Soldiers to a Special Force* (London: Sidgwick & Jackson, 2000), 505–6.
61. *Supplementary Statement on Defence Policy 1967*, Cmnd. 3357 (London, 1967), 4–6.

62. *Statement on the Defence Estimates 1968*. Cmnd. 3540 (London, 1968), 2–3.
63. *Statement on the Defence Estimates, 1975*, CM. 5976 (London, 1975).
64. *Statement on the Defence Estimates 1968*, 29, 33.
65. *Supplementary Statement on Defence Policy 1968*, Cmnd. 3701 (London, 1968).
66. In effect a 20,000-ton aircraft carrier capable of operating a mixed complement of Sea King ASW helicopters and Sea Harrier STOVL aircraft. The Royal Navy currently operates three such vessels.
67. *Statement on the Defence Estimates, 1975*.
68. It is significant that the withdrawal from east of Suez occurred at the same time as NATO began to re-emphasize conventional military capabilities in Europe under the new concept of Flexible Response.

9

THE ROYAL NAVY AND CONFRONTATION, 1963–66

Chris Tuck

From 1963 to 1966, the United Kingdom fought what was, in effect, an undeclared war against the Republic of Indonesia. This chapter will examine the Royal Navy's role in this conflict. It seeks to illustrate the important supporting role that the Navy played in operations. However, it also seeks to demonstrate that, for the Navy as much as for the other services, the struggle that became known as the 'Confrontation' was far more than a regional sideshow. By 1960 the Royal Navy had shifted its focus toward meeting potential limited-war scenarios through strategically mobile forces. Operations like those carried out in 1961 in Kuwait seemed to show the validity of this approach and helped shift the emphasis of the Navy to an east-of-Suez role. As a result, capabilities such as mobility and flexibility became central tenets to meet this strategy as outlined in the 1962 Defence White Paper. Confrontation showed the potential limitations of such a posture. The conflict placed a heavy burden on the Royal Navy, having an impact on all other aspects of its operations. In doing so, it made a direct contribution to the decisions on the UK's east-of-Suez role made by the Wilson government from 1966 to 1968, by widening even further the apparent gap between Britain's commitments and its ability to resource the means to meet them.[1]

The origins of Confrontation

The proximate cause of Confrontation was Indonesian opposition to British, Malayan and Singaporean plans for the creation of a Federation of Malaysia in 1963.[2] However, the general causes of the dispute were more diffuse and related in part to dilemmas in British Southeast Asian policy, and to domestic developments in Indonesia. British defence posture in Southeast Asia was based crucially on the maintenance of the base at Singapore. This base was the means through which Britain could achieve a variety of what it perceived to be critical ends: meeting regional defence commitments such as those to Malaya and Thailand; meeting the growing regional threat from Communism; and sustaining key political relationships with allies such as the United States, Australia and New Zealand.[3] The continuing validity of an east-of-Suez role was central for the Royal Navy, which had reoriented its conventional fleet toward an intervention role.

The creation of the Federation of Malaysia appeared to offer a number of advantages to Britain and its allies. Political extremism was on the rise in Singapore and it appeared as if the relatively pro-British government of Lee Kuan Yew would be pushed by domestic political imperatives to go for full independence or might even lose power completely to the left-wing opposition. If this was the case, the Singapore base would almost certainly be lost and, worse, a Communist regime might take its place, creating fears of a Southeast-Asian Cuba. Conversely, Singapore's inclusion in a wider federation might allow Britain to continue its presence while neutralizing the potential nationalist backlash, allowing Britain to establish a viable defensive framework for the future. However, a key Malayan condition for the creation of such a federation was the inclusion of the British colonies of Sarawak and British North Borneo, with the hope also that Brunei would join. The inclusion of these territories was required by Malaya to balance the ethnic composition of the proposed federation in favour of ethnic Malays, because the federation would otherwise have a Chinese majority.

Initially, Britain did not expect to encounter Indonesian opposition to the creation of Malaysia. Early statements by Indonesia on the project were generally favourable, but by August 1962 with Indonesia committed to political-military action to wrest control of West Irian from the Dutch, this situation had changed. The Indonesian motives for pursuing Confrontation were complex.[4] The Indonesian President, Achmed Sukarno, was undoubtedly committed to reducing the influence of colonial powers in the region and, from an Indonesian perspective, the British plans seemed designed to perpetuate British influence in the region, changing the form of colonial control and not its substance. Sukarno described the Malaysian Federation as 'a country forcibly created by those colonialist powers from which our continent has just liberated itself'.[5] Indonesia was certainly disappointed by Malaysian pronouncements of neutrality over the West Irian issue in January 1962.[6] A policy of confrontation also served some domestic purposes both generally, in terms of focusing domestic interest away from Indonesia's difficult economic circumstances, and specifically, in terms of meeting the nationalist and/or radical agendas of groups such as the Indonesian Communist Party and nationalists within the military and political parties.[7] Inter-service rivalries also contributed to a lack of cohesion in Indonesian policies in the crisis leading up to Confrontation that may well have reduced the chances of a political solution.[8] Wary of provoking a full military struggle with the British, Sukarno instead opted for a policy of *Konfrontasi* (Confrontation), a combination of diplomatic pressure and low-level military activity designed to undermine the creation of the new federation. In December 1962, a revolt in Brunei occurred in which the Indonesians were complicit, having provided material and training. Although a quick British response suppressed this rebellion, Indonesia then embarked on a gradual policy of political and military pressure on the new federation including '…covert military attack, internal subversion, sabotage, economic boycott, anti-foreign riots, international pressure and propaganda and psychological warfare'.[9] Military pressure was used most directly along the 1,000-mile land border separating East Malaysia (as Sarawak and British North Borneo became known after the creation of the federation in August 1963) and Indonesian Kalimantan. From 1964, Indonesian pressure on West Malaysia (Malaya and Singapore) also escalated.

Confrontation and naval power

Maritime forces made an important contribution to the eventual success of Britain's operations in and around Malaysia. The utility of these maritime forces during Confrontation was a function of the unique attributes possessed by maritime power, modified by the particular circumstances of the conflict. In a general sense maritime power offers a range of unique attributes: access to coastal areas through the use of international waters; mobility, due to the fact that two-thirds of the globe is covered with water; versatility, in terms of being able to undertake many different tasks, often concurrently; flexibility in response, if ships are kept at a high state of readiness; adaptability to a variety of roles; sustained reach, thanks to integral logistics support; resilience due to an ability to absorb substantial damage; lift capacity; poise, with an ability to remain in an area for an extended period of time either visible or beyond the horizon; and, through all of these attributes, leverage – an ability to exert often a disproportionate influence on events ashore.[10] However, the Royal Navy's ability to capitalize on the instrumental and environmental advantages of maritime power was influenced by at least three important themes: geography; politics; and the Royal Navy's capabilities relative to those of the Indonesian navy.

Geography shaped powerfully the ways in which the Royal Navy could influence Confrontation. Western Malaysia, though having no land border with Indonesia, was in close proximity to Sumatra and the Rhio islands, so that control of the sea areas around there would constitute the first line of defence against Indonesian attacks. In East Malaysia the main arena was the mutual land border: here maritime forces could adopt a supporting role, making contributions to the defence along rivers and on seaward flanks. Both sides relied on the sea for their major reinforcement and supply routes. Britain required open sea lines of communication from Borneo to Singapore and from Singapore to other theatres. Although local assets became available increasingly over the course of the conflict through the development of Malaysian capabilities, the successful prosecution of the campaign by Britain still depended upon ex-theatre reinforcement. For Indonesia, the sea was also vital. Indonesia is an archipelagic state consisting of more than 13,000 islands. The sea was a vital thoroughfare that linked the disparate parts of the state together. This vulnerability gave the Royal Navy a potentially significant role in deterrence, compellence and naval diplomacy.

The ability of the Royal Navy to exploit the maritime geography of the theatre of operations was shaped by important political controls. British assessments of Indonesia's likely strategy of aggression stressed that a major escalation in the use of force was unlikely, because of Indonesian fears regarding the risks of British retaliation and the alienation of world opinion. Instead Britain believed that Indonesian aggression in Borneo was likely to consist of raids, terrorism and subversion.[11] The threats that needed to be met would therefore include border raids and infiltration, an internal threat from the Clandestine Communist Organization (CCO), internal subversion by elements of the Indonesian minority in Sabah, the dropping of air reinforcements and the landing of armed parties from the sea.[12] Nevertheless, Indonesia had the ability to engage in overt acts should it wish to and so contingencies to take this into account were required.

Britain was constrained greatly in the use that it could make of its military forces to meet this range of Indonesian threats. There was significant concern over the potential impact on world opinion of any British escalation in military force. There were also British worries about introducing more instability into an already fragile region, with turmoil evident in Thailand and Vietnam. Britain also needed to obtain the concurrence of Malaysia, in whose name Confrontation was being fought, and also the acquiescence of important regional allies such as the United States, Australia and New Zealand, all of whom were ambivalent about the adoption of an unduly aggressive policy that might drive Indonesia into Communism. British policy was also shaped by the need to avoid strengthening domestic Indonesian support for Confrontation through measures that might reinforce the perception that Confrontation was, as Sukarno claimed, a struggle against an Imperialist power. Moreover, British policy-makers were cognizant of the need to ensure that, in meeting short-term objectives such as the defeat of Indonesian military probes, Britain did not undermine the attainment of longer-term objectives such as securing a non-Communist and non-aligned Indonesia.[13]

Thus, the overall force posture in which the Royal Navy operated was essentially defensive and deterrent in character with Britain resting its hopes for a successful solution to Confrontation on the build-up of internal pressures in Indonesia that would force Sukarno to compromise. Within this defensive strategy, the British armed forces were tasked with the defence of the border and coastal areas against infiltrators and raiders by land, sea and air; the identification of aggression, covert or overt; control of the border; anti-piracy operations; maintaining the security of bases and lines of communications; anti-terrorist operations; and the preservation of public order.[14] The use of British military power was situated within a wider British strategy that focused on action at the political level to influence world opinion and reduce external aid to Indonesia, and on propaganda and covert measures. The belief by British policy-makers that a solution to Confrontation could not be achieved through military means dictated a military posture that was predicated on the need to defeat and deter Indonesian attempts to infiltrate, sabotage and subvert, but to do so in such a way that it would avoid the necessity for retaliation (and possible escalation). Thus, while it may be true that 'to derive maximum benefit from its navy, a maritime power should be willing and able to seek out the enemy's navy',[15] in the context of Confrontation this simply could not be done: as a result, the uses to which the Royal Navy could be put were highly constrained because of the pervasive influence of political considerations. This meant, for example, that Royal Navy ships were ordered to show 'all possible restraint' in operations and had rules of engagement that stressed the minimum use of force, and even then only in self-defence.[16]

The Royal Navy's ability to achieve control of the sea was also influenced by its capabilities relative to those of its adversary. By early 1962 the Royal Navy had a considerable force deployed as part of its Far East Fleet including a destroyer squadron, a minesweeper squadron, and three frigate squadrons, a submarine division, the aircraft carrier HMS *Ark Royal*, the cruiser HMS *Tiger* and the Commando carrier HMS *Bulwark*.[17] By late 1964 the Far East force included two aircraft carriers (HMS *Centaur* and HMS *Victorious*), one Commando Ship (*Bulwark*), fifteen escorts (including three from Australia and New Zealand), 15 Coastal minesweepers (including four from the Royal Australian Navy), and the Seventh Submarine Division (five submarines and a support ship).[18] This fleet constituted a powerful accretion of maritime power, able to perform a wide range of tasks from surface warfare to air strikes and amphibious assaults. However, this force had to meet many needs. British commitments to the Far East were extensive and included commitments as members of the South East Asia Treaty Organization (SEATO), defence treaties with Malaya and Maldives, direct responsibility for Aden, a commitment to help Commonwealth countries if attacked, and a general need to demonstrate commitment through military presence in the region.

Moreover, the Indonesian navy (*Angatan Laut Republik Indonesia*, or ALRI) was not an insignificant one. From a small force of ships inherited from the Dutch, the Indonesian navy began an expansion programme in 1958 acquiring a range of ships from Italy, Yugoslavia, the United States, West Germany and, particularly, the Soviet Union.[19] In 1963 the Indonesian navy included: one cruiser (Sverdlov class); 17 destroyers and frigates (including Skory- and Riga-class vessels); 12 'W'-class submarines; 30 submarine chasers; six KOMAR-class fast patrol boats each with 10 surface-to-surface missiles; 21 Motor Torpedo Boats; 18 gunboats; 16 minesweepers; 14 larger landing craft; nine oilers, two Submarine tenders; two attack transports/headquarters ships; one supply ship; and 13 Gannet anti-submarine aircraft.[20] The navy had a total strength of 25,000 including 9,000 marines.[21] Since a force of frogmen had been available for operations in West Irian, it was expected by Britain that Indonesia had some demolition and mining capability.[22] Supplementing these naval forces, the Indonesian air force had about 90 jet fighters, 15 Il-28 light bombers and 25 Tu-16 bombers.[23] Most of the Indonesian navy was based at Surabaja naval dockyard. In Kalimantan itself, Indonesian naval forces consisted of half a dozen patrol craft, most based at Pontianak. Larger vessels occasionally visited Balikpapan, and a force of escorts and other vessels was deployed in the area of Tarakan on anti-smuggling and anti-piracy duties.[24] A small proportion of the navy was deployed at short notice near Singapore. Known as the 'Armada Siaga' this force included some submarine chasers, one or two submarines, and one or two of the KOMARs.[25]

Despite its size, the Indonesian navy suffered from many problems. Operational efficiency was not high, and the navy as a whole lacked experience and training: the submarines, for example, were often sighted on the surface even during 'war patrols' and no mine-laying exercises were carried out. Serviceability also tended to be problematic: in late 1963 for example, the majority of the larger ships (the cruiser, seven destroyers, and four frigates) were in refit. Of the 12 submarines, around 4 were operational at any one time. The TU-16s of the Indonesian air force were capable of attacking major surface vessels with missiles and also had a conventional bombing capability, but again it had no experience in carrying out these sorts of operation.[26]

The Indonesian navy had the potential to mount brigade-size amphibious landings but little experience in such operations and only a limited capacity to sustain them logistically. Moreover, Indonesia too was keen to prevent unnecessary escalation because of the political consequences, and so the Indonesian navy was constrained in the uses to which it was put: for example there was no war against mercantile shipping. Instead, Indonesia conducted a long-term programme of harassment and intimidation of Royal Navy ships from shore-based assets such as howitzers in the area of Tawau, and using sampans and patrol craft. In May 1965, for example, a 'Kronstadt'-class vessel trained its guns on HMS *Puncheston* accusing it of being within Indonesia's three-mile limit: Puncheston refused to react.

The sum of these factors was important. The Royal Navy was significantly more powerful than the Indonesian fleet. While the Indonesian threat to sea lines of communication was assessed by the Royal Navy as serious, especially if the Indonesians used their stock of around 10,000 mines, it remained confident that measures were available to deal with this challenge should it emerge. Yet the Royal Navy could not achieve complete control of all sea communications because to do that would require open war, something prevented by political constraints. Nor could the Indonesian navy be ignored because 'if ordered to do so [it] would take the offensive'.[27] The KOMAR-class vessels, for example, posed a significant potential challenge, since they could stand off on the high seas, and then launch missiles into ships in territorial waters. They could be dealt with effectively only by aircraft.[28] Without the immediate possibility of a military solution, it looked as if the commitment that the Royal Navy would have to make might become an increasingly onerous one. The Foreign Office argued in 1963 that military planning would have to be based on three assumptions: that it would not be able to reach a political accommodation with Indonesia; that the Indonesians would not use overt attacks by regular forces (that might justify British retaliation); and that the Indonesians would instead escalate their covert tactics of infiltration, including landings by sea. These assumptions, argued the Chiefs of Staff, placed 'considerable restraints on our ability to bring operations by military means to a quick and successful conclusion. So long as these restraints remain, we face a position in which more and more resources may have to be deployed... this could lead us into severe financial, manpower, and equipment difficulties at the expense of our other commitments'.[29]

The Royal Navy in Confrontation

The Royal Navy had a recent history of operations in the area that became Malaysia: it had made an important, though subsidiary, contribution to operations during the Malayan Emergency of 1948–60. A Royal Navy blockade had helped to reduce the supply of arms to the insurgents. In 1952 HMS *Amethyst* provided fire support 30 miles up the Perak River against a suspected insurgent hideout. In 1954 HMS *Defender* carried out a bombardment against the Johore coast and then steamed nine miles up the Johore River in a naval-presence role. The Navy also made a contribution to tactical mobility through the deployment of No. 848 Squadron of the fleet air arm with its S-55 helicopters.[30] The effort made by the Royal Navy in the clearing of the Brunei revolt, which began in December 1962, was also significant, especially in the early stages. Carrying out the vital role of bulk transport of reinforcements and equipment, the Navy also filled key capability gaps particularly in logistics, riverine and land operations. Moreover, the Royal Navy provided a more general contribution in the shape of naval presence and deterrence. These themes continued as the instability in Brunei gave way to the wider challenge of Confrontation itself. During Confrontation, the Royal Navy made a diverse contribution to success in three general areas. First, the Navy made a direct contribution to military operations, in both East and West Malaysia. Second, the Royal Navy supported British policy through wider naval diplomacy, through activities such as theatre deterrence and presence. Third, the Navy formed a vital part of Britain's contingency planning, widening the scope of options available to British strategic foreign policy-makers.

Operations in East Malaysia

East Malaysia was vulnerable to a range of maritime and riverine threats. Of these, covert infiltration by Indonesian forces was perhaps the most dangerous, but other challenges included Indonesia's potential for overt amphibious landings and the problem of piracy. Covert infiltration was possible by small craft and submarines.

Landings by motorboats could be undertaken from the South Natuna Islands, and from the ports of Sambas and Pontianak in the west and from Tarakan in the east.[31] Although a combination of weather, tides and beach conditions meant that many areas of the coast were not suitable for landings, the coastal areas that were open to potential Indonesian infiltration were nevertheless extensive. The most vulnerable areas were around Tanjong Datu in the West and Tawau in the East. Tawau especially was easily accessed from Indonesia by land or water across Cowie Bay or through inland waterways. Infiltration was made easier in the east because of the extensive cross-border barter trade and by the presence of some 20,000 Indonesian labourers. Tawau was particularly vulnerable because it had no land communications with the rest of Sabah and relied on reinforcement by sea, which was slow, or by air which was dependent on weather and the availability of airfields. As a vulnerable target, Tawau not only needed a garrison but also its own maritime force for coastal defence.[32]

Although covert infiltration was the most significant threat, the Indonesians also possessed a conventional amphibious capability. The threat posed by this was more limited. Aside from the fact that the coastline of Eastern Malaysia was not generally suitable for amphibious operations, the best-equipped ports for supporting such operations were some distance away (Balikpapan at 420 nm and Bandjermasin at 640 nm). In general, support would require large-scale logistic and escort efforts by the Indonesian navy and these would be subject to interdiction by British forces. Also, the Indonesian navy's capabilities in direct bombardment, surface gunnery, torpedo attacks and anti-submarine and air defence were low.[33] Another problem was piracy. This was endemic off the eastern coast of Sabah through the action of Filipinos whose targets were mainly those engaged in the barter trade. Meeting this threat was generally the responsibility of the police, but naval back-up was sometimes required.

The forces directly allocated to East Malaysia to meet these challenges increased progressively from the outbreak of the Brunei revolt in response to the gradual escalation in the nature of the threat. In late 1963, the naval forces in Borneo waters included one escort, two coastal minesweepers and one Malaysian Navy patrol craft. A British/Malaysian boat party at Tawau also maintained boat patrols. The forces deployed to East Malaysia by mid-1964 illustrate the scale of the later commitment. Naval forces based at Tawau included one frigate or destroyer (the Tawau Guard ship), two minesweepers (one Royal Navy, one Malaysian) and four patrol craft/motor launches. Labuan, an island occupied by British headquarters, also had a patrol craft. Forces based at Kuching, in Sarawak, included five minesweepers (three British, two Malaysian).[34] In November 1964, in response to Indonesian infiltration attempts against West Malaysia, a reinforcement of West Malaysia was needed at the expense of the east. At this time the threat to the seaward flanks of East Malaysia also grew, including an Indonesian build-up on Sebatik Island. By March 1965, the available forces included, at Kuching, two minesweepers (one British, one Malaysian), six naval stores tenders and a pinnace. At Tawau, one destroyer or frigate (the guard ship provided by the British, Australian or New Zealand navies), three minesweepers (two British or Australian, one Malaysian) three patrol craft/motor launches (Malaysian), one tanker (from the Royal Fleet Auxiliary) and the Tawau assault group. The Tawau assault group had been created in October 1964 by elements of No. 2 SBS and No. 40 Commando: it consisted of a flotilla of 13 assault craft, supported by five harbour launches with the Governor's yacht acting as headquarters ship.[35] The Navy also crewed a variety of other inshore and river patrol vessels. Co-ordination of these assets with the other elements of the campaign was achieved through the establishment of a joint headquarters, modelled on that established during the Malayan Emergency. Close cooperation was established through daily meetings involving the Director of Borneo Operations (DOBOPS) and his subordinate commanders, including the Commander Naval Forces Borneo (COMNAVBOR).

The tasks performed in support of operations in East Malaysia were shaped by the highly political character of Confrontation: as one of the official summaries of naval operations made clear: 'tasks of direct operational significance were few'.[36] This was true, in the sense that more traditional sea-control activities were not the priority. Contacts with Indonesian naval forces occurred occasionally, but in general Indonesian gunboats kept their distance. Some possible sightings of Indonesian submarines were made.[37] Nevertheless, the Royal Navy carried out a wide range of important activities. One vital role was in transporting reinforcements and bringing in supplies. This was especially important in the early stages of the crisis when the shore-based logistic infrastructure was underdeveloped. Only one port, Labuan, could take ocean-going ships, but it initially had no heavy-duty cranes for loading and offloading. The two other ports were both minor ones: Jesselton, in Sabah, and Kuching in Sarawak. The latter was 21 miles upriver and could be reached by craft no bigger than a small frigate. Minesweepers were used to move troops and supplies such as stores and fuel to support forward helicopter bases, and to ferry reliefs and reinforcements from *Albion* to the shore.

Another vital task was the carrying out of patrols both along the coast and on rivers. These patrols provided general naval presence and boosted locale morale, making a useful contribution to the more general 'hearts and minds' campaign. These patrols carried out a variety of other functions. One was to interdict the supply of weapons to the Clandestine Communist Organization (CCO), an Indonesian-supported insurgent group within East Malaysia. The patrol vessels were drawn mostly from the Sixth Minesweeping Squadron, whose ships were not ideally suited to this role because they were slow and under-gunned, but fast Motor Torpedo Boats (MTBs) and gunboats had been scrapped in the Royal Navy. Activities were also conducted in supporting the Police, for example in patrols up the Rajang River. Here, stop and search operations yielded useful intelligence on the CCO. Much of the effort in Sabah was directed toward anti-piracy operations, for example operations in the Labuk area that involved many craft. Minesweepers also conducted patrols to investigate arms smuggling such as those carried out in 1963 between Tanjong Datu and Kuching.[38]

Sea and river patrols also contributed to anti-infiltration operations. In the Sarawak area, two minesweepers based at Kuching generally carried out naval seaward patrols. These often operated in cooperation with the Long Range Maritime Patrol (LRMP) aircraft. Seaward patrols tended to be concentrated in the Bay of Kuching area out to three degrees north. An improvised force of small craft, including five naval stores tenders, two landing craft and a pinnace, conducted coastal patrols. These patrols extended from Tanjong Datu to Mukah, excluding the coast between Sampardi and Maludam, which was patrolled by the Maritime Police.[39] Naval personnel also manned shore parties that were used to crew river patrol boats. For example, Naval Party Kilo in Western Sarawak was made up initially of part of the crew of the maintenance ship *Hartland Point*. Naval Party

Kilo manned native boats, called Kotaks, armed with Bren guns and operated along rivers and coastal swamps until withdrawn in early 1965 as the availability of police vessels increased. In Sabah, coastal patrols were conducted by the Tawau guardship, one Royal Navy minesweeper, and two Malaysian patrol craft. These were often conducted in association with Long Range Maritime Patrol aircraft. Coastal patrols around Sabah were focused on the area from Lahad Datu south to the Kalimantan border: other areas of the coast were patrolled by vessels from the Maritime Police. The Tawau assault group conducted patrols in the Darvel Bay and Alice Channel areas often in association with the Royal Air Force (RAF). Co-ordination between the Navy and the air force was achieved in Tawau through a Combined Operations Centre. Patrols were often conducted at night using radar and sonar. When contacts were found they would be intercepted, illuminated and then boarded. During the day, RAF aircraft were used to report suspicious craft to the Navy who would then intercept them.[40]

In addition to important bulk transport and patrolling capabilities, Royal Navy assets were an important source for providing tactical mobility along coasts, uprivers and in the air. One of the difficult problems facing British forces in Borneo was transport. East Malaysia had a poorly developed transport infrastructure, partly due to the appalling terrain conditions in large parts of Sabah and Sarawak. Movement by air or water was the most efficient way of shifting troops. Coastal minesweepers played an important role in ferrying troops and equipment up the large rivers: a minesweeper could carry about 200 troops at a time. This capability was especially useful in eastern Sarawak where the River Rajang was navigable up to and beyond the capital of Sibu: there were no roads connecting Sibu with the coast or further into the interior.

Hovercraft also deployed to Borneo in 1965 and were used to move troops and supplies.[41] In addition to moving troops via rivers and the sea, the Royal Navy provided important helicopter support to operations in East Malaysia. Vertical take-off capabilities were vital to the conduct of fluid operations in the jungle. Yet there was a serious shortage of short-range helicopter support: for example, in mid-1964, the brigade deployed in Sabah had only two aircraft and seven helicopters. The latter were Whirlwind 7s provided by the Royal Navy. Arguing for the need for at least 17 more Whirlwind Xs the Chiefs of Staff committee argued that 'Unless and until increases are made, FEAF [Far East Air Force] cannot carry out its tasks without the assistance of the helicopters from ALBION.'[42] In early 1964 most of the Commando ship's helicopters were put ashore and the carrier was then used to ferry RAF helicopter reinforcements from the Mediterranean from October to November 1964. In the 12 months from September 1963 to September 1964 the Whirlwinds conducted 1,279 sorties. Fleet air arm Wessex helicopters provided an additional 2,643 sorties.[43] In addition to providing enhanced tactical mobility for troops, and allowing the maintenance of rapidly deployable reserves, the Royal Navy helicopter force contributed to the 'hearts and minds' campaign. For example 845 squadron's forward base at Nanga Gaat provided a focus for medical and transport support for the local community.[44] Whirlwinds of 846 Squadron and some Wessex helicopters of 845 Squadron were able to rejoin *Albion* once RAF Whirlwinds and Belvederes had been brought in from the Middle East.

In keeping with many other conflicts, the Navy directly contributed to land operations through the deployment of Royal Marines and Special Boat Service (SBS) forces. While the deployment of marines to deal with the Brunei rebellion was just the sort of short-notice emergency that the amphibious forces were designed to meet, the progressive shortage of regular battalions and SAS gradually forced the deployment of the marines as elite infantry units as part of the long-term roulement plan for Borneo. No. 40 Commando was based in Singapore from May 1962 and did tours during every year of Confrontation, being based variously in Sarawak, Tawau, Johore, Serian, Simmangeang and Brunei. No. 42 Commando also did tours every year: in Brunei, Sarawak, Tawau and Lundu.[45] No. 3 Commando Brigade headquarters was also deployed during Confrontation. In July 1963, the Brigade came under Army command and was deployed for the remainder of its tours on jungle operations carrying out the same sort of tasks as the infantry: border patrols, reconnaissance, and aggressive action against Indonesian forces. SBS support was provided by No. 2 and No. 6 Special Boat Squadron. During the conflict they were deployed in a number of roles ranging from covert operations, seaward surveillance, and reconnaissance of beaches and targets, to the conduct of river patrols, operating either on their own or attached to army or marine units. During Confrontation there were debates over the most effective use of SBS forces, in particular whether tasks such as seaward surveillance was the most effective use of their expertise. Later, the SBS were withdrawn from this role and replaced by air and minesweeper patrols, switching instead to covert operations.[46] For example No. 2 SBS worked in cooperation with No. 40 Commando, patrolling the river Rajang. The SBS were also used in a more offensive fashion to carry out reconnaissance of Indonesian beaches and to attack beach defences where necessary. In such circumstances SBS forces were taken by minesweeper or submarine, and deployed in patrols along the coastline.[47] For example between April and July 1965, the SBS successfully carried out three operations against coastal bases in Indonesia, being deployed by submarine for the first two operations and by minesweeper for the third.[48]

While transport and patrol activities, and the provision of additional mobility and ground forces formed the core part of the Royal Navy's contribution to the campaign in East Malaysia, there were other tasks. For example, reports that Indonesian frogmen might be operating from East Sebatik Island, opposite Tawau, led to the training of maritime forces for defence against underwater sabotage.[49] Some search and rescue was carried out: HMS *Zest* rescued the crews of the SS *Salvonia* and the SS *Pompadour* on 20 September 1964.[50] During periods of tension the Tawau guard ship was routinely moved to Wallace Bay to provide Naval Gunfire Support against possible enemy operations.[51]

The diverse contribution that the Navy could make to the defence of East Malaysia is well illustrated by Operation PARROT undertaken in West Sarawak from 18 to 28 April 1963. The aim of this operation was to help cut off the supply of weapons to Indonesian-backed insurgents by confiscating all shotguns from the non-native population. Reinforcements for this operation were brought from Singapore on *Albion*. Minesweepers, including *Alert, Puncheston, Wilkieston, Fiskerton, Dartington*, and *Houghton* then moved the troops upriver. Having disembarked the troops the CMS were then moved to positions such as Lundu, Sibu, Kuching and Sarekei where they would be able to provide a visible presence, and where they would be available to redeploy the troops if required.[52] The flexibility conferred on ground forces by Royal Navy assets was also demonstrated during this operation. Finding a suspected insurgent training camp at the same time as Operation PARROT was under way, *Albion* and four landing craft were used to move elements of the brigade reserve to Sibu to free a Ghurka battalion then engaged in collecting shotguns, which could then be used in an assault on the suspected camp.

Operations in West Malaysia

West Malaysia was separated from Indonesia by sea, making naval forces an integral part of the front-line defence. Indeed, this portion of Malaysia was potentially very vulnerable to Indonesian attack given its proximity to Sumatra and the Rhio islands. Singapore, for example, was only six miles away from the nearest Indonesian territory.[53] However, for nearly a year after the creation of Malaysia in September 1963, Indonesian operations were restricted to East Malaysia, largely because Indonesia recognized the potential political consequences of expanding the conflict. The threat against West Malaysia was confined only to individuals or small groups infiltrating for the purposes of small-scale sabotage or subversion. The burden of meeting this threat fell largely on the Royal Malaysian Police, which was responsible for patrolling the coastal waters. Royal Navy assets, in cooperation with those provided by the RAF and Royal Australian Navy, were deployed 'from time to time' only at the specific request of the Malaysian government. Royal Navy ships and carrier aircraft also made occasional patrols into the South China Sea to shield the east coast of Malaysia, but the only major contact was on 13 April 1964 when an Indonesian submarine was detected.

The Royal Navy's commitment to the defence of West Malaysia escalated from 13 August 1964, when the Malaysian government banned the extensive barter trade that continued between Indonesia and Malaysia across the Malacca Straits and around the Rhio islands, it being felt that this trade helped Indonesian infiltrators evade coastal patrols. The Malaysian and British navies mounted an intense period of suppression operations. Two minesweepers and two other vessels were involved in supporting this operation. On 17 August the Indonesians escalated the confrontation, by conducting their first major operation against West Malaysia, landing more than 100 men at three points on the Western coast of Johore. On 27 August armed boats attacked an ESSO installation off Singapore, attacked a fishing boat and also attacked a Malaysian patrol craft. By this time, on average, the

Royal Navy had a daily commitment of one frigate and two minesweepers to anti-infiltration operations. The increase in threat also led to the deployment of one ship, when available, in an air-defence role. Indonesian attempts against West Malaysia continued. On 2 September 1964 a 96-man parachute landing was carried out near Labis in North Central Johore. On 29 October, 52 Indonesians in five stolen fishing boats landed in the area of Sungei Kesang and on 6 November 10 infiltrated into East Johore, with another 10 armed with explosives landed on Jurong on Singapore Island on 14 November.[54]

The increase in threat required a gradual increase in Royal Navy commitments. By the end of October 1964 four RN escorts were allocated to the defence of West Malaysia. Commonwealth allies could sustain some of the burden of these patrols. Royal Navy patrols were integrated with those of the Malaysian navy and police that provided six patrol vessels and up to thirty police craft. Australian minesweepers were made available for deployment thanks to a political agreement reached at the end of November 1964. In January 1965 the increased requirement for naval assets lead to the commissioning of the 11th Minesweeping Squadron consisting of four Coastal minesweepers and two seaward-defence boats. In March 1965, another two minesweepers were made available thanks to the provision of New Zealand navy crews. By March 1965, 15–18 ships of the British, Australian and Malaysian navies were on patrol each day.

Anti-infiltration operations were an important part of the defence of West Malaysia. As was proved on numerous occasions, if the Indonesians succeeded in landing forces it could take an exceedingly long time to deal with them, given the jungle terrain. On 25 February 1965, 44 well-trained Indonesian police armed with armalites were landed in Southeast Johore. It required five weeks of operations to eliminate them all.[55] It was much more effective to deal with infiltration attempts at sea, either through deterring potential enemy incursions from taking place or by intercepting them. This task was not easy. Command and control of the naval patrol forces proved difficult because of the ad hoc nature of Royal Navy contributions to the defence of the West Malaysian coast. This was dealt with by the creation of the Operational Sub-Committee (Opsco) of the National Operations Committee, which was tasked with co-ordinating the land, sea and air contributions to the defence of West Malaysia.[56] Another difficulty was the lack of purpose-built fast patrol craft in sufficient numbers – Indonesian craft were often faster with lower silhouettes against which radar was difficult to use above 1.5 miles away. This problem was compounded by the numbers of craft that used the straits – given the economic importance of the cross-straits trade, suppressing it was problematic for anything more than a short period of time.[57] Despite these challenges, naval patrols did intercept many of the Indonesian infiltration attempts and almost certainly deterred a good many others. In December 1964 patrols involving HMS *Ajax* and HMAS *Teal* intercepted more than half of the Indonesian operations launched. Many other Indonesian operations large and small were interdicted before they could land. On 8 January 1965 a Malaysian vessel intercepted a tug with 40 Indonesians aboard, killing or capturing all of them. On 4 January *Wilkieston* captured a Sampan off Singapore containing four men and on 25 March Royal Navy ships intercepted three boats with over 40 men. From April to December 1965, 80 per cent of Indonesian infiltrators were intercepted at sea.[58]

In addition to anti-infiltration operations, Royal Navy assets also operated in a number of other roles. Operations in support of land forces were conducted: helicopters from *Bulwark* provided reconnaissance assistance in dealing with the Pontian landings. The SBS also contributed to the defence of West Malaysia: SBS observers and patrol boats covered the approaches from the Indonesian islands near Singapore. They also provided reconnaissance and training for Malaysian commandos. Naval assets were used in proactive operations designed to damage the base areas from which Indonesian infiltrators were launched. From 17 to 19 November Operation TIN CAN was launched in response to a report that Indonesian infiltrators might be using some small islands off East Johore as a base area. HMS *Manxman*, HMS *Kent*, Royal Navy helicopters from No. 814 Naval Air Squadron and elements of No. 42 Commando combined to conduct a search.

Naval diplomacy

In addition to absorbing numbers of smaller craft, the Confrontation campaign also placed a significant burden on large elements of the Far East Fleet in activities not necessarily focused on the direct support of military operations in Malaysia, but nevertheless contributing to the Confrontation campaign as a whole. This contribution fell into the category of naval diplomacy 'the use of naval forces as a diplomatic instrument in support of foreign policy in peacetime and all situations short of full hostilities'.[59] Within this general category of operations two modes of activity can be identified: latent suasion and active suasion.[60] Latent suasion describes the political effects of undirected deployments such as routine patrols. These may have a deterrent effect, and may also have a 'supportive' effect in the sense of reassuring allies. Active suasion refers to the effect of deliberate actions and signals designed either to reassure allies (supportive) or to deter or compel the opposition (coercive).

With regard to latent suasion, the presence of the Far East Fleet sent a powerful political signal of Britain's commitment to Malaysia as well as an implicit threat in the event that Indonesia risked escalation. In addition to routine patrols, the Far East Fleet engaged in maritime exercises, often involving carriers. In June 1965, an amphibious landing exercise was conducted involving a Commando carrier which included an 'opposed' landing.[61] It is impossible to quantify exactly the effect on Malaysia and Indonesia of the continuous theatre presence demonstrated by the Royal Navy. Nevertheless, it remains that Indonesia did not try to use its maritime assets to interfere with British sea lines of communication, through attacks on warships, merchant shipping, or through the use of mines, a fact that was almost certainly due to the presence of the Royal Navy. No Indonesian warships were known to have entered Malaysian territorial waters over the course of the conflict.[62]

Where active suasion was used, the impact of the Royal Navy was more complex. One key role played by the Navy was to challenge Indonesian constraints on freedom of navigation. The Indonesian government claimed a 12-mile territorial limit measured from straight lines joining the outer limits of Indonesia's islands, as well as the right to control the passage of ships up to a further 100 miles out. Having rejected these claims through diplomatic channels, the British government worried that if Sukarno tried to enforce these extensive Indonesian claims, it would require Britain to provide escorts for shipping routes, an occurrence that would put considerable strain on Britain's already stretched resources.[63] In order to demonstrate the right of innocent passage the aircraft carrier *Victorious* and two escorts sailed through the Sunda Straits en route from Singapore to Fremantle in August/September 1964. The sensitivity of such an active use of maritime power was illustrated by the heated debates in Britain regarding the advisability of further attempts to do this, critics stressing the political risks and the military vulnerability of the ships as they passed through the Straits. In the event, on *Victorious*' return visit the Indonesians came up with a compromise, declaring the Sunda Straits a naval exercises area, thus closing it to Britain, but suggesting that the ships came back via the Lombok Straits.[64] Later plans to send *Bulwark* and two escorts on a similar operation were cancelled on the basis that, while there seemed good military reasons for such a passage, the political risks, such as the possibility of strengthening Sukarno when he seemed to be less secure, militated against the idea.[65] Another active use of the navy was its possible role in covert operations. Worried about the failure to bring confrontation to an end, but also aware of problems of escalation as a solution, the British government began to focus on the possibility of pressuring Sukarno by supporting separatists in Sumatra and the Celebes islands. MI6 and British Special Forces were used to destabilize Sukarno's regime.[66] Among the accusations levelled by Indonesia was that Britain was supplying arms to the rebels.[67] In these operations it is likely that submarines, already used for covert SBS insertions elsewhere, may well have been involved.

The Royal Navy and British contingency plans

The commitment made by the RN in the Far East extended further than theatre presence and direct contributions to operations. While Britain assessed that it was unlikely that Indonesia would escalate to all-out conflict, a variety of contingency plans were developed in response to lower-level Indonesian initiatives. As Confrontation became prolonged, these contingencies became even more significant as debates ensued about whether the only way to bring the Indonesians to the negotiating table would be to precipitate escalation.

For example in April 1963, when Indonesian incursions into Kalimantan began in earnest, Plan ALTHORPE was developed. Plan ALTHORPE covered operations designed to destroy Indonesia's air and naval offensive capability in the event of an Indonesian attack. In response to the Indonesian landings in West Malaysia in August and September 1964, two additional contingency plans were developed – Plan MASON and Plan ADDINGTON. Plan MASON was for retaliatory or pre-emptive air and naval gunfire attacks against Indonesian paramilitary bases. Plan ADDINGTON was for air operations designed to destroy the Indonesian air strike capability. Additional contingencies included Plan INSWINGER, the plan for the defence of East Malaysia and Brunei against Indonesian attack, and Plan FLORID, which provided for air attacks on military headquarters and other targets in Kalimantan. Plan HEDGEHOG, another contingency, was for air and naval attacks against selected Indonesian bases, forces and facilities in the Rhio islands and Sumatra. The naval role in these contingency plans was important, particularly the contribution made by the Royal Navy's aircraft carriers in the provision of offensive air power. There were also a variety of movement and theatre-reinforcement plans which would draw on maritime forces for transport and sea-control functions. In the event, these contingency plans were not executed, but on several occasions implementation was seen as imminent. A state of yellow alert, signalling preparation to implement the plans, was called on several occasions – for INSWINGER for example in April 1965, and for ADDINGTON in February 1965. Moreover, as the Indonesian build-up in Kalimantan and Sumatra continued in late 1965 and early 1966, planning for additional 'graduated options' was approved by Ministers to provide more possible military options. These 'graduated options' include possible naval and amphibious operations against Indonesian lines of communication and points of entry in Kalimantan through sea blockades, submarine mining, attacks on shipping, commando/parachute raids, and small-scale sabotage operations.[68]

The burden placed on the Royal Navy by these contingency plans was considerable, because for as long as execution of the plans was regarded as possible, forces to meet them had to be maintained in theatre. Under Plan SPILLIKIN (one of the theatre-reinforcement plans) and Plan ALTHORPE for example, the requirements included two aircraft carriers (or four if operations were prolonged), one Commando carrier (or two if operations were prolonged), 30 escorts, with an additional six escorts if operations were to continue for more than three months. Allowing for refits, training and so forth, another 14 escorts would be needed and another four for operational reserves to cover breakdown and damage. To maintain the capacity to implement ALTHORPE and SPILLIKIN required 58 out of the Royal Navy's total planned escort strength of 90.[69] The consequences for deployments elsewhere would be serious: Persian Gulf commitments would be left to the Amphibious Warfare and Minesweeping Squadrons; no ships would be left on station in the Mediterranean; at best, only one ship would be left in the West Indies; no escorts would be left for the South Atlantic and South America; Home Fleet commitments could be met only at the expense of NATO assignments.[70] The implementation of confrontation contingency plans would mean that it would not be possible to carry out major operations in other theatres, including any plan to support SEATO.[71]

As Confrontation continued, criticism grew within policy-making circles regarding the inability of the UK to bring the conflict to an end. The Royal Navy, it was argued, was only 'broadly just adequate' to meet existing plans and if these forces were required to be maintained for an extended period of time 'it would mean withdrawing ships from all other commitments world-wide'.[72] At a Defence and Overseas Policy Committee meeting in January 1964, the Minister of Defence, Peter Thorneycroft, argued that 'there seemed no possibility of a favourable military solution if we remained on the defensive. It was therefore imperative to find a political solution to the present crisis...Meanwhile the military authorities in Malaysia should plan, first for military action to meet an increased Indonesian threat and, second, for a progressive scale of offensive operations which might become necessary if it was impossible to find a political solution.'[73] However, the first element proved difficult to achieve on terms acceptable to the British government, which feared that in a negotiated settlement, the Singapore base would be compromised. The second element resulted in the development of a range of 'graded contingencies' in order to give the UK and Malaysian governments more options in the event of increases in Indonesian aggression. In discussing possible military measures, roles for the RN were seen in the pursuit, sinking or capture of Indonesian vessels on military operations in Malaysian territorial waters; similar activities on the high seas; the pursuit of Indonesian ships into the Indonesian-claimed 12-mile limit and sinking them there; the sinking of Indonesian vessels on military operations in 'declared areas', i.e. 'those areas publicly declared by the governments concerned in which Malaysia and her allies may take offensive action against any vessel suspected of being engaged in anti-Malaysian activities'. Other options discussed at various times included offensive patrols to within three miles of the Indonesian coast, attacks on small Indonesian craft by patrol boats or frogmen, and attacks by small raiding parties. Discussion was also made of a variety of other measures that would have a psychological effect including additional naval exercises, allowing British submarines to be sighted in strategic waters and other shows of force including the deliberate violation of Indonesian territorial waters.[74] None of these options was implemented, sometimes for operational reasons but generally because of the damaging international political consequences.

By mid-1965 Dennis Healey, the Labour government's defence minister, was arguing that there were two possible alternatives: a 'subtle scheme to provoke an escalation, favourable to us in a military sense, or else subversive action on a large scale to disintegrate Indonesia'.[75] It was recognized by Britain, however, that such actions might well provoke retaliation and thus require reinforcements to be brought into theatre.[76] Eventually, the possibility of looking to escalation for a solution arose: the Commander-in-Chief Far East (CINCFE) argued in October 1965 for the need of 'increasingly severe punitive measures' punctuated by pauses, in order to end Confrontation: in other words a coercive strategy designed to achieve escalation dominance.[77] CINCFE argued that escalation could be made politically acceptable if Indonesia could be provoked into taking action that might justify a counter-response by Britain – for example by sailing Royal Navy ships through Indonesian-claimed waters in the hope that the Indonesians might cause an incident.[78] E.D. Smith comments that the Royal Navy 'played a big part in preventing the Confrontation from being escalated to an all-out war';[79] though broadly true, it is ironic that, for a time at least, the Navy was seen as one possible tool for provoking such an escalation in the conflict.

The burden of Confrontation

The burden that Confrontation placed upon the Royal Navy was exceptionally heavy. This burden included not just those assets committed directly to the defence of East and West Malaysia, but also those that had to be held to meet contingency plans: in fact, virtually the whole of the Far East fleet, making it meaningless to try to distinguish between those elements specifically allocated to Confrontation and those that were not.[80] By mid-1966 Confrontation absorbed 16,000 naval personnel and more than 70 vessels.[81] As such, Confrontation seriously over stretched the Navy, and impinged upon other politically significant commitments, such as SEATO. SEATO plans to deal with external threat contingencies such as plans Four, Six and Seven either could not be executed, or could be executed only with considerable delays.[82] Plan Four, for example, would require the withdrawal of all Naval escorts and minesweepers from Borneo, most of the helicopter capability, and the possible requirement for a Royal Marine Commando.[83] If escalation in Confrontation took place, Britain could not meet the need for reinforcements except at the expense of Middle East and NATO commitments. Overstretch was manifest not just in the difficulty in providing sufficient ships, but also in crewing them: to find only 140 men to man six additional vessels from the reserve in Singapore, minesweepers at home had to be paid off.[84] In 1965, the Chief of the Naval Staff argued that 'our forces are now stretched to the limit'.[85] Britain's position was further undermined when Singapore left the Federation of Malaysia in August of 1965. Criticizing the negative effects of the 'unqualified defence commitment by Britain' to defending Malaysia, Healey argued that 'The key question is not whether or when we leave Singapore, but how to get out of Borneo i.e. how to end our commitment under Confrontation as soon as possible'.[86]

Conclusions

Confrontation eventually ended in August 1966 on terms favourable to the United Kingdom, with its political objectives largely achieved. The key determinant for success was the developing internal problems in Indonesia that led to a military coup and the establishment of a military regime under General Suharto that was generally amenable to British interests. While it is difficult to quantify to what extent British military success helped to foment these difficulties, the military campaign was certainly important in allowing Britain to protract the conflict long enough for these tensions to become decisive. Throughout Confrontation, the Royal Navy made a vital contribution to success. Control of the seas in the Borneo theatre was the sine qua non for the success of the operation. Royal Naval support was vital in reinforcing and sustaining land forces. It made an important contribution to anti-infiltration operations, tactical mobility and policing operations. It was also integral to a range of contingency plans for wider escalation of the conflict. In operating well in its own environment it provided a powerful shaping force to events on land during the campaign.

However this contribution was made at a considerable cost. During a period in which the Navy had been reorienting itself toward the provision of limited-war intervention capabilities, Confrontation posed challenges in terms of scale and role. Although a limited conflict in the strictest sense, Confrontation vastly exceeded the force requirements and longevity of operations such as Kuwait or Aden. Nor was Confrontation an intervention operation: thus the RN's new focus on the strategic benefits of amphibiosity could not provide the relatively cost-effective solution that provided this stance's *raison d'être*. The complex internal and external dimensions of Confrontation simply could not be met through the use of limited intervention capabilities. Indeed, important elements of the Royal Navy's amphibious capability were drawn inexorably into other roles – transport, and support of shore-based helicopters in the case of the Commando carriers, and traditional infantry roles in the case of the Marines.

Overall, Confrontation proved to be a significant setback to British plans to rationalize defence. The Royal Navy had performed very well, providing the vital sea control necessary to win. It had also provided support in variety of specific ways. But the heavily political nature of the conflict made it difficult to apply force decisively. Instead, virtually the whole of the Far East fleet became drawn into a conflict that seriously impaired its ability to act elsewhere, in defence of a strategic concept that increasingly became self-defeating: after all, the Singapore base was supposed to be a means, not an end in itself. Confrontation undermined the Labour government's attempts to rein back defence spending and added new commitments. Indeed, Confrontation brought to a head the contradictions in Britain's position in South East Asia, the consequences of which would turn out to be profound for the Royal Navy. Confrontation, then, was no imperial sideshow: it was a major commitment for the Royal Navy and one that helped further shape the decision to withdraw Britain from its east-of-Suez role.

Notes

1. On the dilemmas facing Britain east of Suez, see Saki Dockrill, *Britain's Retreat from East of Suez: The Choice Between Europe and the World?* (Basingstoke: Palgrave, 2002).
2. For more detail on the political origins of Confrontation see Matthew Jones, *Conflict and Confrontation in South East Asia 1961–1965* (Cambridge: Cambridge University Press, 2002).
3. See John Subritzky, *Confronting Sukarno: British, American, Australian and New Zealand Diplomacy in the Malaysian – Indonesian Confrontation, 1961–65* (London: Macmillan, 2000).
4. See Gregg Poulgrain, *The Genesis of Konfrontasi* (London: C. Hurst, 1998), J.A.C Mackie, *Konfrontasi: The Indonesia-Malaya Dispute 1963–1966* (Oxford: Oxford

University Press, 1974), and Harold Crouch, *The Army and Politics in Indonesia* (Ithaca NY: Cornell University Press, 1978).

5. *Sukarno: An Autobiography* (New York: Bobbs-Merrill, 1965), 307.
6. Public Record Office (PRO) CAB 21/4626, Kuala Lumpur to Commonwealth Relations Office, telegram 60, 24 January 1962.
7. Crouch, *The Army and Politics in Indonesia*, 58–9.
8. Ibid., 60.
9. PRO DEFE 5/149 (Chiefs of Staff Committee Memoranda), COS 73/64, 'Indonesian Intentions and Prospects up to the End of 1966', 28 February 1964.
10. *BR1806: British Maritime Doctrine* (London, 1999), Ch. 2.
11. PRO DEFE 5/143, COS 313/63, 'Planning to Meet Threats to the Borneo Territories', 14 September 1963.
12. PRO DEFE 5/144, COS 376/63, 'Indonesian Confrontation of Malaysia', 15 November 1963.
13. PRO DEFE 5/162, COS 162/65, 'British Policy Towards Indonesia', 20 September 1965.
14. PRO DEFE 5/144, CINCFE 200/63, 'Appreciation of Force Requirements in Sarawak, Sabah and Brunei', 2 November 1963.
15. Colin S. Gray, *The Leverage of Sea Power* (New York: Free Press, 1992), 23.
16. PRO DEFE 5/153, COS 242/64, 'Directive to the Commander in Chief Far East in the Event of Indonesia Attempting to Interfere with Commonwealth Shipping', 20 August 1964.
17. Desmond Wettern, *The Decline of British Seapower* (London: Jane's, 1982), 208.
18. PRO DEFE 5/155, COS 305/64, 'Provision of Forces for Plan Addington', 18 November 1964.
19. PRO ADM 223/724 (Intelligence Reports and papers), 'Quarterly Intelligence Report', April to June 1963, No. 36, July 1963.
20. PRO DEFE 5/151, COS 142/64, 'Indonesian Military Capabilities Against the Borneo Territories', 4 May 1964.
21. PRO DEFE 5/144, COS 388/63, 'Indonesian Military Capabilities Against Malaysia', April 1964.
22. PRO ADM 223/724, 'Quarterly Intelligence Report', April to June 1963, No. 36, July 1963.
23. PRO DEFE 5/143, COS 313/63.
24. PRO DEFE 5/144, COS 376/63, 'Indonesian Confrontation of Malaysia', 15 November 1963.
25. PRO DEFE 5/151, COS 142/64.
26. PRO DEFE 5/144, COS 388/63, 'Indonesian Military Capabilities Against Eastern Malaysia', 29 November 1963.
27. PRO ADM 223/724, 'Quarterly Intelligence Report', April to June 1963, No. 36, July 1963.
28. PRO ADM 1/29144 (Papers of the Admiralty and the Secretariat), Commander-in-Chief Far East to Vice-Chief of the Naval Staff, 10 October 1963.
29. PRO DEFE 5/143, COS 329/63, 'Requirements to Counter Indonesian Action Short of Overt Hostilities', 27 September 1963.
30. E.D. Smith, *Counter-Insurgency Operations 1: Malaya and Borneo* (Shepperton: Ian Allen, 1985), 35.
31. PRO DEFE 5/144, COS 388/63, 'Indonesian Military Capabilities Against Eastern Malaysia', 29 Novermber 1963.
32. PRO DEFE 5/144, COS 364/63, 'Concept of Borneo Operations and Force Requirements', 7 November 1963.
33. PRO DEFE 5/144, COS 388/63.
34. PRO DEFE 5/156, COS 13/65, 'Report on Operations in Borneo', 14 January 1965.
35. PRO DEFE 5/161, COS 131/65, 'Report on Operations in Malaysia', 8 July 1965.

36. PRO DEFE 5/151, COS 166/64, 'Report by Commander-in-Chief Far east on Operations in Borneo', 16 September 1963.
37. PRO DEFE 5/161, COS 131/65.
38. PRO DEFE 5/156, COS 13/65.
39. Ibid.
40. PRO DEFE 5/151, COS 166/64.
41. Wettern, *Decline of British Seapower*, 254.
42. PRO DEFE 5/143, COS 317/63, 'Tactical Air Transport Requirements in the Far East', 20 September 1963.
43. PRO DEFE 5/156, COS 13/65.
44. Wettern, *Decline of British Seapower*, 239.
45. James D. Ladd, *By Land, By Sea* (London: HarperCollins, 1998), appendix 4.
46. PRO ADM 1/29123, SBS 7/11/4, 'Report on No. 2 Special Boat Section, RM Operations', 28 September 1964.
47. James D. Ladd, *SBS: The Invisible Raiders* (London: Arms and Armour Press, 1983), 153–64.
48. PRO ADM 1/29123, HQ 7/11/82. 'Recommmendation for Operational award by JF Mottram, Major, RM CO, HQ 3rd Commando brigade', 10 June 1966.
49. PRO DEFE 5/161, COS 131/65.
50. Ibid.
51. Ibid.
52. PRO DEFE 5/151, COS 166/64.
53. PRO DEFE 5/143, COS 313/63.
54. PRO DEFE 5/161, COS 131/65.
55. Ibid.
56. Ibid.
57. For more details on the problems faced, see annex C (*Problems of Anti-Infiltration Patrolling*) in PRO DEFE 5/157, CINCFE 5/66, 'Quarterly Operational Report', 17 January 1966.
58. PRO DEFE 5/167, COS 44/66, 'Report on Operations in Malaysia', 26 April 1966.
59. *BR1806: British Maritime Doctrine*, 88.
60. Edward Luttwak, *The Political Uses of Seapower* (Baltimore MD: Johns Hopkins University Press, 1974).
61. PRO DEFE 5/167, CINCFE 5/66.
62. PRO DEFE 5/172, CINFE 9/67, 'The Joint Report on the Borneo Campaign', 27 January 1967.
63. PRO DEFE 5/143, COS 319/63, 'Protection of Shipping Against Indonesian Interference', 25 September 1963.
64. PRO DEFE 25/212, Chief of the Defence Staff to Secretary of State for Defence, 6 July 1965.
65. PRO DEFE 13/475, Chief of the Defence Staff to Secretary of State for Defence, 21 July 1965.
66. Paul Lashmar and James Oliver, *Britain's Secret Propaganda War 1948–1977* (Stroud: Sutton, 1998), 1–10.
67. David Easter, 'British and Malaysian Covert Support for Rebel Movements in Indonesia During the Confrontation, 1963–66', in Richard J. Aldrich, Gary D. Rawnsley and Ming-Yeh T. Rawnsley, *The Clandestine Cold War in Asia, 1945–65* (London: Frank Cass, 2000), 201.
68. PRO DEFE 5/157, COS 53/65, 'Graduated Military Operations in Kalimantan', 5 March 1965.
69. PRO DEFE 25/212, Chequers Brief No. 8b, 'Force Levels Required in the Event of Increased Scale of Operations Against Indonesia'.

70. PRO DEFE 11/592, CINCFE 58/65, 'Reinforced Theatre Plan (Far East) No. 5', 21 June 1965.
71. Ibid.
72. PRO DEFE 25/212, Chequers Brief No. 8a, 'Force Levels Required in the Event of Increased Scale of Operations Against Indonesia'.
73. PRO CAB 148/1, minutes of DOPC Meeting, 14 January 1964.
74. PRO DEFE 5/155, COS 321/64, 'Military Measures to Counter Indonesian Confrontation', 30 December 1964.
75. PRO DEFE 25/212, MM/COS 5/65, minutes of Chiefs of Staff Meeting, 6 July 1965.
76. PRO DEFE 5/147, COS 19/64, 'Military Measures to Counter Indonesian Confrontation', 21 January 1964.
77. PRO DEFE 5/162, COS 176/65, 'Measures to Counter Indonesian Confrontation', 21 October 1965.
78. PRO DEFE 25/212, 'Indonesian Confrontation: Speaking Brief for Meeting with Secretary of State', 6 July 1965.
79. Smith, *Counter-Insurgency Operations 1: Malaya and Borneo*, 92.
80. PRO PREM 13/809, Wright to Burrows, 25 March 1966.
81. Eric Grove, *Vanguard to Trident: British Naval Policy Since World War II* (London: Bodley Head, 1987), 267.
82. PRO DEFE 5/144, COS 384/63, 'The Effect of Operations in Eastern Malaysia on our Ability to Meet Our SEATO Obligations', 25 November 1965.
83. PRO DEFE 5/149, COS 80/64, 'Briefs for the ANZAM defence Committee Meeting', 17 March 1964.
84. Wettern, *The Decline of British Seapower*, 248.
85. PRO DEFE 25/212, MM/COS 5/65.
86. PRO PREM 13/431, Healey to Wilson, 13 August 1965.

10

THE BRITISH NAVAL ROLE EAST OF SUEZ: AN AUSTRALIAN PERSPECTIVE

David Stevens

On 26 April 1939 Australia's new Prime Minister – and devoted Anglophile – the Right Honourable Robert G. Menzies delivered his first national broadcast to the electorate.[1] Given at a time of deep global uncertainty, when Australian external policies were practically indistinguishable from those of the British Empire, the address provided a short-hand description of the underlying problem as seen from Canberra. 'In the Pacific', explained the prime minister,

> we have what I might call primary responsibilities and primary risks. Close as our consultation with Great Britain is and must be in relation to European affairs, it is still true to say that we must be to a large extent guided by her knowledge and affected by her decisions. The problems of the Pacific are different. What Great Britain calls the Far East is to us the near north.[2]

There was little original in Menzies's observation; similar statements had been made since well before federation of the Australian colonies in 1901, but this latest repetition underlined the continuing difficulty faced by Australians in having their apparently unique local interests recognized by those residing half a world away. While they might be almost entirely British in heritage and outlook, the small Australian population felt remote from the centre of the Empire, isolated and vulnerable. They inhabited a large island continent on the periphery of Asia, and the potential for invasion by the non-white masses to the north constituted a perennial fear. Since it would be many years before their new nation could generate sufficient resources to deal with such a threat, Australians recognized that they must generally seek some form of Great-Power assistance. As a member of the British Empire, for the first half of the twentieth century Australian sovereignty ultimately depended on the adequate strength of the Royal Navy. Yet, while local politicians freely admitted this dependence they were never wholly confident that their nation's security would be the primary concern of a naval strategy controlled from London.

Such a situation could not continue indefinitely, particularly after the course of the Second World War did much to reinvigorate nationalist feelings. The conservatism that had characterized Australia during the inter-war period once more gave way to a spirit of independence, one which seemed unlikely to be satisfied by the maintenance of traditional ties based on duty, obligation and affection. Within this context of national change, this chapter will examine the gradual divergence of strategic interests and the decline of British naval influence from an Australian perspective. Although the assumption of strategic responsibility and the growth of capabilities independent of the Royal Navy was a long and at times painful process, for the Royal Australian Navy (RAN) it was an essential step in confirming its status as a uniquely Australian institution.

Australian post-war defence policy and the higher defence organization

Popular perception has tended to define the onset of the Pacific War as the watershed in the relationship between Great Britain and Australia. Before the war much had been made of the role of fortress Singapore in Imperial Defence, but the disastrous loss of the capital ships *Prince of Wales* and *Repulse* in December 1941, followed in quick succession by the fall of the Malay peninsula and the island itself, provided many Australians with incontrovertible proof of the failure of pre-war strategic planning. According to this assessment local defence priorities had been badly skewed by the focus on Imperial requirements and the money spent on naval defence between the wars 'largely squandered'.[3] Disillusioned by Sir Winston Churchill's 'inexcusable betrayal',[4] and with their nation left vulnerable to Japanese invasion by the priority given to the Mediterranean, Australians had no choice but to look to the United States for assistance: 'free of any pangs as to our traditional links or kinship with the United Kingdom'.[5]

There was undoubtedly acrimony between the Australian and United Kingdom governments on various strategic issues; however, this critical moment presaged no burning of bridges. More thorough reviews have recognized that neither the Australian people nor their political leaders had any intention of weaning themselves permanently from the Empire.[6] For Australia the wartime relationship with the United States was a matter of mutual convenience, one which had achieved a high degree of friendship and cooperation, but which was only an adjunct to rather than a replacement for Empire cooperation. Australia might be a sphere of American strategic responsibility, but in July 1944 Menzies's successor, John Curtin, informed Churchill that only the British could remedy the South West Pacific Command's weakness at sea. This, he noted, presented an ideal opportunity for the employment of a Royal Navy task force, one 'which could worthily represent Britain in the Pacific, and which would be received with enthusiasm in Australia'.[7] As indeed it was and, as David Brown has observed, for the British Pacific Fleet the Australian people 'brought a new dimension to total war – total hospitality'.[8]

In fact, as Australian authorities turned from the immediate problems of the Second World War to the direction of post-war planning, they remained confident that the policy of cooperation in Empire defence remained sound. Overcentralization had been an obvious weakness, but this could be addressed by greater devolution of responsibility and planning to a more regional basis within a framework of collective defence. Again this was nothing new. As early as 1913, members of the Australian naval staff had suggested that all Imperial forces in the Far East should operate under Australian control.[9] But appropriate machinery was never officially supported, strategic planning essentially remained in Whitehall, and in both 1914 and 1939 the Australian government stood by its agreement to transfer operational control of the RAN's major units to the Admiralty almost automatically after the outbreak of war.

Australia now sought greater leverage in the post-war world, and one of the first practical steps toward establishing a more sophisticated security arrangement came in January 1944 when Australia and New Zealand signed an agreement declaring their intention to establish a regional zone of defence comprising the South West and South Pacific areas and based on the two Dominions.[10] At the Prime Ministers' conference held in London three months later, John Curtin put forward proposals for improved machinery for Empire cooperation, including the formation of an Empire Secretariat. But although the subject was placed on the agenda, Churchill did not trouble to attend the meeting and little progress was made.[11] Disappointed but undaunted, Curtin announced on 23 March 1945 that he had approved the expansion of the Joint Service and Inter-Departmental machinery of the Australian Defence Department. The changes in the Higher Defence Organization might in some ways replicate Britain's joint committees, but were expected to ensure the Australian organization's adequacy to deal with the problems associated with the development of an effective post-war Defence policy, including its relation to cooperation within the British Commonwealth and the United Nations.[12]

Curtin died in July 1945, but much of the policy had been developed by Sir Frederick Shedden, the long-serving Secretary and Permanent Head of the Defence Department, and Curtin's successor Joseph 'Ben' Chifley initiated no significant review.[13] At the next Conference of Prime Ministers in April 1946, Chifley reminded the delegates that the security of the British Commonwealth as a whole, or of any of its members, rested on a number of blended and interrelated factors. First, were the forces placed at the disposal of the United Nations for the maintenance of international peace and security? Second, were the forces to be maintained by each member of the Commonwealth under arrangements for cooperation in Empire Defence? Third, were the forces to be maintained by each member of the Commonwealth to provide for the inherent right of individual self-defence? Finally, there was 'The provision of adequate machinery for Co-operation in Empire Defence, without infringing the determination and sovereign control of its Policy by each member'.[14]

Despite this attempt to create a broader base of responsibility, British military forces were still expected to remain the hard core of Empire Defence. Nevertheless, the widely differing geographical circumstances and diverging interests of the individual Commonwealth members made any attempt to maintain centralized control and direction unworkable. Australia again pushed for a decentralized arrangement, and agreement was eventually reached that cooperation should develop on a regional basis with each nation accepting responsibility for the development and defence of its own area and the strategic zone around it. Between these areas, the protection of lines of communication would be a joint responsibility, but with the Royal Navy likely to play the largest part. Of particular note for Australian planners, Chifley announced that the nation would in future make a larger contribution toward the defence of the British Commonwealth in the Pacific, and that this would be 'by agreement between the United Kingdom, Australia and New Zealand, and thereafter with the United States, and later with other nations with possessions in this area'.[15]

Collaborative defence plans took time to develop, and the lack of consistency in Australian and British Far East policy in the late 1940s made matters doubly difficult,[16] but there were several other important areas of Commonwealth cooperation, chief among which were the setting up of the joint intelligence organization and the establishment of a guided-weapons experimental range in Woomera, South Australia. The latter project was first proposed by Britain in 1945 and eagerly accepted by the Chifley government, which recognized that moving the Empire's weapons-research effort to Australia would not only strengthen defence cooperation, but also ensure Australian access to the new generation of weapons.[17] Equally significant to the Labor administration, however, were the long-term technological and economic benefits to Australia. In the atomic era it seemed possible that Britain might not long survive in a global war. Chifley was already determined to develop local industrial and scientific potential, making the nation as self-supporting as possible while simultaneously providing the widest possible base for a supply structure for the needs of the Commonwealth in the Pacific.[18]

The future navy

How the Royal Navy and its Australian offspring might best adapt to this post-war strategic construct would take some time to discern, for – although reaching its greatest ever numerical strength in 1945 – the RAN was at this point the smallest and weakest politically of the three Australian-armed services and its future growth was by no means assured. Before the Second World War, Australia had endeavoured to maintain its navy as 'an effective and fair contribution to Empire Naval Defence',[19] but in practice the RAN had never received resources commensurate with such an undertaking. Strategically impotent as an independent squadron, for much of the war Australian ships had operated widely dispersed and fully integrated into British and US forces. These ships proved themselves fully equal in seamanship and fighting qualities to those of any navy in the world, but wartime losses had been heavy, and there remained few major units on which to base a post-war fleet. When combined with ageing hulls, the expected dominance of 'push-button warfare',[20] and the apparent absence of any threatening maritime power, there seemed little guarantee that the Navy would regain its traditional primacy in Australian defence planning.

Charged with guiding the RAN through this uncertain period was Admiral Sir Louis Hamilton, who became Chief of Naval Staff (CNS) and First Naval Member of the Australian Commonwealth Naval Board in June 1945. The last British officer to head the RAN, Hamilton was neither a volunteer for the appointment, nor the original first choice. 'The shrewd and diplomatic Hamilton', nevertheless worked hard to smooth the transition from war to peace and maintain the RAN as something more than a token force.[21] Already suspicious of the prevailing push to integrate the services and divide the Defence budget on a more or less equal basis, the Admiral soon identified what he felt was an overemphasis on 'Air Power' as the best defence for an island nation. In response, Hamilton pointed to Australia's thousands of miles of sea communications and reiterated that the 'basic foundation of her defence problem was the protection of the merchant ship'. Only by assisting in the maintenance of the Empire's sea communications could Australia contribute to collective security, obtain overseas reinforcements, and maintain the two-way flow of commerce. Yet, the foundations for reconstruction did not then exist and the post-war RAN remained moribund: 'incapable in modern conditions of operating as an independent force owing to [the] lack of Naval aviation. Moreover, individual ships [are] insufficiently trained in such important activities as Fighter Direction and A/A Gunnery to take their place in an Empire or Allied Fleet.'[22]

To address these deficiencies the RAN's capabilities in destroyers, cruisers and aircraft carriers had to be built up from scratch. There was, however, only a limited destroyer-building programme in place, and before committing to significant post-war expenditure, the Chifley government – like the Attlee administration – wanted time for the full effects of the recent startling developments in science and technology to be assessed.[23] Hamilton worried that the government seemed to be pinning its faith in these new weapons and largely looked on its contribution to Empire Defence 'as being the Guided Weapons Range and the "Higher Defence Machinery" Organisation'. As Hamilton warned the First Sea Lord, Sir John Cunningham, in one of their regular exchanges of correspondence,

> The logical argument then follows that a small population can not do everything, so if they are involved in a war in the future such old fashioned forces as the Navy will be catered for by the Royal Navy and United States Navy, assuming the unlikely event that a modern Navy will be required at all![24]

The acquisition of a Fleet Air Arm was perhaps the most significant hurdle, with the other Australian services wary of the RAN's close ties with the Royal Navy and already pointing to the extravagance of Australia attempting to run two air forces and two training set-ups. A late-war project to acquire a light fleet carrier had foundered on cost grounds,[25] but the Naval Board still hoped to acquire at least two such vessels, which Hamilton regarded as the minimum necessary to sustain a viable national capability.[26] It is noteworthy that the Admiralty Plans Division had been suggesting something similar since at least 1943 as part of a post-war Commonwealth contribution to a Pacific squadron.[27] But the Admiralty's direct influence on force-structure planning was already weakening, and more important to the decision-making process was the support Hamilton generated within the Defence Committee, the Australian government's main advisory body on defence policy. In its 1946 report on the nature and functions of the post-war forces, the committee recommended three major roles for the RAN. The first of these, the provision of a balanced task force, would act as a contribution to collective security. The second role envisaged the provision of a 'sea frontier force' of escort, minesweeping, harbour-defence and surveying craft to maintain sea communications. Finally, the Navy was to be required to maintain assault shipping for combined operations with the Army.[28]

The most powerful figure on the Defence Committee was Sir Frederick Shedden, whose stature was such that he had severed virtually all direct contact between the service Chiefs of Staff and members of the government. Although 'basically sound on Defence problems', Shedden remained to Hamilton, 'merely a civilian and...forced to give way on the score of political expediency'.[29] The government was nonetheless seeking direction, and convincing Shedden was critical to the fulfilment of individual service plans. According to one recent assessment, the Royal Australian Air Force was simply not up to the challenge and failed to develop and articulate an Australian airpower doctrine.[30] By contrast Hamilton discovered that Shedden was a disciple of Admiral Sir Herbert Richmond, and gradually found his relationship with the Secretary advancing 'through the successive stages of "armed neutrality", "co-belligerency" to that of "allies", where we now scratch one another's backs'.[31]

The fruits of this relationship were most clearly seen on 4 June 1947 when Australia's post-war defence policy was finally announced by the Defence Minister, John Dedman. The minister not only confirmed that that the British Commonwealth remained a maritime empire, 'dependent on sea power for its existence', but labelled Richmond the 'greatest modern writer on Imperial Strategy and History' and quoted extensively from his book, *Statesmen and Seapower*:

> Australia's experience in the recent war fully demonstrated the fundamental importance of sea power to our Defence. Owing to commitments in other theatres, the United Kingdom was unable to assign adequate naval forces to the Pacific on the outbreak of war with Japan,...Accordingly, American sea power undertook the role which the Royal Navy similarly

carried out in the Atlantic and Indian Oceans. Thus Allied sea power enabled 'its possessors to exploit all their own resources, to draw upon the resources of the world for the raw materials and finished goods of their needs in war, to carry those goods whither they are needed, and to transport the fighting forces of the other arms to whatever points in the vast theatre of war where they can be most effectively used. Sea power did not win the war itself; it enabled the war to be won. It was, as the British Prime Minister had said, the "foundation" essential to victory'.[32]

In a notable if short-lived turnaround, the RAN was allocated the largest proportion of the Defence budget and received approval to acquire two light fleet aircraft carriers from the Royal Navy. The stated aim was to build a balanced fleet capable of operating either as an independent force for the direct defence of Australia or as a contribution to the wartime seapower of the British Commonwealth. In the latter case, the RAN was still expected to operate under the strategical direction of the Admiralty, but this would be one of the last official statements to include such specific guidance. In addition to the carriers, the five-year plan envisaged an enhanced escort force and additional survey vessels, backed by improved maintenance facilities ashore. Declaring himself 'relatively satisfied' with the announcement, Hamilton summed up the implications in his next letter to Cunningham:

a   It is the first concrete evidence that the British Empire is not going to disintegrate as a world power, and ... is an excellent omen for the future.
b   It means that Australia, for the first time in her history, is going to take a real share in Imperial Defence on a planned basis.
c   To the best of my knowledge it is the first time in history that a democratic Government has committed itself to a 5-year over-all Defence Programme.[33]

Unfortunately, within months the implementation of the plan was proving extremely difficult and in real danger of falling apart. Although the Admiralty had offered Australia two unfinished Majestic-class carriers at a price that equated to the building of just one, no provision had been made in the naval programme for the costs of modernization, which the Admiralty now advised would be necessary in order to cope with the improved performance and increased size and weight of future naval aircraft.[34] Chifley was adamant that the RAN would get nothing over the original estimates and the affair required all of Hamilton's skills to resolve. Aware that he could not rely on the largesse of the United Kingdom Treasury, Hamilton reminded the First Sea Lord of the advantages of establishing naval aviation in Australia, thus allowing British carriers operating in the region full access to maintenance, stores and training facilities.[35] In writing to Chifley, on the other hand, Hamilton stressed the novel strategic situation facing Australia, and hinted that the Royal Navy might not always be available. The RAN, he argued, 'had fallen out of step with modern Navies during the six years of war', yet in the future, responsibility for sea communications in the Southern Pacific and Indian Oceans would largely devolve upon Australia:

> Consequently, it would be prudent to complete the Five Year Plan within the specified time even in the face of rising costs...the Admiralty's interest in the subject is strategic. For more than a century of Australia's existence they were entirely responsible for the sea communications of the Empire, today they wish to ensure there is no gap in that worldwide network. Hence the generous offer of the two most modern carriers at reduced cost implements in a most practical manner the discussions on co-operation in Empire Defence.[36]

The eventual comprise reached was to accept the first carrier, HMAS *Sydney* (ex-*Terrible*) in an unmodernized state, and she was commissioned in December 1948. Within three years she was in action off Korea as a fully effective Commonwealth asset, a remarkable achievement and one due primarily to the generous assistance of the Royal Navy in the provision of training and manpower. The second carrier, HMAS *Melbourne* (ex-*Majestic*), included all the latest carrier developments, but was not delivered until 1955 and at considerably increased cost. In the interim, to allow the RAN's plans for a two-carrier force to proceed, Hamilton's relief, Rear Admiral John Collins, RAN, asked for one on loan. The Royal Navy again responded positively and in recognition of Australia's Korean commitments provided HMS *Vengeance* from 1953 to 1955.

Strategic and operational planning

Notwithstanding Chifley's 1946 declaration on Australia's role in the Pacific, British planners at first regarded the Far East as an unlikely theatre of war, and until 1954 the Australian Chiefs of Staff expected to send a significant part of their forces to support Commonwealth operations in the Middle East.[37] Should a regional threat develop, Australia was assured in secret that British, or should these fail, American forces already in place would screen Australia.[38] Australia, however, sought a more overt commitment and political pressure in both the United Kingdom and Australia gradually forced attention to refocus on Southeast Asia. The shift gained further emphasis as it became clear that in a cold war context the maintenance of regional political and economic stability would be vital, and that the comprehensive security system envisaged in the Charter of the United Nations was not likely to come into existence. Equally certain was that Britain could not afford to retain a significant fleet east of Suez and that in a hot war the hard-pressed Royal Navy would withdraw all its major units to Atlantic and Mediterranean waters – the only arm of the British armed services to be so removed.[39] Indeed, as early as 1948 a British inter-service working party had suggested that the Indian Ocean should become a Dominion responsibility, with an Australian naval command substituted for the British in Singapore.[40]

In a global war against communism, Western strategy specified the security of sea communications linking main support areas with combat theatres as one of its three principal pillars – the others being the security of air bases in the UK, Middle East and Japan, and the security of the main support areas. In April 1948, Defence Minister Dedman announced that Australia's immediate and particular defence interest was the development of the nation as a main support area, and that strategic planning should 'encompass a zone vital to the security of Australia'.[41] Early the following year the government gave approval for the RAN to proceed with planning in connection with the delineation of a zone in which Australia would assume both the initiative for defence planning in peacetime and responsibility for the 'defence of vital sea communications'.[42]

The boundary of the proposed zone included Australia, New Zealand and certain sections of the Far East Station, including Singapore, and soon became known as the ANZAM (Australia, New Zealand and Malaya) Region. ANZAM has since been described as an 'unwritten treaty with unclear objectives and obligations', but it had sufficient substance for Australia's immediate purposes.[43] More importantly, it marked the first step in gaining formal recognition of the primacy of Australia and New Zealand in their own areas of strategic interest. Thereafter Malaya and Singapore became the main military base and the centre of Commonwealth influence in the Far East while both the United Kingdom and New Zealand established Joint Service Liaison Staffs in Canberra accredited to the Defence Department. In the event of war the ANZAM Chiefs of Staff, operating through the Australian Higher Defence Machinery, became the responsible authority.[44]

The main threat to ANZAM sea communications seemed likely to come from the submarines of the Soviet Union. As early as 1946 the Admiralty had warned that the Soviet Pacific Fleet maintained some 60 long-range submarines, all of which might be converted to snorkel operations.[45] Of future concern, the potential enemy had facilities to build submarines at the Pacific ports of Komsomolsk and Vladivostok, while of more immediate interest, the recent Chinese-Russian Treaty of Friendship had resulted in the designation of Port Arthur as a Sino-Soviet naval base.[46] The availability of this ice-free port allowed year round ocean access, and hence removed one of the traditional constraints on Soviet maritime operations in the Pacific.

Although the RAN recognized the threat, it took time for attitudes to mature. Collins, for example, at first regarded the offensive capability embodied in the new carriers as the priority in relation to Australia's commitments under collective defence arrangements. He classified anti-submarine operations as a defensive means of warfare, argued that these could not win a war, and declared it 'a shattering blow' when he discovered that the carriers might 'only' operate 'Trade protection type aircraft'.[47] The Deputy Chief of Naval Staff, Captain G.G.O. Gatacre, RAN, took a somewhat different tack, pointing out that an improved anti-submarine capability for the RAN seemed to be both fundamental and urgent.[48] In a subsequent paper dealing with a 'Balanced RAN', Gatacre could identify no credible offensive role for the carriers, but reminded Collins that defensive measures might have an important offensive aspect. Specifically, the RAN could best contribute to the general Allied offensive by ensuring the safe 'despatch overseas of an expeditionary force and the "uninterrupted outward flow of the products of our main support area"'.[49]

An enduring problem for the RAN was that the number of escorts it had available was hopelessly inadequate. Although not expecting an attack on anything like the scale envisaged in the North Atlantic, assuming responsibility for the naval defence of a wide area in the Indian and Pacific Oceans was no small task. In 1950 even Collins was forced to admit that 'the size and defence requirements of the ANZAM area are rather frightening when one considers the resources available'.[50] That same year the Defence Committee considered a 'Policy and Outline Plan for the Defence of Sea Communications in Australian Home Waters', yet the scope of the ANZAM commitment already foreshadowed the need for a plan that better integrated all available Commonwealth maritime forces. In late 1950 staff officers from the RAN, Royal Navy and Royal New Zealand Navy (RNZN) began writing the 'Plan for the defence of sea communications in the ANZAM region',[51] and by May 1952 the Defence Committee had approved the first edition for forwarding to Britain and New Zealand.[52]

Covering 192 closely typed pages, and focused almost entirely at the operational level, the plan was far more sophisticated than anything previously developed for regional maritime defence.[53] The authors admitted that the plan was defensive, but believed that it provided for the optimum distribution of all available maritime forces. Of greatest significance, national assets were not allocated specifically to either home or Southeast Asian waters, but were instead to be available for operations throughout the region. The division of ANZAM into six clearly defined areas assisted this process.[54] Each area possessed its own Maritime Headquarters and the responsible air and naval commanders exercised joint operational control over both home and regional waters within their boundaries. Regional co-ordination would be effected by a Joint Operations Room in Melbourne with links to all MHQs and the ANZAM Naval Task Fleet.

Despite these efforts, it was clear that the RAN would have faced a difficult problem should a serious threat have developed, but the provision of more assets seemed unlikely. The British Chiefs of Staff were still encouraging Australia's formal commitment to the Middle East, but 'Our Ministers', wrote Collins in October 1951, 'are getting the idea that the Navies of the Commonwealth are more than adequate and that all our efforts should go towards more soldiers and land-based aircraft'.[55] Exacerbating these difficulties, the first post-war decade had seen each of the Australian services overcommit resources and underestimate expenditure. The Korean War briefly brought guidance that the nation must be ready for global war by 1953,[56] but Collins was resigned to future reductions and worried that the RAN might be the first to lose.

The turning point came in April 1954, when the new Defence Minister, Sir Philip McBride, announced that Australian defence policy had been transformed

THE BRITISH NAVAL ROLE EAST OF SUEZ

from preparedness by a critical date to the capacity to maintain defence for the 'Long Haul'. He confirmed that 'While South East Asia is held, defence in depth is provided to Australia and there will be no direct threat, except to sea communications in the form of submarine attacks and minelaying.'[57] Should Malaya fall to the communists, however, Indonesia might follow, and Australia would then find itself within range of enemy bombers. The revised strategic assessment was endorsed by the Defence Committee as a balanced approach, but in practice it placed far greater emphasis on local air defence. Thereafter funds to the Army and Navy were cut specifically to allow for the Air Force build-up. The change was evident not just in the budgetary allocation, but also in the tasks expected of the Navy. McBride's statement marked the completion of the strategic orientation of the RAN to anti-submarine operations and firm guidance that the Fleet Air Arm should not attempt to maintain an independent strike capability. With the RAN unable to get funding for the modernization of *Sydney*, she was successively relegated to flying training, to seamanship training and, by 1958, to reserve.

In fact, the 'long-haul' policy reduced the strength and efficiency of all three services, leaving Australia still dependent on external assistance should local or regional sea communications be seriously threatened. It was a risk that the government appeared more than ready to accept. 'In regard to convoys for Australian Expeditionary forces,' wrote McBride to the British in late 1954, 'the United Kingdom or United States of America should, according to the theatre of strategic responsibility, supplement the strength of the Royal Australian Navy by providing escorts of necessary strength'. The then First Sea Lord, Sir Rhoderick McGrigor, was not so sanguine, warning Collins that:

> Although it is quite true that in the event of a major and direct threat to British territory in the ANZAM region we now visualize that some or all of the Far East Fleet may remain at least initially, in the area, it will be for decision at the time whether any aircraft carrier which may have been sent from the Home or Mediterranean Stations to reinforce the Far East Fleet should remain to assist you in support of your convoys, or whether it should return to N.A.T.O.[58]

The USN's resources were similarly 'not unlimited' and likely to be concentrated elsewhere in the Pacific.[59] Nevertheless, it was toward the US security umbrella that Australia was increasingly turning. Collins had been seeking to make practical arrangements with the Commander-in-Chief Pacific since at least 1948 and, acting on behalf of both the British and Australian Chiefs of Staff, his persistence was finally rewarded. The USN's appreciation of the Soviet submarine threat was significantly serious that it welcomed cooperation with the Commonwealth navies and, in September 1951, Collins signed an agreement with Admiral Arthur W. Radford, USN, that acknowledged the existence of the ANZAM area, and delineated national areas of responsibility for naval control of shipping, reconnaissance, local defence and anti-submarine warfare.[60] The Radford-Collins Agreement

231

functioned purely at service levels and gave Australia no greater influence in US planning, but it did allot a clearly enunciated wartime role for the RAN, one that was relevant to its continuing peacetime presence in Southeast Asia and encouraged the development of direct links with the USN on a variety of operational and technical levels.

The signing of the ANZUS (Australia, New Zealand, United States) Treaty in 1951 likewise reinforced the move toward the United States and finally gave Australia the formal defence alliance it had sought for the Pacific. ANZUS had less immediate practical reality than ANZAM, but it symbolized Australia's willingness to act independently of the Commonwealth, and ensured that the nation became fully integrated with the global alignments of the Cold War. Australia's contribution to collective security subsequently progressed through the arrangements attendant on the Five Power Staff Agency (1953) and SEATO (South East Asia Treaty Organization) (1954) with varying levels of success.[61] SEATO, for instance, aroused US interest in the Southeast Asian area – which previously had been sporadic – and went some way toward achieving Australia's aim of bringing Britain and the United States together in securing peace in the region, yet it did not provide the expected context for joint action.[62] Whatever the contingency planning that occurred within SEATO, Britain was never prepared to contribute directly to the defence of Indo-China, nor the United States to the defence of Malaya.[63] Australia tended to be left standing in the middle, attempting to make a sufficient contribution to each major partner to preserve a sense of obligation without arousing resentment or suspicion in the other.

The FESR and Malayan emergency

At one point the RAN had some 2,000 personnel, or almost 20 per cent of its effective strength, committed to combat operations in Korea, and afterward Australian warships maintained regular armistice patrols. But with only four destroyers and five frigates normally in commission, other activities were severely constrained. Not until the mid-1950s had the forces maintaining the uneasy armistice reduced sufficiently for Australia to make a direct contribution to the defence of Malaya and Singapore under the banner of the Far East Strategic Reserve (FESR). The Strategic Reserve operated within the ANZAM arrangements and gave formal expression to Australia's commitment to a policy now known as 'forward defence'. Menzies was again prime minister and, as he announced in April 1955, the battle against communism had to be carried on 'as far north of Australia as possible'.[64] The attachment of Australian forces to the FESR and their regional basing was the first such commitment in peacetime and hence a significant development in Australian defence policy. In July 1955, the destroyers HMAS *Arunta* and HMAS *Warramunga* began the first naval rotation under the general operational control of the Commander-in-Chief of the Far East Fleet. Thereafter the RAN consistently provided two destroyers or frigates to the Strategic Reserve in addition to at least an annual deployment by an aircraft carrier task group. To all practical purposes these forces became simultaneously a contribution to SEATO.

The FESR's primary role was 'to provide a deterrent to, and be available at short notice to assist in countering, further communist aggression in South-East Asia'.[65] Its secondary role was to help in maintaining Malaya's internal security against the bold policy of hit-and-run terrorism carried out by communist insurgents. Although the Malayan Emergency had been declared in 1948, the greater need had been for infantry and aircraft, and Australian warships took an active part in operations only after their commitment to the FESR. Even then the direct naval role remained relatively small, and more significant from the RAN's perspective was the opportunity to maintain close contact between the Commonwealth navies and ensure the maintenance of standards. As McGrigor had noted in a letter to Collins in 1954, 'the more we can exchange ships and officers, the better it will be'.[66]

Since 1949 the Royal Navy had based three submarines at Sydney for anti-submarine training, and combined Commonwealth exercises routinely took place in Australian and New Zealand waters, but these manoeuvres could not approach the scale and complexity of those held under the auspices of the FESR and SEATO. In April/May 1961, for example, 6,000 American, British and Australian troops, accompanied by a task force of 60 ships and 100 aircraft, staged an amphibious exercise in North Borneo, a formidable demonstration of the strength the US and Commonwealth navies could bring to the region and the level of cooperation already attained. Annual sea-control exercises were also held in the triangle between Singapore, Manila and Bangkok and confidence in Australia's capabilities was such that by the mid-1960s the Flag Officer Commanding HM Australian Fleet was regularly directing such exercises from the carrier *Melbourne* with ships and aircraft of the Royal Navy, RNZN, USN, the Philippines, and Thai navies all taking part.

How relevant this training might be for immediate purposes remained an open question and would lead some observers to conclude that the RAN was becoming rapidly marginalized in Australian Defence planning and in danger of losing direction. In a 1959 announcement on defence reorganization, the Minister for Defence, A.G. Townley, remarked that 'global, or full-scale war remains not impossible, but unlikely, as a deliberate act of policy', whereas 'limited wars could break out in various unstable areas' with little notice.[67] With the government refusing to accept the enormous financial outlay that a successor to *Melbourne* and her air group would entail, Townley added that fixed-wing aviation would be disbanded in 1963 when the carrier became due for a major refit. The problem for the RAN was to balance the emphasis given to different operational tasks depending on whether consideration was being given to its cold war or 'general war' functions.[68] Foreshadowing the impact on force structure, the Australian Director of Plans had written in 1956 of the 'struggle for survival in commission' of the two Battle-class destroyers and three 'Q'-class frigates: 'a matter of resolution between the requirement for the "Cold War" Gun or the "Global War" Anti-submarine ship'.[69]

The broader issue throughout this period was whether Australia should be attempting to provide a balanced navy, essentially a scaled-down version of the Royal Navy or USN, or whether it should attempt to fill specific niche capabilities within an Allied fleet. Of interest within the wider naval context, doubts over the effectiveness of a single carrier operating obsolescent aircraft were not limited solely to Australian politicians and the RAN's sister services. In August 1958, the Admiralty's Plans Division had noted that there was no SEATO requirement for a RAN carrier. Furthermore, 'it cannot be said that there is any vital gap in the Far East or elsewhere, under conditions of Limited War, which the Admiralty is relying on an RAN carrier to fill'.[70] Rather than the expense of running a carrier, the Division thought the Australians might be better off concentrating on an escort fleet of twelve Type 12 frigates and allocating these to regional tasks under central control. An 'integrated interdependent Commonwealth Eastern Fleet' would, it appeared, make the best use of Royal Navy, RAN and RNZN assets in Southeast Asia.

A similar solution had been rejected by Australia in 1919 and was even less likely to be accepted now. Throughout most of the 1950s the RAN's relationship with the USN remained secondary to that with the Royal Navy's Far East Fleet, but the political logic of ANZUS was growing inescapable. Eric Grove has written that the period from 1958 to 1960 marked the decisive end of an era: 'that of unquestioned dependence on British equipment and practices'.[71] While this may be overstating the case, the Australian Navy was certainly expending greater efforts to develop its own independent assessment of force-structure requirements. 'We have no wish to become Americans', wrote the CNS to Lord Mountbatten in March 1956, 'but there is a strong belief in this country that the sensible course for Australians is to acquire war equipment from the USA now. Our very telling reason is that, certainly in global war, our salvation in the Pacific will depend chiefly on the aid of that country. For that we are not less loyal members of the Empire'.[72] Later that year the Naval Board confirmed in an official paper that future developments might make it necessary to turn to the United States 'as the major source of defence equipment'.[73] The defining moment finally came in June 1961 when Townley announced the decision to acquire two Charles F. Adams-class guided-missile destroyers from an American shipyard, the RAN's first major warships that could not be supported from British sources. Neither the Royal Navy nor the USN had every answer needed by the RAN, but the pattern of relationships was changing rapidly and within a decade that with the USN would be the only substantial cooperation with a Great Power navy.

Indonesia and Confrontation

Australia's commitments under the region's collective security arrangements created no specific requirement to proceed with the development of the fleet, and it was not until Indonesia emerged as a possible adversary that the RAN's requests for re-equipment received a more favourable hearing. As the 1950s progressed Australia had become increasingly suspicious of Indonesian designs on New Guinea. Under the terms of the United Nations Charter and Trusteeship, Australia remained responsible for the defence of Papua and New Guinea until independence. Although Australia received American assurances that the ANZUS Treaty would cover the eastern Trust Territories, West New Guinea remained under Dutch control with no such sureties. Australia opposed any acquisition of West New Guinea by force but there were many indications that Indonesia was intent on its annexation. Aggressive Indonesian rhetoric after 1956, the obvious influence of communists in the emergent nation, and a growing program of military acquisitions gave Australian planners credible cause for concern. The development of the Indonesian Navy after 1958 was particularly spectacular. Between 1959 and 1965 the Soviet Union and its allies provided about 100 vessels, including a cruiser, 14 destroyers and frigates, 14 attack submarines, and a dozen missile-armed patrol boats. The transfers raised the dismal prospect of a Soviet-dominated fleet in Southeast Asia, one astride the sea routes between the Indian and Pacific Oceans and with real capabilities if the ships were accompanied by sufficient technical advisers. Worse still, it was soon apparent that modern jet bombers with anti-ship capabilities would accompany the naval transfers.

Australia's 1959 Strategic Basis paper was probably the first to recognize the problem. It acknowledged that, although the nation's ultimate security was linked to its major allies, a range of threats could emerge to national interests that might not involve broader Western concerns. In certain circumstances Australia might have to rely completely on its own defensive and economic capacity for an indeterminate time. The paper concluded that Australia should develop a more balanced force structure, one designed primarily to act independently of allies.[74] Cabinet, which still placed ultimate faith in the alliance relationships with Britain and America, rejected this assessment, but its implications were digested at the service level. The RAN confirmed the pressing need to plan for independent operations in a multi-threat environment.

Fortunately for the RAN, one of its most influential and forward-thinking ministers, Senator John Gorton, was in office. He took on the role of Navy Minister in December 1958 and, by the time he had completed his five-year tenure, the decline of the RAN had been arrested and it was preparing for an enhanced role in regional security affairs. Under Gorton's firm direction, the surface fleet embarked on an unprecedented programme of peacetime expansion, but his most remarkable achievement was a similar turnaround in the fortunes of the Fleet Air Arm. In Cabinet, Gorton successfully argued for the reinvigoration of naval aviation, and the 1961 equipment programme allowed for the purchase of 27 Westland Wessex helicopters. The RAN found the replacement of the fixed-wing aircraft more difficult, but a judicious juggling of flying hours and airframes ensured that the service life of the existing Sea Venoms and Gannets was extended past 1963. By 1964 the RAN had identified two American types as appropriate replacements and acquisition of the Skyhawk fighter-bomber and Tracker anti-submarine aircraft began shortly thereafter.

The key question was whether this transformation would be complete in time. The continuing tension between Indonesia and the Netherlands over West New Guinea resulted in a number of armed clashes in the early 1960s and remained a cause for Australian concern. Nevertheless, since neither Britain nor the United States would support military action on this issue, Australia could exert only limited political pressure. To the relief of all, the two sides came to an agreement in August 1962 for the transfer of sovereignty to Indonesia the following year. Regional antagonisms would not disappear so readily, however. Encouraged by his success, Indonesia's President Sukarno provided support to a rebellion in December 1962 against the Sultan of Brunei. The uprising failed but, in its aftermath, Indonesia adopted a policy of 'Confrontation' toward Malaya and, in particular, to the proposal to unite Malaya, Singapore, Sarawak and Sabah (North Borneo) in an economic and political federation.

In spite of the tensions, the Federation of Malaysia was established in August 1963. Seeing the development as a threat to Indonesia's regional hegemony, Sukarno proclaimed it 'a neo-colonialist plot' imposed on the people against their will. Believing there were pockets of resistance which could be stirred into active revolt, Indonesia extended Confrontation to include a campaign of armed infiltration and physical and psychological sabotage. Although not formally committed to Malaysia by treaty – despite the continuing FESR arrangements – Australia had already declared its willingness to assist with any defence effort. In September 1963 the FESR's naval units were committed to patrol duties against Indonesian infiltration by sea. Early the next year the destroyers and frigates were joined by two of the RAN's new Ton-class minesweepers, which possessed capabilities more accurately matched to the inshore task.

Fears of a major conflict intensified and the RAN's presence grew in proportion to that of the Royal Navy. By May 1966 Australia had twelve warships and 3,584 men in the region, while maintaining a minimum of six vessels in the FESR throughout the year. Joint and combined operational planning included schemes to destroy Indonesia's maritime capabilities, but in the event the Indonesian Navy, suffering from shortages of fuel, stores and technical support, never attempted to contest Commonwealth control of the sea. Repeating the pattern set by the Malayan Emergency, participation by major naval units in Confrontation was often indirect and related to the diplomatic aspects of continued presence and the symbolic use of seapower. Hence in March 1965, the RAN's first missile-equipped escorts, HMAS *Derwent* and HMAS *Parramatta*, joined with *Melbourne* and other Commonwealth forces off the coast of Malaysia in weaponry and other displays. 'Showpiece 65', with the Malaysian prime minister embarked in the carrier HMS *Eagle*, was partly for training, largely to reassure Malaysia, and mostly to send an unmistakable signal to Indonesia of Commonwealth resolve. Confrontation, however, would be the last example of Anglo-Australian naval cooperation in a solely Commonwealth operation.

Britain's rundown and withdrawal

In July 1967, while Australia was committed alongside the Americans in Vietnam, the British announced that they intended to withdraw their military forces as part of their revised 'east of Suez' policy. The announcement was publicly deplored in Australia for, notwithstanding the turn toward the United States, until at least this time many Australians still believed that Britain had an obligation to defend them. Equally shocked were Malaysia and Singapore. Their national forces remained small and ill equipped to deal with a resolute adversary and, like Australia and New Zealand before them, these newly independent nations relied heavily on Britain to guarantee their security. Britain's subsequent decision to complete the withdrawal by 1971 gave even greater urgency to the efforts to find an acceptable solution. Official plans confirmed that the pattern of the rundown would be 'determined by the need to maintain conditions of stability in the area during the period 1968–71 and thereafter, and to facilitate effective cooperation in defence matters between the Commonwealth countries concerned',[75] yet there remained a significant element of uncertainty. John Gorton, by then Australia's prime minister, admitted as much in his Defence statement of 25 February 1969:

> Just a little over a year ago Great Britain announced a considerable acceleration in the pace and scale of the withdrawal of British forces from Malaysia-Singapore...the circumstances under which they may return to assist in an emergency are unknown. For Malaysia, Singapore, New Zealand and ourselves this latest announcement underlined the fact that an era had ended. During the lifetime of any one of us sitting in this House British forces have been stationed in Malaysia-Singapore to keep, or try to keep, peace and stability in that region...Now all that has changed. The major power will be withdrawn. It is no longer a contribution to the efforts of a major power which we will be called upon to make. It is a substitution for the efforts of a major power. And such a substitution must fall short of what previously existed and be of a different character.[76]

The specifics of this character were not immediately obvious. Both Malaysia and Singapore wished Australia and New Zealand to stay, but a decision to retain forces in the area after Britain's withdrawal was without precedent. Further complicating planning was US President Nixon's less interventionist 'Guam Doctrine', announced in 1969, which emphasized 'self-help' in security matters by those regional nations expecting American support. The United States might be ready to stand by their ANZUS obligations, but a contraction of their forward-deployed forces seemed likely, while SEATO, however effective its role in maritime training, was rapidly becoming irrelevant as a mechanism for collective security. Defence Minister Malcolm Fraser summed up these developments on 10 March 1970, when he noted that Australia was entering a new era. The first post-colonial generation had emerged in the newly independent countries to Australia's north and these nations were now in a process of transition. The British withdrawal and American reappraisal meant that Australia was required to put forth a greater effort embodying 'greater independence'.[77]

The rhetoric may have sounded familiar, but the reality of Australia's changing naval strategic position would require some adjustments. The absence of British naval forces based permanently in Singapore was of particular import in view of the development by the Soviet Union of a worldwide maritime capability. Australia could not expect to confront the Soviets at sea, but the increasing activities of their vessels in the Indian Ocean and their 'ability to maintain groups of vessels at sea for unusually long periods' was something that Australian defence policies and planning would need to be taken into account.[78] For the RAN these developments implied an enlargement of its responsibilities and operating areas without the prospect of immediate allied assistance in the event of conflict. Even in peacetime, the loss of regular access to the afloat support services of the Royal Fleet Auxiliary would place constraints on the reach of deployed forces.[79] Arguing that Australia now needed to develop a two-ocean navy, one contemporary analysis agreed that the nation was in 'a totally new, unprecedented situation':

> We can be sad at Britain's withdrawal; we can disparage the broken promises and the unseemly haste; we cannot logically complain that it is taking place. We cannot expect the United States to take over the role of the Royal Navy. We cannot – we do not need to – step into Britain's shoes; we simply need to fill out our own in the Indian Ocean, no less than in the Pacific.[80]

Plans were subsequently advanced to improve Australia's 'maritime capability in the waters around Australia, the Pacific and Indian Oceans and the seas to our north'.[81] Practical measures included the further development of naval infrastructure in Western Australia, while offensive capability was improved by the purchase of an additional two submarines – giving the RAN a total of six – and the doubling of the Skyhawk strength to 20 aircraft. Other projects, such as those to replace *Melbourne*, design a new light destroyer and acquire a fast combat-support ship, were not so successful, but the RAN had made significant progress and thereafter continued its orientation toward more general maritime warfare. Just as important, the re-emergence of the Indian Ocean as a significant factor in Australian defence planning was evidence that strategic concepts had begun to emphasize 'Defence of Australia' over forward defence. This trend toward self-reliance became complete with the election of a new government in 1972, and formed the foundation of Australian Defence policy for the remainder of the century.

Australia and New Zealand had in the meantime both decided to maintain forces in Malaysia and Singapore and noted with some measure of relief that Britain also intended to continue to train and exercise in the region after 1971. A more formal basis for security was provided by the Five Power Defence

Arrangements (FPDA), which involved Britain and its four regional partners and provided for consultation in the event of any threat to Malaysia or Singapore rather than the specific commitment to defence that existed previously. Britain also agreed to maintain a modest permanent force and combine it with contributions from Australia and New Zealand to form a successor to the FESR known as ANZUK Force. This was not a separate defence agreement to the FPDA, but a convenient method of providing a unified command while reducing the logistic and administrative overheads associated with the support of relatively small forces overseas.

The RAN element of ANZUK reflected the Australian commitment to retain forces on a similar scale to those of the previous Strategic Reserve, and included one destroyer or frigate permanently stationed in Singapore, a submarine on rotation in cooperation with the Royal Navy, and the occasional visit of a task group. New Zealand provided one frigate and Britain up to six frigates, together with units on visits. On 1 November 1971, the day following the end of British Far East Command, Rear Admiral D.C. Wells, RAN, assumed command of ANZUK Force. The assumption of such responsibility by an Australian naval officer might be seen as a milestone, but the ANZUK arrangements were transitional and lasted only until 1974. Nevertheless, the FPDA itself proved remarkably resilient and, despite fluctuations in the level of involvement of its members in exercises, has continued to evolve. At the beginning of the twenty-first century the FPDA remains a key element of relations between the five members, and from Australia's perspective still serves its enduring interests in the security of maritime Southeast Asia.[82]

Conclusions

The development of Australia's national identity has been marked by the process of separation from Britain. The naval relationship mirrored this process quite closely and, in what was an extraordinarily dynamic quarter-century, the period 1945–1971 saw the RAN develop from what was often perceived as a detached squadron of the Royal Navy to a balanced and capable national force. These changes occurred at a number of levels, from the training of personnel to the acquisition of equipment, but it was in the assumption of strategic responsibility that the RAN had furthest to journey. Not surprisingly, the post-war history of the RAN was regularly defined by the problems associated with creating an acceptable strategy and matching it to an affordable force structure.

Interwoven with this process of growth and separation by the RAN was the changing regional role of the Royal Navy. In the post-war era Australia's allies periodically attempted to get the nation to do more for regional security. Australia, by contrast, sought to ensure that its allies did not do less, and the continued presence of the Royal Navy played a major role in reassuring Australians that Britain maintained an interest and influence in the region. Today the RAN attempts to integrate seamlessly with USN operations as it once did with the Royal Navy, but it should be kept in mind that there was never a final leaving and that, in addition to a common heritage, some practical ties remain. Australia's eternal challenge is that it is a Western nation in the Asian-Pacific region and its strong links to both Europe and North America are unlikely to be broken. Australia still welcomes the regular deployments of a British Task Force to the region, while the RAN continues to value personnel exchanges and joint exercises with the Royal Navy as a measure of its professional performance.

Notes

1. The author would like to acknowledge the assistance of Commodore James Goldrick, Captain Peter Jones and Alastair Cooper in the preparation of this chapter.
2. Commonwealth of Australia, *A National Broadcast Address by The Prime Minister* (Melbourne: Government Printer, 26 April 1939), 3.
3. See for example A. Stephens, 'The Royal Australian Air Force', in *The Australian Centenary History of Defence*, Vol. II (Melbourne: Oxford University Press, 2001), 138.
4. D. Day, *The Great Betrayal: Britain, Australia and the Pacific War, 1939–42* (North Ryde, NSW: Angus & Robertson, 1988), 1–17.
5. Cited in K. Hack, *Defence and Decolonisation in Southeast Asia: Britain, Malaya and Singapore 1941–68* (Richmond: Curzon, 2001), 74.
6. A. Wyatt, *The Evolution of Australian Foreign Policy 1938–1965* (London: Cambridge University Press, 1968), 24.
7. G. Hermon Gill, 'Royal Australian Navy 1942–1945', in *Australia in the War of 1939–1945* (Melbourne: Collins, 1985), 473.
8. D. Brown, 'The forgotten bases: The Royal Navies in the Pacific, 1945', in D. Stevens (ed.), *The Royal Australian Navy in World War II* (Sydney: Allen & Unwin, 1996), 110.
9. See, D. Stevens, 'Defend the North: Commander Thring, Captain Hughes-Onslow and the beginnings of Australian naval strategic thought', in D. Stevens and J. Reeve (eds), *Southern Trident: Strategy, History and Rise of Australian Naval Power* (Sydney: Allen & Unwin, 2001), 225–41.
10. A. Watt, *Australian Defence Policy 1951–1963: Major International Aspects* (Canberra: Australian National University, 1964), 2.
11. D. Horner, *Defence Supremo: Sir Frederick Shedden and the Making of Australian Defence Policy* (Sydney: Allen & Unwin, 2000), 201–2.
12. Commonwealth of Australia, 'Co-operation in Empire Defence', Memorandum by The Secretary (Melbourne: Department of Defence, 14 December 1945), 8–9.
13. Horner, *Defence Supremo*, 246. Shedden was Secretary of the Defence Department from 1937 to 1956.
14. Commonwealth of Australia, 'Conference of Prime Ministers, London, 1946', Report to Parliament by the Rt. Hon. J.B. Chiefly, MP, Prime Minister of Australia (Melbourne: Government Printer, 19 June 1946), 3.
15. Ibid., 4–5.
16. M.H. Murfett, *In Jeopardy: The Royal Navy and British Far Eastern Defence Policy 1945–1951* (Kuala Lumpur: Oxford University Press, 1995), 153–4.
17. P. Morton, *Fire Across the Desert: Woomera and the Anglo-Australian Joint Project 1946–1980* (Canberra: Australian Government Publishing Service, 1989), 10–11.
18. 'Conference of Prime Ministers, London, 1946', 9.
19. MP 1587/1, 218AO, statement by the Prime Minister on Commonwealth Government's defence policy in the light of the Imperial Conference, 24 August 1937, National Archives of Australia (NAA).

THE BRITISH NAVAL ROLE EAST OF SUEZ

20. A. Stephens, *Power Plus Attitude: Ideas, Strategy and Doctrine in the Royal Australian Air Force 1921–1991* (Canberra: Australian Government Publishing Service, 1992), 95–6.
21. J. Goldrick, 'Selections from the Memoirs and Correspondence of Captain James Bernard Foley, CBE, RAN (1896–1974)', in *The Naval Miscellany, Vol. V* (London: George Allen & Unwin, 1984), 521.
22. ADM 205/74, PRO, letter Hamilton to Sir John Cunningham (First Sea Lord), 18 March 1947.
23. 'Conference of Prime Ministers, London, 1946', 8; Cmnd. 6743, 'Statement Relating to Defence', Presented by the Prime Minister and Minister of Defence to Parliament by Command of His Majesty (London, February 1946), 3.
24. Letter Hamilton to Cunningham, 18 March 1947.
25. See A. Wright, 'Australian Carrier Decisions: the acquisition of HMA Ships, *Albatross, Sydney* and *Melbourne*', *Papers in Australian Maritime Affairs*, No. 4 (Canberra Maritime Studies Program, 1998). In particular Part II – The decision not to purchase a light fleet carrier – 6 June 1945.
26. Goldrick, 'Selections from the Memoirs and Correspondence of Captain Foley', 521.
27. E. Grove, *Vanguard to Trident: British Naval Policy Since World War II* (Annapolis, MD: Naval Institute Press, 1987), 7.
28. A2031, NAA, Defence Committee minute, 19 June 1946.
29. Letter Hamilton to Cunningham, 18 March 1947.
30. A. Stephens, *Going Solo: The Royal Australian Air Force 1946–1971* (Canberra: Australian Government Publishing Service, 1995), 36–7.
31. ADM 205/74, PRO, letter Hamilton to Cunningham, 17 June 1947.
32. Commonwealth of Australia, 'Post-war Defence Policy', statement to Parliament by The Hon. John J. Dedman, MP, Minister for Defence (Melbourne: Government Printer, 4 June 1947), 7.
33. Letter Hamilton to Cunningham, 17 June 1947.
34. See Wright, *Australian Carrier Decisions*, 151–60.
35. ADM 205/74, PRO, letter Hamilton to Cunningham, 27 November 1947.
36. ADM 205/74, PRO, letter Hamilton to Chifley, 19 February 1948.
37. D. Lee, 'The National Security Planning and Defence Preparations of the Menzies Government, 1950–1953', *War & Society* (October 1992), 119–38.
38. Hack, *Defence and Decolonisation in Southeast Asia*, 80.
39. A. Cooper, 'At the Crossroads: Anglo-Australian Naval Relations, 1945–1971', *Journal of Military History* (October 1994), 702.
40. Grove, *Vanguard to Trident*, 47–51.
41. Editorial, 'Five Year Defence Programme', *The Navy* (June 1948), 22.
42. MP 1185/8, 1846/4/336, NAA, minute Captain G. Gatacre (Deputy Chief of Naval Staff) to Collins, 30 March 1949.
43. Anon, paper on the origins of FPDA, Naval Historical Directorate (NHD), Canberra.
44. E. Grove, 'Australian and British Naval Policy in the Korean War Era', in T. Frame, J. Goldrick and P. Jones (eds), *Reflections on the Royal Australian Navy* (Kenthurst: Kangaroo Press, 1991), 254.
45. *Admiralty Maritime Intelligence Review*, November 1946, NHD, Canberra, 26–8.
46. *Australian Station Intelligence Digest*, 28 June 1946, NHD, Canberra, 22–4.
47. ADM 205/69, PRO, letter Collins to Fraser (First Sea Lord), 7 September 1948.
48. MP1185/8, 1937/2/404, NAA, remarks by Gatacre, 4 October 1948 on paper, 'ASW-Review of Present Position'.
49. MP1185/8, 1937/2/404, NAA, paper 'Balanced RAN' by Gatacre, 5 April 1949.
50. ADM 205/72, PRO, letter Collins to Fraser, 26 January 1950.

51. MP1185/10, 5202/21/17, NAA, letter, UK Service Liaison Staff to British Defence Coordination Committee, 5 March 1952.
52. ADM 205/86, PRO, letter, Collins to McGrigor, 14 May 1952.
53. MP 1185/10, 5202/21/22, NAA, 'Plan for the defence of sea communications in the ANZAM region', 8 May 1952, 3.
54. Malayan Area, New Zealand Area, Northwest Australian Area, Northeast Australian Area, West Australian Area, Southeast Australian Area.
55. ADM 205/86, PRO, letter Collins to Sir George Creasy, 2 October 1951.
56. R. O'Neill, *Strategy and Diplomacy, Australia in the Korean War 1950–53*, Vol. I (Canberra: Australian Government Publishing, 1981), 101–4.
57. *Defence Policy and the Programme* (Melbourne, 1954), 1.
58. ADM 205/86, PRO, letter McGrigor to Collins, 3 December 1954.
59. A5954, 46/3, NAA, letter McGrigor to Shedden, 3 November 1954.
60. J. Goldrick, 'The Role of the Royal Australian Navy in Australian Defence Policy, 1945–85', unpublished paper, NHD, Canberra, 9.
61. D. Lee, 'Australia and Allied Strategy in the Far East, 1952–1957', *Journal of Strategic Studies* (December 1993), 551–68.
62. G. Modelski (ed.), *SEATO: Six Studies* (Melbourne: F.W. Cheshire, 1962), 4–5.
63. T.B. Millar, *Australia in Peace and War: External Relations Since 1788* (Botany NSW: Australian National University Press, 1991), 143.
64. Cited in P. Edwards with G. Pemberton, *Crises and Commitments: The Politics and Diplomacy of Australia's Involvement in Southeast Asian Conflicts, 1948–1965* (Sydney: Allen & Unwin, 1992), 169.
65. A4905, NAA, letter McBride to Menzies, 16 May 1955.
66. ADM 205/86, PRO, letter McGrigor to Collins, 29 October 1954.
67. Cited in Modelski, *SEATO*, 80.
68. J. Grey, 'The Royal Australian Navy in the era of "Forward Defence", 1955–75', in D. Stevens (ed.), *In Search of a Maritime Strategy: The Maritime Element in Australian Defence Planning since 1901*, Canberra Papers on Strategy and Defence, No. 119 (Canberra: Strategic and Defence Studies Centre, 1997), 109.
69. MP 1587/1, 495, NAA, note by Director of Plans, 28 May 1956.
70. ADM 1/29326, PRO, Paper, 'The Future of the RAN'.
71. E. Grove, '"Advice and assistance to a very independent people at a most crucial point": the British Admiralty and the future of the RAN 1958–60', in D. Stevens (ed.), *Maritime Power in the 20th Century: the Australian Experience* (Sydney: Allen & Unwin, 1998), 155.
72. Letter, Vice Admiral Dowling to Mountbatten, March 1956, cited in A. Cooper, 'At The Crossroads: Anglo-Australian Naval Relations 1945–1960', BA (Hons) Thesis, University of NSW, 1991, 2.
73. A816/31, 14/301/713, NAA (ACT), 'Strategic Basis of Australian Defence Policy', October 1956.
74. H. Donohue, 'The Evolution of Australian Strategic Defense Thinking', in D. Alves (ed.), *Evolving Pacific Basin Strategies: The 1989 Pacific Symposium* (Washington DC: National Defense University Press, 1990), 269.
75. 'Outline plan for rundown and total withdrawal of United Kingdom forces from Malaysia, Singapore and Brunei by 31st December 1971', Joint Service Secretarial Note No, 102/1968, 2 April 1968, NHD, Canberra.
76. 'Speech by The Rt Hon J.G. Gorton, MP, on Defence' (Canberra, 25 February 1969), 1–2.
77. 'Speech by The Hon Malcolm Fraser, MP, on Defence' (Canberra, 10 March 1970), 1–2.
78. Ibid., 2.

THE BRITISH NAVAL ROLE EAST OF SUEZ

79. It should be noted that RAN ships deploying to Vietnam had at times been refueled by RFA auxiliaries.
80. T.B. Millar, *Australia's Defence* (Carlton: Melbourne University Press, 1969), 127, 131.
81. 'Speech by The Hon Malcolm Fraser, MP, on Defence', 11.
82. Commonwealth of Australia, *Defence 2000: Our Future Defence Force* (Canberra: Defence Publishing Service, 2000), 40.

11

THE RETURN TO GLOBALISM: THE ROYAL NAVY EAST OF SUEZ, 1975–2003

Geoffrey Till

We're goin' 'ome, we're goin' 'ome,
Our ship is at the shore,
And you must pack your 'aversack,
For we won't come back no more.[1]

Sounding the retreat

In the 1960s, Britain was still a major power east of Suez. In 1964, during the Borneo Confrontation, the Royal Navy deployed some 50 warships to the area. In 1968 there were still over 57,000 troops and 14,000 naval personnel permanently deployed east of Suez, rather more, according to some counts than were stationed in West Germany.[2] The Navy itself focused heavily on the amphibious and carrier capacities that were so relevant to this role and confidently anticipated their continuing renewal.[3]

But, of course, navies reflect and illustrate the conditions of the nations they serve, and there were troubles beneath the surface. The 1960s became an uncomfortable time for Britain, and for its navy. The strategic horizon was bleak indeed. The Soviet threat in Europe seemed to be growing and was chillingly exemplified by the ruthless suppression of dissent in Czechoslovakia in 1968. NATO at the time was wracked with dissent about the future role of nuclear weapons and the on-going political differences between France and the United States. For its part, Washington was distracted by the Vietnam war.

For the Royal Navy there was growing concern about the future strategic impact of the very evident growth of the Soviet Navy. Its long-standing submarine and air threat to NATO sealines of communication, the strategic bridge between the United States and its European partners, was being re-enforced by an expanding surface fleet as a result of Soviet procurement decisions in the later 1950s and early 1960s. The growing strength of that surface and submarine challenge in local waters was suggested by the troubling presence of a significant Soviet Mediterranean squadron during the Arab–Israeli wars of 1967 and, especially, 1973.

For the Royal Navy, the danger was twofold. First, there was the continuing issue of the relative priority of the threat to British strategic interests in Europe when compared to those outside it. The signing of the Brussels and NATO treaties, and the deployment *in peacetime* of large-scale forces to Germany, illustrated the 'continentalization' of British defence policy and established the strategic priorities that would dominate the cold war period. Against this, threats to British interests outside Europe would have to play second fiddle and, increasingly, would need to be dealt with by forces designed for, and essentially justified by, their role in the defence of western Europe. Worse still, in an uncertain age stumbling from the heavy reliance on nuclear weapons of the 1950s era of Massive Retaliation to the more prolonged conventional-war options of Flexible Response, it was far from clear what the role of the Royal Navy would be. So, even – or perhaps especially – within the European defence priority, the Royal Navy was under challenge. Traditional emphases on the need to protect Atlantic sea lines of communication, or to support amphibious operations in northern Europe, did not cut much ice with those who believed that any major war with the Soviet Union would quickly become nuclear and be over, one way or another, in a few days.

Of course, viewpoints were not as clear and stark as this and, provided that there were the resources available, compromises between the continental and the global, and between land/air and sea/air priorities within the continental model of British defence could be put together. The problem was that British defence resources seemed to be running dry as well, because of the endemic and deteriorating limitations of the British economy. Increasingly, these strategic pressures were forcing decisions on those reluctant to take them.

The main reason for the withdrawal from east of Suez was quite simple: cost. At a time when its economy was quite clearly in substantial trouble, Britain was 'just another European power'. It simply could not afford to go on with a substantial commitment east of Suez, while spending heavily in the defence of western Europe. A level of expenditure of some 6 per cent per year was unsustainable against the looming economic crisis of 1967/68. Moreover, the focus of British trade was shifting as well; the growth in the relative importance of trade with the rest of western Europe decided the Labour cabinet in 1967 to apply for membership of the Common Market. This symbolized a historic shift in economic policy away from global and toward regional patterns of trade, which made the world east of Suez seem significantly less important.[4]

Moreover, there seemed to be others to whom the burden of securing Western interests east of Suez could be passed, at least to some degree: Australia and New Zealand were willing to associate themselves with security in Southeast Asia; the United States, sweetened by receipt of Diego Garcia, was willing to take over the Indian Ocean, and the Shah of Iran seemed a reliable local power in the Gulf.

Given these surfacing doubts, the costs of the forces needed to sustain the east of Suez role seemed increasingly disproportionate. This was especially true of the Navy's carrier force. Denis Healey maintained that '[b]y far my most difficult equipment decision was to cancel CVA-01, the new strike carrier planned by the navy'. CVA-01's main task was to provide the fleet with air cover when it was operating *outside* the range of friendly shore-based airpower. Broadly, this scenario seemed most likely to apply east of Suez and so the east-of-Suez role, dangerously, began to seem the carrier's chief justification. But it was a justification that could easily be challenged, particularly by the Royal Air Force, which was able to argue convincingly that most places of interest east of Suez were *within* reach of friendly shore-based airpower, provided one or two comforting assumptions about local political support were made. As Healey remarked, the prospect of a sustained naval conflict between British and Soviet naval forces in the straits of Sumatra 'seemed too unlikely to be worth preparing against'.[5]

Accordingly CVA-01 was cancelled, to the intense chagrin of the Royal Navy. While the Navy would be able to run on its existing carrier force until 1975, this historic decision did indeed seem to be the end of an era. It represented the demise of a major naval capability that the Royal Navy had pioneered before the First World War, and as far as Christopher Mayhew, the navy minister who resigned over the issue was concerned, it represented an unacceptable gap between residual east-of-Suez commitments and Britain's capacity to meet them, whatever the air staff might say.

Worse still, the CVA-01 decision did not solve the problem. It merely highlighted it. With the deteriorating economic climate of the late 1960s, a major reappraisal of the east-of-Suez role to which the Royal Navy had devoted so much energy and capital appeared inevitable. It was not simply a question of Britain not having the resources to maintain that role while necessarily devoting so much of its defence effort to western Europe, although that was true. The fact of the matter was that local populations (if not necessarily their leaders) were becoming increasingly hostile to the presence of large numbers of foreign troops on their soil, as was all-too-apparent in Aden for example. Moreover, the new states of the area had access (thanks largely to the Soviet Union) to increasingly sophisticated weaponry that made it more expensive for British forces to remain safely in areas in which they were not wanted.

The end of the Borneo confrontation in 1967, the forthcoming independence of Southern Arabia and an increasing acceptance that this strategic choice could be put off no longer, provided the opportunity for an orderly retreat to be sounded. In July 1967, the Defence White paper as the first part of what was dubbed a 'continuing review' announced the halving of British forces in Singapore and Malaysia by 1970/71 with a full withdrawal to follow. The devaluation crisis of November 1967 accelerated the planned rate of withdrawal through 1968, and in January 1969 Britain's departure from Singapore and Malaysia was fixed at December 1971; the end of the deployment of forces in the Gulf was announced at the same time, with the withdrawal of all but a small force to assist the Sultan of Oman. Plans were also instituted to run down the British commitments to Mauritius and Brunei and to negotiate away the 1955 Simonstown Agreement with South Africa and abandon the naval facilities there.

The final nostalgic display in the Far East took place on 31 October 1971 when Britain's last 'Far East Fleet' off Singapore sailed past its last Commander, Rear Admiral J.A.R. Troup. The fleet comprised the destroyer HMS *Glamorgan*, five frigates, the heavy repair ship HMS *Triumph*, and six RFAs; aircraft from HMS *Albion* and HMS *Eagle* also took part. It was a sad occasion, seemingly closing an era.[6]

The pace of the retreat meant it verged on being a scuttle. As early as 1975, the Defence White Paper could even speak of Britain's 'former aspirations to a world wide role'.[7] As though to symbolize all this, the Ministry of Defence sold off all its desert clothing [much of it dating rather poignantly from the Second World War], clearly assuming that it would not have to fight in such conditions again.[8] It had been, to remodel Sir Eyre Crowe's comment before the First World War, an exercise in the disorderly management of decline.

Second thoughts in the 1970s: the incomplete retreat

The signal to retreat from Britain's global role had, however, been given with the greatest reluctance. As Denis Healey himself told the National Press Club in Canberra in 1966,

> We intend to remain, and shall remain, fully capable of carrying out all the commitments we have at the present time, including those in the Far East, the Middle East, and in Africa and other parts of the world. We do intend to remain in the military sense a world power.[9]

Prime Minister Wilson's reluctance to fall back merely on Europe was well known.[10] Indeed, in some ways, the proof of the pudding was in the eating. The fact that there was a rising trend in the dispatch of British forces to crises around the world (eight instances in 1963, sixteen in 1964, seventeen in 1965) suggested an objective need for this kind of global capability.[11] All sorts of expedients to delay and minimize the inevitable were considered, including building a new air base on uninhabited Aldabra off the coast of Mozambique and constructing new facilities in Australia. But for one reason or another they all came to nought.

Likewise, the Conservative opposition had argued vehemently against the withdrawal from east of Suez and promised to reverse the process when they came to power. They had an opportunity to do this when Mr Heath's government came into office in June 1970. The new government knew that 'Labour had wrought some very considerable changes in defence and our inheritance was very different from the one we had ourselves bequeathed some six years earlier'. The principal pattern to Britain's role east of Suez was to be training assistance, equipment sales, after-sales service and advisory support to local friends. 'It might be less exciting than the ability to launch expeditions beyond palm and pine but it could be self-financing; and it didn't require carrier-borne air support!'[12]

The new Government soon discovered the limits of what they could do, however. 'There was no question of completely putting the clock back; we accepted much of the situation as we found it...'[13] The British economy was still in a parlous state, relations with a United States administration largely preoccupied with getting out of the Vietnam war were strained. Mr Heath, himself, was personally most set on Britain's role in Europe, managing to secure accession to the European Economic Community in January 1972. Moreover, with the beginnings of sectarian violence in Northern Ireland, there arose substantial new demands on defence resources. It was accepted 'that we must concentrate our defence on preserving our own homeland and in contributing whatever we decided to an essentially self-defensive alliance. Defence had come full circle. It was not only to start but almost to end at home.'[14]

Nonetheless, the rate and extent of the retreat from east of Suez was slowed to some extent by Mr Heath's government. It was agreed that Britain would continue to contribute to an ANZUK force in Singapore and Malaysia, would assist in the American construction of a new base on Diego Garcia, and would reactivate the Simonstown Agreement with South Africa. Moreover, the Royal Navy's capacity to support this limited presence was reinforced by a stay of execution for HMS *Ark Royal* until 1978. Most significantly of all, as it turned out, was the April 1973 decision to allow the construction of the famous 'Through-Deck Cruiser' (or 'See-Through-Cruiser as it was known within the Navy) the first of which, HMS *Invincible*, was launched in 1977.[15] This was intended to provide a measure of fixed-wing air support for the Navy in the 1980s, but its justification was not to be a limited form of power projection, but rather to shoot down shadowing Soviet aircraft ('Hack the Shad') and to assist the fleet in its anti-submarine mission.

The return of a labour government in February 1974, continuing economic troubles and a determination to reduce defence expenditure to 4.4 per cent of GNP by 1985, ensured that the rest of the 1970s were a difficult period for the Navy. The long-term surface-combat fleet was in theory reduced by one-seventh, although there was a certain amount of sleight of hand in these 'cuts' which meant that in effect the size of the fleet during the 1970s actually remained surprisingly constant.[16] But the Navy's presence even in the Mediterranean was reduced to a small force of anti-submarine vessels, and base rights in Malta were to be given up by 1979. Most of Mr Heath's east-of-Suez reinstatements were likewise effectively abandoned. Worse still from the ordinary sailor's point of view, newspaper coverage of a visit to South Africa by a task force under Admiral Henry Leach, which included charming pictures of jolly jacks sporting in the waves with various South African lovelies, caused outrage in the Labour party and led to the complete termination of the Simonstown Agreement, this time for good.[17] This came at a time when the Navy was becoming involved in a dour, difficult and essentially unwinnable struggle with Icelandic gunboats over cod in the North Atlantic; the contrast symbolized the humourless realities of naval policy in the late 1970s.

Even so, and despite the end of Confrontation, the withdrawal from Singapore and the end in June 1975 of the 'Beira patrol', the break with the east-of-Suez role and Britain's imperial past was still not clean and complete. A number of over-hangs survived. Hong Kong was the most obvious of these. A new Defence agreement was signed on 18 December 1975, by which the Royal Navy was committed to the defence of the colony until its handover to the Chinese in 1997. This would require the permanent deployment of one frigate and five patrol craft, although the frigate was in fact withdrawn in March 1976. The problem was that although China itself was content to wait until 1997 to enjoy Hong Kong's full benefits, too many of its citizens were much less patient. By 1979 the flow of illegal immigrants was threatening to become a flood. To cope with this, the naval contingent was beefed up with the fast patrol/training boat HMS *Scimitar* for two years, two hovercrafts, a helicopter force operating from an RFA and 3rd Raiding Squadron from 42 Commando, Royal Marines.

This helped, and the pressure eased sufficiently for the Hovercraft squadron to be withdrawn in April 1982. Two years later, the aged Ton-class patrol craft were replaced by the modern Peacock class. In 1988 with the departure of HM Ships *Swallow* and *Swift*, the regular Hong Kong squadron was reduced to three vessels, with Royal Marine support. This force worked closely with the remarkable and unique Hong Kong Maritime Police to deal both with a steady flow of illegal immigrants and especially in the period 1992–96 with fleets of smuggling vessels. These were demanding and hazardous operations that were frequently dangerous too, since professional smugglers would sometimes open fire in their attempts to avoid interception. This commitment and the forces deployed to meet it ended, as arranged, with the return of Hong Kong to China in 1997, ending an era.[18] Ensuring the smooth return of Hong Kong to China remained a major preoccupation of British foreign policy up to the very end, and inevitably embroiled the British in controversial issues over domestic developments in China, and as well the difficult business of the Vietnamese boat-people in the late 1980s and early 1990s.[19]

The vessels engaged in this commitment also from time to time got involved in humanitarian operations of one sort of another and in disaster relief. HMS *Plover*, one of the Hong Kong Peacock-class patrol craft, for example, rescued the crew of the Philippine merchant vessel *Santa Maria* when it grounded on the Pratas Reef, 160 miles south-east of Hong Kong in December 1986. Two years later, HM *Swallow* and *Swift* on passage for the UK rescued 38 South Vietnamese refugees from a sinking boat in the South China Sea, landing them at Singapore. In this, British warships were simply doing what they always do, coming in handy for all sorts of minor support when they happen to be in the area.

The point is, though, that they 'happened to be in the area' a good deal more frequently than the original decision to withdraw from east of Suez might have led people to anticipate. Indeed, a succession of warship cruises and visits was maintained east of Suez, and it was because of this that such low-level humanitarian operations were possible and indeed surprisingly frequent in the 1980s and, especially, the 1990s.[20] To a large degree this was deliberate naval policy, and owed much to the imagination of Admiral Sir Terence Lewin, Vice Chief of the Naval Staff, 1971–74. Lewin acknowledged the national need for an occasional presence east of Suez but argued against the Foreign Office's residual preference for token forces to be permanently stationed around the area. Instead he argued for annual or bi-annual 'Group Deployments' of task forces to cruise the area. Not only would these display British naval power more effectively than the odd minor warship dotted about the place – they afforded much more of an opportunity for British forces to exercise with other navies and indeed with each other in, operationally, a much more useful way. Moreover it would provide Flag Officers with a marvellous chance at independent command.

This argument prevailed, and the first group under Rear Admiral Richard Clayton, sailed in May 1973 for a six-month cruise into the Pacific. Imaginatively it included HMS *Dreadnought*, Britain's first SSN, and a Dutch frigate for some of the time. Preparations for a second such deployment under Rear Admiral Henry Leach set off in the autumn of 1974, comprising the cruiser HMS *Blake*, five frigates, three RFAs and the SSN HMS *Warspite*. The third, under Rear Admiral John Fieldhouse set off in July 1975.[21] The 1975 Defence White paper caused a temporary hiatus in these deployments, but they resumed under the Conservatives in 1979. Task Force 318 under Rear Admiral Conrad Jenkin, indeed was the first to visit the People's Republic of China in 1980 for 30 years.

This very successful pattern was followed for the rest of the century. Their overall purpose was summed up in official press releases in the summer of 1980:

> These deployments enable the royal navy to maintain a capability to operate worldwide, and help to foster links between the Royal Navy and the navies of our friends and allies. The ships also gain valuable experience in operating as a group, as they would in support of NATO in periods of tension or conflict... They also enable the Navy's young sailors, most of them in their late teens to visit distant ports. Their behaviour has been exemplary and ships and men have been warmly welcomed in every port.[22]

This does not mean that these group deployments were without difficulty or occasional controversy, such as Australia's refusal to allow HMS *Invincible* to dock for repairs to her port shaft during the 'Orient Express' deployment of 1983/84.[23] Enhancing the Navy's capacity to conduct task groups at a distance for long periods of time was sometimes made more difficult by the requirement to detach elements for widely separated port visits; occasionally the composition of the group was necessarily limited. (Task Group 318, for example, had no submarine or organic air.) From this point of view, the requirement to exercise with less advanced navies was a limiting factor too. Especially in the early days, Task Group commanders also sometimes complained that the actual objectives of the cruise were not clear to those conducting them or indeed to their hosts who were pleased but sometimes mystified by their presence especially in parts of the world where the British withdrawal of the early 1970s was remembered as both unexpected and sudden.

Before long, explicit support for defence sales was added to the list of requirements and this too took some organizing. Gradually these teething problems were ironed out, and group deployments became increasingly ambitious and professional.

It is hard of course to assess their practical effect but the Foreign and Commonwealth Office, together with its representatives abroad, continued to press for more and more such visits. The deployments covered many thousands of miles, provided hundreds of port visits, produced thousands of media articles, involved hundreds of exercises with dozens of navies and generally meant that the presence of significant British naval forces became a significant, if transient, part of the maritime scene east of Suez.

Generally, this residual presence east of Suez was a response to a number of different imperatives. First of all, the actual process of decolonization and withdrawal itself involved continuing commitments. Hong Kong was the most obvious example, but there were others. In 1980, for example, elements of 42 Commando found themselves in the New Hebrides restoring order immediately before independence. Moreover, the process of de-colonization and Western withdrawal seemed to many to increase levels of international instability, sometimes producing situations that plunged British citizens and British interests into danger, requiring the Royal Navy to stand by in case there was a need to rescue them. British warships stood off Kom Pong Som ready to evacuate British nationals threatened by the Cambodian civil war in March and April 1975, and off Angola for the same reason in the following month. Three years later, two British naval task groups stood off the coast of Iran for three months from December 1978, ready to evacuate British nationals from the civil disorder that led to the fall of the Shah. In 1986, there took place *Operation Balsac* when HM Yacht *Britannia*, RFA *Brambleleaf*, the survey ship HMS *Hydra* and the MV *Diamond Princess* evacuated 1,379 civilians of many different nationalities from Aden, under the protection of the destroyer HMS *Newcastle* and the frigate HMS *Jupiter*.

Second, the Foreign and Commonwealth Office was anxious to maintain relations with erstwhile allies in the region, not least Australia, New Zealand and, most obviously, the United States. The fact that little physical naval power could be delivered in support of these linkages mattered less when local powers were anxious, for their own reasons, that Britain maintain at least a token presence.

The Five Power arrangement for the defence of Southeast Asia was a classic example of this. It brought the forces of Singapore, Malaysia, Australia, New Zealand and the UK together in periodic exercises. The first two countries welcomed and supported the arrangement because it enabled them to cooperate with advanced military forces and, equally important, provided them with a non-controversial channel for close relations between themselves; Australia, New Zealand and the UK supported the commitment because it gave them a continuing toe-hold in a turbulent but fast-developing region. This provided the British with a low-cost means of capitalizing on past experience in the area and of influencing the outcome of events, at least to some extent. Accordingly British involvement in the FPDA's 'Starfish' exercises became a regular feature of task group deployments.

During 'Orient 92' for example, Starfish was conducted east of Malaysia and involved 33 ships, 47 aircraft and a submarine. The British contributed four ships and aircraft from 800, 814 and 849 squadrons.

As far as the Royal Navy was concerned, the Five Power Agreement justified the retention of some basic oiling and supply facilities in Singapore. Moreover, this was a particularly popular place to visit every now and then and the Royal Navy was reluctant to deny itself and its sailors at least a touch of 'fun in the sun' and completely to abandon the outer oceans to the barbarians.

Since fun in the sun was considered recruitment- and retention-positive, providing much relief from cold and stormy operations in the North Atlantic, and since it provided countless opportunities for professional interactions with other navies, this was a perfectly legitimate set of motivations for the Royal Navy to espouse. They did, however, eventually open the Navy to the wounding charge that their function was largely to swan around on a silver sea.

But this was unfair in that in so doing the Royal Navy was simply reflecting a residual sense in senior political circles that Britain was more than just another medium European power. In many ways this reflected the reluctance with which the labour government had 'abandoned' the east-of-Suez role in the first place.

Margaret Thatcher, the Navy and the east-of-Suez role

The Navy's fortunes and the relative importance assigned the east-of-Suez role once again mirrored a shifting context when Mrs Thatcher's Government came to power in May1979. At this time, a certain momentum was developing on the continent from which the European Union eventually emerged. Plainly, the new government with its Atlanticist proclivities, most marked in the Prime Minister herself, would need to keep a close watch on all this. At the same time, there was a growing sense of threat from the Warsaw Pact in Europe, unhappily allied with a reluctant appreciation that cutbacks in defence expenditure were needed in order to help make possible the radical reform of government finances and the nation's economy on which Mrs Thatcher was plainly set.

This suggested that while Europe and NATO would remain the top priority in British defence, there was a pressing need for a review of the manner in which related defence activity was conducted and of its cost. Equally obviously, expenditure on forces that could only be justified by the east-of-Suez role would be looked at with special scepticism. The results of all this for the Royal Navy became clear when, after extensive debate about Britain's security priorities and requirements during the first two years of the Thatcher government when 'British defence policy, epitomised by the Nott Defence Review of 1981, focussed almost entirely on Europe, with only token gestures to the world role'.[24] British defence rested on the four pillars of wartime roles:

- Nuclear defence
- The maritime commitment to the Eastern Atlantic

- The land/air commitment to the Central front
- The defence of the UK base.

An amphibious contribution to NATO's Northern Flank was sometime considered an extra half-pillar.

Since in fact there were now relatively few defence assets that could *only* be justified by the east-of-Suez role, little of the necessary defence savings could be extracted by any further rundown in this area. Accordingly, as far as the Royal Navy was concerned, the political battle to win was the one about its roles in a NATO context where the Soviet Union and its allies were the main adversaries. This wartime function was a response to the gravest threat that Britain faced. The Navy thought it could do no other than acquiesce in the general view that the country had to focus on the most serious threat, rather than on the most likely. In Mrs Thatcher's words, the hard logic was perfectly clear: 'No one...at the meeting openly contested that the NATO central front was bound to be the decisive area. Scenarios of conflict in the Third World might be more likely: but only on the central front could the war be lost in an afternoon.'[25]

The sense that the East/West divide in Europe was the strategic centre of gravity was reinforced by Mrs Thatcher's view that the Soviet Union and its allies were responsible for many of the troubles in the Third World anyway, or at least hoped for significant profit from them.

In this context the Royal Navy had four main roles: the containment of the ships and submarines of the Soviet Northern and Baltic fleets; the reinforcement of northern Norway and/or Denmark; the provision of anti-submarine warfare [ASW] support for the NATO strike fleet; and the direct and indirect defence of reinforcement and re-supply shipping coming across the Atlantic. All of these roles required sophisticated assets able to survive and win in an increasingly hostile environment and to be able usefully to interoperate with the US Navy.

As far as the Royal Navy was concerned, this justified a first-class balanced fleet of carriers, a significant destroyer and frigate force, a mix of diesel- and nuclear-propulsion submarines, an amphibious force and a mining force – in addition to the nuclear-submarine deterrent force that it also happened to operate. The Navy's leaders rapidly discovered that these comfortable assumptions were not shared by their Defence Secretary, John Nott.

Mr Nott argued that unless corrective steps were taken, a war in Europe would be over before the United States and Canada would be a position to send over reinforcements in the first place, not least because British ammunitions stocks on the central front were so low.[26] He was sceptical of the operational relevance of NATO's Northern Flank in such a situation (although its political significance was a different matter altogether!). And even if it did, after all, prove necessary to take action against a Soviet northern fleet deploying into the North Atlantic, Mr Nott was persuaded by a set of operational analysis statistics provided by Professor Sir Ron Mason, his Chief Scientific Adviser – but regarded by the Navy as being extremely dubious – that a blockade across the Greenland-Iceland-UK gap conducted by nuclear-propelled submarines and maritime patrol aircraft, cued by the undersea SOSUS submarine surveillance system, would do the job perfectly well. The Royal Navy's expensive and generally under-armed surface ships and aircraft carriers were simply not cost-effective, and were the obvious area for drastic cuts.

The initial debate focused on the fate of the carrier HMS *Invincible*. There were two aspects to this issue. The first was the ship's utility in general war with the Soviet Union, about which Mr Nott was deeply sceptical. The second was its continued value for a role out-of-area. John Nott claimed to have been perfectly persuaded 'about the value of carriers in a climate of low-intensity warfare or in meeting local crises around the world'.[27] In this he was reinforced by the Navy's own abiding interest in its east-of-Suez role. There is some evidence that it was Admiral Lewin himself who persuaded the Defence Secretary about the value of this activity. The Defence White Paper gave some prominence to the east-of-Suez role, specifically identifying the value of the carriers for it:[28] 'Britain's own needs, outlooks and interests... give her a special role and a special duty in efforts of this kind'. It emphasized that 'the Royal Navy has a particularly valuable role' in this regard, detailing the Armilla patrol, and the continuing value of group deployments east of Suez.[29] But this, of course, was not the point:

> I did not see how we could afford three carriers in planning for a high-intensity war against the Soviets, nor how at that time we could afford to equip ourselves, in priority, for an out-of-area low-intensity war – not least because the protection of the carriers required a flotilla of supporting frigates, of which we had few in number anyhow.[30]

In Mr Nott's view there were definite limits to what the country could afford in maintaining capacities that were useful for the east-of-Suez role but which could not be justified independently by their wartime role in Europe. In the circumstances, two carriers and their supporting escorts were acceptable, but three, together with a definite commitment to replace the Navy's assault ships, were not.

Alarmed by its failure to convince Mr Nott of the error of his ways, the Navy eventually responded with some alternative sets of savings proposals. The more radical of these was a set of propositions challenging the priority assigned to the commitment of the army and the RAF to continental Europe. In the political circumstances then prevailing, this was unrealistic, even though drastic reductions in the size of the British Army of the Rhine were in fact considered.[31] Almost equally unrealistic was a series of suggestions that focused on running down just some of those capabilities that had special utility for the east-of-Suez role, namely the scrapping of HMS *Endurance*, the Royal Yacht HMS *Britannia*, both of the LPDs, HM ships *Fearless* and *Intrepid*, and the disbandment of the Royal Marines. Although these suggestions were (perhaps as expected) not taken, the fact that they were made illustrates the extent to which the Royal Navy felt constrained to focus in this debate on its role in the maritime defence of western Europe, at the expense of its role east of Suez.[32] One small symbol of this was the 1981 scrapping of the heavy-repair ship HMS *Triumph* (once a light carrier) whose role hitherto had been to service warships east of Suez.[33] Paradoxically, this ship would probably have been extremely useful during the Falklands conflict a year later.

Circumstances had produced a curious situation in which the Navy and the Defence Secretary both felt constrained to adopt attitudes to the east-of-Suez role that were not quite what they really thought. The Navy rather underplayed its allegiance to the role. John Nott was quite right when he said: 'The Royal Navy took it as the unquestioned view of their role that they were to reach out worldwide, performing the traditional "blue water" role of safeguarding British interests and British shipping all around the world.'[34]

Certainly, the Navy did not abandon the east-of-Suez argument altogether. In briefing papers that he prepared for Mrs Thatcher for example, the First Sea Lord, Admiral Sir Henry Leach, pointed out that '[a]t a time when the capability to deter Soviet aggression outside Europe is becoming increasingly important it makes no sense to slash the only part of our defence capability which can contribute to this deterrence on a continuing day-to-day basis'.[35] But nonetheless this was a comparatively small part of his case against the cuts. Like most people at the time, Sir Henry accepted that the defeat of Soviet power was Britain's top strategic priority and that, basically, the European theatre was where this would have to be done. In this, he was following generations of naval officers who concluded that Britain's capacity to defend its interest outside Europe depended first and foremost on its capacity to control the waters around it. In the classic formulation, the Navy needed to secure its capacity to control the sea by defeating the Soviet Navy before exercising that control east of Suez. The requirements of war had to take precedence over those of peace, however uneasy that peace might be. These were ancient and time-honoured traditions, perhaps, but true for all that.

In the event, his campaign failed. The Nott review sought major reductions in the size of the destroyer/frigate fleet and reduced the carrier fleet to two, with HMS *Invincible* being offered to Australia. The Survey ship HMS *Endurance* was to be scrapped. There was a deal of sleight of hand in these cuts too, since they were only expected really to come into effect from 1985 onward and in the meantime ships ordered in the last months of the Callaghan government and the replacement of Falklands losses obscured the real purport of the review. Interestingly, also, there was little attempt to build up the SSN and MPA blockading force across the Greenland-Iceland-UK gap that provided so much of the apparent rationale for the cuts in the post-1985 surface fleet.

For his part, John Nott was persuaded to show rather more enthusiasm for the east-of-Suez role than he really thought justified. No doubt this was partly because the navy's withdrawal from this role went against the grain as far as Mrs Thatcher was concerned. Her government had come to office strong in the belief that Britain's destinies could not be confined to the parish-pump politics of western Europe. Mrs Thatcher herself had a global view, was profoundly Atlanticist in her assumptions and clearly wanted to revive Britain's role east of Suez. The fall of the Shah of Iran in 1979 had deprived the West of a friendly power that could be trusted to look after Western interests in an important and turbulent area, now apparently under increasing threat with the emergence of radical Islam on the one hand and the apparent expansion of Soviet power – as exemplified by its invasion of Afghanistan – in the same year. In response, the United States set up a Rapid Deployment Joint Task Force that eventually led to the creation of a new Central Command dedicated to the defence of American interests in the area. From the start, Mrs Thatcher was keen to participate in all this, was interested in earmarking British forces for the purpose and was keen for Britain to continue to provide equipment training and advice to friendly Gulf states. 'Repeatedly', she claimed afterwards, 'events have demonstrated that the West cannot pursue a policy of total disengagement in this strategically vital area'.[36]

John Nott's predecessor Francis Pym had likewise hoped that the Navy could re-enter the Indian Ocean, provided in this case that the German navy were able to shoulder more of the maritime burden in the Atlantic.[37] John Nott was broadly sympathetic to this line as well. In evidence of this, the original decision to scrap the LPDs was reversed after a visit to Portsmouth by John Nott in which the Navy went out of its way to demonstrate the ship's value in the disaster-relief and service-assisted evacuations that so characterized contemporary conceptions of the east-of-Suez role.[38]

But Mr Nott was only sympathetic up to a point. For him that key point was that the navy's historic fascination for events outside the area should not be allowed to skew Britain's defence efforts within it. He became increasingly concerned about this prospect when the successful Falklands campaign seemed to him to be giving the east-of-Suez role undue prominence. This was reinforced by continuing scepticism about the importance of maritime power, relative to land/air power in the defence of western Europe.[39]

Reviving commitments in the 1980s

This desire to reactivate an east-of-Suez role, at least to some extent, focused mainly on the Gulf – partly in consequence of Britain's historic involvement in the area, partly because of its turbulence, and partly because of its oil. The notion that Britain and other members of the Western community could rely on Iran as a proxy defender of regional stability disappeared with the Iranian Revolution of 1979. One immediate consequence of this was the Armilla patrol, an acceptance of the need to maintain a visible Royal Navy presence in the Gulf of Oman and the Straits of Hormuz. HMS *Coventry* began the first patrol on 7 October 1979. Initially, it was felt that this would require the maintenance of four destroyers or frigates east of Suez. But this would require extensive RFA and other support and represented a huge distraction for a surface fleet struggling to cope with the demands of extensive modernization and the growing challenges of the Soviet Navy in Europe's northern waters. In 1981, the force was reduced to two destroyers or frigates east of Suez in 1981, just as the Iran–Iraq war began.

Thereafter the composition and activity of the force waxed and waned according to circumstances, but showed a gradual tendency to increase throughout the 1980s, more or less in line with the increasing impact on Gulf tanker traffic of the war between Iran and Iraq. In 1982, in fact, it reduced to one Royal Navy warship, when the arrival of HMNZS *Canterbury* and *Waikato* allowed the British to detach one frigate for the Falklands campaign and its aftermath. Thereafter, however, the force gradually increased through the 1980s. From 1984 it was expanded by a Royal Marine Air Defence detachment armed with Javelin surface-to-air missiles to increase the force's capacity to deal with air attack in the Gulf. In the same year the Operation Armilla Accomplice (later re-titled Operation CYMNEL) series of annual exercises began. These exercises rehearsed preparations to provide a stand-by force of minesweepers for use in the Gulf. The first exercise took place in the Mediterranean, and it was this force that was diverted to the international campaign to clear the Suez Canal in August 1984. Patrols west of the Straits of Hormuz increased in 1986 as the frequency of air and other Iraqi and Iranian attacks on merchant ships increased, and an additional destroyer or frigate was added to the force from March 1987. Royal Navy Explosive Ordnance disposal teams were increasingly called upon to deal with unexploded missiles on damaged merchant ships. The Operation CYMNEL minesweeping force – in the shape of four MCMVs, the support ship HMS *Abdiel*, the forward repair ship RFA *Diligence* and an RFA oiler – eventually appeared in the Gulf in September 1987 and remained throughout 1988, joining with the Belgian, Dutch, Italian and French vessels in the informal European minesweeping squadron that swung into action in the Gulf after the Iranian-Iraqi ceasefire of August 1988. On the completion of this task, British minesweepers were withdrawn from the area in February 1989, followed by the Royal Marine Javelin detachment in March.

The British Armilla patrol in fact mounted the biggest single effort in the escort (or accompaniment) of tankers in and out of the Gulf. Initially this service was extended only to British- or British-related flagged ships but after February 1988, this was extended to foreign-flagged ships substantially in British ownership. To the end of hostilities, the British accompanied 1,026 tankers – more than all the other Western navies put together. In February 1988, for example, the Armilla patrol accompanied 60 transits compared to the US Navy's fifteen, the French seven and the Italians' five. The work was conducted with a low-key emphasis in as non-provocative and reassuring manner as possible, and seemed often in some distinction to the more proactive style of the US forces in the area.[40] It was hot, steamy work requiring considerable delicacy of touch and probably needing more in the way of reserve back-up than was generally available – but it succeeded.[41]

The permanent deployment of naval forces to the Gulf Area reinforced the pattern, already discernible in the 1970s, of British warships getting involved in things simply because they happened to be in the area. In August 1983, for example, HMS *Andromeda*, HMNZS *Waikato* and RFA *Grey Rover* stood by the Chagos archipelago when Mauritian vessels intruded into the British Indian Ocean territory. During this period, there were also a number of maritime rescues of one sort or another.[42] The need for an out-of-area capability seemed further proved by the Falklands campaign of 1982. This at least was the contention of the maritime lobby that argued with more vigour than historical accuracy that the proposed naval cuts had inspired the Argentine assault in the first place. Mrs Thatcher saw it as a confirmation of both the necessity, and more importantly the possibility, of Britain maintaining a defence capability outside the narrow bounds of European defence. 'Certainly no one who lived through that campaign could be in any doubt about the importance of a country such as Britain with far-flung interests being able to project its military power swiftly and effectively across the globe.'[43]

She remained convinced that 'British policy "East of Suez" still matters', pointing out the area's growing economic importance, reminding the British of their historic ties and common interests with Australia and speculating that the newly industrialized countries of the region would welcome more European, and particularly more British contact 'as a counterweight to the other dominant influences in the region – the United States, China and Japan'.[44]

The Falklands factor, as it became known, made Mr Nott's navy cuts seem – in the words of a *Times* leader of the period – to be as 'politically unsound' as they were 'strategically ill-founded'.[45] Mr Nott accordingly fought an increasingly lonely campaign to prevent the slow return to a set of priorities that seemed to him more akin to Britain's imperial past than to the rude and brutal necessities of a cost-effective contribution to the defence of western Europe. The Falklands campaign, he argued, was an aberration and should not be the basis of British defence planning. His opposition to 'posturing with ship deployments in foreign ports to emphasise our ability to punch above our weight' and 'neo-imperialist do-goodery' was clear from his autobiography even twenty years later.[46]

Indeed, the continental tradition in British defence thinking has continued ever since. In 1997, for instance the leading historian Corelli Barnett wrote that

> We should focus our future defence budget and defence policy on contributing first-class armed forces with first-class equipment to the collective defence of the NATO area as defined in the original 1949 North Atlantic treaty. It is time that we put an end to overstretch – both of our national pretensions and of our long-suffering armed forces.[47]

Another stage in the re-emergence of the east-of-Suez role was nonetheless suggested by the 1983 Defence White Paper, which unlike its predecessors devoted a whole section, not just a paragraph or two, to the world 'Beyond the NATO Area' and which reviewed the recent role of the Royal Navy in the Lebanon, and especially in the early stages of the Iran–Iraq war. The 1984 White Paper likewise drew attention to the purchase of support ships 'to provide afloat support for naval vessels operating at great distance from their bases…[and to give]…a considerable enhancement to the "out of area" capability of the destroyer/frigate force and of conventional submarines'.[48] However, while the rundown of the Cold War may have provided an opportunity for a strategic transformation in Britain's security priorities in the long run, it brought about a host of pressing concerns in Europe in the short term. As a glance at Mrs Thatcher's autobiography reveals, the future of Europe in the new era dominated her foreign policy concerns. While there was a growing recognition of the importance of Britain's interests east of Suez, Europe was still the major preoccupation. Exactly the same priorities can be detected in her successor Mr Major's government too. He spent many months of his six and a half years at No. 10 in foreign travel, much of it in attempting to secure Britain's global interests, but in the end it was Europe that commanded his destiny.[49]

Nonetheless, the most urgent foreign policy issue at the time of Mrs Thatcher's downfall and Mr Major's arrival was the need to respond to Iraq's invasion of Kuwait in August 1990. Mrs Thatcher was under no doubt that this aggression needed to repelled, that this was 'no time to go wobbly'[50] and that Britain had a major role to play in seeing the matter through. Within an hour of the news coming through, she ordered British warships at Penang and Mombasa to join HMS *York* (from the Armilla patrol), which was already in the Gulf. And before her departure, she ordered Britain's biggest military deployment into the area for decades.

The Gulf War of 1991 and the sanctions-enforcement campaign which proceeded it became Britain's biggest commitment of forces east of Suez for 30 years and marked at least temporarily a complete reversal of the rolling decisions to retreat in the 1960s. Britain deployed some 45,000 personnel to the area during 'Operation Granby'. As part of an international maritime coalition of 13 non-Arab navies, the Royal Navy deployed eleven destroyers/frigates, two submarines, ten mine-countermeasures vessels, three patrol craft, 11 Royal Fleet Auxiliaries and three naval air squadrons to the immediate operational theatre, not counting further forces acting in indirect support in the Mediterranean and elsewhere. This was less than 10 per cent of the Coalition's total maritime strength even though the British naval contribution was the second largest force after that of the US Navy.

By the time of the ceasefire, the Royal Navy had challenged 3,171 merchant ships and boarded 36. The build-up of forces required a huge sea-based logistical effort involving 146 merchant ship round trips. British ships, especially the Type 42 destroyers HM Ships *Gloucester* and *Cardiff*, operated 'up-threat' with leading US and Kuwaiti units. Helicopters from these two ships and from HMS *Brazen* helped destroy the bulk of the Iraqi navy in the so-called 'Battle of the Bubiyan Channel' while the large British MCM force conducted extensive precursor and post-conflict mine-clearance operations. Other surface units provided air defence and logistical support. All concerned emphasized the benefit of experience derived from the Armilla patrol.[51]

Although the Gulf campaign of 1990/91, and its aftermath remained one of the Navy's biggest operational preoccupations of the 1990s, it did not preclude a substantial role in the Adriatic, nor the maintenance of routine activities, such as the programme of Task Group Deployments to the Far East. Not surprisingly, though, this resulted in a very great increase in operational tempo, which put the

Continuing constraints in the Thatcher/Major era

The Royal Navy recognized that the emergence of the US Navy's *The Maritime Strategy* could be a means for breaking away from the limited defensive operations centred upon the Greenland–Iceland gap that had been envisaged in the Nott era, and for entering into demanding, ambitious 'forwards operations' with the US Navy.[53] This implied a need for just the sophisticated and balanced fleet for which it had argued during the Nott Defence Review. To engage in these demanding operations against Soviet submarines, aircraft and surface ships in Europe's inhospitable northern waters demanded well-equipped and modern warships, ASW carriers and a sizeable amphibious force. The Navy used the opportunity to replace losses sustained during the Falklands campaign to claw back some of the assets conceded during the Nott Review and to ready themselves for these new and exciting alliance developments. Although once again their professional focus was on high-intensity operations against the Soviet navy in northern waters, the requirement would produce a fleet that would, of course, have considerable potential for lesser operations east of Suez. And with the collapse of the Soviet Union in 1989 and the consequent end of the cold war, this is precisely what they got.

This process of recovery was not, however, all plain sailing under Mr Nott's successors Michael Heseltine and George Younger. The economic bubble of the mid-1980s burst; by the end of the decade the conditions were considered 'dismal ... with deep-seated troubles'.[54] Accordingly, the search for defence costsavings carried on for the remainder of the 1980s. These were particularly noticeable in regard to the renewal of the amphibious and mining fleets.[55]

It was the same story for the early 1990s, a period in which commitments grew while naval resources fell. The money devoted to defence dropped to 2.8 per cent of GDP while naval manpower fell by some 20 per cent. Yearly editorials in *Jane's Fighting Ships* produced by the redoubtable Captain Richard Sharp continually bemoaned the fact that low frigate/destroyer replacement orders meant that the fleet was in effect being reduced by stealth. In 1991 he pointed out that only three frigates and one overdue SSBN had been ordered since mid-1988, whereas maintaining the escort fleet at the level agreed in consequence of the Nott review actually required three to four orders per year. In 1992 he complained:

> It becomes depressing year after year to have to praise British naval competence in far-flung places while searching in vain in Defence White Papers for an acknowledgement that what sailors and marines have to spend their time doing is recognized as their primary purpose. Neither

are there sufficient resources being allocated to allow the continuation of all the present tasks at the same level, or even the maintenance of the same high standards.[56]

He likewise lamented the long delay in the replacement of the two LPDs *Fearless* and *Intrepid*, although promises had been made in 1987, and worried about when the Navy would be able to consider the eventual replacement of the three Invincible-class carriers. The gap between the navy's commitments and the forces it had with which to meet them seemed to him to be widening dangerously.

However, things began to improve in 1994 when the LPH HMS *Ocean* was ordered, together with the upgraded FRS 2 Sea Harrier. 1995 saw a substantial bottoming-out with orders at last for the two new Assault ships, the last batch of Type 23 Duke-class frigates, a new advanced SSN the Astute-class, seven MCM vessels and a new Survey Ship.

The 1990s: accelerating interest in a wider world

The success of the Gulf campaign of 1990/91 increased the sense that Britain had a special interest, and indeed a special responsibility to play a major role outside its immediate area helping 'to avert a slide into disorder'.[57] The widespread assumption was that the professional proficiency of its armed forces, its diplomatic experience and expertise and its special relationship with the United States would allow it 'to punch above its weight'.

The process of renewed globalism was further reinforced by the election of a Labour Government in 1997. The new prime minister, Tony Blair, ordered a Strategic Defence Review (SDR) 'to re-assess Britain's security interests and defence needs and consider how the roles, missions and capabilities of our Armed forces should be adjusted to meet the new strategic realities' of the post-cold war world. The review was intended to be inclusive of all shades of opinion and foreign-policy-led, rather than predetermined by any a priori assumptions about how much money Britain could afford to spend on defence. It was to be derived from first principles, and nothing was to be taken for granted, with the exception of the need for the UK to maintain a national nuclear deterrent.

Among the many striking conclusions of this review were the following:

- It was an uncertain world, likely to produce a range of unpredictable threats.
- Britain as a leading trading power was so deeply immersed in the globalized economic system that if the British did not go to the crisis, the crisis would come to them.
- The most likely area in which these threats might arise and in which the British could make a significant contribution were Europe, the Mediterranean and the Gulf.
- Because it was impossible to predict in advance what might be required, there should be a shift toward military planning based on developing and

maintaining capabilities that were likely to be useful rather than on existing commitments.

- A capacity to engage in expeditionary operations was likely to be the most useful of these military capacities, and so should be given a high priority.[58]

The implications of this set of conclusions were enormous. They illustrated the extent to which the decisions of 1968 had been turned on their head. The British were in effect signalling that their role in the Gulf during the 1980s and in the Iraq war of 1990/91 was no aberration. The British were now back 'east of Suez' with a vengeance.

As though to make the point crystal clear, the Ministry of Defence embarked on a series of policy initiatives that were designed further to shift the Royal Navy's preoccupations rather away from war *at* sea to war *from* the sea and to build up the expeditionary capacity which this revived global role plainly required. First, there was a commitment to replace Britain's three existing carriers with two much larger ones capable of operating the latest aircraft. This represented the clearest possible reversal of the original decision to abandon CVA-01 back in 1966, which had inevitably led to the further decision for Britain to withdraw from east of Suez. It was, indeed, a quite historic decision. It was accompanied by equally historic decisions to merge the fixed-wing and rotary aircraft of the three services as a means of boosting the aerial support available for sea-based intervention operations, to which the very successful LPH HMS *Ocean* had already made a significant contribution. The other major and even more distinctive element of an expeditionary capability, the fleet's amphibious force was also to be reinforced with the decision to replace, at last, the two LPDs HMS *Fearless* and HMS *Intrepid* and to build four new Bay-class amphibious landing ships. The Ministry of Defence also ordered six roll-on/roll-off ships to beef up its capacity to support distant operations logistically. Finally, it was decided to set up a Permanent Joint Force Headquarters with the remit of planning and preparing for a variety of military contingencies around the world. This was but part of a determined drive toward 'jointery' which was intended to ensure that British forces in expeditionary operations would work together as cost-effectively as possible. All this was also encapsulated in British maritime doctrine. The second edition of BR 1806 appeared in 1999 and confirmed that 'the focus of maritime attention has undoubtedly shifted towards littoral operations in support of operations ashore'.[59]

Nothing in politics is clear-cut, however! Doubts and limitations remained. One set of concerns centred on the feasibility of plans and the likely cost of the two new carriers and their considerable reliance on the success of the American Joint Strike Fighter programme. There was concern about the carriers' cost impact on the rest of the naval programme, with much speculation in the press and elsewhere that it could require substantial cutbacks in the Navy's 32-strong frigate and destroyer force, and maybe a reduction in the navy's 12-strong nuclear attack submarine fleet.[60] The early retirement of the upgraded Sea Harrier force likewise led to worries about the costs of the new emphasis on expeditionary operations. Moreover, the limitations of Britain's capacity to engage in these demanding operations, especially in contrast to the overwhelming power of the United States, emerged in deficiencies in the conduct of the Saif Sareea exercise in Oman in 2002 and in the later Afghanistan operation. Concerns ranged from worries about the extent to which British equipment was sufficiently adapted to operating in desert conditions to logistical delays in moving military personnel and equipment into the operational area.[61]

But perhaps the most significant doubts arose in consequence of the terrorist attacks on Washington and New York on September 11 2001. If the original idea behind the SDR had been to put time and space between the crisis and its prospective Western victims by moving forward in expeditionary operations intended to deal with the threat at source, the attacks of 9/11 indicated that international terrorists could outflank such reactions asymmetrically and strike at the very heart of the system they resented. This led to concerns that Britain and other Western states should perhaps withdraw their forces from danger, seek to interfere less and focus instead on the demands of homeland defence. In some circles, the attack led to the view that instead of focusing upon dealing with terrorism as the symptoms of the problem, the West should concentrate more on the resentments against a globalized trading system that were its fundamental cause. This would require a focus on non-military action and might even imply less emphasis on military activity and military spending east of Suez, rather than more.

The issues led the Ministry of Defence to reconsider its Strategic Defence Review and to add a 'new chapter' that would take account of the events of 9/11 and come to some conclusions about what Britain's defence response to it should be.[62] What emerged, in general effect, was a reaffirmation of the conclusions of the original review. Britain needed to maintain forces that could be used to 'prevent, deter, coerce, disrupt or destroy' international terrorists and the regimes that harboured them. This put a premium on British military forces engaged in 'deterrence' operations designed to prevent such problems from arising; if that failed, Britain required high-intensity war-fighting capacities in order to conduct find-and-strike operations. Afterward Britain should be able to conduct post-crisis 'stabilization' operations to prevent the original problem re-emerging later. Most significantly, Britain needed to be able to do all this at longer range, and usually in conjunction with allies, often with the United States in the lead.[63]

It seemed likely that this would require a widening of areas of concern outside the confines of Europe, the Mediterranean and the Gulf that had originally been envisaged in the SDR. The Defence Secretary, Geoff Hoon, variously declared that

> Furthermore,…the attack on 11 September…has demonstrated that we cannot dictate the geographic areas where our interests may be engaged…
> This means that, in future, we may be engaged across a different, and potentially wider canvas than we perhaps envisaged even at the time of

the Strategic Defence Review ... [T]he attempt to delineate in the future where threats might arise is going to be even more difficult than it ever was ... a threat could come from any quarter of the world and we have to be in a position to deal with it.[64]

In fact, this aspect of New Chapter work in effect retrospectively acknowledged that this widening process had in fact already taken place, not least with sustained sea-based operations in Sierra Leone and East Timor.

Nonetheless, the extent to which Britain and its navy had returned to its historic role east of Suez was amply demonstrated through the late 1990s and into the twenty-first century by a continuing presence in the Gulf to enforce UN sanctions on Iraq, to enforce the no-fly zone, and to engage in periodic pressure on Saddam Hussein to desist from pressurizing Kuwait and/or to abandon his programme of weapons of mass destruction. This involved a significant presence ashore, especially in Kuwait, constant maritime patrolling in the Gulf and the regular launching of air and sometimes cruise-missile strikes on military targets in Iraq.

Substantial as this role in the Gulf actually was, it was to expand still further in the early years of the twenty-first century. The al-Qaeda attack on Washington and New York led to 'Operation Enduring Freedom' initially against the Taliban regime in Afghanistan and more generally against international terrorism everywhere. Considering that Afghanistan was a land-locked country over 400 miles from the sea, even so, the fact that its two most convenient neighbours were disinclined to act as hosts for substantial overland assaults on Afghanistan, meant that the operation had a substantial maritime component. The strategic policy of the British Government made inevitable a substantial Royal Navy role in its support.

Profiting from a fortuitous large-scale exercise in Oman, Saif Sareea II, which itself was one of the biggest naval operations since the Falklands war, the British deployed a substantial force into the Bay of Bengal in order to assist, while maintaining their share of international operations in the Gulf to maintain the sanctions regime against Iraq, intercept drugs and other smugglers and deal with any terrorist-related maritime activity they encountered. 'Operation Veritas' was initially to be led by HMS *Illustrious*, then off Salalah in Oman; the ship was re-roled in five days into a helicopter carrier and led a British naval task force to the area.[65] In due course, elements of 45 Commando Royal Marines conducted 'Operation Jacana', Britain's largest combat deployment since the 1991 Gulf War. This was new and relatively unfamiliar territory for the British whose previous experience in Afghanistan had not been happy. Moreover, this was a different kind of war, against a faceless adversary rather than a formal state and in comparison very open-ended and all-embracing.

By contrast, 'Operation Telic', Britain's substantial involvement in the 2003 campaign against Iraq, was in many ways to finish off uncompleted business in the Gulf. It involved a force of some 30 warships, submarines and RFAs headed by an amphibious task group centred on a re-roled HMS *Ark Royal* and HMS *Ocean*, 50 helicopters and 5,000 naval personnel, plus a substantial force of

Royal Marines deployed ashore. Another major logistical effort was required, supported this time by some 64 merchant ships. The retasking of the task group's major ships symbolizes the extent to which the Royal Navy's preoccupation has shifted from power at sea (against the Soviet Navy of Cold War days) to power from the sea (in support of expeditionary operations ashore). That at a very early stage in the campaign the British chartered two salvage ships and sent the RFA *Sir Galahad* into Umm Qasr with humanitarian supplies signifies the variety of demands that this expeditionary concept will require.[66]

Different though these two campaigns were they both were facilitated by a presence East of Suez that had by now become routine again. 'Operation Veritas' was made easier by 'Saif Sareea II'; HMS *Ark Royal* flagship of 'Operation Telic' was diverted to this task having originally been scheduled to lead the latest large-scale Task Group Deployment to the Far East. These events, and the reversal of British defence preoccupations they implied, simply demonstrated what Lord Carrington called 'the sheer unpredictability of international life' and the necessity to 'be as ready for the unforeseen as can be managed'.[67] As things turned out, the Royal Navy was, despite everything, sufficiently ready to cope with the consequences of a major shift in British defence policy back toward its maritime origins in a manner that could not have been foreseen 30 years earlier.

Conclusions

If, with the advantage of hindsight we can see that the Royal Navy's historic retreat from east of Suez is in fact therefore much better seen as an example of *reculer pour mieux sauter*,[68] why was this necessary and how was it possible? The British concluded that they simply could not disengage completely from the area, because it contained too many interests deemed crucial to Britain's prosperity and security. Moreover, the relative priority of those interests rose, as the Cold War declined, and the direct and indirect impact of distant troubles on Britain's domestic prospects became more obvious.

The turn-around became more possible, first and foremost because shifts in the strategic environment allowed a reallocation of resources from the one area to another, and because the impressive recovery of the British economy meant there was less pressure on defence resources than there had been even as late as the mid-1980s. Even so, the proportion of overall government expenditure and of Gross Domestic Product that was devoted to defence expenditure at the end of the twentieth century, some 2.4 per cent, was still at levels that are, by historical standards, quite modest and which are in some respects still declining. Moreover, the rate is slightly less than the world average of 2.6 per cent.[69]

However the money devoted to defence was spent rather more efficiently than it had been in the past, and certainly more efficiently than in some other comparable countries. The professional structure of their forces allows the British to spend far more on equipping and training their military personnel than can France, Germany or Italy. In real capability terms, Britain spends about 50 per cent more on defence than either France or Germany, even though this represents a smaller proportion of GDP than, for example, is the case with France.[70] Defence management reforms, introduced with increasing speed through the period, but especially from Michael Heseltine's time as Defence Secretary, have contributed to this. Finally, the determined stress on jointery from the mid-1990s onward has paid dividends in the conduct of expeditionary operations. Taken together this represents significant improvement on the conduct of the business of defence in 1975. At this time, inter-service relations were rancorous (especially between the Royal Navy and the Royal Air Force[71]), civilians and service people in the Ministry were separate communities and the management of defence was inefficient. Generally, most people thought the situation much better a quarter of a century later.

One result of all the reforms, however, was a substantial loss to the Navy, and to the other two services as well, of much of their independence. The Navy had increasingly to think of itself as part of an integrated team, and this was not an easy adjustment. Nonetheless, the Navy benefited significantly from the fact that many of the expeditionary operations in which it became involved – the Falkands, the Former Republic of Yugoslavia, Sierra Leone, East Timor, all three wars in the Gulf and Afghanistan – all had a very significant maritime component. And in them the capacity of the Royal Navy to influence events was greatly aided by its ability to cooperate with the other two services, and as experience accumulated to build up expertise in the conduct of expeditionary operations. This was all very different from circumstances in the mid-1970s when the Navy's presence east of Suez did indeed savour of a pleasant and generally fairly undemanding imperial afterglow. Twenty-five years later the Royal Navy's presence east of Suez had become more business-like, more worthwhile if perhaps less fun. It looked more sustainable too – but as ever, only time will tell whether the return to globalism east of Suez will continue to be seen as the best policy for Britain to pursue and whether the resources necessary to its conduct will continue to be made available. And, once again, the first indication of this may prove to be the fate and the extent of the Royal Navy's carrier programme.

Notes

1. Rudyard Kipling, 'Troopin' – quoted in Denis Healey, *The Time of My Life* (London: Penguin, 1989), p. 278.
2. See Cmnd. 3540, *Statement on the Defence Estimates 1968* (London, February 1968).
3. Eric Grove, *Vanguard to Trident: British Naval Policy Since World War II* (London: Bodley Head, 1987), 267, 253.
4. David Sanders, *Losing an Empire Finding a Role: British Foreign Policy Since 1945* (Basingstoke: Macmillan, 1990), 228–31.
5. Healey, *Time of My Life*, 275–6. A particularly useful summary of the CVA-01 issue may be found in Grove, *Vanguard to Trident*, 270–5.
6. Grove, *Vanguard to Trident*, 307–8.
7. See Command (Comd) Paper 5976, *Statement on the Defence Estimates, 1975* (London, March 1975), 13.

8. House of Commons Defence Committee, *A New Chapter to the Strategic Defence Review Vol. II: Oral and written evidence* (House of Commons, May 2003) [Hereafter HCDC Vol. II], 25.
9. Healey, *Time of My Life*, 292.
10. M. Dockrill, *British Defence Since 1945* (Oxford: Blackwell, 1988), 86–7.
11. Figures derived from Cmnd. 2901, *Statement on the Defence Estimates, 1966*, part 1, the Defence Review (London, February 1966).
12. Lord Carrington, *Reflect on Things Past* (London: Collins, 1988), 217–19.
13. Ibid., 218.
14. Ibid., 219.
15. Dockrill, *British Defence Since 1945*, 101–4.
16. Grove, *Vanguard to Trident*, 324.
17. Henry Leach, *Endure No Makeshifts; Some Naval Recollections* (London: Leo Cooper, 1993), 158–9.
18. Full details of this may be found in Captain Peter Hore, ed., *Royal Navy and Royal Marines Operations 1964 to 1996* (London: MOD, Maritime Strategic Studies Institute, 1999). For the Hong Kong Police, see Iain Ward, *Mariners: The Hong Kong Marine Police Force, 1948–97* (Exeter: IEW Publication, 1999).
19. Mark Stuart, *Douglas Hurd: The Public Servant* (Edinburgh: Main Dream, 1998), 345–65.
20. See Hore, *Royal Navy and Royal Marines Operations 1964 to 1996*.
21. Richard Hill, *Lewin of Greenwich: The Authorised Biography of Admiral of the Fleet Lord Lewin* (London: Cassell, 2000), 248–51, 281, 283, 287.
22. MOD Press Releases of 19 May and 23 July 1980.
23. Grove, *Vanguard to Trident*, 384.
24. Andrew Dorman, 'Reconciling Britain to Europe in the next millennium: the Evolution of British Defense Policy in the post-Cold War Era', *Defense Analysis*, 17 (2001), 191.
25. Margaret Thatcher, *The Downing Street Years* (London: HarperCollins, 1993), 250–1.
26. Testimony of Field Marshal the Lord Bramall at the ICBH Witness Seminar Programme's 'Nott Review' of 20 June 2001, transcript, 50–3.
27. John Nott, *Here Today Gone Tomorrow: Recollections of an Errant Politician* (London: Politico's, 2002), 229.
28. Cmnd. 8288, *The United Kingdom Defence programme: The Way Forward*, paragraph 34; Hill, *Lewin of Greenwich*, 337.
29. Cmnd. 8288, paragraphs 32 and 34.
30. Nott, *Here Today Gone Tomorrow*, 229.
31. Testimony of Field Marshal the Lord Bramall at the ICBH Witness Seminar Programme's 'Nott Review' of 20 June 2001, transcript 51, 58–9.
32. Andrew Dorman, 'John Nott and the Royal Navy: the 1981 Defence Review Revisited', *Contemporary British History*, 15 (2001), 101, 104, 115.
33. Ibid., 55.
34. John Nott, *Here Today Gone Tomorrow*, 211.
35. Leach, *Endure No Makeshifts*, 207–10, 254.
36. Thatcher, *Downing Street Years*, 162; Dorman, 'John Nott and the Royal Navy', 101.
37. Pym talks of Indian Ocean Role, *Daily Telegraph*, 2 April 1980. Cited in Andrew Dorman, *Defence Under Thatcher* (Basingstoke: Macmillan, 2002), 33.
38. Ibid., 112.
39. John Nott, 'Our Defences all at Sea' and 'Planning for the future', *TheTimes*, 5 and 6 October 1987.
40. George P. Politakis, *Modern Aspects of the Laws of Naval Warfare and Maritime Neutrality* (London: Kegan Paul International, 1998), 567.

41. For an excellent review, see Captain P.J. Mclaren, 'The Gulf Re-visited – Why?', *Naval Review* (July 1990).
42. Details may be found in Hore, *Royal Navy and Royal Marines Operations 1964 to 1996*.
43. Thatcher, *Downing Street Years*, 251.
44. Ibid., 501.
45. *The Times*, 21 June 1982.
46. Nott, *Here Today Gone Tomorrow*, 243.
47. *Sunday Times*, 26 October 1997.
48. Cited in Grove, *Vanguard to Trident*, 387.
49. John Major, *John Major: The Autobiography* (London: HarperCollins, 1999), 514.
50. Thatcher, *The Downing Street Years*, 816–28.
51. House of Commons Defence Committee, *Preliminary Lessons of Operation Granby 17 July 1991*, testimony of Commodore Christopher Craig and despatch by Air Chief Marshal Sir Patrick Hine, Joint Commander of the Operation, 29 June 1991.
52. Admiral Sir Benjamin Bathurst, 'The Royal Navy – Taking Maritime Power into the New Millennium', *Journal of the RUSI* (August 1995).
53. Although this strategy was only publicly articulated in a special edition of the *Proceedings of the US Naval Institute* in January 1986, it was under development from 1979, and the US Navy's growing intention to adopt a more proactive and ambitious strategy in European and Pacific waters was increasingly well known. NATO's Concept of Maritime Operations [CONMAROPS] developed in parallel.
54. Major, *John Major: The Autobiography*, 136, 167, 202.
55. Dorman, *Defence Under Thatcher*, 144–7.
56. His editorials have been conveniently gathered and printed together as Captain Richard Sharpe RN, *Jane's Fighting Ships Forewords 1988–2000* (London: Jane's, 2002).
57. Douglas Hurd, 'Britain's Role in Fighting the New World Disorder', *DailyTelegraph*, 30 January 1993.
58. *The Strategic Defence Review* (London, July 1998).
59. *British Maritime Doctrine: BR 1806,* 2nd Edn (London: TSO, 1999), 3.
60. House of Commons Defence Committee, *A New Chapter to the Strategic Defence Review; Sixth Report 2002–03*, Vol. II (hereafter SDR), 15.
61. Ibid., 20, 25, 41.
62. Statement on the SDR New Chapter, HC Deb, 18 July 2002, col. 460.
63. SDR New Chapter, Vol. 1, paragraph 11.
64. Speeches at King's College, London, 5 December 2001, and the Chatham House, 10 March 2003.
65. 'UK Boosts Commitment for Afghanistan', *Jane's Defence Weekly*, 31 October 2001.
66. 'RN Key to Supporting Land Forces in Iraq', interview with Rear Admiral David Snelson, *Jane's Navy International*, May 2003.
67. Carrington, *Reflect on Things Past*, 224.
68. To withdraw in order to charge again.
69. Figures derived from *The Military Balance 2001–2002* (Oxford: IISS, 2002), the *2001 Yearbook* of the Stockholm International Peace Research Institute (Stockholm, SIPRI, 2002) and evidence presented by Professor Malcolm Chalmers to the House of Commons Defence Committee in October 2002; House of Commons Defence Committee, SDR, 150–5.
70. Chalmers, 152.
71. Leach, *Endure No Makeshifts*, 163.

SELECT BIBLIOGRAPHY

Agbi, S. Olu, 'The Pacific War Controversy in Britain: Sir Robert Craigie Versus the Foreign Office', *Modern Asian Studies*, 17 (1983), 289–517.

Airlie, S., *Thistle and Bamboo: The Life and Times of Sir James Stewart-Lockhart* (Hong Kong: Oxford University Press, 1989).

Albion, R.G. (Reed, R., ed.), *Makers of Naval Policy, 1798–1947* (Annapolis MD: Naval Institute Press, 1980).

Aldrich, Richard J., *The Key to the South: Britain, the United States, and Thailand during the Approach of the Pacific War, 1929–1942* (Oxford: Oxford University Press, 1993).

Aldrich, Richard J., Rawnsley, Gary D. and Rawnsley, Ming-Yeh T. (eds), *The Clandestine Cold War in Asia, 1945–65* (London: Frank Cass, 2000).

Alves, D. (ed.), *Evolving Pacific Basin Strategies: The 1989 Pacific Symposium* (Washington DC: National Defense University Press, 1990).

Asada, Sadao, 'From Washington to London: The Imperial Japanese Navy and the Politics of Naval Limitation', *Diplomacy and Statecraft*, 4 (1993), 147–91.

Asada, Sadao, 'The Revolt against the Washington Treaty: The Imperial Japanese Navy and Naval Limitation, 1921–1927', *Naval War College Review*, 46 (1993), 82–97.

Attwell, Pamela, *British Mandarins and Chinese Reformers: The British Administration of Weihaiwei (1898–1930) and the Territory's Return to Chinese Rule* (Hong Kong: Oxford University Press, 1985).

Babij, Orest M., 'The Second Labour Government and British Maritime Security, 1929–1931', *Diplomacy and Statecraft*, 6 (1995), 645–71.

Babij, Orest, 'The Making of Imperial Defence Policy in Britain, 1926–1934', Unpublished Dphil. thesis, Oxford, 2003.

Baer, G.W., *One Hundred Years of Sea Power: The United States Navy, 1890–1990* (Stanford CA: Stanford University Press, 1994).

Barnes, Capt. A.A.S., *On Active Service with the Chinese Regiment* (London: Little, Brown, 1902).

Barnett, C., *Engage the Enemy More Closely* (New York: Norton, 1991).

Beasley, W.G., *Japanese Imperialism* (Oxford: Oxford University Press, 1991).

Beaver, P., *The British Aircraft Carrier* (New York: Patrick Stephens, 1982).

Beck, Peter, 'Politicians versus Historians: Lord Avon's "Appeasement Battle" Against "Lamentably, Appeasement-Minded" Historians', *Twentieth Century British History*, 9 (1998), 396–419.

SELECT BIBLIOGRAPHY

Bell, Christopher, ' "Our Most Exposed Outpost": Hong Kong and British Far Eastern Strategy, 1921–1941', *Journal of Military History*, 60 (1996), 61–88.

Bell, Christopher, ' "How are we going to make war?" Admiral Sir Herbert Richmond and British Far Eastern War Plans', *Journal of Strategic Studies*, 20 (1997), 123–41.

Bell, Christopher, 'Thinking the Unthinkable: British and American Naval Strategies for an Anglo-American War, 1918–1931', *International History Review*, 19 (1997), 789–808.

Bell, Christopher, *The Royal Navy, Seapower and Strategy between the Wars* (Basingstoke: Macmillan, 2000).

Bell, Christopher, 'The "Singapore Strategy" and the Deterrence of Japan: Winston Churchill, the Admiralty and the Dispatch of Force Z', *English Historical Review*, 116 (2001), 604–34.

Bennett, Gill, 'British Policy in the Far East 1933–36: Treasury and Foreign Office', *Modern Asian Studies*, 26 (1992), 545–68.

Beresford, Lord C., *The Break-Up of China* (London: Harper & Bros, 1899).

Berridge, G.R., Keens-Soper, Maurice and Otte, T.G., *Diplomatic Theory From Machiavelli to Kissinger* (Basingstoke: Palgrave, 2001).

Best, Antony, *British Intelligence and the Japanese Challenge in Asia, 1914–1941* (London: Macmillan, 2002).

Black, I. McD., RCNC, 'Fuelling at Sea', *North East Coast Institution of Engineers and Shipbuilders*, 68 (1951–2), 15–23.

Bodley, R.V.C., *Admiral Tōgō: The Authorized Life of Admiral of the Fleet, Marquis Heihachirō Tōgō, O.M.* (London: Jarrolds, 1935).

Booth, A., 'Britain in the 1930s: A Managed Economy?', *Economic History Review*, 40 (1987), 499–521.

Booth, A., *British Economic Policy, 1931–49: Was There a Keynesian Revolution?* (London: Harvester Wheatsheaf, 1989).

Borg, Dorothy, *The United States and the Far Eastern Crisis of 1933–1938* (Cambridge MA: Harvard University Press, 1964).

Boulger, D.C. 'Wei-hai-Wei and Chusan', *Fortnightly Review*, 78 (October 1905), 656–64.

Bourne, Kenneth and Watt D. Cameron (eds), *British Documents on Foreign Affairs: Reports and Papers from the Foreign Office Confidential Print: Series E: Asia, 1860–1914* (Frederick MD University Publications of America).

Brassey, T.A. (ed.), *The Naval Annual 1899* (Portsmouth: Griffin, 1899).

Buck, D.D., 'The Siege of Tsingtao', *Orientations*, 8 (1977), 32–43.

Butler, J.R.M., *Grand Strategy, Vol. II; September 1939–June 1941* (London: HMSO, 1957).

Butler, R., Woodward, E.L., Bury, J.P.T., Medlicott, W.N., Dakin, D. and Lambert, M.E. (eds), *Documents on British Foreign Policy, 1919–1939* (London: HMSO, 1966).

Cagle, Malcolm W. and Manson, Frank A., *The Sea War in Korea* (Annapolis: Naval Institute Press, 1957).

Cantwell, J., *Images of War: British Posters 1939–45* (London: HMSO, 1993).

Carey, Capt. P.C.S. Tupper RN, 'Fuelling At Sea', *Journal of the Royal United Services Institute*, 91 (1946), 8–17.

Carley, Michael Jabara, 'Anti-Bolshevism in French Foreign Policy: The Crisis in Poland in 1920', *International History Review*, 2 (1980), 410–31.

Carlton, David, 'Great Britain and the Coolidge Naval Conference of 1927', *Political Science Quarterly*, 83 (1968), 573–98.

SELECT BIBLIOGRAPHY

Carter, Rear Admiral W.R., *Beans, Bullets And Black Oil* (Washington DC: Dept of Navy, US Government, 1953).

Chalmers, Rear Admiral W.S., *The Life and Letters of David, Earl Beatty: Admiral of the Fleet, Viscount Borodale of Wexford, Baron Beatty of the North Sea and of Brooksby* (London: Hodder & Stoughton, 1951).

Charmley, John, *Chamberlain and the Lost Peace* (London: Hodder & Stoughton, 1989).

Chung, Ong Chit, *Operation Matador Britain's War Plans against the Japanese 1918–1941* (Singapore: Times Academic Press, 1997).

Clavin, Patricia, *The Failure of Economic Diplomacy: Britain, Germany, France and the United States, 1931–36* (New York: St Martin's, 1996).

Clavin, Patricia, ' "The Fetishes of So-Called International Bankers": Central Bank Co-operation for the World Economic Conference, 1932–3', *Contemporary European History*, 3 (1992), 281–311.

Clavin, Patricia, 'The World Economic Conference 1933: The Failure of British Internationalism', *Journal of European Economic History*, 20 (1991), 489–527.

Clowes, William Laird, *The Royal Navy: A History From Earliest Times to the Death of Queen Victoria* (London: Chatham, 1997).

Commonwealth of Australia, *A National Broadcast Address by The Prime Minister* (Melbourne: Government Printer, 26 April 1939).

Commonwealth of Australia, 'Co-operation in Empire Defence', Memorandum by The Secretary (Melbourne: Department of Defence, 14 December 1945).

Commonwealth of Australia, 'Conference of Prime Ministers, London, 1946', Report to Parliament by the Rt. Hon. J.B. Chiefly MP, Prime Minister of Australia (Melbourne: Government Printer, 19 June 1946).

Commonwealth of Australia, 'Post-war Defence Policy', statement to Parliament by The Hon. John J. Dedman, MP, Minister for Defence (Melbourne: Government Printer, 4 June 1947), 7.

Commonwealth of Australia, *Defence 2000: Our Future Defence Force* (Canberra, Defence Publishing Service, 2000).

Cooper, A., 'At the Crossroads: Anglo-Australian Naval Relations, 1945–1971', *Journal of Military History* (October 1994), 65–88.

Costigliola, F.C., 'Anglo-American Financial Rivalry in the 1920s', *Journal of Economic History*, 37 (1977), 911–34.

Cowman, Ian, 'Main Fleet to Singapore? Churchill, the Admiralty, and Force Z', *Journal of Strategic Studies*, 17(2) (June 1994), 79–93.

Cowman, Ian, 'Defence of the Malay Barrier? The Place of the Philippines in Admiralty Naval War Planning, 1925–1941', *War in History*, 3 (1996), 398–417.

Crouch, Harold, *The Army and Politics in Indonesia* (Ithaca NY: Cornell University Press, 1978).

Cunningham, Viscount of Hyndhope, Admiral of the Fleet, *A Sailor's Odyssey* (London: Hutchinson, 1951).

Dallek, Robert, *Franklin D. Roosevelt and American Foreign Policy, 1932–1945* (New York: Oxford University Press, 1979).

Darracott, J. and Loftus, B., *Second World War Posters* (London: Imperial War Museum, 1972).

Darwin, John, 'Imperialism and the Victorians: The Dynamics of Territorial Expansion', *English Historical Review*, 112 (1997), 75–102.

Davis, C.B. and Gowen, R.J., 'The British at Weihaiwei: A Case Study in the Irrationality of Empire', *The Historian*, 113 (2000), 22–36.

SELECT BIBLIOGRAPHY

Day, D., *The Great Betrayal: Britain, Australia and the Pacific War, 1939–42* (North Ryde NSW: Angus & Robertson, 1988).

Dedman, John J., MP, *Minister for Defence* (Melbourne: Government Printer, 4 June 1947).

Dedman, John J., *Defence: Outline of Future Policy 1957,* Cmnd. 124 (London: HMSO, 1957).

Dedman, John J., *Defence Policy and the Programme* (Melbourne: Government Printer, 1954).

Dingman, Roger, *Power in the Pacific: the Origins of Naval Arms Limitation* (Chicago, IL: University of Chicago Press, 1976).

Dockrill, Michael and McKercher, Brian (eds), *Diplomacy and World Power: Studies in British Foreign Policy, 1890–1950* (Cambridge: Cambridge University Press, 1996).

Dockrill, S., *Britain's Retreat from East of Suez: The Choice between Europe and the World?* (Basingstoke: Palgrave, 2002).

Drummond, Ian, *The Floating Pound and the Sterling Area, 1931–39* (Cambridge: Cambridge University Press, 1981).

Eccles, Rear Admiral Henry E., *Logistics In The National Defense* (Harrisburg PA: Stackpole, reprint 1989).

Edwards, P., with Pemberton, G., *Crises and Commitments: The Politics and Diplomacy of Australia's Involvement in Southeast Asian Conflicts, 1948–1965* (Sydney: Allen & Unwin, 1992).

Ehrman, J., *History of the Second World War United Kingdom Military Series Grand Strategy* (London: HMSO, 1956).

Ehrman, J., *Cabinet Government and War, 1890–1940* (Cambridge: Cambridge University Press, 1958).

Endicott, Stephen, *Diplomacy and Enterprise: British China Policy, 1933–1937* (Manchester: Manchester University Press, 1975).

Erdmann, A.P.N., 'Mining for the Corporate Synthesis: Gold in American Foreign Economic Policy, 1931–1936', *Diplomatic History,* 17 (1993), 171–200.

Esherick, Joseph W., *The Origins of the Boxer Uprising* (Berkeley CA: University of California Press, 1987).

Esherick, Joseph W., 'Essence of Parliament', *Punch Magazine* (28 May and 2 July 1898).

Esthus, R.A., *Double Eagle and Rising Sun: The Russians and Japanese at Portsmouth in 1905* (Durham NC: Duke University Press, 1988).

Esthus, R.A., *Explanatory Statement on the Navy Estimates 1956–1957,* Cmnd. 9697. (London: HMSO, 1956).

Farrell, Brian and Hunter, Sandy (eds), *Sixty Years On: The Fall of Singapore Revisited* (Singapore: Eastern Universities Press, 2002).

Ferris, John R., 'Treasury Control, the Ten Year Rule and British Service Policies, 1919–1924', *Historical Journal,* 30 (1987), 859–83.

Ferris, John R., *Men, Money and Diplomacy: The Evolution of British Strategic Policy, 1919–1926* (Ithaca NY: Cornell University Press, 1989).

Ferris, John R., '"The Greatest Power on Earth": Great Britain in the 1920s', *International History Review,* 13 (1991), 726–50.

Field, James, *A History of UN Naval Operations: Korea* (Washington DC: GPO Naval Historical Center, 1982).

Finney, Patrick (ed.), *The Origins of the Second World War* (London: St Martin's, 1997).

Fisher, John, *Curzon and British Imperialism in the Middle East, 1916–19* (London: Frank Cass, 1999).

Fisher, John, 'Five Year Defence Programme', *The Navy* (June 1948), 41–66.

Fleming, Peter, *The Siege at Peking* (London: Hart Davis, 1959).

SELECT BIBLIOGRAPHY

Fletcher, Roger, 'An English Advocate in Germany: Eduard Bernstein's Analysis of Anglo-German Relations, 1900–1914', *Canadian Journal of History*, 13 (1978), 209–35.

Frame, T., Goldrick, J. and Jones, P. (eds), *Reflections on the Royal Australian Navy* (Kenthurst: Kangaroo Press, 1991).

French, David, 'Perfidious Albion Faces the Powers', *Canadian Journal of History*, 28 (1993), 177–88.

Friedman, Norman, *The Post War Naval Revolution* (London: Conway Maritime Press, 1986).

Gill, G. Hermon, 'Royal Australian Navy 1942–1945', in *Australia in the War of 1939–1945* (Melbourne: Collins in association with the Australian War Memorial, 1985).

Goldman, Emily O., *Sunken Treaties: Naval Arms Control between the Wars* (University Park PA: Pennsylvania State University Press, 1994).

Goldrick, J., 'Selections from the Memoirs and Correspondence of Captain James Bernard Foley, CBE, RAN (1896–1974)', in *The Naval Miscellany*, Vol. 5 (London: George Allen & Unwin for the Naval Records Society, 1984).

Goldrick, J., 'The Role of the Royal Australian Navy in Australian Defence Policy, 1945–85', unpublished paper, Naval History Directorate, Canberra.

Goldstein, Erik and Maurer, John (eds), 'Special Issue on the Washington Conference, 1921–22: Naval Rivalry, East Asian Stability and the Road to Pearl Harbor', *Diplomacy & Statecraft*, 4 (1993).

Goldstein, Erik and Maurer, John (eds), *The Washington Conference, 1921–22: Naval Rivalry, East Asian Stability and the Road to Pearl Harbor* (London: Frank Cass, 1994).

Gooch, J., *The Plans of War: The General Staff and British Military Strategy* (London: Routledge & Kegan Paul, 1974).

Gooch, J., *The Prospect of War: Studies in British Defence Policy, 1847–1942* (London: Frank Cass, 1981).

Gooch, J. and Temperley, H.W.V. (ed.), *British Documents on the Origins of the War, 1898–1914* (London: HMSO, 1926–38).

Gray, Colin S., *The Leverage of Sea Power* (New York: Free Press, 1992).

Grove, E., 'Australian and British Naval Policy in the Korean War Era', *Admiralty Maritime Intelligence Review* (November, 1986), 3–10.

Grove, E., *Vanguard to Trident: British Naval Policy Since World War II* (London: Bodley Head, 1987).

Hack, K., *Defence and Decolonisation in Southeast Asia: Britain, Malaya and Singapore 1941–68* (Richmond: Curzon, 2001).

Hagan, Kenneth J., *This People's Navy* (New York: Collier Macmillan, 1991).

Haggie, Paul, *Britannia at Bay: The Defence of Britain's Far Eastern Empire, 1931–1941* (Oxford: Clarendon, 1981).

Hallett, Rear Admiral C.C. Hughes, 'Naval Logistics in a Future War', *Journal of the Royal United Services Institute*, 95 (1950), 238.

Hallett, H.S., 'The Partition of China', *The Nineteenth Century*, 43 (January 1898), 154–64.

Halsey, W.F., Fleet Admiral and Bryan, J., *Admiral Halsey's Story* (New York: Whittlesey House, 1947).

Hamil, Ian, 'Winston Churchill and the Singapore Naval Base, 1924–1929', *Journal of Southeast Asian Studies*, 11 (1980), 277–86.

Hattendorf, B. and Jordan, Robert S. (eds), *Maritime Strategy and the Balance of Power* (New York: St Martin's, 1989).

Henrikson, A.K., 'The Geographical "Mental Maps" of American Foreign Policy Makers', *International Political Science Review*, 1 (1980), 496–530.

273

SELECT BIBLIOGRAPHY

Herwig, Holger H., *'Luxury' Fleet: The Imperial German Navy 1888–1918* (London: Allen & Unwin, 1980).

Hildebrant, Vice-Admiral, 'Capture of the Taku Forts by the Allied Forces, 17 June, 1900', 'Ward Room', trans. *United Service Magazine*, XXVIII (October 1903–March 1904), 11–17.

Hinsley, F.H. (ed.), *British Foreign Policy under Sir Edward Grey* (Cambridge: Cambridge University Press, 1977).

Hooker, Nancy H., *Moffat, Jay Pierrepont, 1896–1943* (Cambridge MA: Harvard University Press, 1956).

Hooker, Nancy H. *The History of The Times* (London: The Times, 1947).

Horner, D., *Defence Supremo: Sir Frederick Shedden and the Making of Australian Defence Policy* (Sydney: Allen & Unwin, 2000).

Howarth, O.J.R. and Herbertson, A.J. (eds), *The Oxford Survey of the British Empire, Vol. II, Asia* (Oxford: Clarendon, 1914).

Hyam, R., *Elgin and Churchill at the Colonial Office, 1905–1908* (London: Macmillan, 1968).

Johnston, R.F., *Lion and Dragon in Northern China* (London: John Murray, 1910).

Johnston, R.F., *Twilight in the Forbidden City* (London: Gollancz, 1934).

Jones, Matthew, *Conflict and Confrontation in South East Asia 1961–1965* (Cambridge: Cambridge University Press, 2002).

Kennedy, Greg (ed.), *The Merchant Marine in International Affairs, 1850–1950* (London: Frank Cass, 2000).

Kennedy, Greg, *Anglo-American Strategic Relations and the Far East, 1933–1939* (London: Frank Cass, 2002).

Kennedy, Greg, 'Neville Chamberlain and Strategic Relations with the US during his Chancellorship', *Diplomacy and Statecraft*, 13 (2002), 95–120.

Kennedy, Greg, 'Becoming Dependent on the Kindness of Strangers: Britain's Strategic Foreign Policy, Naval Arms Limitation and the Soviet Factor, 1935–1937', *War in History*, 11, 1 (2004), 79–105.

Kennedy, Gregory C. and Neilson, Keith (eds), *Incidents and International Relations: People, Power, and Personalities* (Westport CT: Praeger, 2002).

Kennedy, Paul M., *The Realities Behind Diplomacy: Background Influences on British External Policy, 1865–1980* (London: Allen & Unwin, 1981).

Kennedy, Paul, *The Rise and Fall of British Naval Mastery* (London: Macmillan, 1983).

Kennedy, Paul, *The Rise and Fall of the Great Powers: Economic Change and Military Conflict from 1500–2000* (New York: Random House, 1987).

Keyes, Roger, *Adventures Ashore & Afloat* (London: George Harrap, 1939).

Kimball, Warren F., *Forged in War: Roosevelt, Churchill, and the Second World War* (New York: W. Morrow, 1996).

King, Admiral E. and Whitehall, W., *Fleet Admiral King: A Naval Record* (London: Eyre & Spottiswoode, 1953).

King-Hall, L. (ed.), *Sea Saga: Being the Naval Diaries of Four Generations of the King-Hall Family* (London: Victor Gollancz, 1935).

Kiyoshi, Inoue, *Nihon teikokushugi no keisei* (Tokyo: Iwanami Shoten, 1972).

Kleinfeld, Gerald R., 'Nazis and Germans in China 1933–37: The Consulate and the German Community in Tsingtao', *Canadian Journal of History*, 15 (1980), 229–47.

Kubicek, R.V., *The Administration of Imperialism: Joseph Chamberlain at the Colonial Office* (Durham NC: Duke University Press, 1969).

Kunz, D., *The Battle for Britain's Gold Standard in 1931* (London: Croom Helm, 1987).

SELECT BIBLIOGRAPHY

Kunz, D., 'When Money Counts and Doesn't: Economic Power and Diplomatic Objectives', *Diplomatic History*, 18 (1994), 451–62.

Kuramatsu, Tadashi, 'The Geneva Naval Conference of 1927: The British Preparation for the Conference, December 1926 to June 1927', *Journal of Strategic Studies*, 19 (1996), 104–21.

Ladd, James D., *SBS: The Invisible Raiders* (London: Arms and Armour Press, 1983).

Ladd, James D., *By Land, By Sea* (London: HarperCollins, 1998).

Landsdown, John, *A History of UN Naval Operations: Korea* (Worcester: Square One Publications, 1992).

Lashmar, Paul and Oliver, James, *Britain's Secret Propaganda War 1948–1977* (Stroud: Sutton, 1998).

Lawson, Sir W. and Gould, F.C., *Cartoons in Rhyme and Line* (London: T. Fisher Unwin, 1905).

Lee, D., 'The National Security Planning and Defence Preparations of the Menzies Government, 1950–1953', *War & Society* (October 1992), 119–38.

Lee, D., 'Australia and Allied Strategy in the Far East, 1952–1957', *Journal of Strategic Studies* (December 1993).

Lepsius, J., Mendelssohn-Bartholdy, Albrecht and Thimme, Friedrich (eds), *Die grosse Politik der europäischen Kabinette, 1871–1914* (Berlin: Deutsche Verlagsanstalt, 1922–7).

Lethbridge, H.J., 'Sir James Haldane Stewart Lockhart: Colonial Servant and Scholar', *Journal of the Hong Kong Branch of the Royal Asiatic Society*, 12 (1972), 68–9.

Leutze, J.R., *Bargaining for Supremacy: Anglo-American Naval Relations, 1937–1941* (Chapel Hill NC: University of North Carolina Press, 1977).

Lloyd, Trevor, 'Ramsay MacDonald: Socialist or Gentleman?', *Canadian Journal of History*, 15 (1980), 67–82.

Louis, William Roger, *British Strategy in the Far East, 1919–1939* (Oxford: Clarendon, 1971).

Lowe, Peter, 'The British Empire and the Anglo-Japanese Alliance 1911–1915', *History*, 54 (1969), 212–25.

Lowe, Peter, *Great Britain and Japan 1911–1915: a Study of British Far Eastern Policy* (London: Macmillan, 1969).

Luttwak, Edward, *The Political Uses of Seapower* (Baltimore MD: Johns Hopkins University Press, 1974).

Lyttelton, E., *Alfred Lyttelton: An Account of His Life* (London: Longmans, 1917).

MacGregor, David, 'Former Naval Cheapskate: Chancellor of the Exchequer Winston Churchill and the Royal Navy, 1924–1929', *Armed Forces and Society*, 19 (1993), 319–34.

Mackay, Ruddock F., *Fisher of Kilverstone* (Oxford: Clarendon, 1973).

Mackie, J.A.C., *Konfrontasi: The Indonesia–Malaya Dispute 1963–1966* (Oxford: Oxford University Press, 1974).

MacMurray, J.V.A. (ed.), *Treaties and Agreements with and Concerning China, 1894–1919* (New York: Oxford University Press, 1921).

Maiolo, Joseph A., *The Royal Navy and Nazi Germany, 1933–39: A Study in Appeasement and the Origins of the Second World War* (London: Macmillan, 1998).

Makoto, Ikuta, *Nihon rikugun shi* (Tokyo: Kyōikusha, 1980).

Marder, Arthur J., *Old Friends, New Enemies: The Royal Navy and the Imperial Japanese Navy* (Oxford: Oxford University Press, 1981).

Marks, Sally, 'Ménage à Trois: The Negotiations for an Anglo-French-Belgian Alliance in 1922', *International History Review*, 4 (1982), 524–52.

SELECT BIBLIOGRAPHY

Marsh, P.T., *Joseph Chamberlain: Entrepreneur in Politics* (New Haven CT: Yale University Press, 1994).

Martel, Gordon, 'The Meaning of Power: Rethinking the Decline and Fall of Great Britain', *International History Review*, 13 (1991), 662–94.

Masato, Miyachi, *Kokusei seijika no kindai Nihon* (Tokyo: Yamakawa Shuppankai, 1995).

Mayhew, C., *Britain's Role Tomorrow* (London: Hutchinson, 1967).

McDermott, John, 'Sir Francis Oppenheimer: "Stranger Within" the Foreign Office', *History*, 66 (1981), 199–207.

McKale, Donald M., 'Weltpolitik versus Imperium Britannica: Anglo-German Rivalry in Egypt, 1904–14', *Canadian Journal of History*, 12 (1987), 193–207.

McKercher, B.J.C., 'A Sane and Sensible Diplomacy: Austen Chamberlain, Japan and the Naval Balance of Power in the Pacific Ocean, 1924–1929', *Canadian Journal of History*, 21 (1986), 187–213.

McKercher, B.J.C., '"Our Most Dangerous Enemy": Great Britain Pre-eminent in the 1930s', *International History Review*, 13 (1991), 751–83.

McKercher, B.J.C. (ed.), *Arms Limitation and Disarmament: Restraints on War, 1899–1939* (Westport CT: Praeger, 1992).

McKercher, B.J.C., 'From Enmity to Cooperation: The Second Baldwin Government and the Improvement of Anglo-American Relations, November 1928–June 1929', *Albion*, 24 (1992), 65–88.

McKercher, B.J.C., 'No Eternal Friends or Enemies: British Defence Policy and the Problem of the United States, 1919–1939', *Canadian Journal of History*, 28 (1993), 257–94.

McKercher, B.J.C., *Transition of Power: Britain's Loss of Global Pre-eminence to the United States, 1930–1945* (Cambridge: Cambridge University Press, 1999).

McKercher, B.J.C. and Moss, David J. (eds), *Shadow and Substance in British Foreign Policy, 1895–1939: Memorial Essays Honouring C.J. Lowe* (Edmonton: University of Alberta Press, 1984).

Middleton, R., *Towards a Managed Economy: Keynes, the Treasury and the Fiscal Debate of the 1930s* (London: Middleton, 1985).

Millar, T.B., *Australia's Defence* (Carlton: Melbourne University Press, 1969).

Millar, T.B., *Australia in Peace and War: External Relations Since 1788* (Botany NSW: Australian National University Press, 1991).

Mills, William C., 'The Chamberlain-Grandi Conversations of July–August 1937 and the Appeasement of Italy', *International History Review*, 19 (1997), 594–619.

Miner, N.J., 'Tale of Two Walled Cities: Kowloon and Weihaiwei', *Hong Kong Law Journal*, 12 (1982), 179–202.

Ministère des Affaires Étrangères (ed.), *Documents diplomatiques français, 1871–1914* (Paris: Imprimerie Nationale, 1930–46).

Modelski, G. (ed.), *SEATO: Six Studies* (Melbourne: F.W. Cheshire, 1962).

Moretz, Joseph, *The Royal Navy and the Capital Ship in the Interwar Period: An Operational Perspective* (London: Frank Cass, 2002).

Morison, S.E., *History of the USN in WWII, Vol. XIII: The Liberation of the Philippines* (Oxford: Oxford University Press, 1959).

Morton, P., *Fire Across the Desert: Woomera and the Anglo-Australian Joint Project 1946–1980* (Canberra: Australian Government Publishing Service, 1989).

Mouré, Kenneth, 'The Limits to Central Bank Co-operation, 1916–36', *Contemporary European History*, 3 (1992), 259–79.

SELECT BIBLIOGRAPHY

Murfett, Malcolm, *Fool-Proof Relations: The Search for Anglo-American Naval Co-operation during the Chamberlain Years, 1937–1940* (Singapore: Singapore University Press, 1984).

Murfett, M.H., 'Living in the Past: A Critical Re-examination of the Singapore Naval Strategy, 1918–1941', *War & Society*, 11 (1993), 73–103.

Murfett, M.H., *In Jeopardy: The Royal Navy and British Far Eastern Defence Policy 1945–1951* (Kuala Lumpur: Oxford University Press, 1995).

Murfett, Malcolm H. (ed.), *The First Sea Lords: From Fisher to Mountbatten* (Westport CT: Praeger, 1995).

Murfett, Malcolm H., Miksic, John N., Farrell, Brian P., Shun, Chiang Ming (eds), *Between Two Oceans: A Military History of Singapore from First Settlement to Final British Withdrawal* (Oxford: Oxford University Press, 1999).

Myakishev, Lieut., 'The Capture of the Taku Forts', *Journal of the Royal United Service Institution*, XLV (January to June 1901), 730–44.

Myakishev, Lieut., 'The Neglected Estate of Wei-hai-Wei', *Fortnightly Review*, 75 (March 1904).

Neilson, Keith, ' "Greatly Exaggerated": The Myth of the Decline of Great Britain before 1914', *International History Review*, 13 (1991), 695–725.

Neilson, Keith, ' "Pursued by a Bear": British Estimates of Soviet Military Strength and Anglo-Soviet Relations, 1922–1939', *Canadian Journal of History*, 28 (1993), 190–207.

Neilson, Keith, *Britain and the Last Tsar: British Policy and Russia, 1894–1917* (Oxford: Clarendon, 1995).

Neilson, Keith, 'The Defence Requirements Sub-Committee, British Strategic Foreign Policy, Neville Chamberlain and the Path to Appeasement', *English Historical Review*, 158 (June 2003), 651–84.

Neilson, Keith, 'Defence and Diplomacy: The British Foreign Office and Singapore, 1939–40', *Twentieth Century British History*, 14, 2 (2003), 138–64.

Neilson, Keith and Kennedy, Greg (eds), *Far Flung Lines: Studies in Imperial Defence in Honour of Donald Mackenzie Schurman* (London: Frank Cass, 1997).

Nicholas, H.G. (ed.), *Washington Despatches: Weekly Political Reports From the British Embassy* (Chicago IL: University of Chicago Press, 1981).

Nichols, J., 'Roosevelt's Monetary Diplomacy in 1933', *American Historical Review*, 56 (1988), 295–317.

Nichols, J., 'Nimitz Visits British Pacific Fleet', *USNIP*, 71 (July 1945), 10–12.

Nish, Ian H., *The Anglo-Japanese Alliance: The Diplomacy of Two Island Empires 1894–1907* (London: Athlone, 1966).

Nish, Ian H., 'The Royal Navy and the Taking of Weihaiwei, 1898–1905', *Mariner's Mirror*, 54 (1968), 13–24.

Nish, Ian, *Alliance in Decline: A Study in Anglo-Japanese Relations 1908–23* (London: Athlone, 1972).

Nish, Ian (ed.), *Britain and Japan: Biographical Portraits* (Folkstone: Japan Library, 1994).

Nish, Ian and Kibata, Yoichi (eds), *The History of Anglo-Japanese Relations: Volume 1: The Political-Diplomatic Dimension, 1600–1930* (Basingstoke: Macmillan, 2000).

O'Brien, Phillips Payson, *British and American Naval Power: Politics and Policy, 1900–1936* (Westport CT: Praeger, 1998).

O'Brien, Phillips Payson (ed.), *Technology and Naval Combat in the Twentieth Century and Beyond* (London: Frank Cass, 2001).

Offer, A., 'The British Empire, 1870–1914: A Waste of Money?', *Economic History Review*, 46 (1993), 243–6.

SELECT BIBLIOGRAPHY

O'Halpin, Eunan, *Head of the Civil Service: A Study of Sir Warren Fisher* (London: Routledge, 1989).

d'Ombrain, N., *War Machinery and High Policy: Defence Administration in Peacetime Policy, 1902–1914* (Oxford: Oxford University Press, 1973).

O'Neill, R., *Strategy and Diplomacy, Australia in the Korean War 1950–53,* Vol. I (Canberra: Australian War Memorial and Australian Government Publishing Service, 1981).

Otte, T.G., 'Great Britain, Germany, and the Far Eastern Crisis of 1897–8' *English Historical Review*, 110 (November 1995), 1157–79.

Otte, T.G., 'A Question of Leadership: Lord Salisbury, the Unionist Cabinet and Foreign Policy Making, 1895–1900', *Contemporary British History*, 14 (Winter 2000), 1–26.

Otte, T.G. (ed.), *The Makers of British Foreign Policy: From Pitt to Thatcher* (Basingstoke: Palgrave, 2002).

Otte, T.G., 'Neville Chamberlain and Strategic Relationships with the United States During his Chancellorship', *Diplomacy & Statecraft*, 13 (2002).

Otte, T.G., '"Not Proficient in Table-Thumping": Sir Ernest Satow at Peking, 1900–1906', *Diplomacy & Statecraft*, 13 (June 2002), 161–200.

Otte, T.G., *Global Transformation: Britain, the Great Powers and the China Question, 1894–1905*, forthcoming.

Otte, T.G., '"Avenge England's Dishonour": Parliament, Byelections, and Foreign Policy in 1898', forthcoming.

Otte, T.G. and Pagedas, Constantine A. (eds), *Personalities, War and Diplomacy: Essays in International History* (London: Frank Cass, 1997).

Ovendale, Ritchie, *'Appeasement' and the English Speaking World: Britain, the United States, the Dominions, and the Policy of Appeasement, 1937–1939* (Cardiff: University of Wales Press, 1975).

Owen, R. and Sutcliffe, B. (eds), *Studies in the Theory of Imperialism* (London: Longman, 1972).

Oye, K.A., 'The Sterling–Dollar–Franc Triangle: Monetary Diplomacy, 1929–1937', *World Politics*, 38 (1985), 173–99.

Parker, R.A.C., *Chamberlain and Appeasement: British Policy and the Coming of the Second World War* (New York: St Martin's, 1993).

Patterson, A. Temple, 'A Midshipman in the Boxer Rebellion', *The Mariner's Mirror*, 63 (1977).

Peden, George C., *British Rearmament and the Treasury, 1932–1939* (Edinburgh: Scottish Academic Press, 1979).

Peden, George C., 'The Burden of Imperial Defence and the Continental Commitment Reconsidered', *Historical Journal*, 27 (1984), 32–50.

Peden, George, *The Treasury and British Public Policy 1906–1959* (Oxford: Oxford University Press, 2000).

Pelkovits, N.A., *Old China Hands and the Foreign Office* (New York: Macmillan, 1948).

Pelz, Stephen, *Race to Pearl Harbor: the Failure of the Second London Naval Conference and the Onset of World War II* (Cambridge MA: Harvard University Press, 1974).

Perras, Galen Roger, '"Our Position in the Far East would be Stronger without this Unsatisfactory Commitment": Britain and the Reinforcement of Hong Kong, 1941', *Canadian Journal of History*, 30 (1995), 231–59.

Peter, Gyorgy, 'Central Bank Diplomacy: Monagu Norman and Central Europe's Monetary Reconstruction after World War I', *Contemporary European History*, 3 (1992), 233–58.

SELECT BIBLIOGRAPHY

Piggott, F.S.G., *Broken Thread: An Autobiography* (Aldershot: Gale & Polden, 1950).

Polmar, N., *Aircraft Carrier: A Graphic History of Carrier Aviation and its Influence on World Events* (London: Macdonald, 1969).

Post, Gaines Jr, *Dilemmas of Appeasement: British Deterrence and Defence, 1934–1937* (Ithaca NY: Cornell University Press, 1993).

Potter, E.B., *Nimitz* (Annapolis MD: Naval Institute Press, 1976).

Poulgrain, Gregg, *The Genesis of Konfrontasi* (London: C. Hurst, 1998).

Pratt, Lawrence, 'The Anglo-American Naval Conversations in the Far East', *International Affairs*, 47 (1971), 745–63.

Prince, Stephen, 'The Contribution of the Royal Navy to the United Nations Forces during the Korean War', *Journal of Strategic Studies*, 17 (1994), 94–120.

Ragsdale, Hugh, 'Soviet Military Preparations and Policy in the Munich Crisis: New Evidence', *Jahrbücher für Geschichte Osteuropas*, 47 (1999), 210–26.

Robbins, K., 'Sir Edward Grey and the Empire', *Journal of Imperial and Commonwealth History*, 1 (1973), 218–19.

Roberts, G., 'A Soviet Bid for Coexistence with Nazi Germany, 1935–1937: The Kandelaki Affair', *International History Review*, 16 (1994), 466–90.

Rock, W.R., *British Appeasement in the 1930s* (London: Edward Arnold, 1977).

Rodger, N.A.M., *Naval Power in the Twentieth Century* (Basingstoke: Macmillan, 1996).

Roi, Michael, *Alternative to Appeasement: Sir Robert Vansittart and Alliance Diplomacy, 1934–1937* (Westport CT: Praeger, 1997).

Roskill, Stephen, *Naval Policy between the Wars* (London: Collins, 1968–76).

Roskill, S.W., *The War at Sea, 1939–45*, Vol. III (London: HMSO, 1976).

Rothwell, V.H., *British War Aims and Peace Diplomacy 1914–1918* (Oxford: Clarendon, 1971).

Rothwell, V.H., 'The Mission of Sir Fredrick Leith-Ross to the Far East, 1935–1936', *Historical Journal*, 18 (1975), 147–69.

Rothwell, V.H., *Anthony Eden: A Political Biography, 1931–57* (Manchester: Manchester University Press, 1992).

Saburō, Toyama, *Nihon Kaigun shi* (Tokyo: Kyōikusha, 1980).

Scammel, Claire M., 'The Royal Navy and the Strategic Origins of the Anglo-German Naval Agreement of 1935', *Journal of Strategic Studies*, 20 (1997), 92–118.

Schlesinger, A.M., *The Coming of the New Deal* (Boston: Houghton Griffin, 1959).

Shay, R., *British Rearmament in the Thirties: Politics and Profits* (Princeton NJ: Princeton University Press, 1977).

Siegel, Jennifer, *Endgame: Britain, Russia and the Final Struggle for Central Asia* (London and New York: I.B. Tauris, 2002).

Sigwart, Capt. E.E., *Royal Fleet Auxiliary* (London: Adlard Coles, 1969).

Simpson, M. (ed.), *The Somerville Papers: Selections from the Private and Official Correspondence of Admiral of the Fleet Sir James Somerville*, Publications of the Navy Records Society, Vol. 134 (Aldershot: Scholar Press, 1995).

Smith, E.D., *Counter-Insurgency Operations 1: Malaya and Borneo* (Shepperton: Ian Allen, 1985).

Speller, Ian, *The Role of Amphibious Warfare in British Defence Policy, 1945–1956* (Basingstoke: Palgrave, 2001).

Sprout, H. and Sprout, M., *Toward a New Order of Sea Power: American Naval Policy and the World Scene, 1918–1922* (New York: Greenwood, repr. 1976).

Sprout, H. and Sprout, M., *Statement on Defence 1962: The Next Five Years, Cmnd 1639* (London: HMSO, 1962).

SELECT BIBLIOGRAPHY

Sprout, H. and Sprout, M., *Statement on the Defence Estimates 1966. Part 1. The Defence Review,* Cmnd. 2901 (London: HMSO, 1966).

Sprout, H. and Sprout, M., *Statement on the Defence Estimates 1968.* Cmnd. 3540 (London: HMSO, 1968).

Sprout, H. and Sprout, M., *Statement on the Defence Estimates, 1975,* Cmnd. 5976 (London: HMSO, 1975).

Stephens, A., *Power Plus Attitude: Ideas, Strategy and Doctrine in the Royal Australian Air Force 1921–1991* (Canberra: Australian Government Publishing Service, 1992).

Stephens, A., *Going Solo: The Royal Australian Air Force 1946–1971* (Canberra: Australian Government Publishing Service, 1995).

Stephens, A., 'The Royal Australian Air Force', in *the Australian Centenary History of Defence,* Vol. II (Melbourne: Oxford University Press, 2001).

Stephens, Lt-Col. T., 'A Joint Operation in Tanganyika' *RUSI Journal,* 637 (February 1965), 17–28.

Stevens, D. (ed.), *The Royal Australian Navy in World War II* (Sydney: Allen & Unwin, 1996).

Stevens, D. (ed.), *In Search of a Maritime Strategy: The Maritime Element in Australian Defence Planning since 1901,* Canberra Papers on Strategy and Defence, No. 119 (Canberra: Strategic and Defence Studies Centre, 1997).

Stevens, D. (ed.), *Maritime Power in the 20th Century: the Australian Experience* (Sydney: Allen & Unwin, 1998).

Stevens, D. and Reeve, J. (eds), *Southern Trident: Strategy, History and Rise of Australian Naval Power* (Sydney: Allen & Unwin, 2001).

Subritzky, John, *Confronting Sukarno: British, American, Australian and New Zealand Diplomacy in the Malaysian–Indonesian Confrontation, 1961–65* (London: Macmillan, 2000).

Sukarno, Sukarno, *Sukarno: An Autobiography* (New York: Bobbs-Merrill, 1965).

Sun, E.Z., 'The Lease of Wei-hai-Wei', *Pacific Historical Review,* 19 (1950), 277–83.

Sun, E.Z., *Supplementary Statement on Defence Policy 1967,* Cmnd. 3357 (London: HMSO, 1967).

Sun, E.Z., *Supplementary Statement on Defence Policy 1968,* Cmnd. 3701 (London: HMSO, 1968).

Sydenham, Lord, *My Working Life* (London: John Murray, 1927).

Tarling, Nicholas, *Britain, Southeast Asia and the Onset of the Pacific War* (Cambridge: Cambridge University Press, 1996).

Taylor, A.J.P. (ed.), *Lloyd George: Twelve Essays* (London: Hamish Hamilton, 1971).

Templewood, Samuel John Gurney Hoare, 1st Viscount, 1880–1959, *Nine Troubled Years* (London: Collins, 1954).

Thompson, J., *The Royal Marines: From Sea Soldiers to a Special Force* (London: Sidgwick & Jackson, 2000).

Thorne, Christopher, *The Limits of Foreign Policy. The West, the League and the Far Eastern Crisis of 1931–33* (New York: Putnam, 1973).

Till, G. (ed.), *Seapower at the Millennium* (Stroud: Sutton, 2001).

Tomes, Jason, *Balfour and Foreign Policy: The International Thought of a Conservative Statesman* (Cambridge: Cambridge University Press, 1997).

Toshiaki, Ōkubo and Inone Mitsusada (eds), *Nihon rekisshi taike 4: kindai 1* (Tokyo: Yamakawa Shuppansha, 1987).

Tracy, Nicholas (ed.), *The Collective Naval Defence of the Empire, 1900–1940* (Aldershot: Ashgate, for Navy Records Society, 1997).

SELECT BIBLIOGRAPHY

Trask, David F., 'Woodrow Wilson and International Statecraft: A Modern Assessment', *Naval War College Review*, 36 (1983), 57–68.

Trotter, Ann, *Britain and East Asia, 1933–1939* (Cambridge: Cambridge University Press, 1975).

Vian, Sir Philip, Admiral of the Fleet, *Action This Day* (London: Frederick Muller, 1960).

Waddington, G.T., 'Hassgegner: German Views of Great Britain in the Later 1930s', *Historical Association*, 81 (1996), 22–39.

Watt, A., *Australian Defence Policy 1951–1963: Major International Aspects* (Canberra: Department of International Relations, Australian National University, 1964).

Watt, D.C., (ed.), *Personalities and Policies: Studies in the Formulation of British Foreign Policy in the Twentieth Century* (Westport CT: Greenwood, 1965).

Watt, D.C., *What About the People? Abstractions and Reality in History and the Social Sciences* (London: London School of Economics and Political Science, 1983).

Watt, D.C., 'Wei-hai-wei: Its Value as a Naval Station', *Blackwood's Magazine*, 165 (June 1899), 1069–77.

Wesley-Smith, P., *Unequal Treaty, 1898–1997: China, Great Britain and Hong Kong's New Territories* (Hong Kong: Oxford University Press, 1980).

Wettern, D., *The Decline of British Seapower* (London: Jane's, 1982).

Wheeler, Capt. C.J., USN, 'We Had the British Where We Needed Them', *United States Naval Institute Proceedings*, 72 (12 December 1946), 1584.

Wildenberg, Thomas, *Gray Steel and Black Oil: Fast Tankers and Replenishment at Sea in the U.S. Navy 1912–1992* (Annapolis MD: Naval Institute Press, 1996).

Williamson, P., *National Crisis and National Government: British Politics, the Economy and Empire, 1926–1932* (Cambridge: Cambridge University Press, 1992).

Willmott, H.P., *Empires in the Balance: Japanese and Allied Pacific Strategies to April 1942* (Annapolis MD: Naval Institute Press, 1982).

Willmott, H.P., 'Just Being There', Paper presented to the Institute of Historical Research for the Julian Corbett Prize in Modern Naval History, 1986.

Willmott, H.P., *Grave of a Dozen Schemes* (Annapolis MD: Air Life Publishing, 1996).

Wilson, H.W., 'Front-Bench Invertebrates', *National Review*, 31 (April 1898), 300–1.

Winton, J., *The Forgotten Fleet* (Warhurst: Douglas-Boyd Books, reprint 1991).

Wright, A., 'Australian Carrier Decisions: the Acquisition of HMA Ships, *Albatross, Sydney* and *Melbourne*', *Papers in Australian Maritime Affairs*, No. 4 (Canberra: Maritime Studies Program, 1998).

Wright, Arnold (ed.), *Twentieth Century Impressions of British Malaya: its History, People, Commerce, Industries and Resources* (London: Lloyd's Greater Publishing Co., 1908).

Wyatt, A., *The Evolution of Australian Foreign Policy 1938–1965* (London: Cambridge University Press, 1968).

Yōichi, Hirama, *Nichi-Ei domei: domei no sentaku to seisui* (Tokyo: PHP Shinsho, 2000).

Yorke, R.S., 'Wei Hai Wei, Our Latest Leasehold Possession', *Fortnightly Review*, 64 (1898), 4–6.

Young, Leonard K., *British Policy in China 1895–1902* (Oxford: Clarendon, 1970).

Young, Leonard K., 'Zakhrat Germanie Kiao-chao v 1897 g.', *Krasni Arkhiv*, 87 (1928).

INDEX

Abyssinia 97, 105
Acland, Francis Dyke 11
Aden 184, 188–9, 193, 203, 216, 246, 251
admiralty 10, 13–16, 23, 25, 42,
    53, 63, 65, 67, 73–9, 81–2, 91,
    95–108, 121, 124, 128, 129, 140,
    146, 148, 155, 157, 184–8, 191, 193,
    195, 223
Afghanistan 76, 256, 263, 266
Air Ministry 122, 183–6
Air Staff 120, 122
Aldabra 184
Alexander, A.V. 107
Alston, Beilby 68
Amoy Incident 51
Amphibious Warfare Squadron 180
Andrewes, Rear Admiral 162, 165
Anglo-Chinese Convention
    of 1907 63
Anglo-Japanese Alliance 36, 38, 50,
    52–6, 62–76, 93
Anglo-Japanese Treaty 68
ANSUK 239, 248
ANZAM 229–32
ANZUS Treaty 232, 234
Aoki, Viscount 47
Arab–Israeli Wars 245
Ardagh, Colonel Sir John 11,
    12, 15
Aritomo, Yamagata 47
Armilla patrol 256–7
Armistice 163
Ashton-Gwatkin, Frank 66
ASIS 162, 167, 170
Atago 44, 46
Australia 70, 73, 104, 129, 138, 140,
    143, 162, 181, 184, 200, 202, 221–40,
    245, 251

Bahrain 182
Balfour, Arthur 9, 10, 17, 22, 24, 26–7,
    70–2, 80
Balikpapan 205–6
Bangkok 233
Barstow, Sir George 70, 73
Battenberg, Lord Louis of 56
Bayley, Captain 46, 53
Beach, Sir Michael Hicks 7
Beatty, Lord David 48, 53–4, 74–5, 77
Begg, Admiral Varyl 191
Beira Patrol 188
Bentinck, C.H. 67
Berlin 9
Bertie, Francis 6, 10
Birkenhead, Lord 76
Blair, Tony 261
Borneo 73, 136, 188–9, 201, 206,
    208–9, 216
Borneo Confrontation 244, 246
Boxer Protocol 38
Boxer Uprising 15, 18, 35–56
Bridge, Admiral Sir Cyprian 16, 53, 56
Bridgeman, William 77
Brind, Admiral Sir Patrick 162
British and American Tobacco
    Company 21
British Legation 40–3
British North Borneo 200–2
British Pacific Fleet 128–9, 133–49, 156,
    169, 172, 223
Brodrick, St John 15, 16
Brooke-Popham, Sir Robert 125
Bruce, Rear-Admiral James 46–7
Brunei 109, 182, 200, 205–6, 214, 245
Brussels Conference 104
Buller, Admiral, Sir Alexander 9
Burma 134

INDEX

Cabinet Defence Committee   180
Callaghan, Captain George A.   50, 53
Campbell, Francis   22
Canada   77, 253
Carles, Consul   41, 43
Ceylon   178
Chamberlain, Austin   68, 73–4
Chamberlain, Joseph   7–10
Chamberlain, Neville   81, 92–8, 101,
    104–5, 107
Chatfield, Admiral Sir A. Ernle
    99–101, 103
Cheefo   8–10, 17, 21
Chiefs of Staff   75, 98–9, 130–1, 179,
    183, 204
Chifley, Joseph   223–5, 227–8
China   6–8, 11, 13–27, 36–7, 41, 44–5,
    49–56, 63, 69, 74, 80, 98, 102–4, 132,
    134, 163, 249, 258
China Expeditionary Force   15
China Question   5
China Squadron   15, 35–56, 107
China Station   23–5
Chinese Board of Foreign Affairs   8, 20
Chinese-Russian Treaty of
    Friendship   229
Chinnampo   164
chunking   52
Churchill, Winston   26, 68–9, 71, 74–8,
    107, 124, 130–6, 143, 149, 222–3
Chusan islands   13, 15, 17, 42
Clandestine Communist
    Organization   202, 207
Clarke, Colonel G.S.   11, 23–5
Clayton, Rear Admiral Richard   250
Clifford, Rear Admiral   168
Cold War   258
Collins   229–33
Colonial Defence Committee   11, 13–14
Colonial Office   16–19, 21–5, 66
Committee of Imperial Defence   11, 21,
    23–4, 63, 68, 70–8, 91, 93–9
Communism 2002   202
confrontation   199–217, 249
Coolidge Conference   76, 78
Cox, H. Bertram   20
Cradock, Christopher   48, 53–4
Craigie, Sir Robert   97, 105
Crowe, Sir Eyre   68, 74, 247
Cunningham, Admiral John   130–1, 137,
    139–40, 147, 225, 227
Curtin, John   222–3

Curzon, George Nathaniel   7, 8, 16, 27,
    65, 68–9
Cyprus   184
Czechoslovakia   244

Danckwerts, Rear-Admiral Victor H.   107
Dedman, John   226, 229
Defence Committee   226
Defence Requirements
    Sub-Committee   94–6, 100–1, 104–5
Diego Garcia   248
Dewa, Rear-Admiral   47
Dickens, Rear Admiral G.C.   99
Dorward, Colonel Arthur   15, 48–9
Double Stance   181–2, 194
Dreyer, Admiral Sir Frederic   99

East Malaysia   201, 205–7, 209, 214, 216
East Timor   264, 266
Eastern China Railway   37–8
Eden, Anthony   97, 105, 132
Egypt   163, 178, 189
Elgin, Earl of   24–5
Eliot, Sir Charles   67, 72
Endymion   50
Ernle-Earle-Plunket-Drax, Admiral
    Sir Reginald   99
European Economic Community   248

Falkland Islands   195, 255–6, 258,
    260, 266
Far East Fleet   232
Far Eastern *Dreibund*   5
Far Eastern Strategic Reserve   232–3,
    239, 269
Federation of Malaysia   199–200,
    216, 236
Festing, Field Marshal   183
Fieldhouse, Rear Admiral John   250
Fifth Army Division   47
Fighting Ships Committee   78
First World War   26, 62, 82
Fisher, Commodore   156
Fisher, Sir Warren   78, 92, 94–5, 100–1
Fitzgerald, Rear Admiral Charles C.P.
    9–10
Five Power Agreement   252
Five Power Defence Arrangements
    238–9, 251
Fleet Air Arm   226, 231, 235
Fleet Train   131, 156, 158, 162–4, 168
FO2FE   166–8, 171

283

INDEX

Force 'Z' 118–25
Foreign Office 10, 19, 21–3, 42, 51–2, 62, 64–5, 69, 74–6, 80–2, 91, 95–7, 100–8, 131–2, 147–8, 204, 250–1
Foreign Office's Political Intelligence Department 63
Four Power Treaty 71–2, 80
France 5, 15, 23, 72, 103, 172, 244, 265–6
Fraser, Admiral Sir Bruce 18–43, 129, 146–8
Fraser, Malcolm 237
Frewen, Vice-Admiral 184–5
Fukushima, General 49
Future Fleet Working Party 191

Gaselee, Lieutenant General Alfred 50–1
Gatacre, Captain G.G.O. 229
Geddes, Sir Auckland 67, 69
Geneva 76–7, 80, 82
George, Lloyd 68–9
Germany 4–11, 17, 19, 20–4, 52–3, 67, 69, 73, 97, 129, 149, 245, 265–6
Gonnohyōie, Yamamoto 47
Gorton, John 235, 237
Green, Lt John 51
Greene, Sir William Conyngham 64
Grenada 163
Grew, Joseph 105
Grey, Sir Edward 24–6, 63–4
Gulf of Akaba 163
Gulf of Oman 256
Gulf of Pechili 6, 9, 13, 17

Halifax, Lord 105, 107, 132
Halsey, Admiral William 133, 139, 145–7
Hamilton, Admiral Sir Louis 225–6
Hampden, E.M. Hobart 67
Hampton, T.C. 103
Hankey, Sir Maurice 71–2, 80, 93, 102
Harding, A. John 20
Hardinge, Sir Charles 64
Hare, George Thompson 16–17, 19
Harris, Air Marshal Sir Arthur 123
Hayao, Captain Shimamura 55
Healey, Denis 190–2, 215–16, 246–7
Heath, Mr 247–8
Heihachirō, Vice-Admiral Tōgō 55
Hermes 183
Hitler, Adolph 80

HM Ships *Cardiff* 259
HM Ships *Gloucester* 259
HM *Swallow* 249
HM *Swift* 249
HMAS *Arunta* 232
HMAS *Derwent* 236
HMAS *Melbourne* 228, 233, 236, 238
HMAS *Sydney* 228, 231
HMAS *Warramunga* 232
HMNZS *Canterbury* 257
HMNZS *Waikato* 257
HMS *Abdiel* 257
HMS *Albion* 180, 182, 189, 193–4, 197, 199, 210, 247
HMS *Algerine* 53
HMS *Amethyst* 205
HMS *Andromeda* 257
HMS *Ark Royal* 183, 186, 194, 203, 248, 264–5
HMS *Athabaskan* 160
HMS *Aurora* 46, 48
HMS *Barfleur* 41, 48
HMS *Blake* 250
HMS *Brazen* 259
HMS *Britannia* 254
HMS *Bulawayo* 157–8, 160, 167, 172
HMS *Bulwark* 180–2, 192, 194, 203, 212–13
HMS *Cambrian* 189
HMS *Centaur* 189, 203
HMS *Centurion* 42
HMS *Coventry* 256
HMS *Defender* 205
HMS *Dreadnought* 250
HMS *Duke of York* 160
HMS *Eagle* 183, 193, 236, 247
HMS *Endurance* 254–5
HMS *Fame* 43, 46
HMS *Fearless* 180, 254, 261–2
HMS *Glamorgan* 247
HMS *Glory* 166
HMS *Illustrious* 264
HMS *Intrepid* 180, 254, 261–2
HMS *Invincible* 248, 250, 254–5
HMS *Isis* 51
HMS *Ladybird* 165, 167, 171
HMS *Ocean* 261–2, 264
HMS *Parramatta* 236
HMS *Pigmy* 51
HMS *Plover* 53
HMS *Prince of Wales* 107, 118–25, 222
HMS *Puncheston* 204

284

INDEX

HMS *Repulse* 107, 118–25, 222
HMS *Striker* 181
HMS *Theseus* 166
HMS *Tiger* 203
HMS *Triumph* 162, 165–6, 247, 255
HMS *Tyre* 165
HMS *Unicorn* 166
HMS *Vengeance* 228
HMS *Victorious* 203, 213
HMS *Warspite* 250
HMS *Whiting* 46
HMS *York* 259
Hong Kong 5, 13, 17, 19, 22, 25, 43, 64,
    67–8, 72, 74, 103, 129, 160–8, 170,
    188, 192, 195, 249, 251
Hong Kong and Shanghai Banking
    Corporation 42
Hong Kong New Territories 5
Hong Kong Regiment 48
Hoon, Geoff 263
Hopkins, Harry 132
Hopkins, Sir Richard 92–3
Hsiku Arsenal 48
Hull, Cordell 132
Hayuntao 9

Imperial Japanese Army 134
Imperial Japanese Navy 119
Imperial Railways of North China 42
Inchon 164–6
Indian Army 50
Indian Ocean 66, 130, 184
Indonesia 200–4, 209, 212, 215, 234–6
Indonesian navy 203–7, 235
Industrial Intelligence Committee 98, 102
Intervention and Amphibious Capability
    Working Party 192–3
Iran 256–7
Iranian Revolution 256
Iraq 257–8, 259, 262, 264
Island Strategy 184, 186
Ismay, General Sir Hastings 123, 140
Italy 97, 105, 203, 265

Jamaica 163
Jamieson, J.W. 20–1
Japan 5–6, 22, 24, 26, 53, 62–9, 72,
    74–6, 79–83, 91, 94, 96–107, 128–34,
    139, 143–6, 149, 162, 164, 166, 170,
    229, 258
Japanese Army 46
Jellicoe, Admiral 53–4

Jenkin, Rear Admiral Conrad 250
Jih-tao 10–11
John, Admiral Caspar 181
Johnston, Reginald 5
Johore 205, 209–10, 212
Joint Chiefs of Staff 135
Joint Intelligence Committee 99, 102
Joint Planning Committee 122
Joint Services Seaborne Force 181,
    183–6, 194
Jordan 178
Joy, Admiral 162, 165
Jutarō, Komura 44

Kalimantan 201, 203, 213–14
Kasagi 44
Kellogg–Briand Pact 78
Kelly, Admiral Sir John 99
Kerr, Lord Walter 40, 47, 51–3
Ketteler, Baron von 49
Keyes, Roger 43, 46, 53
Kiaochow Bay 4–8, 21–2, 24–5
Kimmel, Admiral 107
Kinkaid, Admiral Thomas 139
King, Admiral Ernest J. 128, 134–8, 140,
    142–6
Knatchbull-Hugesson, Sir Hughe M. 102
Korea 24, 154–77, 228, 230, 232, 269
Korean War 154–6, 158, 160–1, 164–5,
    168–9, 173, 230
Kowloon New Territories 22
Kuching 207, 210
Kure 164–6, 168, 171
Kuwait 181–2, 192, 195, 199, 217, 259
Kyushu 135

Landing Ship Logistic 180
Landing Ship Tanks 180
Lansdowne, Lord 19–20
Lao-ho San 20
Leach, Admiral Henry 248, 250, 255
League of Nations 65–7, 73, 80
Leahy, Admiral 137
Lebanon 258
Legations in Peking 47–9
Lewin, Admiral Sir Terence 250, 254
Lewis, J.F. 12–13
Liaotung peninsula 53
Libya 178
Lindsay, Sir Ronald 103
Liukung-tao 10–12, 16, 27
Lockhart, James Stewart 16, 20–1, 25

INDEX

London Naval Conference 1935   79,
   81–2, 94–6, 100–2, 104
Lothian, Lord   106
Lucas, Charles Prestwood   16–17, 19,
   22, 24–5
Luce, Admiral David   190–1
Lumsden, Lieutenant-General
   Sir Herbert   140
Lutai Canal   49
Lyttelton, Alfred   19, 22

MacArthur General Douglas   134,
   139–45
McBride, Sir Philip   230–1
MacDonald, J. Ramsay   73, 79–80, 96
MacDonald, Sir Claude   6, 9–10, 40–4
McGrigor, Sir Rhoderick   231, 233
Madden, Sir Charles   76, 78
Major, John   259
Malaya   104, 118–19, 163, 199–201, 203,
   229, 231–3, 236
Malayan Emergency   205–6, 233, 236
Malaysia   116, 200, 202, 204–5, 210, 212,
   236–9, 246, 248, 251–2
Malaysian Navy   206, 210–11
Maldives   203
Malta   248
Manchukuo   93
Manchuria   21, 36–7, 50–1, 53, 56
Manila   233
Manus   140–5
Marshal, General George   133
Masato, Miyachi   37
Masirah   184
Mason, Ron   253
Mauritius   247
Mayhew, Christopher   191, 246
Menzies, Robert G.   221, 232
Mitchell, Brigadier-General Billy   118
Mitsuzane, Captain Nagamine   44
Mombasa   192
Moncrieff, Admiral Scott   168
Moore, Sir Arthur   25
Motoomi, Lieutenant-General
   Yamaguchi   50
Morimura, Captain   40
Moscow   76
Mountbatten, Lord   179–80, 234
Murray, Sir Oswyn A.R.   99

Nagasaki   55
Nanking   42, 52

NATO   172, 178, 194–5, 214, 216,
   252–3, 258
Netherlands, The   236
New Guinea   235
New York   263
New Zealand   73, 104, 162, 200, 202,
   223–4, 229, 233, 237, 239, 245, 251
Newchwang   50–1, 53
Nimitz, Admiral Chester   128–30, 133–4,
   136–48
Nine-Power Treaty   72, 80
Ningchang   41
Nixon, President   237
Noel, Sir Gerard   19
Nordmark   157
North Borneo   200, 233, 236
North Korea   154, 162
North, Admiral Sir Dudley   123
Nott Defence Review   252, 254, 260
Nott, John   253–6

O'Conor, Sir Nicholas   6–7
Octagon Conference   129, 135–8
Okinawa   139, 141, 144–5, 162
Oman   263–4
Ommanney, Sir Montagu   19
Open Door   42, 54
Operation Cymnel   257
Operation Enduring Freedom   264
operation ICEBERG   139, 141–6,
   156, 170
Operation MUSKETEER   179

Pacific Ocean   66, 70
Pacific War   62, 155
Panay   102
Paris Peace Conference   26, 63
Parlett, H.G.   67
Pearl Harbor   72, 98, 102–3, 106, 109,
   138, 143, 156, 164
Peiho River   45–6, 48
Peking   5–11, 13, 17, 20, 25–6, 37–50, 55
Percy, Lord Eustace   63
Persian Gulf   163
Philippines   107
Phillips, Admiral   119–21, 123–5
Pike, Air Marshal Thomas   183
Pontianak   203, 205
Port Arthur   5–14, 18, 21, 229
Portsmouth peace treaty   23
Pulford, Air Vice-Marshal C.W.H.
   119–21

286

INDEX

Pusan   165
Pym, Francis   256

Radford–Collins Agreement   231
Radford, Admiral Arthur W.   231
Rawlings, Vice Admiral Sir Bernard   140, 144–5
Refuelling at sea   158–60, 166, 172
RFA *Brown Ranger*   162, 164
RFA *Charlotte*   162, 164
RFA *Diligence*   257
RFA *Fort Rosalie*   164
RFA *Green Ranger*   162, 164
RFA *Grey Rover*   257
RFA *Sir Galahad*   265
RFA *Wave Chief*   162, 164
Richmond, Admiral Sir Herbert   226
Roberts, Field Marshal Earl   16
Rockhill, William W.   20
Roosevelt, Franklin D.   92, 98, 102–7, 135–6
Ross, Sir Fredrick Leith   92
Royal Air Force   121–3, 135, 179, 182–6, 190–1, 193–4, 198, 210, 246, 254
Royal Australian Air Force   226
Royal Fleet Auxiliary   158–73, 180, 206, 238
Royal Marine Javelin   257
Royal Marines   40–1, 179, 186–8, 209, 254
Royal Navy   35–56, 63, 71, 80, 99–108, 119–25, 128–50, 154–73, 178–95, 199–217, 222, 224, 244–66
Runciman, Walter   98, 102, 104
Russia   5–11, 15–19, 36–8, 42, 44, 50, 53, 55–6, 62, 65, 67, 73, 76, 78–80, 149
Russo-Japanese War   18, 37, 62

Sabah   207–8, 236
Saif Sareea   263–5
St Petersburg   6, 7, 44
Salisbury, Lord   6–9, 37, 40, 42, 47, 52, 76
Sandys, Duncan   180
Sarawak   200–1, 206–9
Sasebo   165–8, 170
Sasebo Shipbuilding Company   165
Satow, Sir Ernest   19–20, 22, 55
Scott, Bishop   41
Scott, Charles   44
Scott–Muravev agreement   14
Sea of Japan   162

Second Navy Bill   37
Second World War   118–19, 123, 128–9, 150, 154–5, 157–8, 161, 170–1, 178, 183, 223
Selborne, Lord   53
SEXTANT conference   129
Seymour, Vice-Admiral Sir Edward   9, 11–13, 16, 40–7, 51–2, 54–5
Shanghai   18, 21, 52–3
Shanghai Crisis, 1927   36
Shanhaikuan   50–1
Shantung   8–9, 17–18, 20–1, 26, 52
Shedden, Sir Frederick   223, 226
Shirai, Lieutenant Yoshimi   118
Sierra Leone   264, 266
Simon, Sir John   80
Simonstown Agreement   247–8
Singapore   54, 66–8, 70, 72–5, 78–9, 81, 93, 99, 103, 106–7, 119–21, 129, 136, 165–6, 168, 170, 180, 182, 184, 192, 199, 200–1, 203, 209–10, 212–13, 215, 216, 222, 228–9, 232–3, 236–9, 246–9, 251–2
Singapore Strategy   70, 82
Singora   119
Sino-German Convention   22
Sino-Japanese War   4
Slessor, Air Marshal Sir John   123
Smith-Dorrien, Commander A.H.   12
Snowden, Philip   79
Somerville, Admiral Sir James   123, 144
South Africa   38–40, 247–8
South African War   15, 37, 40, 54
South East Asia Treaty Organization   203, 214, 217, 232–4, 237
South Korea   162
Soviet Navy   244, 255, 265
Soviet Union   178, 203, 229, 235, 238, 245–6, 253–4, 260
Spruance, Admiral Raymond   139
SS *Choysang*   164
SS *Wuseheh*   165
Stimson, Henry   80
Strategic Defence Review   261, 263
Suez   36, 178–9, 181–2, 184, 187–8, 190, 191, 193–4, 199, 217, 228, 237, 244–66
Suez Canal   179, 257
Suharto, General   216
Sukarno, Achmed   200, 202, 213, 236
Sumatra   201, 210, 214
Sydney   142–3, 156

287

INDEX

Tahsieh, Wang   25–6
Taiwan   51
Taku   41–3, 45–8, 51, 55
Taku Bar   35, 46, 51, 55
Taku Forts   46, 48, 50, 52
Talienwan Bay   7, 9
Tanganyika   5, 189, 192
Tarakan   203, 205
Tawau   205–6, 208–9
ten year rule   63, 77–80
Thailand   184, 199, 202
Thatcher, Margaret   252–61
Thorneycroft, Peter   183, 186, 215
Three-Party Disarmament Committee   79
Tientsin   17, 21, 40–6, 49, 52, 97
Tientsin Defence Force   48
Tientsin Station   48
Tilley, Sir John   65
Tirpitz   129
Tokyo   23, 40, 47, 62, 66–7, 71, 76, 78, 80, 93, 105, 135
Tongku   45–6
Townley, A.G.   233
Treasury   62, 70–9, 81–2, 91–9, 108, 190
Troup, Rear Admiral J.A.R.   247
Tse-t'ung, Mao   39
Tsingtao   4, 20
Tsungli Yamên   8, 10, 40
Twelve-month Plan   134
Twenty-One Demands to China   63
Tyrrell, William   76

United Nations   169, 235
United States   62–9, 71–9, 90–104, 131–3, 154, 200–3, 222, 224, 231–3, 236–7, 245, 253, 256, 258, 263
United States Navy   98–108, 128, 131, 136–9, 143, 146–50, 154, 158, 160–8, 172–3, 231–4, 239, 253, 260
Upcott, G.C.   78
US Pacific Fleet   106–7
US Task Force   77, 162, 165
USS *Missouri*   145

Vansittart, Sir Robert   100, 104
Vian, Sir Philip   145
Vietnam   202, 237, 244
Vietnam War   248
VSIS   162, 163

Waldersee, Field Marshal Count von   50
War Office   14–16, 25, 43, 66, 186
Warren, Pelham   52
Warsaw Pact   252
Washington Naval Treaty   72, 80, 92–3, 101–2, 195
Watkinson, Harold   186
Way Ahead Committee   179
Weihaiwei   4–27
Weihaiwei Gold Mining Company   20
Wellesley, Sir Victor   68
Wells, Read Admiral D.C.   239
West Germany   203, 244
West Irian   200, 203
West Malaysia   10–11, 13, 16, 201, 205–6
West New Guinea   235–6
Whitehead, J.B.   47
Willis, Admiral   124
Wilson, Prime Minister   247
Winant, John G.   132
Wogack, Colonel   45
Wolseley, Field Marshal Lord   14
Woosung   52

Yalu River   165
Yangtson   44
Yangtze   9, 13, 52–4
Yangtze Valley   40, 42, 52, 54
Yellow Sea   160, 162
Yew, Lee Kuan   200
Yokosuka   165
Yorke, R.S.   13
Yugoslavia   203, 266

Zanzibar   189
Zuckerman, Professor   185

eBooks – at www.eBookstore.tandf.co.uk

A library at your fingertips!

eBooks are electronic versions of printed books. You can store them on your PC/laptop or browse them online.

They have advantages for anyone needing rapid access to a wide variety of published, copyright information.

eBooks can help your research by enabling you to bookmark chapters, annotate text and use instant searches to find specific words or phrases. Several eBook files would fit on even a small laptop or PDA.

NEW: Save money by eSubscribing: cheap, online access to any eBook for as long as you need it.

Annual subscription packages

We now offer special low-cost bulk subscriptions to packages of eBooks in certain subject areas. These are available to libraries or to individuals.

For more information please contact webmaster.ebooks@tandf.co.uk

We're continually developing the eBook concept, so keep up to date by visiting the website.

www.eBookstore.tandf.co.uk